Mastering Digital Photography and Imaging

Mastering™ Digital Photography and Imaging

Peter K. Burian

San Francisco • London

Associate Publisher:	Dan Brodnitz
Acquisitions Editor:	Bonnie Bills
Developmental Editor:	Willem Knibbe
Production Editors:	Dennis Fitzgerald, Erica Yee
Technical Editor:	Tim Grey
Copyeditor:	Pat Coleman
Compositor:	Side By Side Studios
Proofreaders:	Laurie O'Connell, Nancy Riddiough
Indexer:	Ted Laux
Book and Cover Designer:	Mark Stuart Ong, Side By Side Studios
Cover Illustrator/Photographer:	Sandune by Peter K. Burian/Camera photo used by permission of Konica Minolta Photo Imaging U.S.A., Inc.

Library of Congress Card Number: 2003115578

ISBN: 0-7821-4290-7

Manufactured in the United States of America

10 9 8 7 6 5 4 3 2 1

Foreword

In my nearly three decades as a professional photographer, I've seen some incredible changes in the way we make images. When I started in newspaper work, there were still cigar-chomping old-timers on the street who lugged WW II-era Rollei twin lens reflex cameras fitted with big, manual, potato-masher style strobes to shoot check passings, ribbon cuttings, and yes, even house fires. Why? Because they just couldn't get the hang of using 35mm gear. Needless to say, those guys went the way of dinosaurs and typewriters.

I, on the other hand, was a total gearhead who embraced every new bit of technology that came down the pike. First it was thyristor strobes that put out just the right amount of light. Then TTL metering modes and flash control, then autofocus, then "smart"flash which effortlessly blended flash and available light calculations. With each new innovation, there I was on the cutting edge, fully embracing and understanding the technology and how it could make my image-making easier, quicker, and more efficient.

And then came the digital revolution.

Back then, I was the guy with the stogie and the PRESS card stuck in the hatband of my fedora, hopelessly lost in the jungle of a new technology I neither understood nor wanted. Every aspect was bewildering, and I literally howled as I struggled with Curves, Levels, Histograms, RAW, DPI, PPI, not to mention computer freezeups, crashes, and upgrades. Just when it all got to be too much, I reached out to my friend Peter Burian.

In a calm and sensible way, Peter walked me through the digital minefield, in no-nonsense, photographer-to-photographer language that I could understand. Peter demystified the process without oversimplifying it, literally talking me back off the ledge of becoming a terminal Luddite. I used to think, "wouldn't it be great if everyone had a Peter Burian to guide them into the digital age?"

Now, in the form of this book, you do. While most instructional guides are either hopelessly elementary or written so only a software engineer could decipher it, Peter has managed to walk the middle line. And unlike a lot of other how-to writers, he's not afraid to tell it like it is; when he gives you a bit of advice, you know it's something that he has tried and made work. His writing reflects that most rare commodity in the Tower of Babel that is digital photography advice: an informed and evenhanded opinion.

And so, dear reader, thanks to the 15th century miracle of moveable type and the printing press, you've got access to one of the true masters of this very 21st century practice of digital photography. I can think of no one better to guide you. And Peter, if you wonder why I hardly ever call or e-mail you anymore, you have only yourself, and this book, to blame!

Bob Krist
New Hope, Pennsylvania

Bob Krist is an award winning freelance photographer who works regularly on assignment for magazines such as *National Geographic Traveler, Smithsonian, Islands, Caribbean Travel* and *Life* and *GEO Saison.* Krist's book *Spirit of Place: The Art of The Traveling Photographer* was hailed by American Photographer magazine as "the best book about travel photography we've ever read." Bob Krist is also a contributing editor with *National Geographic Traveler* and *Islands* as well as travel photography columnist with *Outdoor Photographer* magazine. He teaches travel photography at the Maine, Cuba, and Tuscany Photo Workshops.

To Bev, for understanding why I no longer want a "real job,"
and to Katie and Julie, who bring joy to our lives.

Acknowledgments

Although only one name is on the cover, this book was not a solitary venture; an entire team made it possible. I want to thank the staff at Sybex, including Bonnie Bills who motivated me in the early stages, Dennis Fitzgerald who patiently but persistently kept me on track, editor Willem Knibbe who daily challenged me to make the text more incisive and readable. Others who contributed their talent include Mark Ong, Susan Riley, Pat Coleman and Rodney Koenke. I am particularly grateful for the assistance of technical editor Tim Grey, a Photoshop instructor and the author of *Color Confidence* (Sybex, 2004) who brought vast technical wisdom to this project.

Thanks to the companies who provided product photos to illustrate certain sections and to Fred Miranda of FM Software, the Adobe Photoshop CS beta support team, and Josh Haftel of Nik Multimedia Inc. for supplying software and to Brian Levey of ColorVision Inc. for providing calibration hardware and software.

No one arrives suddenly at a stage where he has the expertise and the credibility to author a technical book such as this. Although I sometimes claim to be self-taught, I must acknowledge those who contributed to my education in photography: Géza Gaspardy, Maria Zorn, Arthur Morris, instructors at Sheridan College, and my current technical advisors, Ellen Anon and Tim Grey.

For helping me to achieve a measure of credibility, I am particularly grateful to those who gave me the first "breaks" in what eventually became a full-time career: Jenni Bidner, Bill Hurter, Bob Shell, Bonnie Paulk, Jacques Thibault, Jacques Dumont, Marti Saltzman, and Rob Sheppard. I also want to thank John Agnone, my editor during his tenure at National Geographic Books, travel photographer Bob Krist who became my mentor, and my current magazine editors: Anita Dammer and Darwin Wiggett of *Photo Life*, Robert Keeley of *Australian Photography*, and George Schaub of *Shutterbug* and *e-DIGITAL PHOTO*. My deepest thanks to all these individuals and to others not mentioned here.

And a final hug to those who will not have an opportunity to see this book, my father Dr. Ignac Burian and my mother Edith Gaspardy. I know how proud you would be, and I wish you were here to acknowledge your role in this achievement.

Contents

Landhaus
Saxler
HOLZ
AM DOM

Introduction

As recently as five years ago, photography was experiencing a decline. Many photo enthusiasts were abandoning their camera systems and darkrooms, switching to a point-and-shoot camera for the few obligatory snapshots during seasonal events. Often, the primary family camera was a disposable model, not designed for high image quality but popular because of convenience and price. Despite the introduction of the Advanced Photo System, a small film and camera format designed to make picture taking more "fun," interest in the still image and in the "same old" equipment was waning. Digital cameras and printers were available, of course, but they failed to attract many consumers due to high prices, mediocre image quality, and the perception that imaging software was "too complicated."

For the most part, the picture in 2004 is quite different, thanks to more affordable, user-friendly digital equipment and software that's also vastly more sophisticated. According to a prediction by InfoTrends (www.infotrends.com), digital camera sales should reach nearly 53 million this year. My own anecdotal evidence may be even more persuasive. Today, virtually all my friends—both snap shooters and photo hobbyists—own digital equipment. They're shooting frequently enjoying both photography and scanning as well as the benefits of image enhancement and printmaking. The few holdouts will probably add digital cameras to their systems by the end of this year.

Clearly, digital cameras have revitalized photography. And, yes, any image capture with a still camera qualifies as photography, a term drawn from the Greek words for *photo* and *graphia*, translated as "writing with light." Whether the image is formed in silver halide crystals or electronic pixels, the process of picture taking is quite similar and equally rewarding. In that case, why does the title of this book refer to "imaging" as well? Because some topics relate to processes that are purely digital in scope, such as scanning images, manipulating them with software, making the right computer and software selections in the digital darkroom, creating digital prints, and sharing electronic images using the Internet. Although these are essential aspects in digital photography, none are available to the purely analog photographer. Consequently, we have decided to categorize them under the term "imaging."

Some pundits maintain that "the medium is the message," echoing a comment made by media guru Marshall McLuhan in the 1960s; they're implying that we buy digital gear because we love electronic gadgets. That may be true for a few consumers but not for most photo enthusiasts or even for snap shooters. The joy of photography does not lie in the equipment (or medium) that we use but in the images that we make, photos that capture memories or allow us to exercise our creativity.

Naturally, the digital medium offers benefits over film-based photography. First, there's the immediacy of viewing our images, a few seconds after they are recorded. (A Polaroid camera offers immediacy too, but with substantially lower image quality and without the other advantages.) We can show the pictures to our friends, evaluate them, and reshoot immediately if they're not technically or creatively satisfying. Whether we use a digital camera or scan our conventional photographs, digital imaging also affords a vast range of image-enhancement opportunities as a secondary creative outlet. In the digital darkroom, we can achieve effects that were extremely difficult or impossible to achieve with an enlarger and caustic chemicals. Finally, there's no need to make trips to a lab for film, processing, or printing.

If you use an ultrahigh-resolution camera or film scanner, advanced enhancing techniques, and a top-rated photo printer, your images can be superior to those made with conventional methods. Even if you take snapshots with a $299 digital camera and make prints with a $99 inkjet photo printer, you should be satisfied. Your pics should be as good or better than what you expect from 35mm film and prints made by a high-volume photofinisher. Don't want to bother with printmaking? No problem. Many retailers, including major chains such as WalMart, can make excellent prints from your image files using one of the new digital labs; you can also order digital prints online, from services such as www.ofoto.com or www.shutterfly.com.

If you're reading this book because you're planning to buy digital equipment—or considering an upgrade to your current gear—you'll find many pages of advice on various aspects of hardware and software. Start by reviewing the chapters on cameras, scanners, printers, and the digital darkroom: the computer and software that you'll want in order to take full advantage of the medium. Then, move on to the chapters on techniques for capturing technically excellent images with a camera or scanner, for enhancing them so they'll meet your highest expectations, and for sharing them with others through the Internet or gallery-quality prints suitable for framing.

Already own all the gear that you'll need? In that case, avoid the temptation to skip the chapters on equipment because they contain information and methods on getting the most from each item.

That brings me to discussing the slant of this book. You'll find that it explains technology, image formats, features, and methods unique to digital capture, as well as concepts such as color management, exposure control, depth of field, and more. Some books omit certain of these topics or gloss over them, believing that many readers would find them "too complicated." Granted, the concepts are not simple, but they are essential for a full understanding of the entire process of capturing, enhancing, and sharing your images. Working with a technical consultant and a knowledgeable editor, I have tried to present the technical information in a manner that will satisfy the experienced photographer and computer user, without overwhelming the novice.

But more important, we have collaborated to bring you *knowledge*: interpretations of technical facts and recommendations that will help you select the most suitable equipment and techniques. In every chapter, I have tried to make this book valuable in terms of insights and practical tips based on extensive experience with techniques and tools that help to make better images. There's an old expression that says, "You can take this advice to the bank." It is my profound hope you'll find the advice in this book equally valuable as well as inspiring in your own image making. It's all presented from the perspective of a photographer and intended to help you master all the essential aspects of digital photography and imaging.

Good luck and all the best in your own image making.

Peter K. Burian
Toronto, Canada, 2004

About the Author

Peter K. Burian is a full-time photographer and writer, a long-time contributor to photographic magazines such as *Shutterbug*, *e-DIGITAL PHOTO*, *Australian Photography*, and *Photo Life*. Most of his articles are test reports of photographic equipment, predominantly *digital* equipment for the past several years. Burian is the co-author of ten other books, including eight Magic Lantern Guides to SLR camera systems, the *National Geographic Photography Field Guide: Secrets to Making Great Pictures* available in ten languages, and *Camera Basics: Getting the Most From Your Autofocus Camera*. The author has made many presentations to photographic associations, most recently on all aspects of digital photography and imaging. Although best known for his writings on photo techniques and equipment, he is a prolific photographer, primarily specializing in outdoor subjects, including nature, travel, and active lifestyles. He continues to add images weekly to his vast file of conventional and digital photos, and his work is marketed for editorial and commercial publication by two agencies, Corbis Images and The Stock Connection. Peter K. Burian lives in a small town near Toronto, Canada, with his wife, Bev, and their daughters, Julie and Katie; he can be reached at pkburian@hotmail.com.

Chapter 1: Introduction to Digital Cameras

Chapter 2: Scanners

Chapter 3: Software

Chapter 4: Printers

Chapter 5: Choosing a Photo Printer

Courtesy Nikon, Inc.

Essential Digital Imaging Equipment

In Part One, we will consider the equipment that is used for digital photography and other aspects of imaging: cameras, scanners, computers and pertinent software, basic accessories, as well as photo printers. You will not want or need everything that I'll discuss, and some of it might be well above your current budget. In that case, consider some of the content as reference material for later use or simply to give you an appreciation for the latest equipment and the most sophisticated capabilities that are available.

CHAPTER one

Introduction to Digital Cameras

Unless you plan to digitize *existing photographs with a scanner, as discussed in Chapter 2, you'll need a digital camera—often called a digicam—if you want to make digital images. In some respects, these cameras are similar to their 35mm counterparts. They include most of the same features, but gain many others that are exclusive to the digital process.*

At first glance, a digicam may seem expensive compared with a 35mm film camera. That's true, but it can offer better value in the long run, at least for photographers who shoot a great deal. Because digicams store images on a memory card, there's no need to pay for film or processing; think of the card as "reusable film." Granted, you'll want prints of some images, but this is cheaper than paying to print every picture on a roll of film. Digicams are also a lot more fun than 35mm cameras. At a party, for example, you can snap a lot of pictures and show them to friends on the camera's color display immediately. Delete any rejects and take some pics over again if you're not happy with the poses or expressions. Many cameras will even record short video clips.

In this chapter, I'll discuss how digital cameras work, the various types of digital cameras, their primary capabilities, and some of the features that are unique to digital cameras. If you are thinking of upgrading to a newer, more advanced or different type of digital camera, the following sections can help guide your purchasing desision.

How Digital Images Are Captured

When you turn the camera on and press the shutter button, the aperture in the lens opens to allow light to strike the light-sensitive sensor to record a picture. All digital cameras use these electronic sensors to capture photographic images. There are a variety of sensor types, including CCD (charge-coupled device), CMOS (complimentary metal oxide semiconductor, see Figure 1.1), and LBCAST (Lateral Buried Charge Accumulator and Sensing Transistor Array). All these very technical names describe the different methods used by each type of sensor to accomplish the same goal. That goal is to record the scene before the lens using an array of pixels (an acronym for picture elements) on the sensor to store the tonal and color values of the final image.

Figure 1.1: Several types of sensors, of various sizes, are used for image capture in digital cameras.

RECOMMENDATION: CMOS or CCD Sensor?

For practical purposes, there is no substantial difference between the imaging capabilities of a technically advanced CCD and CMOS sensor. Each type has some claimed advantages, but both can produce a high level of image quality. While some very cheap, low-resolution models, including "toy" cameras intended for children, may include *low grade* CMOS chips, this is not relevant for our purposes. The types of cameras that I'll discuss in this book all incorporate sensors that are technically excellent. Nearly all compact digicams employ a CCD sensor, while some digital SLR (Single Lens Reflex) cameras employ a CMOS sensor. When considering several digital SLR cameras, the type of sensor should not be a high-priority item in your deliberations.

Although digital cameras can record images in full color, the individual pixels on the sensor can't actually measure color values. They can measure only the intensity of the light striking the pixel, not the color properties of that light. Therefore, filters are placed in front of the pixels so that each can measure only one of the three primary colors (red, green, and blue) of light. (Sony has introduced a sensor that captures *four* colors, adding "emerald" (resembling cyan) as the fourth color, but this is not yet in widespread use.) The filters are arranged in a specific order, most commonly using the "Bayer" pattern in which there are twice as many green pixels as red and blue.

When the light projected by the lens comes in contact with the imaging sensor during exposure, the light-sensitive pixels accumulate an electrical charge. More light striking a particular pixel translates into a stronger electrical charge. The electrical charge for each pixel is converted into a specific value based on the strength of the charge so that the camera can actually process the data.

Each pixel in a digital image must contain values for all three of the primary colors to accurately describe the final color of the pixel. Because each pixel on the imaging sensor records only the value of one of those colors, the other values must be calculated based on surrounding values. For most captures this is done within the camera. The final image data can then be written to the camera's memory card as an image file. An exception to this is the RAW capture format, discussed later in this chapter. When we shoot in a camera's RAW capture mode, the actual pixel values are recorded and stored in a special data file that needs to be processed using special software (in your computer) to convert it to an image format.

Another type of imaging sensor, made by Foveon (www.foveon.com), is not yet in general use in digital cameras. (At the time of this writing, only the Sigma SD series SLR cameras incorporate this sensor.) Called the X3, it records all three primary colors of light (red, green, and blue) at every pixel. (Other sensors record only one color per pixel, as discussed earlier.) Consequently, cameras with the X3 sensor do not need to interpolate color data and do not need the filter discussed earlier. The first X3 sensor contains 3.43 million pixels, but for every pixel location, there is a stack of three "photo detectors" for a total of 10.29 million. This technology is complex, and it does have some advantages, as I discovered while testing the Sigma cameras. Technically a 3.43 megapixel camera, it produced a level of image quality that I would expect from a 5 megapixel camera, suitable for making 11 × 16.5" prints of excellent quality. Foveon has developed X3 chips of even higher resolution, and some of these may be available in digital cameras by the time you read this book.

The Megapixel Issue

Regardless of the type of sensor, the more pixels, the more information that is being captured. High resolution translates to digital photos with well-defined detail, great clarity, and an impression of high sharpness. Most digicams (see Figure 1.2) today capture images with a sensor that has at least 1 million pixels, also called one megapixel, and you can find professional SLR cameras with more than 10 megapixels for making ultra-high-resolution images. In practical terms, more megapixels translates to larger prints of high quality.

Figure 1.2: Compact digital cameras are available with image sensors ranging from 1 to 6 megapixels.

Courtesy Nikon, Inc.

How Many Megapixels Do You Need?

You can find compact cameras with resolution ranging from 1 megapixel to 8 megapixels. Generally speaking, you will want to look for a camera with the highest resolution available in your price range if you plan to make prints. How much resolution do you need r to make a beautiful inkjet photo? The following list provides a rule of thumb as to what you'll need to make photographic quality prints of certain sizes, using the highest resolution and the lowest JPEG (named after the Joint Photographic Experts Group) compression capture mode for one of the better cameras in each resolution range.

- **Cameras with 1 megapixel sensors** are suitable for very good 4 × 6" prints and acceptable 5 × 7 prints.
- **Cameras with 2 megapixel sensors** should allow you to make very good 5 × 7" prints and acceptable 8 × 10" prints from your best images.
- **Cameras with 3 megapixel sensors** generally produce images suitable for good 8 × 10" prints; the best 3 megapixel cameras can produce image quality suitable for making acceptable 11 × 14" prints.
- **Cameras with 4 megapixel sensors** should produce images that are suitable for fine 8.5 × 11" prints that you'll be proud to show and share. With images from the best 4 megapixel cameras, you should be able to make very good 11 × 14" prints.
- **Cameras with 5 or 6 megapixel sensors** are intended for those who want high quality in 13 × 19" prints and very close to photo quality in slightly larger prints.

Few photo printers can generate prints larger than 8.5 × 11". Unless you plan to buy a larger format printer or often crop image files extensively (calling for greater enlargement of the smaller files), you should be very satisfied with a top-rated 4 megapixel compact digicam. If you plan to exhibit prints or sell images, or if you are extremely critical as to quality, you might want to consider models with even higher resolution. In SLR cameras, 5+ megapixel resolution has become the norm as discussed later.

Image Recording Formats

Before moving on to a review of the various types of digital cameras, it's worth considering the various image capture modes that are mentioned in subsequent sections.

JPEG Capture Format

The most common image recording format used by digital cameras is JPEG. This popular format can be opened with virtually any imaging software in a computer. The JPEG format includes compression in order to reduce the size of the file to allow more images to be recorded on a memory card. When the file is opened in the computer, the data is uncompressed.

JPEG Format Issues

JPEG is a "lossy" format, meaning that it always causes a loss of information in the image. To produce a smaller file size, pixel values may be changed. This is most commonly done by breaking the image down into blocks, typically 16 × 16 pixels, and then finding the most efficient way to describe the color within those blocks. That may involve changing pixel values so that the data can be described more efficiently.

continues

Higher amounts of compression applied to a JPEG image will result in a smaller file size, but it will also result in more information being lost in the process. That translates into a loss of detail in the image, as well as the creation of "artifacts." These artifacts are visible as blocks of color in the image that don't blend in well with the surrounding area. For example, you might see bright blocks of pixels in dark areas along a high-contrast edge in the image.

Although the loss of detail and creation of artifacts can be a serious problem, they are usually not an issue if you use the minimal amount of JPEG compression. Therefore, I recommend that you avoid using settings that will cause the camera to apply a high level of compression. Stick with the camera's top JPEG quality mode such as Ultra Fine or Best.

Digital cameras offer several choices for recording JPEG images with options for Resolution (number of pixels) and for Quality (compression ratio.) You can choose to make a large, high-resolution image with low compression—often denoted in the camera's menu as Large/Fine or Large/Super Fine—for optimal image quality. Or you can choose to make a lower-resolution image with a higher compression ratio for situations in which quality is not your primary concern. Cameras usually offer many combinations of resolution and compression, although some cameras simplify the process, offering only general image-quality options such as Best, Good, Normal, and E-mail. The Best option, for example, produces the highest resolution and lowest compression ratio.

RECOMMENDATION: Save Your JPEGs as TIFFs

After downloading JPEG images to your computer, save them as TIFF (Tagged Image File Format), using the "Save As" feature in your image editing software. TIFF is an excellent choice for archiving image files as discussed in Chapter 9Save the TIFF files as your "master files." If you need a small file of any image for Internet use, simply downsize a TIFF file for that purpose and *save it under another file name* as a JPEG. Retain your master file as you would save a negative in 35mm photography for subsequent use for other purposes.

Granted, there will be occasions when you'll select a low-resolution/higher-compression capture mode. You may decide to do so when you want certain photos to make only small prints, when you want photos only for Internet use, or when all your memory cards are almost full and have inadequate capacity for larger files.

RAW Capture Format

In addition to JPEG capture modes, digital SLR cameras, and some prosumer-level compact digicams, include a special capture mode referred to as RAW mode. When you select this option, the camera captures raw data from the sensor and saves it in a proprietary file format. The data is often compressed, using a lossless algorithm. After RAW images are downloaded from the camera to a computer, they must be converted to a standard image file format, such as TIFF, that is recognized by image-editing software. The conversion process requires special software that is included with the camera and also available from companies such as Adobe and PhaseOne.

Aside from slightly higher image quality than the best JPEG option, the primary advantage of the RAW capture mode is great latitude for correcting factors such as exposure and color rendition *before converting the RAW data to an image format*. Most of the RAW

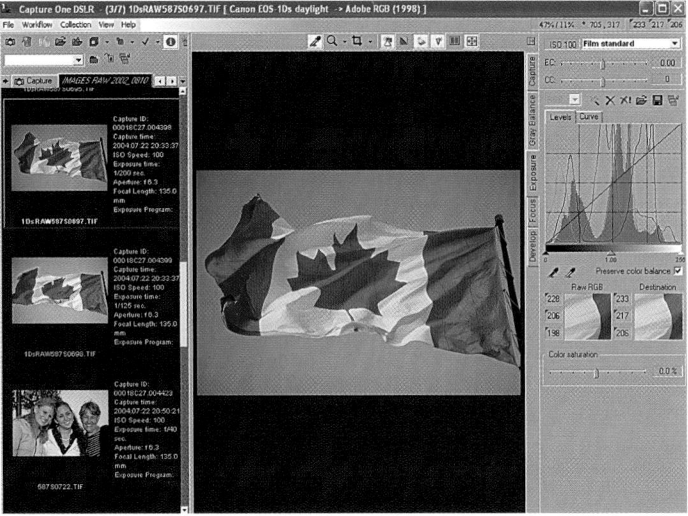

Figure 1.3: RAW images must be converted to a conventional image format, such as TIFF, using special software. Most such software includes a wealth of image-enhancing capabilities; those intended for color and exposure correction are the most valuable.

conversion programs (see Figure 1.3) offer features for adjusting brightness, white balance, and color saturation as well as other parameters, including sharpness and contrast.

Granted, images captured in JPEG or TIFF format—fully processed in-camera—can be adjusted with conventional image-editing software such as one of the Adobe Photoshop programs. However, any major corrections to exposure and color rendition are more effective when applied to raw data that has not yet been processed. Should you ever make an error that produces a RAW image that's too dark, that's too bright, or that has a strange color cast, it can probably be corrected quite effectively with the RAW converter software.

RECOMMENDATION: Use RAW Capture Mode for Large Prints

Although the best JPEG capture mode can produce very good to exceptional image quality (depending on the camera), a RAW image is superior in this respect. If your camera offers an option for capturing images in RAW format, use this feature when you want the finest possible image, such as when you intend to make large prints. A RAW image file maintains a higher level of quality than an image made in JPEG when the file size is increased in the RAW conversion software or later with image-editing software. Consequently, you will be able to make larger prints that are suitable for framing.

RAW image capture offers another advantage: it records the image with 12-bit color depth instead of 8-bit used in other capture modes. Image files with the higher bit depth contain billions rather than millions of possible colors, so they exhibit a wider range of tones and colors for the best detail and smoothest gradations. When using the RAW image converter software to convert the image to a conventional TIFF format, you can choose to save images in 8-bit or 16-bit depth. I'll discuss this topic in far more detail in Chapter 9.

TIFF Capture Format

A few digital SLR cameras include an option to record images in TIFF format. A TIFF image is comparable in quality to a RAW image, but is substantially larger. I can see only one benefit to using this capture mode: you don't need to convert the image using special software. The drawbacks outweigh this benefit, however. Because each file size is so large, your memory card will hold fewer images. In TIFF capture, you cannot shoot more than one image in a sequence. Also, image processing time is extremely long, which can be very frustrating.

RECOMMENDATION: The "Best" Capture Mode

Some photographers, particularly those specializing in landscapes, prefer to use TIFF capture instead of the RAW format. They tolerate the long, in-camera processing time because they do not

continues

want to spend extra time at a computer converting RAW images. That is a personal decision, but in my view, the drawbacks of the TIFF capture mode outweigh its benefits. Frankly, JPEG capture, in the high-resolution/highest-quality setting of a top-rated camera, is a fine choice for most images. Use the RAW capture mode (with cameras that include this option) if you plan to make oversized prints, of even higher quality, or if you want the other benefits offered by this format. Do note, however, that most compact digicams do not offer any still-image recording option other than JPEG. Some prosumer cameras offer only a TIFF or only a RAW capture alternative. If one of these is important to you, check the specifications carefully before buying a camera.

Digital Camera Classes

Visit a large photo retail store, and you'll find three major types of digital cameras: compact models with a built-in lens, larger cameras that accept interchangeable lenses (see Figure 1.4), and even larger models designed to accept a large digital back accessory. The latter two types of cameras and their lenses are expensive, and the accessory digital backs are even more expensive. Because such equipment is primarily intended for commercial applications and studio use, I will discuss it only briefly.

COURTESY OF SIGMA CORPORATION

Figure 1.4: Lenses such as this 15–30mm zoom are useful with a digital SLR camera for achieving ultrawide-angle effects despite the "focal length magnifier" factor.

Single-use digital cameras—as well as very inexpensive low-resolution digital cameras—are also available, but these do not produce high-quality images, so they will not be covered in this book.

Lens Focal Lengths

Virtually every digital camera—except for a few professional SLR models—incorporates a sensor that is smaller than a 35mm film frame that is a common reference standard. Consequently, any lens produces a narrower angle of view, or greater apparent magnification, with such digital cameras. That's why you often see zoom lenses with marked focal lengths such as 7.6mm to 22.8mm in a compact digicam. This is roughly equivalent to a 37–111mm zoom lens on a 35mm camera, although the *exact* effective focal lengths depend on the digicam's actual sensor size.

With a digital SLR camera, the extent of the focal length magnification factor also depends on the image sensor size. A typical factor is about 1.5x, making a 300mm lens equivalent to a 450mm lens, and a 20mm lens equal to a 30mm lens. Some cameras produce a different focal length magnification factor: 1.3x or the more common 1.6x, for example, and a full 2x with the Olympus E-1 camera that employs a sensor that's smaller than average in digital SLR cameras.

This factor is useful if you often photograph distant subjects, because you may not need to buy an expensive super telephoto lens. But for true wide-angle effects, you'll need very short lenses. That's why short focal lengths are becoming more common, with lenses such as the 14mm, the 15-30mm, and 16-35mm zooms and the Olympus 11–22mm zoom.

Most compact digicams include a feature called "digital zoom" in addition to the true "optical" zoom. When you access digital zoom, the camera crops the image electronically, saving only the central area and discarding numerous pixels. Although many cameras' processors then add pixels, through interpolation, image quality deteriorates noticeably. I recommend against using the digital zoom feature unless high image quality is not your primary goal.

Figure 1.5: Compact digicams are available in many sizes, from tiny to quite large, and in various configurations.

COURTESY OF FUJIFILM USA

Compact Digital Cameras

The most common type of digital camera (see Figure 1.5) includes a built-in lens and flash unit, an LCD monitor for viewing images, and an optical viewfinder—a small window for viewing the scene—above the lens that will actually take the picture. Although cameras of this type are often called point-and-shoot models, this term is valid only for the inexpensive, basic models. Consequently, I'll refer to cameras with a built-in lens as compact cameras to distinguish them from the larger SLR models that accept interchangeable lenses.

Viewfinders and LCD Monitors

Some of the affordable compact digital cameras do not include an optical viewfinder. With such models, use the LCD monitor for viewing your subject while composing photos. Naturally, you can use this viewing technique with any compact digital camera–instead of using the viewfinder–but battery consumption will be substantially higher when the monitor is always on.

Although most digital cameras include an optical viewfinder, some models–particularly those with a built-in zoom lens with very long focal lengths–incorporate an electronic viewfinder (EVF) instead. An EVF is actually a small LCD monitor that allows you to see the image that the sensor will capture. The view through an EVF is not as sharp, crisp, and bright as it is through an optical viewfinder, but this is a standard feature in cameras with long (built-in) zoom lenses.

There is an advantage to using the LCD monitor on the camera back, or an electronic viewfinder, when composing your images in extreme close-up photography. Because you view the subject through the taking lens, the view is accurate. You see exactly what the lens sees, without the parallax error that occurs when viewing the subject through a secondary lens (optical viewfinder) that is above the primary lens. This allows for accurate framing, capturing the desired subject area instead of an area above it.

Especially in the 3+ megapixel categories, you can find three levels of compact digital cameras: basic, advanced, and prosumer. Basic models are designed primarily for snap shooting and simplicity of operation. Extensively automated, they allow little control over the image, except, perhaps, for adjusting the overall brightness and white balance.

Figure 1.6: Compact digicams usually include a few analog buttons, switches, and dials and many electronic controls, usually accessed via a menu button.

The advanced cameras include a wealth of capabilities, from fully automatic, to semiautomatic to fully manual operating modes. They may also include overrides for controlling factors such as sharpness, contrast, the intensity of color rendition, and more, as discussed in a later section.

The more expensive prosumer models are loaded with extra features (see Figure 1.6). Many such cameras also accept optional accessories, including wide-angle and telephoto lens adapters, filters, and high-powered accessory flash units.

If you buy one of the latest compact digital cameras, it will probably include all the essentials: a built-in 3x optical zoom lens and flash unit, automatic focusing, a color LCD monitor for viewing your photos, a memory card for storing images, a CD with software, cables for connecting the camera to your computer and to a TV monitor, plus a battery. Some camera kits include rechargeable batteries and a charger; others include only single-use batteries. If a camera that uses single-use batteries accepts rechargeables, you'll want to purchase a set, plus a spare set, along with a suitable charger.

Digital camera kits include only a low-capacity memory card that may hold no more than a dozen images made in the camera's best-quality capture mode. Just as you would buy extra film for a 35mm camera, you'll want to buy at least one memory card. Think of the card as "digital film." A 64MB card is a good start with a 1, 2, or 3 megapixel camera, but for a 4, 5, or 6 megapixel camera, you'll want a card with 256MB capacity.

Compact Digicam Pros and Cons

Compact digital cameras are the most popular type by far, and that's understandable considering their advantages over the SLR cameras that accept interchangeable lenses.

- They are more affordable and offer a better value because a lens is built-in (see Figure 1.7), and is not an extra cost option.
- Their smaller size and weight allows for greater portability and greater convenience with a built-in lens.
- They are less complex.
- They are available in a broader range of choices in brand, price, megapixels, and capabilities.

Figure 1.7: Common in compact digicams, a 3x zoom lens includes focal lengths ranging from moderately wide angle to short telephoto and is useful for many types of subjects. (Settings: Image on left made at 37mm equivalent; image on right made at 111mm equivalent.)

Although these advantages are certainly meaningful, compact cameras are not ideal in all respects. Consider the following issues:

- A built-in zoom lens is not nearly as versatile as a wide range of SLR system lenses ranging from fisheye to super telephoto.
- Only a few compact digicams, usually the most expensive models, accept filters, lens adapters, and accessory flash units.
- Compact cameras have fewer capabilities and options than SLR cameras.
- Few models are available with resolution higher than 5 megapixels.
- The smaller sensors in compact cameras, with their smaller pixels, do not produce image quality comparable to that produced by SLR cameras.
- In extreme close-up photography, models with an optical viewfinder do not produce accurate framing. You must use the LCD monitor to compose your images in such situations.

Interchangeable Lens SLR Cameras

A digicam with a built-in lens can be convenient, but many photographers prefer an SLR that accepts a full series of lenses (see Figure 1.8). The term Single Lens Reflex refers to the fact that you view the scene through the same lens that takes the picture. A system of mirrors in a prism reflects the image to the camera's viewfinder so there is no need for a secondary viewing lens above the "taking" lens. Because you view the subject through the "taking" lens, framing is more accurate in close-focusing without the parallax error that occurs with a separate viewfinder. The view is also bright and crisp because the viewfinder is optical and not electronic.

Figure 1.8: A digital SLR system includes cameras and a variety of lens types and accessories such as flash units.

A Note on Terminology

As mentioned earlier, compact digicams—with built-in long telephoto zoom lenses—also offer through-the-lens viewing, but these employ a small LCD screen (EVF) in the viewfinder. Such cameras are also SLR models, but in practice, the term *SLR* is generally used only when discussing the cameras that accept interchangeable lenses and employ a prism for through-the-lens viewing. Consequently, I'll use the term SLR only when discussing cameras that accept interchangeable lenses. An SLR camera system includes lenses from ultrawide-angle to super telephoto, allowing you to achieve any desired effect. They have other advantages over the compact cameras. Typically, SLRs offer more advanced digital and conventional capabilities and more options to image capture format. Although an SLR camera can be complicated, it can also be as simple as you want, in its fully automatic program mode with image adjustment controls at the default settings.

Figure 1.9: One of the primary advantages of a digital SLR camera over a compact digicam is faster speed in framing and in autofocus. This benefit is particularly important in action and wildlife photography.

Most digital SLR cameras include the capabilities that serious photographers expect: high-speed continuous focus for tracking action subjects (see Figure 1.9); built-in flash plus compatibility with accessory flash units; automatic, semiautomatic, and manual modes; numerous overrides for controlling every aspect of an image; depth-of-field preview for assessing the range of sharp focus; and a great deal more. They offer at least two recording formats: JPEG for small image files even in high=resolution imaging and a proprietary RAW mode for very high picture quality without excessively large image files. Many even include a third option: TIFF image capture for the finest image quality, though as discussed previously, this can result in slow recording times and huge files that quickly fill up a memory card.

Most digital SLR camera kits include the camera body, a cable for connecting the camera to your computer, a CD with software, rechargeable battery and charger, and possibly a low-capacity memory card. A lens is not included, although some retailers sell kits, at a higher price, that include an affordable zoom lens that will get you started if you do not already own suitable lenses.

Four years ago, the most affordable digital SLR camera cost as much as a good used automobile and boasted an image sensor with only 2 million pixels. Today, you can buy a 6-megapixel digital SLR for $1000, and it will generate much larger image files than its precursor, with substantially higher resolution.

Digital SLR Camera Pros and Cons

As the "cons" in the compact camera section imply, a digital SLR camera offers benefits, particularly in terms of superior image quality and versatility. Although lens adapters—used with a prosumer digicam—can be useful, SLR cameras accept a far more comprehensive range of lenses; these also produce higher image quality than lens adapters.

A digital SLR camera body is certainly more expensive than a compact camera, and it does not come with a lens. If you already own a Canon, Sigma, Pentax, or Nikon autofocus SLR camera, with suitable autofocus lenses, your lenses will be compatible with a digital SLR camera of the same brand. In that case, your investment need not be excessive. And the investment will pay off in the long run, because you'll save money on film and processing.

Finally, you'll find that most of the SLR models are loaded with all the capabilities and overrides that will satisfy advanced photographers. The best cameras produce images with ultra high resolution, suitable for beautiful prints as large as 13 × 19", and even larger if the images are enhanced and printed with some expertise.

RECOMMENDATION: Compact Digicam or Digital SLR Camera?

An SLR camera, plus lenses, costs far more than a compact digicam with a built-in lens, and an SLR is larger, heavier, and substantially more complex. Hence, this is not the right choice for everyone. But if you're a photo enthusiast who uses a 35mm SLR camera when shooting film, you'll certainly want to consider a digital SLR camera. ($899 and up, plus lenses.) In addition to the creative and problem-solving abilities available with a variety of lenses and extra features, an SLR camera offers another significant benefit over a compact model: superior image quality because it employs a larger image sensor—with larger recording pixels—than a compact digicam.

If you will not need the additional versatility available with a wide range of (expensive) lenses and the extra capabilities available with an SLR camera, or if you do not plan to make very large prints, a highly rated compact digicam should meet your needs. Look for test reports on the Internet to determine which specific models are "best."

For the maximum versatility with a compact digicam, consider one of the 4+ megapixel prosumer models that boasts many of the same capabilities as SLR models and also accepts wide-angle and telephoto lens adapters as well as accessory flash units. Although the accessories are not inexpensive, they do increase a camera's versatility. Some digicams include a wide range (6x to 10x) optical zoom lens, and one of these cameras may provide all the focal lengths that you will want. The only drawback is that such cameras use an electronic (instead of optical) viewfinder, and not everyone finds an EVF convenient to use.

Professional Studio Cameras

Professional photographers working in a studio often use medium- and large-format film cameras that accept interchangeable lenses and digital backs (see Figure 1.10) with 11 to 20+ megapixel resolution for making massive image files for commercial purposes. In addition to the high cost of the cameras and lenses, the digital backs are prohibitively expensive for the majority of photo enthusiasts. If you are interested in learning more about such equipment, visit the websites of manufacturers such as Creo (www.creo.com), PhaseOne (www.phaseone.com), Kodak (www.kodak.com), Fujifilm (www.fujifilm.com), and Mega Vision (http://acme.mega-vision.com).

Figure 1.10: Some medium-format film cameras accept a digital back. This type of equipment is expensive and is designed to meet the needs of portrait and commercial studio photographers.

Choosing the Right Compact Digital Camera

If you have decided that a compact digicam is the right choice, and you're ready to shop for a new camera, which models should you consider? Frankly, far too many cameras are on the market to answer that question, with new models introduced every month and others discontinued. The answer also depends on your own needs, budget, preferences, and the types of subjects that you often photograph.

In this section, I'll discuss many digicam capabilities and comment about the value of each feature. After reading the following, you should know which capabilities you consider most important. Make a list of these features. While reviewing the specifications of several models (within your budget) on a photo retailer's website store, refer to the list; eliminate cameras that will not meet your needs. This process should help you to narrow the field to a few cameras that you'll want to check out in person at a well-stocked retail store.

Popular Compact Digicam Features

Digital cameras with built-in lenses generally include most or all of the following capabilities. The high-end prosumer cameras often include some esoteric features as well, but these are not common and are of little interest to most photographers.

Resolution

Presumably, you have already determined the resolution that you will require, and can afford, so you know whether you want a camera with a 3, 4, 5, or higher megapixel sensor. Do note that some cameras, particularly a few Fujifilm FinePix models, include a mode that produces images with double the resolution: 6 megapixels with a 3 megapixel camera, for example. This is achieved through "interpolation": adding extra pixels by copying existing pixels. Although this feature can be somewhat useful, the resulting images do not provide double the image quality.

Recording Options

As mentioned earlier, JPEG is the most common image-recording format. If you appreciate the benefits of the RAW format discussed earlier, and do not mind spending extra time at your computer converting RAW images, look for a camera that also includes a RAW capture mode.

Zoom Lens

Most digicams include an optical zoom lens (see Figure 1.11), usually a 3x model such as a 38–114mm equivalent. This type is convenient because it allows you to switch from wide-angle to telephoto framing in a second or two. A few cameras include a 4x or 5x optical zoom lens, for greater effective "reach," and an optical viewfinder. You can also find digicams with a much longer lens: a 6x or 8x zoom. These allow you to fill the frame with more distant subjects, but such cameras are larger, more expensive, and employ an Electronic Viewfinder (EVF). Frankly, unless you often photograph distant subjects, and find that you are comfortable with using an EVF, I would recommend sticking with a camera that includes a 3x, 4x, or 5x zoom lens and an optical viewfinder.

Figure 1.11: Digital cameras with a built-in zoom that extends to long focal lengths— like this Minolta model's 28–200mm equivalent lens — incorporate an electronic viewfinder and not the more common optical viewfinder.

Focus Options

Autofocus is standard, and most current cameras employ a "wide area" or "multipoint" autofocus system that can set focus even on a subject that is not in the center of the frame. This useful feature allows you to shoot quickly, without first centering the subject. It also encourages better composition, with the subject placed off-center in more of your pictures. Many cameras offer another valuable option, allowing single sensor selection for more accurate control over the exact point of focus—on the eyes in a portrait photo, for example.

Many cameras also include autofocus options for "landscape" (for infinity focus) and "macro" (from 1" to 5", for example.) Useful for subjects that are extremely close, or very far, from the camera, these are usually accessed with an analog control. If you select one of these, remember to reset the camera to conventional autofocusing afterward.

Still rare in compact cameras, Continuous Autofocus mode allows the camera to continuously change focus as you point the lens toward subjects at different distances. This feature is primarily used to reduce the time delay between pressing the shutter button and the instant of exposure. It is not the same as the Continuous "tracking" focus available with SLR cameras, for follow-focusing in action photography. A compact digicam's Continuous focus system may be able to keep up with the motion of a slow-moving subject, such as a person walking, but it will not produce sharp images of faster motion.

More and more digicams also offer a rudimentary manual focus system that allows you to preset focus for any of several distances; such systems are not very versatile or convenient to use. This is not a feature you will need unless you often photograph landscapes, a situation in which the ability to set focus to a specific distance can be essential.

ISO Setting

Most cameras have an automatic ISO (for International Organization for Standardization) feature that adjusts sensitivity depending on the brightness of the light. In low light, it sets a high ISO (such as 400) in order to allow for shooting at fast shutter speeds to prevent blur from camera shake. In bright light, when a fast shutter speed can be set at any ISO, the system sets a low ISO (such as 100) for the best image quality.

ISO is a term that was intended for application to photographic film and denotes the sensitivity of a film to light. (The ISO system replaced the older ASA numbering system.) A low ISO film has low sensitivity to light, and a high ISO film has high sensitivity and can record a correct exposure at a faster shutter speed. The terminology has been applied to digital cameras as well, a logical step, because the concept is identical.

The majority of cameras also offer manual ISO control for making your own settings: ISO 100, 200, and 400, for example. As discussed in the following paragraph, this is an important control but not available with all cameras; I would not buy a camera that omits this feature. Higher ISO options are available with some cameras, but are not really necessary for most of us. They may be useful for those who must often shoot in very low light—without flash or a tripod—when high image quality is secondary to getting a sharp, well-exposed shot.

Select ISO 100 for the best image quality and ISO 200 for fast shutter speeds on cloudy days. Reserve the ISO 400 (or higher) settings for low-light situations. A high ISO setting will provide faster shutter speeds for sharper pictures, but image quality will be much lower due to digital noise caused by the need to amplify the signal at the sensor. This noise resembles grain in images made with film, but is generally more objectionable because of the random colors it produces within the image. If possible, use ISO 100, and mount the camera on a table-top tripod in low light; with nearby subjects, use electronic flash. Then, you won't need to worry about camera shake, and you'll get better image quality.

Operating Modes

In addition to a basic Program (fully automatic) mode, many digicams include several other options. Extra Program modes, designed for good results with a suitable aperture/shutter speed combination for specific types of subjects, are great for aim-and-shoot simplicity. In my experience, the following Program modes are most often useful: Landscape, Portrait, and Sports.

If you're an experienced photographer, you'll also want a semiautomatic Aperture Priority mode that allows you to select a specific f/stop with the camera setting the correct shutter speed to maintain a good exposure. Set a wide aperture (such as f/2.8 or f/4) to blur away a busy background, using the longest zoom setting. Or select a small aperture (such as f/8 or f/11) and a wide-angle zoom setting to maintain sharpness from the foreground to the background in a city scene or a landscape. Some Program modes can achieve a similar effect but Aperture Priority mode gives you greater control.

A Shutter Priority mode is also common, and this feature allows you to set a fast or slow shutter speed, while the camera sets a correct aperture. Some cameras also include a fully manual mode that requires you to set both the aperture and shutter speed, guided by some indicator provided by the light meter. This feature is slow to use and is intended only for the most-experienced photographers.

White Balance Control

All digicams include an Auto White Balance feature that automatically adjusts for the type of ambient light: sunny, cloudy, household lamps, and so on. The automatic systems do not always provide ideal results, and some images will have an undesirable color cast. Consequently, most cameras include specific settings to match common lighting conditions. The more options, the better. Simply select the one that best matches the lighting, and you should get excellent images without a color cast. A few prosumer cameras also offer a Custom or Manual Preset White Balance option that allows you to "teach" the camera to render whites as white in a difficult lighting condition—under the sodium-vapor lamps found in some sports arenas, for instance. This feature is most useful if you often photograph under uncommon lighting conditions.

Light-Metering Options

To calculate a correct exposure—good brightness level—digital cameras generally employ a sophisticated "evaluative" or "multi zone" metering system. These evaluate the lighting pattern, ignore ultrabright or extremely dark areas, and set a good to excellent exposure in most situations. The most successful of these systems are highly reliable and may be all that most digicam owners require.

Experienced photographers who are familiar with the use of the less automated Center-Weighted metering system will want a camera that also includes this feature. Some exposure compensation will usually be required for good exposures with light- or dark-toned subjects. Spot Metering is also common in advanced and prosumer cameras and is intended for metering a small subject area such as a spot-lit performer against a dark stage. This feature requires some expertise in selecting an area to meter and in knowing when to increase or decrease exposure; hence, it's intended only for use by experienced photographers.

Exposure Compensation

Regardless of the type of metering system, in some situations a camera will not provide the ideal exposure; some pictures may be excessively dark or bright. That's why an exposure compensation dial is standard equipment for controlling image brightness.

This feature allows you to take a picture, check the image in the LCD monitor, and make adjustments for reshooting. If the image is too dark, set a +0.5 exposure compensation level and shoot again. If the image was too bright, set a -0.5 exposure compensation level before reshooting. Sometimes, you may need to use a higher level of compensation for optimal exposures; most cameras offer a range from -2 to + 2 , for a significantly darker or brighter image. Some allow you to select from an even wider range, such as -4 to +4, but you will rarely (if ever) need that capability.

It's not always possible to accurately determine whether the exposure was correct by checking the image on the LCD monitor. Image brightness can vary depending on the lighting conditions when viewing the monitor. Ideally, you should view the image in shade and not in direct sunlight. Some prosumer digicams include a "histogram" display, a feature that allows you to more accurately evaluate exposure, particularly loss of detail in shadow and highlight areas. The histogram is discussed in the "SLR Camera Capabilities" section.

Autoexposure bracketing (AEB) is another common advanced feature; when it's selected, the camera takes three images in a sequence, varying the amount of exposure by a preselected amount: for metered exposure, overexposure, and underexposure. This can be useful if you want to shoot quickly and are not sure if you need to set exposure compensation.

If shooting in a camera's RAW capture mode, you will not often need to use exposure compensation or bracketing. Using the RAW converter software in a computer, you can increase or decrease exposure by up to -2 or +1. That is adequate for most images, in my experience.

Flash Modes

Cameras with built-in flash include common settings such as Auto mode for flash when needed, Off mode for use when flash is not appropriate, and Red-Eye Reduction mode that can help reduce red-eye. Other useful modes worth looking for include Daylight or Forced flash, which triggers flash in bright conditions and is useful for brightening shadow areas, such as those cast over a person's face by the bill of a hat. Slow Sync flash is intended for long exposures with flash, perhaps to photograph a person in front of a city skyline at night. (Use a tripod to prevent blurry pictures caused by the long exposure.) Finally, a few cameras offer Flash Exposure Compensation or Flash Intensity Adjustment; this feature is most valuable for decreasing flash output outdoors, for a subtle flash effect that yields a more professional look.

If you often photograph distant subjects, you will want to use a high-powered flash unit with greater effective "reach" than the tiny, built-in flash. In that case, look for a camera that's designed to accept an accessory flash, generally only one that's made by the camera manufacturer.

LCD Monitor

Although this is a standard feature—for composing images and for viewing images that you have previously taken—some monitors are better than others. The best monitors are large (at least 1.8" diagonal), with high-image resolution (at least 100,000 pixels) and have an antireflection coating for greater ease of viewing in bright light. Some cameras offer Playback Zoom for enlarging portions of the monitor image to check sharpness; this can be a valuable feature.

Power Sources

Digital cameras devour batteries, especially when the LCD monitor is used often, making the familiar alkalines virtually useless because of their low power output. You'll want a camera that accepts high-capacity batteries either in the AA size or some unusual size/shape in a proprietary battery pack. Rechargeable Lithium Ion or Ni-MH (Nickel Metal Hydride, see Figure 1.12) batteries are the most practical since they offer high-power capacity, last a long time, and can be reused. Avoid cameras that accept only nonrechargeable lithium batteries because those are expensive to replace.

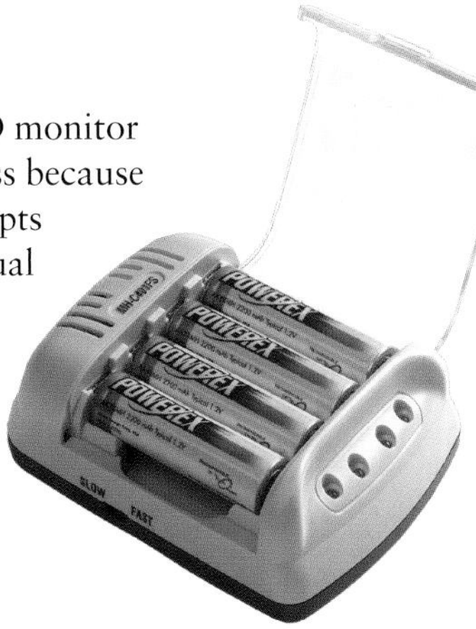

Courtesy of Maha Energy Corporation

Figure 1.12: Many digital cameras accept the rechargeable Ni-MH batteries in AA size. This type is inexpensive, offers high-power capacity, and can be recharged at least 500 times.

RECOMMENDATION: Get Extra Batteries

You'll want an extra battery pack or a set of batteries to prevent frustration caused by loss of power. Check the price of this accessory. The rechargeable Ni-MH AA batteries are quite affordable, but some of the proprietary battery packs are very expensive. If you shoot a great deal and will often need to change batteries, you'll probably want a camera that accepts rechargeable Ni-MH AA batteries. Buy several packs. In a pinch, you may also be able to use universally available alkaline AAs, although they may not last for many shots, especially when using the camera's LCD monitor for framing your images.

Storage Media

Digital cameras store images on removable, solid-state flash memory cards (see Figure 1.13). Several formats are available: CompactFlash, SmartMedia, xD-Picture Card, Memory Stick, SecureData (SD), and the very similar MultiMedia (MMC) cards are the most common today. (Cameras that accept SD cards are generally compatible with MMC cards too.)

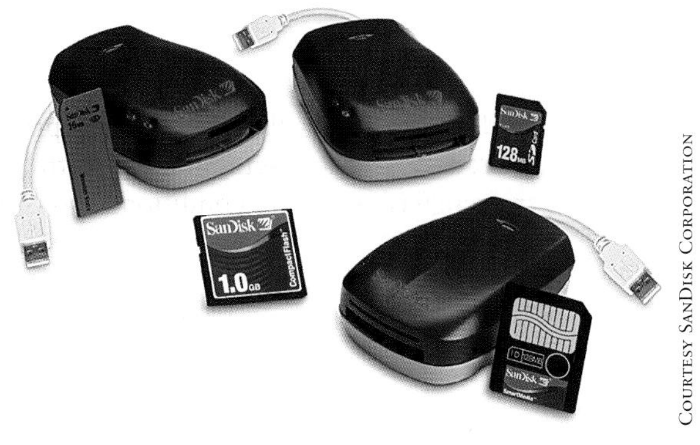

Courtesy SanDisk Corporation

Figure 1.13: Several types of memory cards are available, varying in size, thickness, and shape. You can also find memory card readers (discussed later in this chapter) that accept one or more types of cards; these accessories offer great convenience in downloading images taken with a digital camera.

Each type of card is different in size and shape, and with a few exceptions, cameras accept only one type of card. With compact digicams, there is really little advantage to one type of medium over another. All are available in maximum capacities of at least 256MB. Some cards are more expensive than others, however, so you might want to do a quick search on the Internet for current prices of various types of cards. Especially if you plan to buy several extra cards, use this information before deciding to buy a specific camera.

Other CompactFlash Issues

Some high capacity CompactFlash cards are designated as Type II, indicating that they are thicker than the conventional Type I card. Before buying one of these, check your camera owner's manual to make sure that it's compatible with Type II cards. CompactFlash cards with more than 2GB capacity are not only thicker (Type II) but use a new type of file system called FAT32; most current digital cameras support only the FAT16 file system. Check the card manufacturer's website for compatibility information about your camera before buying a card with a capacity of 2GB or more.

Some cameras also accept Microdrive media. These resemble a thick, Type II CompactFlash card, but contain a miniature hard drive, with moving parts, instead of solid-state flash memory. Only certain cameras—generally those that accept Type II CompactFlash cards—are compatible with Microdrives. Frankly, I recommend using CompactFlash cards in any event; they generally record data more quickly and are more rugged because they have no moving parts.

Other Features

When reviewing the specifications for any camera, check to see whether it accepts filters, so you can use filters such as a polarizer to reduce glare and to enrich blue skies. (Some cameras require an accessory tube for mounting filters.) Check whether batteries and charger are included in the kit.

Connectivity information can be important too when it comes time to hook up the camera to your computer to download images. If your computer includes a USB 2.0 port, for ultrahigh-speed data transfer, look for a camera that is fully USB 2.0 compatible. It will also support the earlier USB 1.1 connection that is more common on many computers, but the images will download at a much slower rate. Another high-speed option is a FireWire connection, which is standard on new Macintosh computers but not common on Windows-based computers.

Because it can be a hassle to hook up the camera whenever you want to transfer images, you will probably want to buy a memory card reader accessory. These cost $20 and up, and some models accept several types of memory cards. You can leave this accessory plugged in to one of your computer's USB or FireWire ports. Whenever you are ready to download images, simply insert the memory card into the card reader's slot. In that case, the accessory's connectivity information (not the camera's) will be the relevant factor.

RECOMMENDATION: Most Important Compact Digicam Features

Unless you need some additional capabilities for specific reasons, I suggest considering a 4+ megapixel camera with the following features: Aperture Priority and some program modes, the essential flash options (always on and off and red-eye reduction), JPEG recording mode, evaluative (multizone) light metering, the best possible LCD monitor, at least 4 White Balance and ISO options, wide-area autofocus with a single sensor option, a 3x or 4x zoom lens, and an optical viewfinder. Nice-to-have features include compatibility with filters and accessory flash units, Continuous Autofocus, and a RAW capture mode.

Choosing the Right Digital SLR Camera

Digital SLR cameras—resembling 35mm SLR cameras—are available in two ranges: professional and consumer. In this book, I will only briefly mention the pro cameras and will concentrate on the models that target consumers (see Figure 1.14). These are quite rugged and include all the features that the majority of photo enthusiasts require. They accept numerous lenses that allow for automatic or manual focusing, are compatible with accessory flash units, and are powered by high-capacity battery packs or (less commonly) by rechargeable AA batteries.

At the time of this writing, most are 5 or 6 megapixel cameras, although, the Sigma SD-9 and SD-10 incorporate a unique Foveon brand 3.43 megapixel sensor with 10.29 million "color photodetectors," discussed earlier. (For more information on this technology, visit the Foveon site at www.foveon.com.)

The professional SLR cameras (see Figure 1.15) are even more rugged, built like a tank to withstand pro caliber abuse. They include additional capabilities of interest to working professionals, such as news and sports photographers. Two types are available: models that produce ultrahigh resolution (more than 10 megapixels) and models that offer ultrahigh framing rates (such as 8 frames per second). A few pro cameras incorporate a full-frame sensor (the same size as a 35mm film frame) and do not produce the focal length magnification factor discussed earlier.

The pro cameras are also substantially more pricey than the consumer models; they cost double, triple, and even five times more, depending on the models compared. Although it's worth checking out the pro cameras on the Nikon, Canon, and Kodak websites as a matter of interest, I suspect that 95% of you will buy one of the consumer-oriented SLR cameras that I will discuss. (www.nikonusa.com, www.usa.canon.com, www. www.kodak.com).

COURTESY OLYMPUS AMERICA INC.

Figure 1.14: Digital SLR cameras resemble 35mm SLR cameras and include most of the same features, but they are more complex because they include the additional components required for digital imaging.

COURTESY NIKON INC.

Figure 1.15: Professional digital SLR cameras are heavier, larger, more expensive, and more rugged than consumer cameras. They are also faster, with a very high framing rate that makes them competitive with 35mm SLR cameras.

By the time you read this, cameras that were current at the time of writing may have been discontinued and replaced with new models with different feature sets. That's why I rarely discuss specific models in this book. You may find more advanced cameras, with higher resolution or higher speed, as well as more affordable models with fewer features and lower resolution. Still, the basic features will probably be similar.

SLR Camera Capabilities

All the features mentioned in the "Common Compact Digicam Features" section apply to digital SLR cameras, but there are additional capabilities. You'll often find more ISO options (higher and lower), numerous custom functions for tailoring camera operation to your own preferences, extras such as depth-of-field preview for visually assessing the range of apparent sharpness at any f/stop, high-speed continuous AF for tracking fast motion, and more. All these are fairly typical SLR features, although not every camera includes all of the same capabilities.

You'll want to consider some additional factors if you are thinking of buying an SLR camera (see Figure 1.16) or debating as to the type of camera that might be best for you.

COURTESY OF FUJIFILM USA

Figure 1.16: Digital SLR cameras include more capabilities than most compact digicams and different types of controls. They are more versatile but also more complicated to operate.

Additional Overrides Digital cameras typically feature numerous overrides of digital image parameters. Some models, for example include a full range of options for adjusting white balance, sharpness, contrast, color hue, tone, and saturation, as well as color balance fine-tuning. Other cameras offer fewer options. Review the specifications for all cameras that you are considering before making a final decision.

Frankly, you may not need all the overrides available in the most-full-featured cameras, especially if you often plan to shoot in the RAW capture mode, as discussed earlier. That's because you can adjust important image parameters using the conversion software. Even when shooting in JPEG or TIFF capture mode, there is really no need for an in-camera control for sharpness or color saturation; both parameters are best adjusted with image-editing software in your computer.

Most digital SLR cameras and many prosumer compact digicams include a feature called a histogram that can help you evaluate exposure. Some cameras can exhibit the histogram in both the Capture and Playback mode, while others offer it only in Playback. This feature can be useful for accurately evaluating image exposure, particularly highlight and shadow detail.

Color Space Options A color space defines the range of colors available for a particular digital image. Because of the way digital image files are organized, they can contain only a limited number of total colors. Therefore, only a portion of the total visible spectrum is available. That portion is the color space.

Two standard color spaces are available. Most digital cameras make use of the sRGB (standard Red, Green, Blue, a color space that is ideal for Internet use.) This color space is a great choice for images that will only be displayed on a monitor, but it is not ideal for printed output. Many, digital SLR cameras offer the option of recording images in the Adobe RGB (1998) color space, which provides a wider range of colors than sRGB and is more appropriate for printed output.

Granted, you can shoot in sRGB color space and later convert the images to Adobe RGB (1998) in your computer, providing a broader range of colors while editing the image. This is not ideal because an image recorded in sRGB does not capture colors that are outside this color space, but within the Adobe RGB (1998) color space. Consequently, it's worth looking for a camera that includes both color space options. Use Adobe RGB mode for shooting images that you plan to print; if you want to use some of the same pictures for e-mail or a web page, simply convert them to sRGB with image-editing software.

Speed Issues Because they are designed for serious photography, digital SLR cameras typically offer higher framing rates than most compact digicams: 3 frames per second or faster is common. Especially if you often shoot sports or other action, check the specifications for the maximum frame rate as well as the "burst depth": the maximum number of frames that you can shoot per burst in high-resolution capture modes.

Lens Compatibility Every digital SLR camera accepts only lenses with a specific lens mount, usually only autofocus lenses. Nikon, Fuji, and Kodak cameras take Nikon AF mount lenses; Canon cameras require EF mount lenses; Pentax cameras are fully compatible with Pentax AF mount lenses and partially compatible with some Pentax mount manual focus lenses; Sigma cameras require SA mount lenses made only by Sigma; and the Olympus digital SLR cameras are compatible only with the new series of Zuiko Digital lenses from Olympus. If you already own lenses that will be compatible with certain digital SLR models, you will probably want to consider one of those cameras.

Flash Unit Compatibility Most digital SLR cameras are equipped with a built-in flash unit that is not very powerful. If you need more power output, you'll need an accessory flash unit that is specifically dedicated to the camera for full compatibility.

You may already own a flash unit that is compatible with a 35mm camera made by a certain manufacturer, but this flash unit may not be compatible with a digital camera. For example, Nikon digital cameras require DX series flash units, Canon cameras require EX series flash units, and so on. (Information about flash unit compatibility is available on the camera manufacturers' websites.) While other flash units—designed for 35mm cameras of the same brand—may also work, they may not work properly, or some of the functions may not operate. Buy the right flash unit, and you'll have access to a vast range of professional lighting effects, as discussed in Chapter 6.

RECOMMENDATION: Most Important SLR Digicam Features

Unless you have specialized needs, I suggest a consumer grade 5+ megapixel SLR camera that includes at least the following capabilities. The camera should include a full set of operating modes, three exposure metering options, the primary overrides mentioned in the "Additional Overrides" section, high-speed continuous autofocus, 3+ frames per second framing rate, ISO options from 100 to 800, an Adobe RGB (1998) color space option, JPEG and RAW capture modes, a histogram display at least in Playback mode, and depth-of-field preview.

CHAPTER two

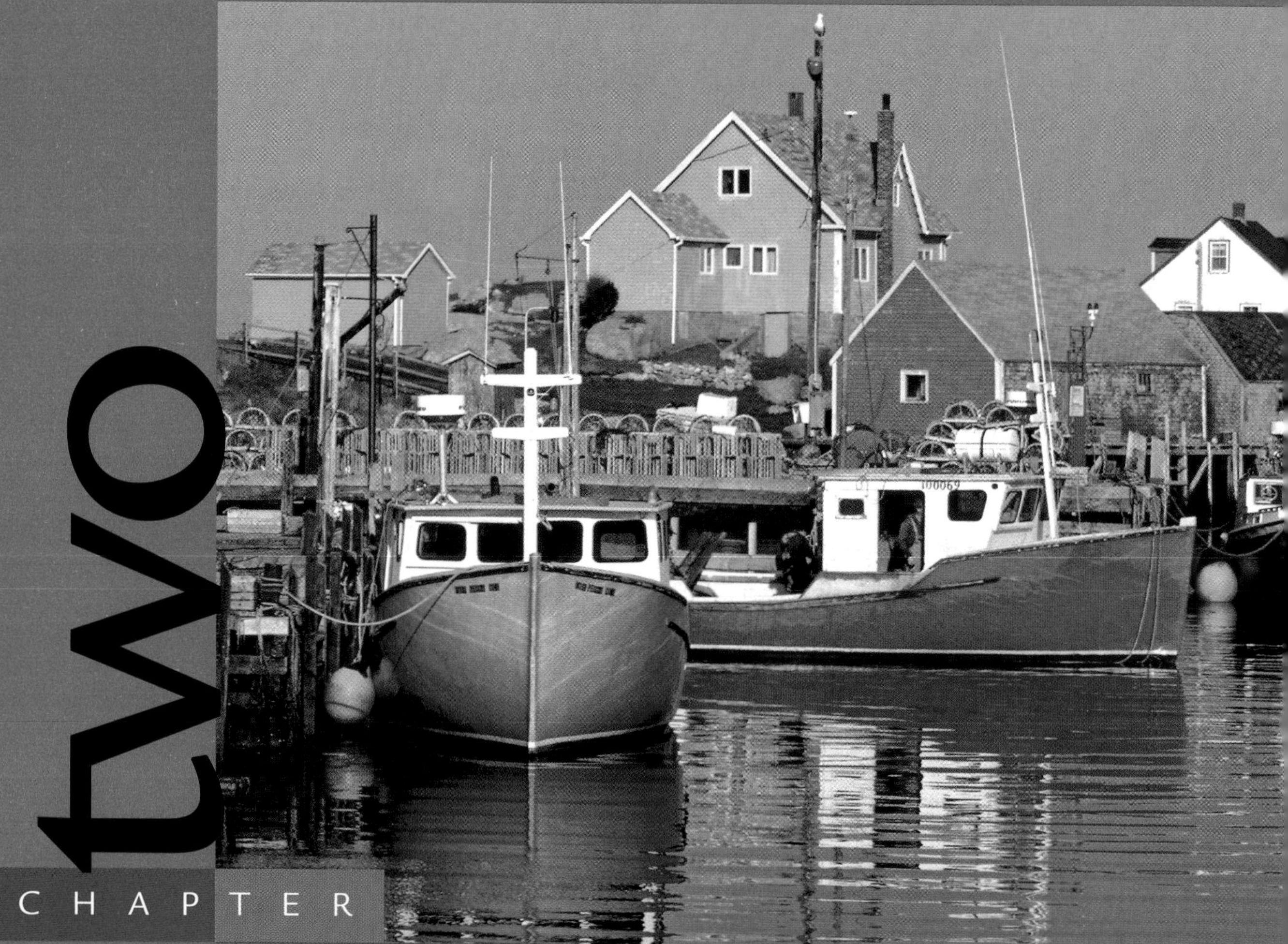

Introduction to Scanners

Although digital cameras are *certainly useful and convenient, a scanner remains a popular accessory. That's because many families and serious photographers are still shooting with a film camera but want digital images of their favorite photos. Even those of us who have switched to a digital camera usually own a scanner for digitizing the many negatives, color slides (the image on the left was scanned from a 35mm slide), and photographic prints that we have accumulated over the years.*

In this chapter, I'll discuss the types of scanners—as well as the commercial scanning services—that are available for consumers, and provide tips on selecting a scanner to meet your needs. We'll get into more advanced scanning issues, as well as techniques, in Chapter 8.

The Types of Scanners

A scanner is a piece of hardware designed to convert a document, a page from a book or a magazine, a piece of film, a photograph, or any flat artwork into an electronic image file format that can be transferred to a computer. Some scanners allow you to scan three-dimensional objects as well. Since this book is about photography and photo-oriented equipment, I'll emphasize the concepts and equipment that apply to digitizing negatives, color slides, and photographic prints.

Scanners operate by illuminating the original and reading the light with an imaging sensor like those used in digital cameras. Two primary types of scanners are available for consumer use—flatbed scanners and film scanners. Flatbed scanners are intended for scanning prints and other artwork but are often available with a "transparency adapter" for scanning

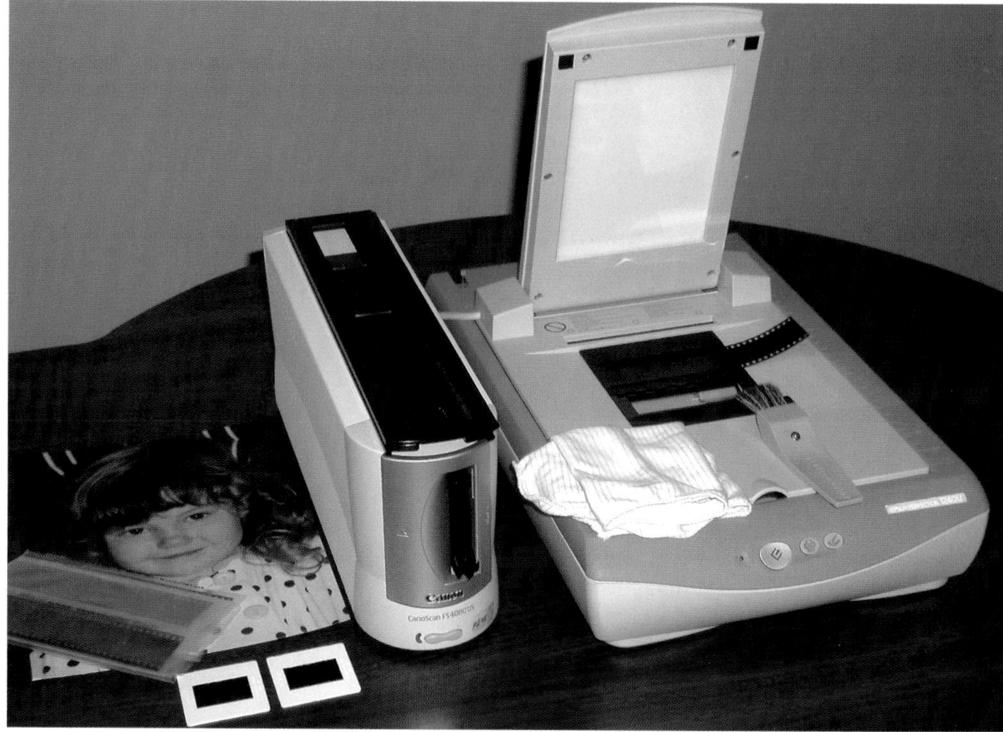

Figure 2.1: The primary scanners intended for consumers are the dedicated film scanners and the flatbed scanners, including those with an adapter for scanning negatives and transparencies.

film; the adapter illuminates the slide or negative from above. When using a flatbed scanner (see Figure 2.1), the light is reflected off the print and onto the imaging sensor.

Dedicated film scanners accept only film and are optimized for making scans from negatives and transparencies. During the scanning process, light is passed through the transparent slide or negative onto the imaging sensor. In both types of scanners, the sensor reads the intensity of the light striking it, using three passes or three rows of sensors to read individual values for red, green, and blue.

Scanner capabilities and features vary widely. As you would expect, the most expensive models—within any scanner-type category—offer the most features and produce the highest image quality.

Figure 2.2: In addition to the familiar flatbed designs, you can find newer scanner models that are particularly compact or very slim.

Flatbed Scanners

Resembling a photocopier with a lid and a glass plate where you can place a photo, a flatbed scanner is the most popular type (see Figure 2.2). Designed to scan photos as large as 8.75 × 12", most flatbeds are quite affordable and easy to use, and they come with software that is very user friendly. Some even offer "one touch" scanning; you can press one button to get an acceptable to good scan. Fortunately, most such scanners also offer a manual mode that provides some scan adjustment controls for factors such as brightness, contrast, and color rendition.

Flatbeds are available for as little as $50 for a low-resolution model (1200 × 2400 dpi) and for $400 and up for a high-resolution model (3200 × 6400 dpi) with extra features and more sophisticated scanner software. If you plan to use a flatbed scanner primarily for scanning prints, high resolution is not a critical issue. In fact, rarely would you want to scan a print at a resolution higher than about 600 dpi.

Another important issue is the bit-depth of the scanner, which determines the range of colors the scanner can distinguish. The best scanners are able to scan at 48 bits, but even 36-bit scanners can provide excellent scans. A 24-bit scanner offers the minimum color range needed for scanning photos.

The transparency adapter hardware required to digitize slides and negatives is included with some high-end models and is an extra-cost accessory with certain flatbeds in the medium price range.

Dedicated Film Scanners

Designed to scan negative and transparency film exclusively, most film scanners (see Figure 2.3) accept only 35mm format film and, with an adapter, the smaller Advanced Photo System (APS) format film. A few models are available that accept medium-format film as well.

The typical film scanner for 35mm film offers 2700 to 2900 dpi resolution, makes image files as large as about 28MB when set to the highest optical resolution, and costs $300 and up. (See the "Primary Scanner Features" section for a discussion of resolution issues.) Several 4000 dpi models are also available, and these can make scans in excess of 50MB. They cost $1000 and up. Models with even higher resolution are becoming available as well, such as the Minolta DiMAGE Scan Elite 5400, a 5400 dpi scanner. Scanners that also accept medium-format negatives and transparencies are generally also 4000 dpi models, and these can make image files in excess of 100MB, depending on the size of the original. They cost $2400 and up.

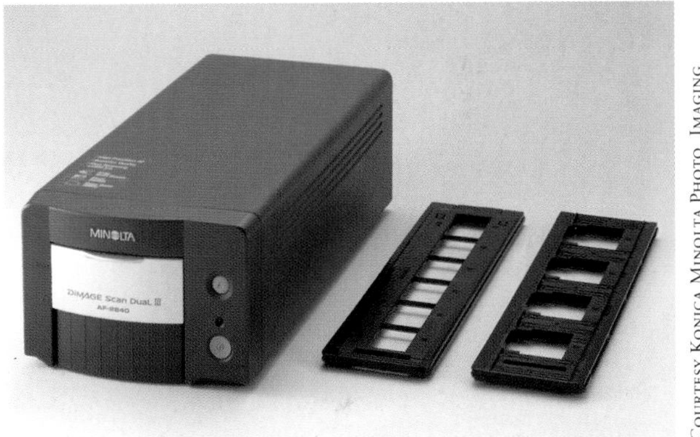

Courtesy Konica Minolta Photo Imaging U.S.A., Inc.

Figure 2.3: Dedicated film scanners are intended for photographers who want to make high-quality, high-resolution scans from 35mm or larger-format negatives and transparencies.

In addition to the common 8-bit per channel depth mode (often called 24-bit), many of the latest film scanners also offer an option to scan in a 12-bit per channel color mode (often called 36-bit), producing a file with 16-bit color (16 bits per channel). When this option is selected, the image file size is doubled. Although you might not want to create such large files, higher bit-depth means more tonal and color information in the final image file. This provides more latitude for adjustments to the image, helping to ensure smooth gradations of tone and color in the image even after significant editing. Additional recommendations will be provided on working with 16-bit color in Chapter 9.

Film scanners usually include sophisticated scanner software packages (discussed in the "Primary Scanner Features" section). For anyone with some experience using the advanced features of image-editing software—such as Curves and Levels—the similar software tools can be invaluable for making scans that are close to perfect, as discussed in Chapter 8.

Other Types of Scanners and Scanning Services

In addition to the flatbed and film scanners made for consumer use, you can find expensive, ultrahigh-resolution "upright" ($15,000) and "drum" ($80,000+) scanners. These are intended for use by studios, publishers, advertising or stock agencies, and service bureaus for generating massive image files with up to 11,000 dpi resolution. They are prohibitively expensive for most photo enthusiasts. If you occasionally need ultrahigh-resolution scans, look for a service bureau in your area that offers this service, do a web search, or check the ads in some of the digital photography magazines. Expect to pay at least $100 for an ultrahigh-resolution drum scan.

Courtesy Epson America, Inc.

Figure 2.4: Ultrahigh-resolution upright and drum scanners are prohibitively expensive, but most serious photographers, and even some professionals, find that a high-quality 4000 dpi film scanner ($1000+) meets the majority of their 35mm needs with image files in excess of 50MB.

More affordable scanning services are available for making digital image files from 35mm slides or negatives; these are offered by a growing number of labs that process film. The labs use a variety of equipment for making low to moderately high resolution scans (Figure 2.4). Expect to pay a few dollars per scan plus an extra fee for the cost of the CD used to store your images.

Some labs will make scans using a system such as the Photo-CD from Kodak Digital Science Photo (www.kodak.com/global/en/professional/products/storage/pcdMaster/aboutPCD.jhtml) or another proprietary service. Order scans from your negatives or slides and the lab will charge a dollar or two per scan plus a fee for the CD. A Photo-CD will include images in six levels of resolution from 128 × 192 pixels to 2048 × 3072 pixels. The latter—when made from a razor-sharp slide or negative—is adequate for making good 11 × 16" prints and good prints in sizes up to 13 × 19".

Some service bureaus offer the Kodak Pro Photo CD Scan service that produces even higher resolution with six different resolutions per image up to a 72MB file (4096 × 6144 pixels). (This service costs about $10 per scan plus a fee for the CD. Check out www.kodak.com/global/en/professional/products/. If you do not need high-resolution scans, you might select the Kodak Picture CD option instead, for scans with 1024 × 1536 pixel resolution (www.kodak.com/global/en/professional/products).

Primary Scanner Features

Since flatbed and 35mm film scanners are by far the most popular, and also the most practical for photo enthusiasts, I'll emphasize these types. The basic features of both types of scanners are similar, although each has some unique features. The following are the most important features you'll need to consider when shopping for a flatbed or a dedicated film scanner.

Resolution

Just like digital cameras, some scanners can produce higher resolution than others: more pixels per inch (abbreviated as ppi) in an image file. The more pixels per inch, the more picture information and the larger the image data file. The higher resolution is useful if you want to produce large prints of high quality.

Although the correct term to denote resolution is ppi (pixels per inch), manufacturers routinely use dpi (dots per inch). This is actually a misnomer, but since it is becoming universally accepted, I will also discuss scanner resolution in dpi. Whenever you think of scanners, however, think of their resolution in terms of the number of pixels per inch.

With flatbed scanners (see Figure 2.5), resolution is generally stated with two numbers, such as 1200 × 2400 dpi optical resolution. That's because a scanner offers higher resolution (more pixels) in the horizontal direction than in the vertical plane. Its processor then "interpolates" (generates extra vertical pixels) so you get a properly scaled image. In any event, it's the first number that's the most meaningful and the most useful when comparison shopping. (With film scanners, only a single dpi numeral is used to denote resolution.)

When reviewing a scanner's specifications, you may find some higher resolution numbers as well, such as 9600 × 9600 dpi "enhanced resolution" or "interpolated resolution." This indicates that the scanner software can employ algorithms to interpolate the image, artificially increasing the number of pixels by a substantial amount.

Figure 2.5: The highest optical resolution currently available in consumer-grade flatbed scanners is 4800 × 4800 dpi. In 35mm film scanners, 5400 dpi is available, and medium-format film scanners offer a maximum of 4000 dpi.

Ignore enhanced or interpolated resolution data when comparing scanners. Optical resolution is a far more realistic reflection of the image quality. You are far better off scanning at maximum optical resolution and then scaling the image up using image-editing software if you need a larger image than the scanner can produce.

RECOMMENDATION: Scanner Resolution

How much resolution do you need? Consider the following as a rule of thumb.

Optical resolution of 1200 × 2400 dpi is adequate in a flatbed scanner ($100 or less) that will be used to scan photographic prints. If you plan to scan slides and negatives, you'll want a flatbed with at least 2400 × 4800 dpi resolution ($200+) if you want to make prints larger than 8.5 × 11".

In a dedicated film scanner, look for a high-quality machine with 2700 dpi to 2900 dpi optical resolution ($500+); the resulting scans should allow you to make prints as large as 10 × 15". If you need ultrahigh-resolution scans for making larger prints, or if you demand superior quality, you may be a candidate for one of the 4000 dpi machines ($750+).

Dynamic Range

Another important factor is the "dynamic range," or "density range," which refers to a scale of brightness values from pure white to black. It determines the number of tones, from pure white to darkest black, that the scanner can see. A scanner with a high dynamic range will produce images with more detail in highlight and shadow areas than a scanner with a lower dynamic range. Scanner manufacturers provide data on dynamic range in numerals, often between 3 and 4.5. The specifications for some inexpensive scanners do not provide this data; in that case, you can assume that the dynamic range is very low. A scanner with a high dynamic range offers three benefits. It captures far more detail in bright areas of an image; it differentiates between various shades of black; and you'll get less of a digital noise pattern in shadow areas. Even a slight difference in dynamic range numbers—3.4 versus 3.2, for example—is substantial. That's because the scale is logarithmic; every 0.1 increase represents a factor of 2. Consequently, a scanner with a dynamic range of 3.4 will produce images with greater detail in shadow and highlight areas than a machine with a dynamic range of 3.2.

RECOMMENDATION: Minimum Dynamic Range

A dynamic range of 3 is more than adequate for scanning photographic prints. If you plan to scan negatives, 3.2 is the minimum you'll want. Because a slide or a larger transparency contains more contrast than a negative, look for a scanner that offers a dynamic range of 3.4 or, preferably, 3.6. Some film scanners' specifications boast a dynamic range that's higher than the theoretical maximum of 4; this capability exceeds the range of tones in a slide or negative.

However, in actual practice I've found that even when a scanner has a dynamic range that *should* enable it to record all tonal values in the original, some information is lost. It's worth buying a film scanner with the highest dynamic range available in your price range. This will ensure that the machine can capture as much detail as possible, but doesn't guarantee that it will capture the full range of tones present in the original slide or larger transparency.

Color Depth

Also called bit-depth, this factor determines the number of colors that a scanner can see. The higher the bit-depth, the more accurate the colors in the scanned image, with full rendition of the subtle differences between similar colors. Most scanners offer color depth of at least 8 bits per channel—for red, green, and blue, the three colors used in imaging. This is often denoted as 24-bit color depth in the specifications. This level is adequate for most purposes, because it records "true color": more than 16.7 million distinct colors, at least in theory.

A variety of factors can limit the range of colors that are actually recorded when scanning. Also, when you enhance the image in image editing software, additional color information is eroded. Therefore, higher bit-depth is preferable, particularly for images that will be edited significantly.

Some high-end scanners offer much higher color depth, producing image files with 16 bits per channel or 48 bits in total; at this setting, the scanner can record more than 281 trillion possible colors, in theory. In actual practice, far fewer colors will be recorded, but you'll still have considerably more information than you'll find in a 24-bit image.

Few image-processing programs can work with color depth higher than 24 bit, and inkjet printers will sample the data down to 8 bits per channel before printing. Adobe Photoshop 7 allows you to work with 16-bit per channel images, but with significant limitations. The latest version of Photoshop, called CS, allows you to use most of the software's tools and utilities when working with the high-bit files, so you can take advantage of high-bit scans to produce images with smoother gradations of tone and color.

RECOMMENDATION: Color Depth

Since 36-bit color depth is commonly available, I can't recommend a film scanner that offers only 24-bit capability. If you're a serious photographer who wants to produce the best possible prints from scans, check out scanners with 48-bit color depth to take advantage of the additional range of tones and colors they can capture.

Included Software

More and more new scanners include software for automatically removing dust specks and scratches (see Figure 2.6). Some also include features for automatically restoring color in faded photos and/or reducing the apparent graininess of scans made from a slide, a negative, or a print. These features can save a lot of time in correcting image defects in your image-editing

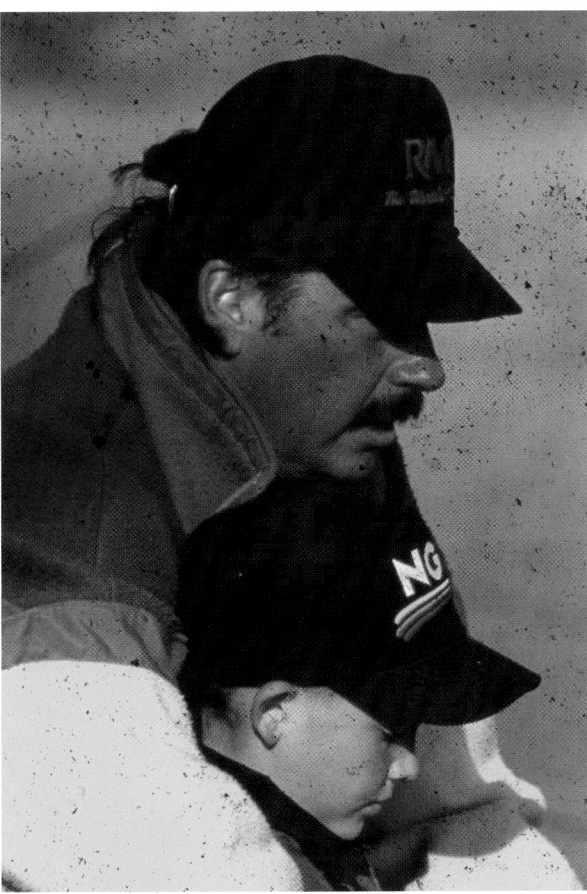

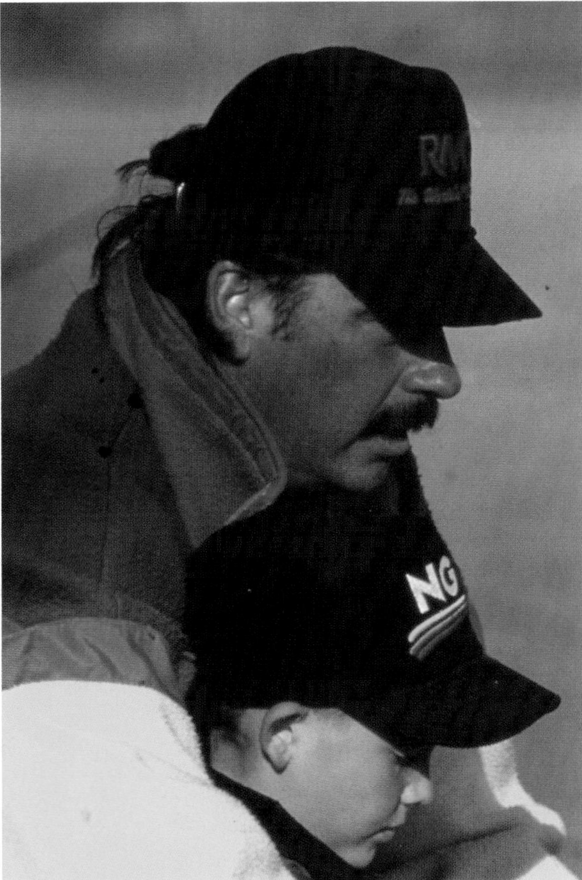

Figure 2.6: Scanner software that includes features for correcting image defects can be useful. Most photographers find the dust/scratch removal software valuable. For the image on the right, Digital ICE^3 was applied to eliminate defects.

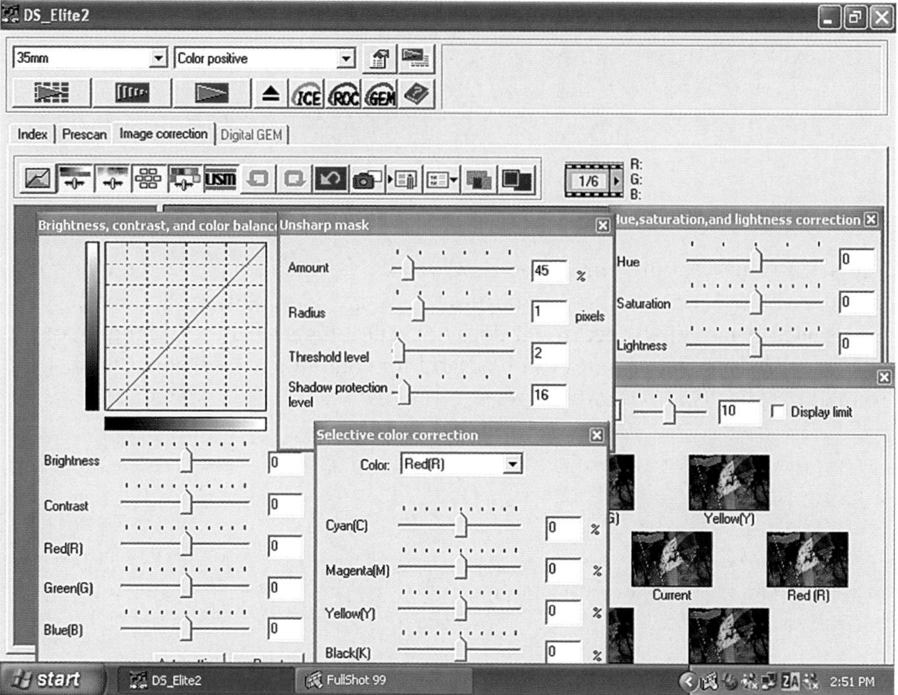

Figure 2.7: The medium- to higher-priced scanners often include sophisticated and versatile image-enhancement and editing features. Many of the tools are similar to those you would expect to find in one of the Adobe Photoshop programs, while others are intended for multisampling and for correcting image defects.

software later, but they do slow the scanning process and generate scans that are slightly or noticeably "soft," depending on the specific technology used.

High-end film scanners also include multisampling capability used to produce scans with less digital noise in dark areas. This process will cause the scan to take considerably longer, as the scanner must scan the image multiple times and then compare the results. Any pixel values that differ from one scan to the next are determined to be noise, and dealt with accordingly by the software.

Finally, some scanners include sophisticated software that includes a wide range of advanced image-enhancement tools (see Figure 2.7). Although most scanners intended for photo scanning provide *some* such tools, the high-end models include far more sophisticated options. These provide a much greater degree of fine control over all aspects of an image: contrast, sharpness, color balance and saturation, sharpness, highlight and shadow detail, and so on.

RECOMMENDATION: Included Software

A dust and scratch removal system—particularly one with sophisticated technology such as Digital ICE³ and the new ICE⁴—can produce clean scans without degrading image sharpness to a great extent. I rarely find the color-restoration and grain-reduction features necessary, but you might want this technology if you plan to scan many old, faded photos or very grainy film or photographs.

A multisampling feature is useful for scanning slides or negatives that contain very dark areas. If you frequently photograph night scenes or areas with deep shadows, consider buying a scanner with a multisampling feature to minimize digital noise in the dark areas.

continues

Highly sophisticated software, with the types of tools you might find in a program such as Adobe Photoshop, is beneficial for serious photographers who want to make the best possible scans. Before buying a midrange to expensive scanner, make sure that it includes versatile scanner software with numerous capabilities; Chapter 8 includes more specific recommendations on this issue.

Speed

As you would expect, some scanners are faster than others, producing a digital file with the same number of pixels in less time. The specifications provide an estimate as to scanning speed, but this is usually unrealistic because it does not reflect high-resolution scanning of a photograph. Nonetheless, such estimates can be useful for comparing one scanner with another as long as the specifications indicate the method used by both manufacturers to calculate speed.

Expect to pay more for a fast scanner than for a slow scanner. And remember that actual scanning speed will depend on a number of factors, including the speed of your computer, the type of connectivity (ultrafast USB 2.0 or Firewire versus USB 1.1, for example), and the use of features that require additional processing by the scanner software. When activated, image defect correction tools and multisampling can significantly increase scanning time, particularly when several of the features are used.

RECOMMENDATION: Scanner Speed

Use scanners' speed specs only for comparison purposes; expect much longer actual scan times. If you're considering a dedicated film scanner, check out models that allow you to load at least four slides or six negatives at one time, perhaps with an extra-cost accessory. This "batch scanning" will save a lot of time.

If you intend to make many scans, especially high-resolution scans, it's worth paying more for a fast machine. But remember that you need a fast computer and the right connectivity to take advantage of high-speed data-transfer features.

Connectivity

Current scanners are generally designed for connecting to a computer with a USB (Universal Serial Bus) connection, with some higher-end scanners using a FireWire (IEEE 1394) connection. (IEEE stands for Institute of Electrical and Electronics Engineers, a coordinating body that establishes telecommunications standards.) Both types of connectivity are much faster than the earlier parallel port connectivity. They are also much simpler and more reliable than the SCSI (Small Computer System Interface) connectivity that was common at one time on high-end scanners but could be difficult to manage for inexperienced users.

Naturally, for a USB scanner you will need a computer with a USB port, a common feature on computers made in the past few years. (You can add USB connectivity with an optional card, if necessary.) The USB connectivity offers great simplicity; plug the scanner in and load the accompanying software, and you can start making scans in a few minutes.

The USB 1.1 technology was standard for many years, and it offers fast data transfer. Some scanners are now sold with the newer USB 2.0 connectivity that offers much faster data transfer. Don't worry if your computer doesn't have a USB 2.0 port and card because a

USB 2.0 system is fully backward compatible; it will work with a USB 1.1 computer port, at the slower speed, of course.

A few high-end scanners also offer FireWire (or IEEE 1394) connectivity. We will likely see future scanners supporting the new FireWire 800 standard, which will double the speed of FireWire connections.

How Fast is USB 1.1, USB 2.0, and FireWire?

According to manufacturers' specifications, USB 1.1 has a maximum data transfer rate or throughput of 12Mbps (megabits per second) while USB 2.0 offers a maximum 480Mbps transfer rate, and FireWire offers a maximum of 400Mbps. Based on this data, you might expect USB 2.0 connectivity to be 40 times faster than USB 1.1. Based on my experience when scanning photographs, USB 2.0 connectivity is about 4 times faster than USB 1.1; in other words, a scan is completed in about one-quarter the time. Although USB 2.0 should be faster than FireWire, the latter is actually slightly faster in actual use, because of "the additional overhead of USB 2.0," according to one expert. I find the difference to be negligible and can recommend either form of connectivity.

RECOMMENDATION: USB 2.0 Connectivity

Data transfer through a USB 1.1 connection is a slow process but is not particularly troublesome if you make low resolution scans, without a large amount of data that must be transferred. If you plan to buy a high-resolution scanner and intend to make scans that produce 20MB or larger image files, you will want a machine with USB 2.0 or FireWire connectivity. If your computer does not currently offer support for USB 2.0 or FireWire, upgrade it with the necessary hardware. You can do so for less than $100. Since most computer accessories—such as cameras and memory card readers—connect to a computer with a USB cable, you'll find USB 2.0 connectivity to be a more practical addition than FireWire support.

Figure 2.8: Some of the latest flatbed scanners, such as this Epson model, include a transparency adapter. Many others accept an optional accessory adapter.

PHOTO COURTESY EPSON CANADA LTD.

Transparency Adapter

Standard flatbed scanners are not designed to digitize a transparent negative, slide, or larger transparency. To do so, you'll need a model with a "transparency adapter" that has its own light source. Some new flatbed scanners (see Figure 2.8) are sold with the necessary adapter, sometimes built-in, while others offer it as an extra-cost accessory.

RECOMMENDATION: Transparency Adapter or Film Scanner?

A dedicated film scanner can produce much higher quality scans than a flatbed with transparency adapter, but not everyone can justify owning both types of machines. Also, high-quality film scanners, particularly those that accept medium-format negatives and transparencies, are expensive. Nonetheless, if you primarily need a scanner for digitizing many 35mm slides and negatives, save up for a dedicated film scanner.

A flatbed scanner with a transparency adapter can be versatile, allowing you to scan prints as well as negatives and transparencies of all sizes, typically up to 4 × 5". If you generally scan medium-format or larger film, you may not need more than 2400 × 4800 dpi resolution even for making 16 × 24" prints. That's because the original is quite large and will not require much magnification. If you plan to scan tiny 35mm slides and negatives with a flatbed with an adapter, you'll need a scanner with at least 2400 dpi resolution for the quality that you'll want in order to make good 8 × 10" prints. Look for a 3200 × 6400 dpi flatbed with adapter if you plan to make larger prints, of high quality, from 35mm film.

CHAPTER three

Computer Setups for Digital Imaging

Since you are reading a book *about digital imaging, I'll assume that you already own a computer. Chances are, you can get started with some imaging—downloading images from a digital camera, scanning, and image editing—with your current computer. It might require some upgrades, and you might also be thinking of buying a new computer. This chapter will take a look at what upgrades are most useful and worthwhile and at what type of computer, monitor, and peripherals are best for digital imaging. With the right equipment, digital imaging can be enjoyable, without the frustration caused by slow processing, lockups, and crashes.*

Windows or Macintosh?

If you want to start a heated debate among a group of computer enthusiasts, simply pose the question, Which is better: a Macintosh or a Windows-based computer? After an hour of listening to the resulting commentary, you'll probably still have no idea as to which is better in general or which is most suitable for digital imaging. To save you the time and confusion, I'll answer the question in one sentence: for the digital imaging enthusiast, one type of computer is just as suitable as the other.

At one time, Macintosh computers were definitely the leaders in digital imaging for several reasons:

- Most of the best imaging software was available only for the Mac.
- A Mac was far easier and more convenient to operate than a PC with a DOS-based operating system.
- The Mac's graphical interface was ideal for digital imaging.
- Macs offered superior color management and graphics tools.

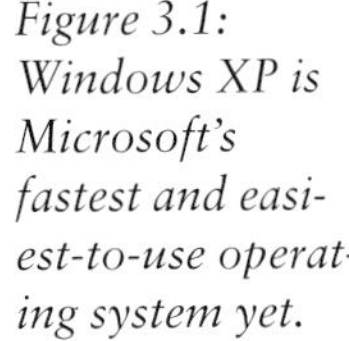

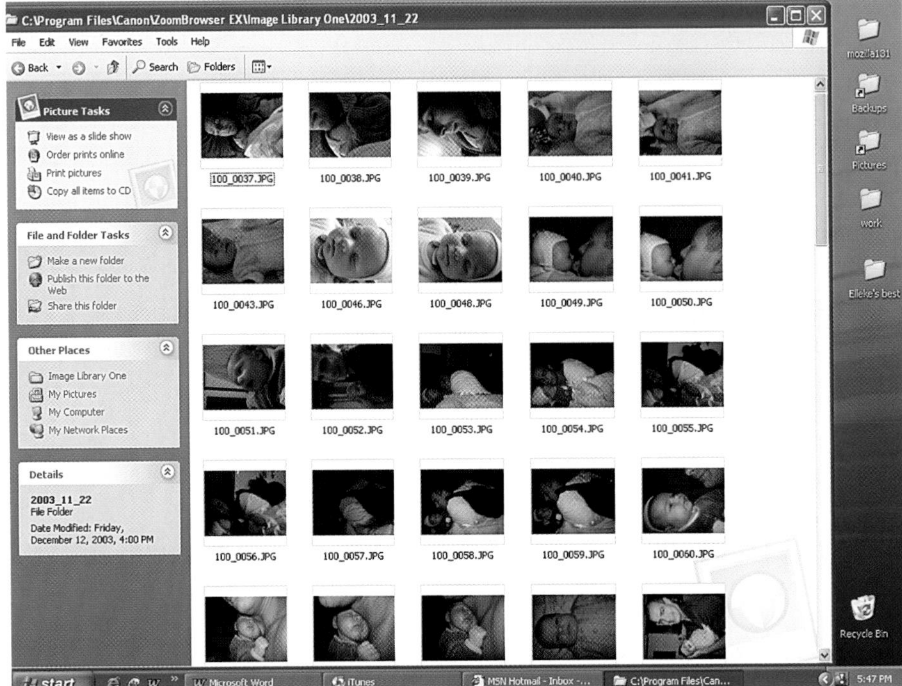

Figure 3.1: Windows XP is Microsoft's fastest and easiest-to-use operating system yet.

In many respects, Windows has caught up; particularly with Windows XP, this platform is fast, effective, and convenient for digital imaging (see Figure 3.1). Although Macs at the highest end of the price range may have some advantages in power and speed, these are not significant considerations for the vast majority of imaging enthusiasts.

Nearly all current digital cameras, scanners, and peripherals are compatible with both operating systems. Most of the software programs designed for some aspect of digital imaging are available for both systems, although some, especially low-end programs, are initially introduced only for Windows. When deciding which platform might be most suitable for your needs, think about the following issues.

Familiarity What platform are you currently using? If you are familiar and comfortable with one operating system, you may not really want to change to an entirely different system. You might also want to stick with your current system because most of the software that you own will not be compatible with the other operating system.

Which platform are your friends using? It's worth owning the same operating system as they do, in case you ever need help or advice. Unless you live in a major city, you might also want to ask the repair facilities in your area as to the support they offer for each platform.

Software Issues While this is changing, some software, for imaging and other purposes, is only available for Windows or Mac, not both. Do some research on the Internet as to the software that you want and its availability for the platform that you are considering.

Budget After checking prices at retailers and web stores such as www.dell.com, www.sonystyle.com, and www.apple.com, ask yourself, Which platform offers the best value for the money in my price range?

The "Cool Factor" Do you absolutely love the design of one type of computer and find another to be old-fashioned or boring? Aesthetic considerations such as this are not frivolous, especially when you're spending a lot of money and plan to spend a great deal of time working with your new system. Do not underestimate the value that pride of ownership can provide.

RECOMMENDATION: Windows versus Macintosh

What is the bottom line on the best operating system for digital imaging? In my view, both are ideal for this purpose. The Mac may be preferable for some professional photographers because most stock photo agencies, as well as photo buyers, ad agencies, and publishers, use Macintosh computers. On the other hand, I own a Windows PC, as do many of the imaging enthusiasts and professional photographers that I know. Since both Windows and Mac operating systems can work with JPEG, TIFF, and Adobe Photoshop PSD image files, compatibility is not a problem even in my business of stock photography and the production of illustrated articles for publishers in several countries. Address the issues discussed earlier before making your decision, and you will be satisfied whether you buy a Mac or a Windows-based system.

Desktop Computer Components

A desktop computer system (see Figure 3.2) will include the following major components.

A Microprocessor, or CPU (central processing unit) The central "brain" of the computer; performs the mathematical operations that are at the heart of all tasks the computer handles. A high-speed CPU, with a clock speed of 2 to 3GHz (gigahertz, or billions of cycles per second) is common in Windows-based computers. The Mac employs a different system architecture, so a 1 to 2GHz processor offers similar performance.

Random Access Memory (RAM) Provides temporary storage of data required by your software. The computer uses RAM in a way that is similar to the way you might use a scratch piece of paper to work out a math problem. With any type of computer, a lot of RAM helps ensure fast processing and reduces the risk of lockups and crashes.

Hard Drive A magnetic disk that provides permanent storage of information in your computer; this is where you save files. Because image files and imaging software programs consume large amounts of space on a hard drive, high capacity is essential. Although a 40GB hard drive is standard on midrange computers, it's worth paying a bit extra to upgrade to a 100GB hard drive. If the hard drive that you buy proves inadequate in the future, you can add an extra hard drive. Most of the current hard drives are very fast, able to potentially read or write more than 100MB per second.

PHOTO USED WITH PERMISSION OF SONY CORPORATION

Figure3.2: You can purchase a desktop computer system in customized form, including the specific components you want.

Figure 3.3: CRT monitors are much larger and heavier than LCD monitors but are preferable for digital imaging.

Monitor Provides a visual display of data and images in your computer. Two types of monitors are available for desktop computers, the conventional CRT (cathode ray tube) monitors (see Figure 3.3) and the slimmer and lighter LCD (liquid crystal display) monitors. (Laptop computers use LCD monitors, but these are also available for desktop systems.) Solid state LCD monitors employ pixels made of liquid crystals instead of using the CRT's conventional electron gun and phosphors. An LCD monitor provides a sharper, smoother, crisper view. The advertised size is also the real size of the display, because the edges are not blocked by the monitor case as with CRT monitors. But CRT monitors have advantages too, and some of these make them preferable for serious imaging: they cost much less than a comparable LCD monitor, display more vibrant colors, and have wider viewing angles. CRT monitors can also support a wide range of resolutions with no loss in image quality, which is not possible with LCD monitors.

A 19-inch or larger monitor is useful because it allows you to see a more of an image when it is enlarged. It also allows you to see more of the image area when software control panels and dialog boxes are open, and it makes it easier to view two images that are open simultaneously. Useful monitor features include a fast refresh rate, 100Hz for example, to prevent screen flicker, and a small dot pitch (a measurement of like-colored dots on a monitor; the lower the number, the higher the image quality). Conventional CRT monitors with a low dot pitch, such as 0.26 and especially 0.24mm, produce a crisp and sharp image because the individual pixels are closer together.

Video Card Produces the actual signal that is used to display an image on your monitor. A powerful card with at least 32MB of Video RAM (VRAM) ensures that your screen redraws quickly to reflect any changes you make to the image. When you use a higher resolution and higher bit-depth for your monitor display, more memory is required for the video card to be able to process the data quickly. Many cards today are even more powerful with at least 64MB of RAM.

Peripherals Which can include a floppy disk drive, a CD or DVD drive (including support for writing to those disc types), a second hard drive, a memory card reader, an all-purpose or photo printer, and perhaps a tablet and stylus (see Figure 3.4) to use in place of a mouse with photo-editing to provide more control.

Using a Tablet and Stylus for Image Editing

For many photo-editing tasks, you'll find that you need to exercise precise control over the mouse. In those situations, you might prefer to use a stylus because you manipulate it with your fingers as you would a pen, rather than moving your whole hand with a mouse. In addition to allowing more control over cursor movement, the stylus is pressure sensitive. This allows a whole new area of control. Applying varying degrees of pressure can control the size, hardness, or other attributes of the various brush tools used in photo-editing software.

The Wacom (**www.wacom.com**) brand of tablets all include a stylus and wireless mouse. If you're just getting started with digital imaging and want to experiment with an inexpensive tool, the Wacom Graphire series offers good performance at a reasonable price ($100 and up). However, its tablet does not provide adequately high resolution for detailed work. Instead, I would recommend one of the Wacom Intuos tablets, which range in sizes from 4" × 5" to 12" × 18" and in price from $250 to $750. The 9" × 12" model is an excellent compromise between available surface area and the amount of desk space consumed.

Basic Hardware for the Digital Darkroom

Digital imaging calls for a high-speed processor, plenty of RAM, and a high-capacity hard drive for storing large image files. Unless you will be working with many huge files (50MB or larger) or editing digital video, you should be satisfied with a "basic" system. For typical imaging needs—frequently working with image files as large as 30MB in Adobe Photoshop and for making prints as large as 13" × 19"—the following midrange desktop system should certainly be adequate.

Consider these recommendations as a starting point in your own research as to the type of equipment you want to investigate. Check web stores for specifics on the latest models and current prices. By the time you read this, faster and more advanced processors may be available in a similar price range; shop around to get the most for your budget.

Wacom Technology Corporation

Figure 3.4: A tablet and stylus system offers precise control over many aspects of digital-image enhancement.

Windows-Based Computers

In a Windows-based computer system (see Figure 3.5), preferably preloaded with Windows XP, consider an Intel Pentium 4 or comparable processor (2.6GHz or faster) with 512MB RAM, a 60GB or larger hard drive, a video graphics card with at least 32MB VRAM and a 19-inch CRT monitor with low (0.24mm) dot pitch and fast (75Hz or higher) refresh rate. The computer should be equipped with USB ports, preferably the ultrafast USB 2 connectivity as discussed in Chapter 2. You will also want a high-speed 40x12x48x CD "burner"drive for writing images to a CD for long-term storage. (A 40x12x48x machine offers a Write speed of 40x, a ReWrite speed of 12x, and a Read speed of 48x.)

A package of this type should cost less than $2000. It will provide high speed in opening software programs and image files and applying software tools and filters and will allow you to open several image files at one time without fear of frequent lockups or crashes.

If your budget is tight, you might look for a system with a 17-inch monitor, a 40GB hard drive, 256MB RAM, and 24x10x24x CD recordable/rewritable drive, saving several hundred dollars. This is the minimum I would recommend for anyone who will often work with large image files.

Macintosh Computers

In a Mac, you might want to consider an iMac model with 1GHz Power PC G4, 64MB video card, 80GB hard drive, 512MB RAM, and a 17-inch widescreen LCD monitor. You should be able to find one for less than $2000.

High-End Hardware for the Digital Darkroom

If you will frequently be working with huge image files of 50MB or larger, making oversized prints, or editing digital video, you'll want to consider a very powerful and ultrafast computer

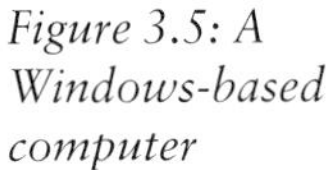

Figure 3.5: A Windows-based computer

system. The following recommendations are only examples of the type of equipment that you might want to consider. By the time you read this, more advanced processors, more RAM, and more hard-drive capacity will be available with even higher speed; shop around to find the ultimate equipment available at the price you're willing to pay.

Windows-Based Computers

Look for the fastest possible Intel Pentium 4 or comparable processor (3.0GHz or higher clock speed), 1GB or more RAM, a 120GB or larger hard drive, a video card with 64MB VRAM that supports multiple monitors, a DVD-R/CD-R combo drive for archiving images on a CD or higher capacity DVD, a 21-inch monitor, and perhaps a second monitor. Expect to pay at least $3500 for a system such as this.

You might also want a second monitor to double the area of your "desktop," useful when you want to view two or more images, for comparison purposes, at a large size. If the computer does not support a second monitor, you'll also need a special video card for dual output, such as a Matrox Millenium G550 (www.matrox.com), which costs about $125.

Macintosh Computers

Consider the PowerPC G5 with dual 2GHz processor, 1GB RAM, 160GB hard drive, graphics card with at least 64MB RAM, DVD-R/CD-RW drive, and 20-inch flat panel monitor. Expect to pay about $4500 for a system of this type, more with upgrades and an extra monitor. If you buy another Mac computer without support for multiple monitors, you'll need a video card that supports dual outputs, such as the Radeon 7000 Mac Edition (www.mirror.ati.com), which costs about $125.

Laptop Computers

Laptop computers are similar in concept to desktop computers but are substantially smaller and more portable. Laptops (see Figure 3.6) are also more expensive than desktop systems, and the LCD monitors of most models are not very useful for image editing; contrast is lower, and even a slight change in viewing angle can significantly affect the relative display brightness.

Although a laptop is not the best choice as your primary machine for image editing, it is convenient for traveling. If you decide to buy one, look for a model with a processor that is as fast as that in your desktop computer and includes as much RAM. A lower-capacity hard drive should be adequate unless you plan to store numerous massive image files in your laptop. Because a laptop's monitor is less than ideal for image viewing, plan to save the image editing for completion after you return home. Use your desktop computer, with its superior monitor, for image enhancing.

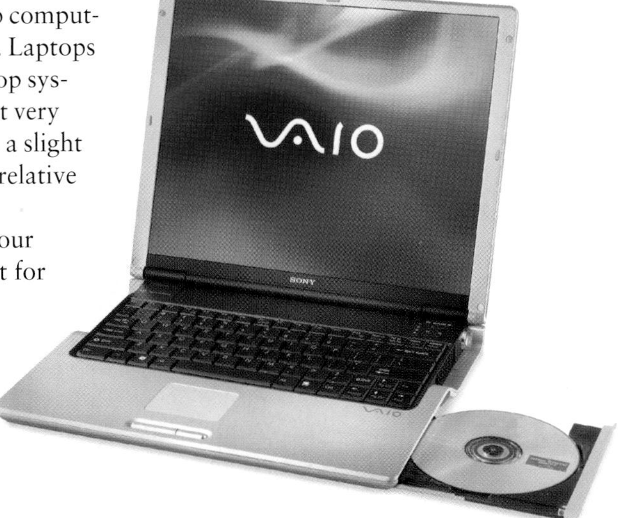

Photo used with permission of Sony Corporation

Figure 3.6: Although a desktop computer with a CRT monitor is preferable for digital imaging, a laptop computer is certainly convenient when traveling.

Upgrading Your Current Computer

So far in this chapter, I've discussed the type of computer that you might want to buy if you're ready to replace your current system. If that is not practical at this time, because of budget constraints, you might need to upgrade your current computer. Most computers made in the past few years are upgradeable, at least with some components. Theoretically, you might be able to upgrade every component, but that would probably cost more than purchasing an entire new system. Consider some of the following upgrades, selecting the one or two that will provide the greatest value or solve your most serious problem.

- Add extra RAM to increase the speed of adjusting your images, particularly with large files. This is the most valuable upgrade in terms of computer performance. Expect to pay about $100 for 256MB of RAM, although prices for RAM tend to drop relatively quickly with time.
- Replace the processor with a faster one of the same type. You will need to determine what type of processor is supported by your main board (motherboard). Each type of processor has a unique arrangement of pins for connecting to the main board. Also, there may be limitations on the voltage or clock speed supported. Be sure to confirm compatibility and any specific installation options required to upgrade this component before attempting to replace the processor.
- Replace your video card with a newer card, one with at least 32MB of VRAM and, ideally, 64 video MB RAM ($50 to $100). Even better, replace your existing card with one that supports multiple monitors, as discussed earlier.
- Add a fast CD burner if your computer does not already have one. You can find 40x12x48x CD-RW models for less than $100. Also review the section "Data Storage Options" in this chapter for other peripherals, such as DVD burners.
- Add USB ports if your computer does not already include this connectivity, preferably with ultrafast USB 2 ports. (You can buy the necessary accessories for less than $50.) If your computer is equipped with a USB 1.1 system, upgrade to USB 2 if you have a camera, a scanner, a memory card reader, or an external drive that supports USB 2 connectivity. You'll want at least four USB ports, preferably front ports so you don't need to access the back of your computer to plug in various devices. If you later find that you need more ports, for additional devices, you can add a hub accessory (available for about $50).
- Replace your monitor if it does not offer adequate color fidelity, contrast range, or brightness. Don't skimp on this purchase. You will probably want to keep the monitor for some years, even after you buy a new computer, and you'll spend many hours looking at your images on the monitor. Check the section on Desktop Components in this chapter for advice on the type, size, and monitor features that might best meet your needs for digital imaging.
- Add an additional hard drive if you are running out of space to store your images. Especially if you're working with a high-resolution digital camera or are producing particularly large prints, your image files will be large. As the number of images on your hard drive adds up, all available space may be consumed. It is important to have free hard drive space to use as temporary storage; if you are running low on space, a second hard drive can help.

RECOMMENDATION: Replace Your Computer

Be sure to check the specifications and requirements for any new hardware upgrades that you are considering; make sure they are compatible with your computer before you attempt an upgrade. As you research the available components and their prices, compare the upgrade costs to the cost of replacing your computer with a new and faster model. In many cases, it makes more sense to buy a new computer with considerably better performance and a warranty than to upgrade your existing computer. As with the purchase of other components for your digital darkroom, I strongly encourage you to research carefully and read reviews to ensure you are getting components you can trust to perform as you expect.

Data Storage Options

Whether you scan photos or shoot with a digital camera, and regardless of the type of computer that you use, one issue is worth thinking about. Where should you store the image files?

A computer's internal hard drive is a convenient location for storing images, but you won't want to use it as your only method of storage. Image files consume a great deal of space, so the hard disk will eventually fill up. Computers can crash, so there's always a risk of losing data. In the following sections, you'll find information on some of the options that you might want to consider as a redundant method of backup.

External Hard Drive

Instead of filling up the computer's internal disk with image files, some photographers prefer to buy an additional hard drive. Many desktop computers allow you to add a second internal unit, but the other option is an external hard drive (see Figure 3.7). This accessory usually plugs into a computer with a USB or FireWire cable. Unlike an internal hard drive, an external unit is portable, so you can take it with you when traveling or use it to access your images elsewhere if your computer should fail.

Figure 3.7: An additional hard drive, whether internal or external, is an affordable means of adding a large amount of storage space to your computer.

An external hard drive is a useful accessory for storing images, but like any device, it is not fail-safe. Be sure to back up your images using an additional external hard drive or other media such as CDs or DVDs.

CD Burners

Most every computer made in the past few years includes a CD drive (see Figure 3.8) that allows you to "read" data on CDs and to write or "burn" data to CD's if the device is also capable of this function as most are.

Two types of discs are available: the conventional recordable CD (CD-R) and the newer rewritable CD (CD-RW). Most recent CD burners accept both types of discs. CD-RW discs offer one benefit over CD-Rs: you can write new data to this type of disk by overwriting any old data. However, CD-RW media are not as reliable as CD-Rs, and I do not recommend their use for archival storage of your important images.

This optical medium uses a laser to burn data into discs with capacity of about 700MB. The process is fairly quick: it takes about two minutes to write a full 700MB of data to a CD-R with a 40x CD-R drive. CD-Rs are also inexpensive, costing less than 40 cents each when purchased in bulk. Most CD-Rs will be reliable for at least 30 years, and some are archival: they should last for 100 years. This medium offers a high degree of compatibility: a CD-R can be read by any other CD drive and by most DVD drives.

Photo used with permission of Sony Corporation

Figure 3.8: A CD recorder (or burner) and CD-Rs are an affordable solution for those who want moderately high capacity for "backup" storage.

RECOMMENDATION: CD-RW versus CD-R

A CD burner and CD-Rs are affordable, making the CD-R option the most cost effective method of saving digital images for the long term. Because of their "universal compatibility," CD-Rs are great for sending huge image files to friends who have a CD drive. Avoid using CD-RW discs for storing images. These are much less stable. Because there are no reliable estimates for the longevity of CD-RW media, stick with CD-R discs. The CD-Rs offer the best and most-affordable solution for photographers who need to archive their images.

Buy only CD-R media of the highest quality, such as Mitsui Gold Standard and Verbatim DataLifePlus, to minimize the risk of recording failure and for long-term archival storage. When recording your most valuable images, burn each CD-R twice. Keep one copy handy for quick access, and store another in a different physical location for safekeeping.

DVD Burners

Based on a similar optical technology to CDs, drives for reading DVDs are common, especially in laptop computers. If you want to store images to DVDs, you'll need a DVD recorder, or "burner." This device writes data to a DVD with ultrahigh capacity—as much as 4.7GB or 9.46GB on a dual-sided disc, with the possibility of higher-capacity discs in the future. As with CDs, two types of DVDs are available: write-once and rewritable. Since many DVD burners can also record and play CDs, these devices are certainly versatile.

There are several DVD formats, so you can run into compatibility problems. Discs that are recorded in one format may not be recognized by machines that support only another format. Fortunately, a few manufacturers have started addressing the compatibility problem with their latest DVD recorders that support multiple formats.

At $150, multi-format DVD burners are affordable, but the discs are a lot more expensive than CDs. (DVDs can cost $4 and more, though the cost per megabyte of storage versus CDs is about the same.) The 4x DVD burners offer fast data recording to write-once discs. Note that the speed ratings for DVD drives are not the same as for CD drives. A DVD drive that can burn at 1x offers performance equivalent to about 36x on a CD burner.

RECOMMENDATION: DVD Drives

Because of its ultrahigh capacity, DVD is attractive for photographers who produce many extremely large image files. However, the lack of a clear standard creates a potentially serious problem. For storing numerous large images that only you will need to access, DVD is a great solution. However, if you need to send image files to other people, you'll want to burn them to a CD-R because of its universal compatibility. Fortunately, virtually all DVD burners can also write to (and read) CD media, so I recommend buying a DVD drive that offers this option.

Removable Magnetic Media

Several companies make accessory drives for saving data usually in a cartridge or disk. Iomega Zip drives (see Figure 3.9), for example, accept 100MB to 750MB disks. The disks are far more expensive than CD-R media ($15 for a 750MB Zip disk) and physically larger. Magnetic media are also not as rugged or as archival as a CD or a DVD. For moderately long term storage of image files, Jaz and similar disks can be useful. The cartridges are not as universal as other storage formats, so accessing files could be an issue in the future.

Courtesy Iomega Corporation.

Figure 3.9: Zip disks, available with capacity as high as 750MB, can be useful for temporary backup or transport of image files.

RECOMMENDATION: Magnetic Media

Magnetic media can be reused many times, and data transfer is quick, useful for temporarily backing up part of your hard drive. Because of its many drawbacks, when compared with the CD-R, I do not recommend removable magnetic media for long-term image storage.

CHAPTER four

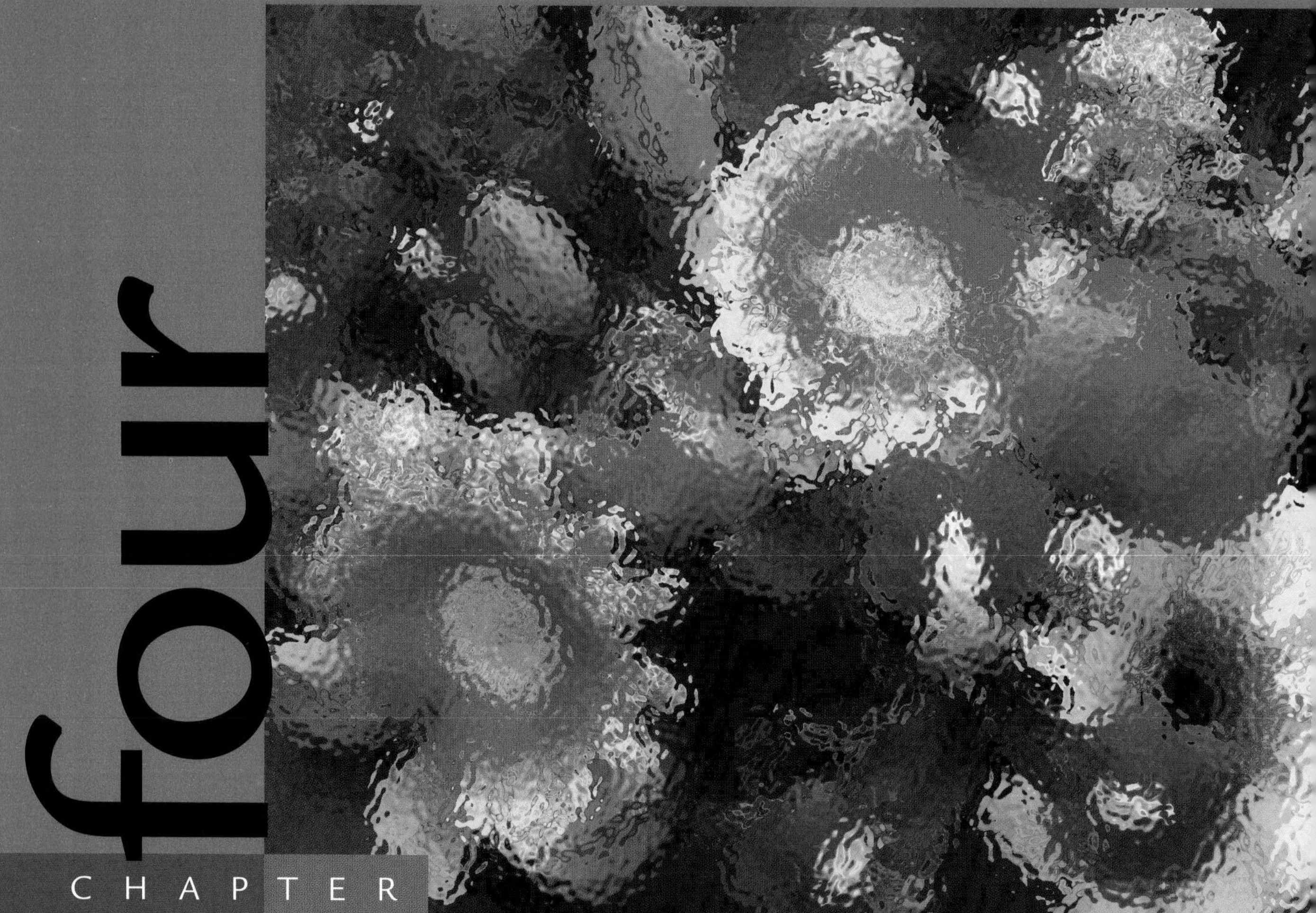

Software for the Digital Darkroom

In virtually every chapter *of this book, you'll find reference to image-editing software. Such programs are integral to the process because digital photos are captured and saved as data files, requiring a computer and software to acquire images from a camera and then to store, manage, catalog, enhance, and resize them for printing or other purposes. As discussed in Chapter 9, image enhancement is the most valuable feature from a technical and creative perspective. Just as the traditional darkroom gave us extensive control over our conventional images, the digital darkroom, powered by image-editing software, provides a great deal of control over our electronic images.*

A vast assortment of software is available for digital imaging, ranging from free to expensive, each with its own set of features. It is impossible to cover all these in a few pages. Consequently, I'll discuss the most popular and useful programs, particularly those targeting photo enthusiasts, and provide a personal evaluation as to the effectiveness of each. More extensive coverage would fill an entire book, and indeed, many books have been written about some of the programs. Instead of trying to replicate those, I'll introduce the most useful software, starting with the multipurpose products and moving on to those designed for archiving images and those intended for producing specific image-enhancing effects.

Affordable Image Editors

If you search the Web for the "best" imaging software, you'll be tempted to buy Photoshop CS (Creative Suite), the most powerful program and the one that most professional photographers and studios use. As discussed later, this $649 product certainly has merit, but it is expensive and complicated. You can get excellent results with more affordable software, often without a steep learning curve. Most photo enthusiasts can find at least one image-editing program in the under-$129 category that will meet or exceed, their needs (see Figure 4.1).

Figure 4.1: Some of the image-editing programs bundled with digicams are quite versatile but uncomplicated in their operation.

If you buy a digital camera, it will be bundled with software for convenient downloading of images, a file browser for viewing and filing images, plus software for some basic image editing: cropping, color, brightness and contrast adjustment, and some other enhancement features. These programs are often proprietary, designed for a specific camera manufacturer; there are far too many to even list in this chapter. Other camera, scanner, and printer kits include third-party software, from manufacturers such as ArcSoft, Adobe, or ACDSee,. These programs may not be the latest versions available or may be limited editions that do not include all of the functions available with software that you can purchase.

RECOMMENDATION: Work With the "Bundled" Software

The image editor that was included with your new camera, scanner, or printer may or may not be the one that you'll want for long-term use. Still, it is worth experimenting with the bundled software, especially if you are new to digital imaging. Read the instruction manual and become familiar with its enhancing features and its interface. After extensive use, you should be able to critically evaluate the various pros and cons of the software. Which of its functions are especially valuable and which features is it missing? Which aspects of its controls do you find convenient and which are frustrating? Make notes and compile a "wish list" for your next image editor.

Once you have completed this preliminary evaluation process, read some online reviews of image-editing programs in your price range to become familiar with their additional functions and methods of operation. Narrow your list of choices to a few image editors and visit the manufacturers' websites. After reviewing their lists of features, look for free trial downloads or "demo versions" of their software. The ability to "play before you pay" allows you to assess the versatility of several brands of programs, as well as the logic and the convenience of the user interface that each provides. The only drawback? Some image editors are certainly not simple to use, and the instruction manuals—available on some, but not all, manufacturers' websites—can be daunting.

That's one reason you'll want to read product reviews written by imaging experts with the experience that's required to comment on the effectiveness of several brands of software and the logic of operation of each type. As a starting point, consider the comments on the most popular image editors in this chapter, starting with the affordable programs.

Adobe Photoshop Elements 2

A bestseller in the affordable category, Photoshop Elements 2 (see Figure 4.2) costs $99 and is included in a few high-end digital camera kits at no extra charge. You can also download a trial version for free, at www.adobe.com/digitalimag. Featuring a user interface that's based on the full version of Photoshop, Elements 2 includes many of the valuable capabilities of its more expensive counterparts.

Although Elements is not the simplest software to use, it's worth starting with this one if you believe that you will eventually want to upgrade to Adobe Photoshop CS, the "gold standard" in image-editing software. Become proficient with Elements' features and method of operation, and you will find the transition to CS relatively uncomplicated. Like other affordable programs, Elements does not include all the capabilities of Photoshop CS, so you may well want to upgrade as you become more advanced in image editing.

Initially, you might want to use Elements 2 to import photos from digital cameras, CDs, and scanners. Then, organize them using File Browser so that you can preview, sort, rotate, and rename the photos. Take advantage of the automatic correction of contrast/brightness and color balance. Try the Quick Fix options for making more precise adjustments (using sliders) to brightness, color rendition, focus, and so on and to make corrections with tools such as Fill Flash, Adjust Backlighting, and Rotate Image. Be sure to try the easy-to-use Red Eye Brush Tool to improve pictures of people and pets.

Figure 4.2: In many respects, Photoshop Elements 2 is similar to Photoshop CS, making this affordable software a suitable training ground for those who will later want the professional program.

The Value of "Unsharp Mask" and "Layers"

Two features, often mentioned in this chapter and discussed at length in Chapters 9 and 11, warrant a brief explanation here. Both are useful for image editing.

Unsharp Mask (USM) is the most effective sharpening tool for most types of images. In addition to producing a natural-looking effect, USM is more versatile than other sharpening tools that set a predefined sharpening level. The USM in most programs lets you set a desired level of sharpening, as appropriate for a particular subject type. (A portrait image, for example, generally calls for less sharpening than a city scene.) For photo and imaging enthusiasts, I would not recommend any image-editor without an adjustable USM utility; keep this in mind when scanning the specification charts of programs that you are considering.

A more advanced feature, layers is also more complex. In a nutshell, programs that support layers let you make duplicate copies—or layers—of an image. (See Figure 4.2 for a Photoshop Elements 2

continues

screen showing layers open for image editing.) You can then work on those copies, instead of the actual image. When satisfied with the changes to the layers, you can combine the layers and merge them into the image, completing your project. Although the "layering capability" or "layers support" is not an essential feature in your first image editor, it does make a program more versatile.

Access the menus for more advanced options such as layers, filters, including Unsharp Mask as well as artistic filters, and a Cloning Brush tool to remove imperfections. Elements also lets you automatically blend multiple images into seamless panoramas; design greeting cards; apply frames, edges, and drop shadows to your photos with simplicity; paint with realistic brushes; add other special effects; and print multiple photos in different sizes on the same sheet of paper. If you ever need guidance, select the instant-access help files, read Smart Messages that provide simple context-sensitive help, or use the how-to recipes that you can display by typing keywords. There's even a Do It For Me option that can alleviate complexity for some functions.

For a full course on maximizing the potential of this program, see *The Hidden Power of Photoshop Elements 2* by Richard Lynch (Sybex 2002).

Jasc Paint Shop Pro

One of the most powerful image-editing programs available in the affordable category, Paint Shop Pro (version 8 or later) costs only $99 and is sometimes compared to Photoshop 7, the professional Adobe software that was available until the release of Photoshop CS. Although Paint Shop Pro see (Figure 4.3) does not include all the functions of Photoshop 7, it is impressive, boasting numerous advanced and sophisticated capabilities. In addition to extensive

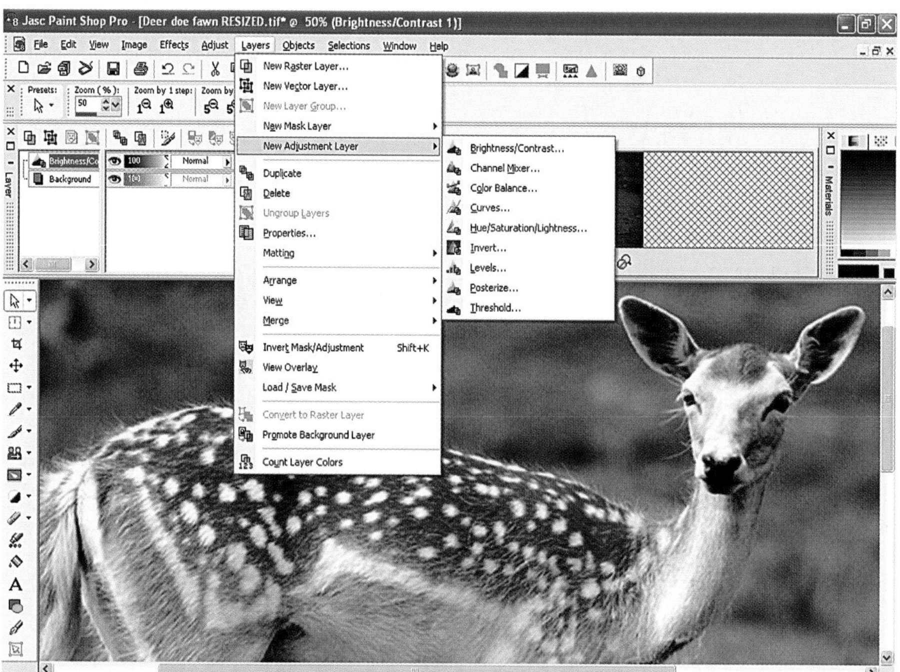

Figure 4.3: Offering many professional-caliber features, Paint Shop Pro is surprisingly affordable.

image enhancement, this Jasc software allows for unlimited undo levels for canceling the effects of previously applied tools. Many other professional-caliber tools—including a vast number of filters and paint brushes, color matching to colors from another image, plus masking and full layering capabilities—are also available.

And yet, Paint Shop Pro includes many features designed for simplicity, such as a one-click Photo Fix button, an easy-to-use red-eye removal tool, and a template-based printing feature for novices. Automatic adjustment tools are available for color balance, for contrast and saturation adjustment, for removing small scratches, and for fade correction for old photos, plus a JPEG artifact remover for enhancing heavily compressed images. The Learning Center guides the user through many complex tasks, such as straightening a crooked photo, fixing perspective distortion caused by a wide-angle lens, or erasing large areas of a single color.

Despite its low price, Paint Shop Pro offers a wide array of advanced features, including some tools for creating web graphics, but its primary image-adjustment tools are surprisingly easy to use. Some of the capabilities (such as animation) that are mentioned in reviews do not target photo enthusiasts. Try the free demo that's available at www.jasc.com, and you may decide that you prefer this program over Photoshop Elements 2.

You'll find that its interface is entirely different from that of any Adobe program. Some users find the Jasc software easier to use initially, although others consider Paint Shop Pro more complicated in general, probably because it includes more functions than Elements. In any event, this is one of those image editors that might meet your needs for many years, perhaps indefinitely, if you take advantage of any upgrades that Jasc offers in the future.

Microsoft Digital Image Pro

Despite the "pro" designation, this $99 program is designed for great simplicity and convenience of operation, with most functions accessed via icons. Microsoft's wizard interface options are also useful for guiding you through tasks, including a variety of creative ways to present images. But don't let the apparent simplicity fool you; this is a powerful image-editing program that includes many capabilities (see Figure 4.4). A few of the image-enhancing tools worth noting include Smart Erase for removing unwanted objects, Unsharp Mask with great control over the exact effect, Add Fill Flash and Reduce Backlighting, Airbrush, and Blending Brush to eliminate flaws and blemishes in people pictures, red-eye correction, and more. Naturally, you'll find the usual features for correcting color, contrast, and brightness, plus a new feature: manual adjustment of shadows, midtones, and highlights by individual color channel.

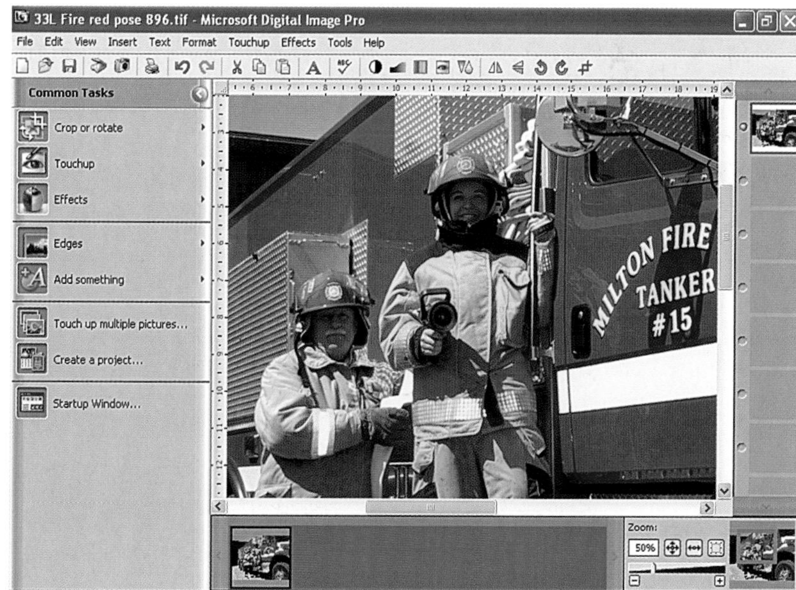

Figure 4.4: Designed for maximum simplicity of operation with its icon-driven interface, Microsoft Digital Image Pro is suitable for both families and photo enthusiasts.

Microsoft Digital Image Pro also includes many special effects tools and filters. Other features include photo and art brushes and tools for creating borders, mats, and frames for your images. You can also choose from numerous photo projects for making calendars, photo albums, flyers, greeting cards, postcards, invitations, and more. For additional specifics on features, visit the Microsoft website at www.microsoft.com/products/imaging/products/. I think you'll be amazed by the wealth of capabilities, including a file browser and advanced tools such as layers and Gaussian Blur, useful for blurring away a cluttered background.

In my estimation, Microsoft Digital Image Pro will especially satisfy families who appreciate its many special effects, projects, and fun features. It should also appeal to some photo enthusiasts because of the many options for enhancing images, especially people pictures. Because this software targets those who are inexperienced in image editing, it does not include some of the professional-caliber functions of Elements 2 or Jasc Paint Shop Pro; on the other hand, it is certainly easy to use and offers many auto-assist features.

Ulead PhotoImpact

Designed for managing, enhancing, and sharing photos, PhotoImpact (version XL or later) includes a sophisticated image browser and organizer, more web-page production tools than most photo-editing programs, many print layout options, and numerous correction and creative options (see Figure 4.5). Some of the image-enhancement tools include "intelligent" photo correction with suggestions for fixing common problems, for great ease of use. First-time PhotoImpact users might want to buy the 45-minute video tutorial, which includes seven project lessons that can facilitate the learning process; it's available for $36 as a download from the Ulead website.

It's worth taking advantage of that tutorial, because this image editor provides many professional-caliber tools, such as retouching brushes and filters for correcting color, exposure, shadow detail, lens distortion, and other parameters. This $90 product includes some valuable features such as the High Dynamic Range tool that produces extra detail in highlight and shadow areas. Visit www.ulead.com for more information.

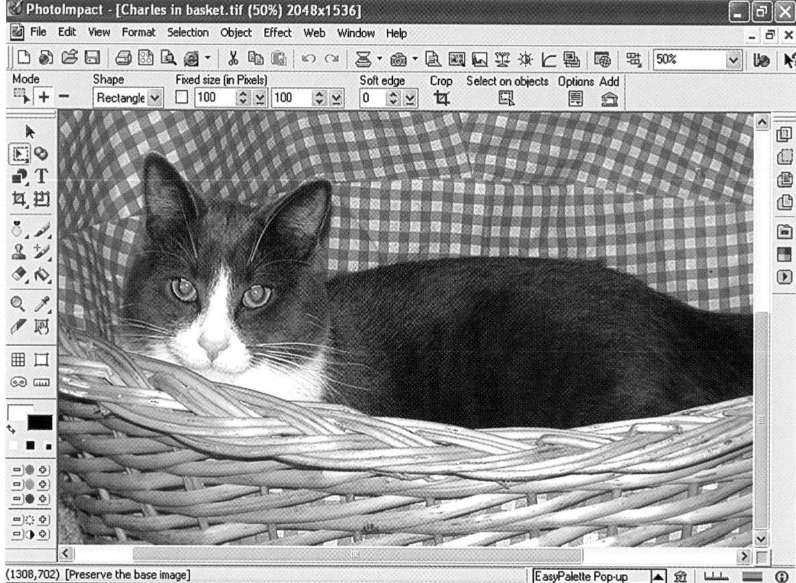

Figure 4.5: Although it is designed with the ease-of-use that novices want, PhotoImpact is surprisingly versatile in its browser and image editing capabilities.

Roxio PhotoSuite

Those who want a basic, simple-to-use program at a bargain price ($20) often select this software. Designed for "photo editing without a learning curve," this product makes it easy to transfer photos from a camera, organize them in albums, and correct some technical problems such as red eye and poor exposure or color with one click (see Figure 4.6). PhotoSuite also offers more advanced image-enhancement tools too such as cloning and special effects. Families will appreciate the various printing layouts and templates for projects such as making calendars. For added value, PhotoSuite includes Roxio Easy CD creator for convenient recording of images or slideshows to a CD plus a CD-label creator. Get more information at www.roxio.com.

Figure 4.6: Offering the lowest price among popular image editing programs, PhotoSuite is an excellent value.

RECOMMENDATION: Buy the "Right" Image Editor

As the preceding sections on the popular programs indicate, there are many options in the under-$129 category; search the Web, and you should be able to find a dozen others. But which is the *best* of the affordable image editors? To a great extent, the answer depends on your own subjective preferences, your actual needs, and your definition of a user-friendly interface. Do the research suggested in the introduction, and it's unlikely that you will make a wrong choice.

Based on my experience and my own subjective judgment, I'll make the following suggestion. If you are looking for software for family use, start by checking out Microsoft Digital Image Pro and Roxio PhotoSuite. Both include user-friendly tools for correcting common image problems as well as features for creating projects. My own daughters use Digital Image Pro and find it "easy, fun, and great for fixing pictures."

If you are a serious imaging enthusiast or developing in that direction, you might want to consider Adobe Photoshop Elements 2 instead. Although this image editor involves a steeper learning curve, it offers a significant advantage: its interface is nearly identical to that of the high-end Photoshop programs. Become familiar with Elements, and many of your operating skills will be transferable. If you start with another program instead, the transition to Photoshop CS will be substantially more difficult, with a much steeper learning curve.

The skills-transfer factor may not be relevant to the majority of digital imaging enthusiasts because any of the highly versatile programs will meet their needs for many years, perhaps indefinitely. On the other hand, it is something to think about before investing a great deal of time and effort into becoming an expert with any brand of software, other than Adobe. If you decide to use Elements 2 for your own image-editing needs, I recommend buying a second program for your family: one that is more user friendly and includes additional features, such as templates for many projects that families enjoy.

Professional Image Editors

Some imaging and photography enthusiasts reach a point where they decide that they need the additional capabilities of a professional program that has the most powerful tools available for image management and enhancement. Among advanced digital photo enthusiasts and professional photographers or studios, two feature-rich image-editing programs have proven to be the most popular: Corel Photo-Paint (version 11 or newer) and the bestselling Adobe Photoshop CS, the latest version that replaced Photoshop 7.

Corel Photo-Paint

Available as part of the CorelDRAW Graphics Suite that also includes graphic design/page layout software and software for creating web graphics and Macromedia Flash movies, Photo-Paint is highly advanced software. It allows the user to work with layers (described earlier) and includes a vast range of tools, each allowing for precise control. Many are useful for photo editing, and the program includes numerous image-adjustment filters as well, for achieving effects such as sharpening (with four tools), blurring, smoothing, softening, and a great deal more. The Corel software is also compatible with many so-called Photoshop plug-in filters, useful for expanding its versatility.

Although intended primarily for professionals, Photo-Paint includes some features of value even for snap shooters, such as automatic red-eye removal. Although not simple to use, Photo-Paint employs a logical interface with convenient menus, buttons, icons, and other controls). A customization feature even allows the user to change the interface to resemble that of Photoshop.

At the time of this writing, Photo-Paint (see Figure 4.7) was not available as standalone software and could be purchased only as part of the CorelDRAW Graphics Suite 11,

Figure 4.7: Part of the CorelDRAW Graphics Suite, Photo-Paint is a pro-caliber image program.

for about $400, including CorelDRAW 11 (graphic design and animation software) as well as R.A.V.E. 2 (for web graphics design.) Some photographers are using Graphics Suite as their primary image editor, often because of its many tools for creating graphics for web and other applications.

Adobe Photoshop CS

Adobe's Photoshop program has dominated the world of advanced digital-image editing for more than 10 years; many serious imaging hobbyists, as well as most professional photographers, use some version of this software. The latest, Photoshop CS, an upgrade over Photoshop 7, is the most robust, versatile, and desirable version to date; it boasts an incredible variety of tools from automatic, to simple, to complex and fully controllable. Though not simple to use by any means, Photoshop features a logical interface, as shown in Figure 4.8, that is convenient to use.

Photoshop CS boasts virtually every capability that a graphic designer, publisher, or commercial studio will ever need, but many of its features specifically target the photographer (see Figure 4.9). Although it provides many uncomplicated ways to adjust your images—such as Auto Contrast, Auto Levels, and Auto Color correction, plus a tool that can be used for red-eye removal—Photoshop also includes advanced tools that don't limit what you can achieve. A veritable cottage industry has developed over the years, providing videos, seminars, workshops, and books—such as *Photoshop CS Savvy* by Steve Romaniello (Sybex, 2004)—on getting the most from this complex, multifaceted software.

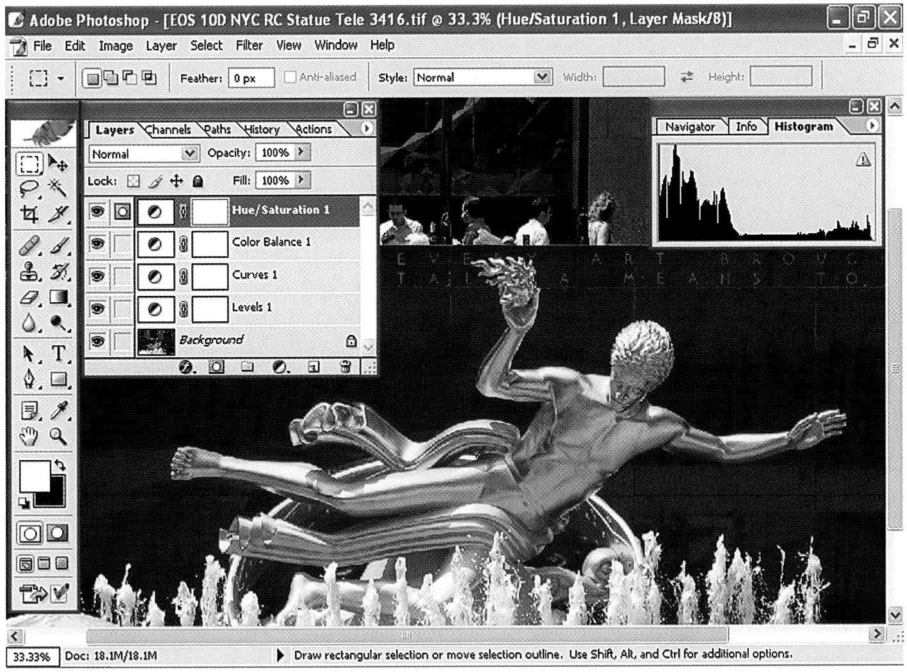

Figure 4.8: Photoshop CS is the reigning champion among advanced image editors because of its vast power and versatility.

If you can imagine a change to your image, there is a way to produce that change in Photoshop. Some of the most significant features of this image editor include the following.

- Greater support for layers than any other software, including new Photo Filter adjustment layers.
- Several retouching tools that make it easy to professionally remove dust, scratches, extraneous elements, facial blemishes, and other flaws. One of these tools, the Healing Brush, is similar to the Cloning Brush tool, but was designed to preserve color, tonality, and texture of the area under repair.
- Approximately 100 filters that allow you to improve or manipulate virtually every aspect of an image.
- Wide range of color correction tools.
- Comprehensive support for working with 16-bit files, for greater color accuracy than with the standard 8 bit color depth.
- A useful Shadow/Highlight adjustment tool for modifying dynamic range, by increasing highlight or shadow detail, without affecting midtone detail unless that is also desired.
- Live Histogram, available for each individual color channel if desired, for evaluating exposure, for viewing changes that occur as you adjust an image, with continuous feedback.
- Built-in raw image converter and enhancer utility that is compatible with raw data files generated by most cameras. This converter includes a wealth of image-correction features.
- A versatile and sophisticated File Browser.

These features merely scratch the surface of this professional software. For a full description of the benefits, visit the Adobe website at www.adobe.com/digitalimag/main.html. Photoshop CS is priced at $649. Registered owners of a previous full version of Adobe Photoshop (but not Elements) can upgrade to CS for $169.

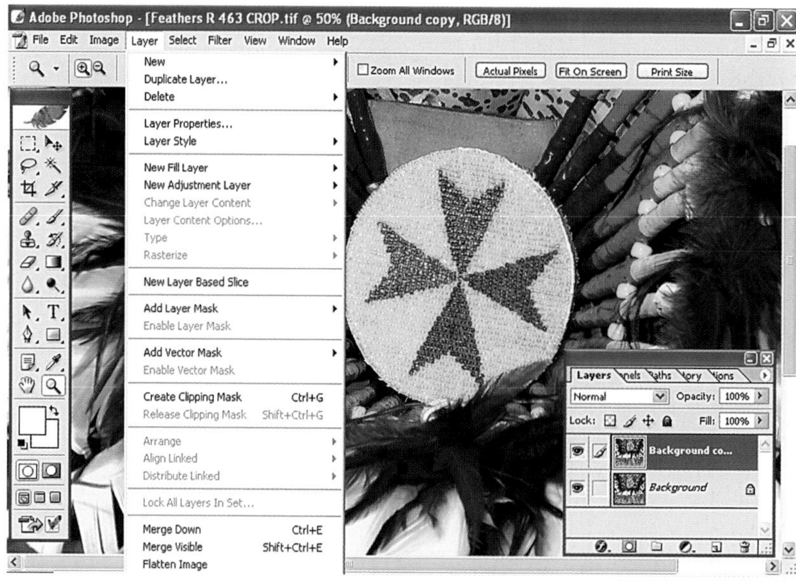

Figure 4.9: For specifics on the new features of Photoshop CS, visit the Adobe website. Many advanced photographers consider comprehensive support for 16-bit files the most valuable new feature.

RECOMMENDATION: The Best Image Editor

Judging by the overwhelming acceptance by photographers and the rave reviews it has received from all quarters, Adobe Photoshop deserves its bestseller status. The new CS may seem expensive at $649, and many of you will probably want one of the affordable programs discussed earlier. The $169 upgrade fee offers good value for anyone still using earlier versions of a full Photoshop program, especially for those who will benefit from the new, built-in raw image converter. This converter is faster and more versatile than most similar programs bundled with digital camera kits.

Although Corel Photo-Paint is also powerful, I prefer the Adobe Photoshop programs, particularly CS, for three reasons: greater versatility, faster speed, and greater dedication to the specific needs of photographers. This is a personal judgment based on limited experience with Photo-Paint and extensive familiarity with the Adobe products. You might want to look around on the Web for other opinions, especially if you want software that is more affordable than Photoshop CS and need the special features that are included in Corel Photo Suite 11.

Plug-In Software for Image Enhancement

As mentioned earlier, many all-purpose image-editing software programs can be made even more versatile, with the addition of software available from after-market suppliers. Although they are referred to as Photoshop plug-ins, many (but not all) are compatible with other programs, such as Corel Photo-Paint, Microsoft Digital Image Pro, JASC Paint Shop Pro, and Ulead PhotoImpact. (If any of the plug-ins are of interest to you, check the distributors' websites for up-to-date compatibility information with the software that you are using.) Designed to extend the capabilities of the image editor, plug-ins (see Figure 4.10) can provide more effective methods for taking care of certain tasks or can add new features, often special effects.

Plug-ins are usually called filters, because they were originally designed to simulate special effects that can be achieved by using certain filters on your camera's lens when taking pictures. Many of the newer plug-ins are actually far more versatile, producing creative, or stylized, effects that cannot be achieved with photographic filters. Thousands of digital filters and other types of plug-ins are available, generally on distributors' websites, where you can purchase them via a download to your computer.

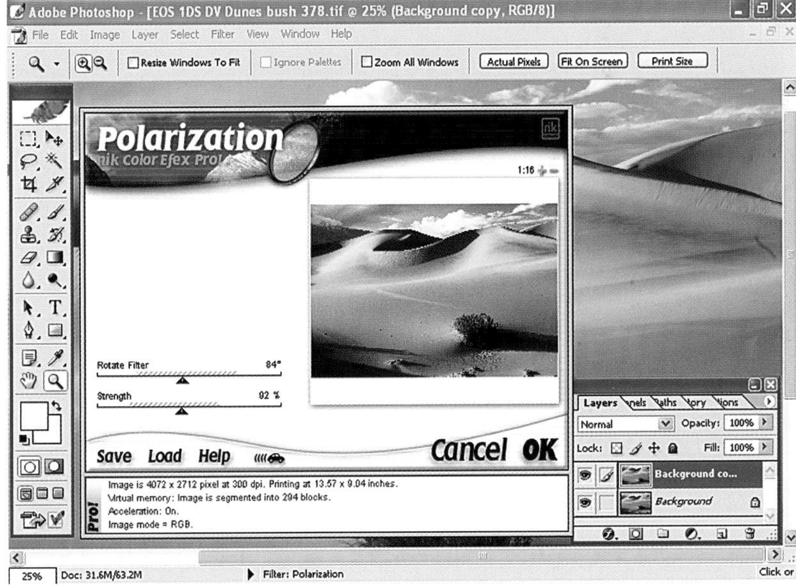

Figure 4.10: Most plug-ins are designed to produce special effects, and they can be useful, but I consider the image-correction plug-ins particularly valuable.

Most are intended for creating special effects: adding a body of water to a landscape image, creating fantasy effects, making abstracts from conventional images, adding fireworks or lightning bolts, and so on. These can be fun, but I recommend starting with plug-ins that are effective in image enhancement: professional-caliber sharpening, improving color balance or saturation, pulling detail out of shadows and highlight areas, and so on.

When you purchase a plug-in, the download and installation process should be quite simple. Generally, you'll run an installation program that automatically installs all required files. In some cases, you might need to copy a file yourself into the Adobe Photoshop Plug-In folder. The plug-in distributor's website should provide instructions on the downloading process and on where to find their product on your image editor's menu; it usually appears under Filters or in the Actions palette.

Considering the overwhelming number of plug-ins available, I find it virtually impossible to make recommendations as to which you might want to try. However, in my unscientific survey of friends who are serious photographers or digital-imaging enthusiasts, the products in the following sections are often mentioned. After receiving their recommendations, I have tested the most popular plug-ins, often using the free download samples that are available, and I can vouch for their effectiveness.

Some plug-ins are quite expensive because they are available only in full packages that include many tools or because they are of professional caliber and based on costly and time-consuming development. Many plug-ins are available for $100 or less, and some are particularly affordable because they offer only a single function, such as image sharpening. The following have received rave reviews from my photographer friends, and in most cases, I share their views.

Extensis Intellihance Pro This set of plug-ins was designed to help you find the right color, brightness, contrast, and sharpness for any image. Select a tool, and the software displays your image, plus eight copies, each with a different level of correction so you can see variations side by side. When you select the sample that appears closest to ideal, the software makes the necessary corrections to your image. This is a quick way to improve your images without a lot of trial-and-error attempts. Although the package is expensive at $200, it has been highly rated in several published reviews. For more information, visit www.extensis.com.

Neat Image Pro Several companies offer plug-ins or stand-alone software designed to reduce digital noise; I have found Neat Image Pro plug-in (version 2 or later, priced at $60) to be the most effective with images made at high ISO (International Organization for Standardization) or during long exposures. This digital filter can also reduce noise and film grain in scanned images and is somewhat useful for reducing JPEG artifacts in overcompressed images. Neat Image Pro (see Figure 4.11) provides full control over the level of filtration from low to high, allowing for any desired effect. Because operation is not intuitive, follow the basic steps provided at www.neatimage.com to prevent frustration; also try the free demo version.

Nik Multimedia Plug-Ins This company offers many plug-in kits, including two that are used by many professional photographers. Color Efex Pro includes 55 filters for enhancing, optimizing, and stylizing your images. The most useful tools include filters for making impressive color and lighting enhancements in seconds with convenient sliders and preview images. Filters are also available for enhancing blue skies, for converting color images into beautiful black-and-white images, for simulating the effect achieved by a polarizing filter, and a great deal more. Though this software is not inexpensive, at $300, I can strongly recommend Color Efex Pro because of its many problem-solving, enhancing, and stylizing tools. Nik also offers individual packs with fewer filters, at $109; one of these might meet all your needs. Get details at www.nikmultimedia.com.

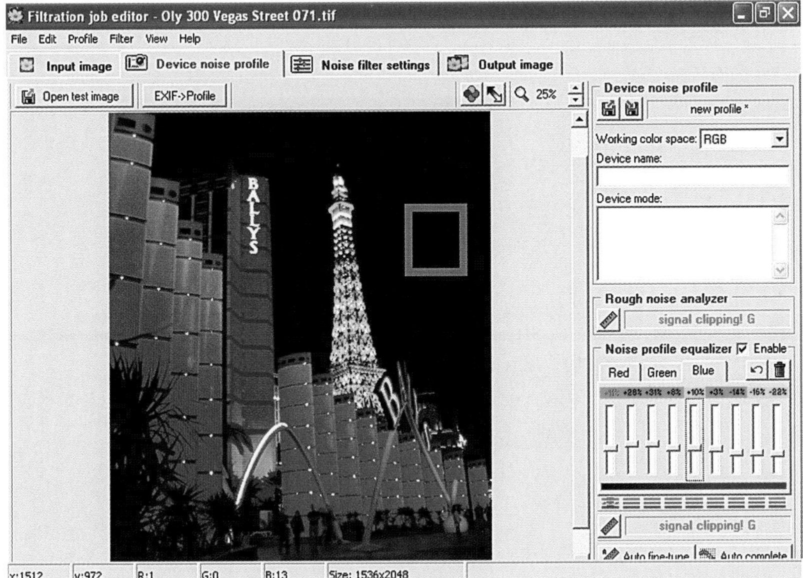

Figure 4.11: One of the most effective noise-reduction software programs on the market, Neat Image Pro is extremely versatile, offering a wide range of user-selected settings.

Nik also markets a Sharpener series of plug-ins for image sharpening. When used with Photoshop (or some other software), these produce professional-caliber results quickly, employing sophisticated options with multiple steps to preserve maximum image quality. I found Nik Sharpener Pro Inkjet to be the most useful for optimally sharpening images that I plan to print at specific sizes and resolution settings. This plug-in sells for $170.

Nik Dfine This Nik Multimedia package of plug-ins includes various tools for correcting several types of digital noise and for minimizing JPEG artifacts. The noise-reduction tools are effective and include many options for achieving precisely the correction that will produce the best results. Other features include corrections for exposure errors caused by back lighting and poor color balance or saturation, a Quick Fix tool, and a great deal more. Considering all its capabilities, this software is quite a value at $100.

Vivid Details Test Strip This plug-in was designed to help the user find the ideal color balance for their images by producing a test strip: a series of variations on any image, with different degrees of color correction and exposure. Test Strip (see Figure 4.12) provides a large thumbnail of your image as well as several other versions, examples of the image with different levels of color adjustment. Move a slider to see the effects of small changes. This visual comparison system makes it relatively easy to select the adjustment levels that seem to produce the most pleasing results. Other features allow for convenient viewing of changes in brightness or shadow/highlight detail. List price is $179, but this plug-in is often available from retailers for less than $100. For more information, visit www.vividdetails.com.

Defect Removal Plug-Ins Mentioned in other chapters, Digital ROC, SHO, and GEM are included with some scanners but plug-in versions are also available from Kodak's Austin Development Center. Each of these products sells for $80, but discounts are often available at www.asf.com.

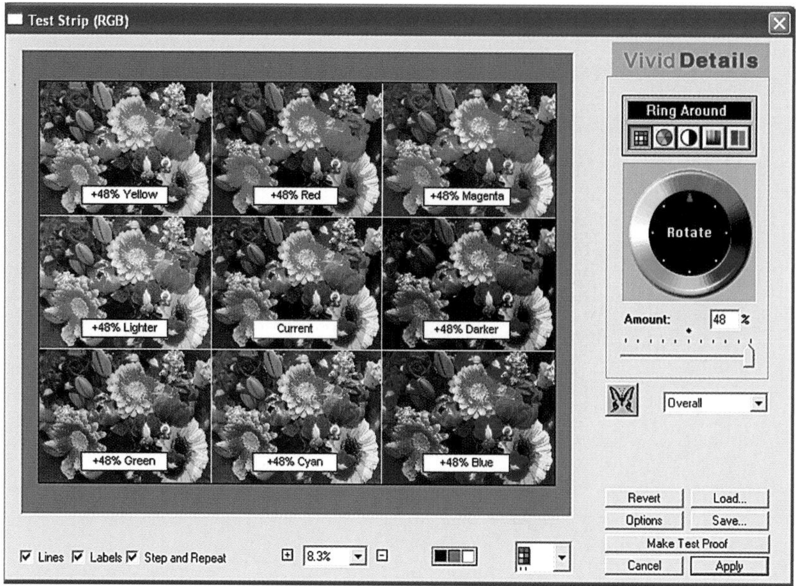

Figure 4.12: Employing a ring-around display, Vivid Details Test Strip allows you to compare the effect that any change in color balance will produce in your image.

Digital ROC was designed to improve images with incorrect color balance, including those made under tungsten and fluorescent lighting, and does an acceptable job of this task. It is also quite effective with scans of faded photographs, automatically restoring much of the original color.

Digital SHO can reveal some extra detail in shadow areas, in images with exposure problems caused by backlighting, uneven flash illumination, and partial shade. Digital GEM automatically reduces digital noise and grain without causing excessive softening or blurring; you can use a Clarity slider to sharpen or soften the image. I find that GEM tends to oversoften images and introduce some artifacts, but it can be useful for improving images that are extremely grainy.

FM Software Plug-Ins Fred Miranda of FM Software markets a line of plug-ins that is both effective and surprisingly affordable. Ranging in price from $10 to $20, these plug-ins are compatible with most Photoshop programs, as specified at www.fredmiranda.com/software. I consider the following two the most useful.

Intellisharpen Pro This is an advanced plug-in that employs many steps in Photoshop quickly, with great simplicity. Select a desired level of sharpening, based on your estimate, and it produces professional-caliber sharpening; if the effect is not what you intended, simply undo the function and try again at a different intensity level. Considering the low price, this plug-in is impressive, because it sharpens without increasing digital noise or creating a halo around high-contrast subject edges and without sharpening an out-of-focus background or the sky. Although Intellisharpen Pro does not include a preview screen, I soon learned to estimate the sharpening level that is appropriate for any image that I plan to print.

Shadow Recovery Professional Plug-In (SR Pro) Miranda designed this plug-in to increase detail in shadow areas (see Figure 4.13). This product lightens dark areas, revealing detail, without affecting highlight and midtone areas, at a desired intensity level from low to very high. An Add Shadow Contrast tool option increases image contrast

Figure 4.13: Few image editors (except Photoshop CS) offer a versatile tool for recovering shadow detail. The SR Pro plug-in does, and its multistep process is simple and fully variable.

without compromising detail in midtone and highlight areas. Finally, two other options allow for reducing digital noise in shadow areas, useful for images made at high ISO or during long exposures. The results look natural and are easy and quick to achieve without the complicated masking techniques used by Photoshop experts.

DV Pro Photographers who appreciate the high overall saturation produced by Fujichrome Velvia film can simulate a similar effect in their digital images with the DV Pro plug-in. This FM Software product offers many saturation levels (and also desaturation levels) and supports 16-bit images. Using this automatic multistep tool is preferable to simply increasing overall color saturation in Photoshop, because that can increase noise and artifacts and cause a color shift. By enhancing colors individually within the red, blue, and green color channels, DV Pro produces superior results and does so just as quickly.

RECOMMENDATION: The Value of Plug-Ins

As hinted earlier, some of the image-enhancing and correction features offered by plug-ins can be achieved using the tools in the advanced image-editing software programs. (Naturally, many plug-ins also provide features, particularly special effects, that are not available with most image editors.) However, the process can be quite complex, calling for a great deal of time and expertise to produce professional-caliber results. The most sophisticated and intelligent plug-ins can produce comparable results in seconds. Many include sliders for adjusting the amount of correction, and some offer preview screens that let you visually assess the effect that any change will produce.

Before buying plug-ins, do some research as to their exact features and try to find published reviews that provide a detailed evaluation of the effectiveness and ease of use of the products you are considering. I recommend starting your research on the Plugin Site at **www.thepluginsite.com**. Operated by Harald Heim, this site provides some reviews of plug-ins and image-editing software, links to many distributors, news about recently released products, a gallery of effects, discussion boards, and more.

File Browser Software

Most digital cameras and scanners are bundled with file browser software, designed for convenience in downloading images to your computer (see Figure 4.14). Typically, the software also allows you to view thumbnails, rename images, move images to other folders in your computer, and, often, to find images quickly. Some programs include additional features for cropping, for rotating or delete images, for making minor corrections, and so on. A bundled browser with good functionality may well meet all your needs, but if not, you can find great stand-alone browsers. They generally include the functions mentioned, and some offer even more features and greater convenience of operation.

There are far too many programs of this type to discuss here or even to list. The following products are both popular and worth considering if your bundled software lacks the advanced capabilities that you want:

- DownloaderPro (for automated image downloading) (www.breezesys.com)
- BreezeBrowser with many browser features, from Breeze Systems (www.breezesys.com)
- Jasc Paint Shop Photo Album (www.jasc.com)
- Adobe Photoshop Album (www.adobe.com)
- CompuPic Pro (www.photodex.com)
- ThumbsPlus (www.cerious.com)
- ACDSee (www.acdsystems.com)
- ImageStore (www.ttlsoftware.com)
- Ulead Photo Explorer (www.ulead.com)

These file browser programs generally cost $28 to $50, although some, such as CompuPic Pro, are priced at $80 or more.

Figure 4.14: The browser software that's bundled with digital cameras is generally quite basic, designed for a few specific functions.

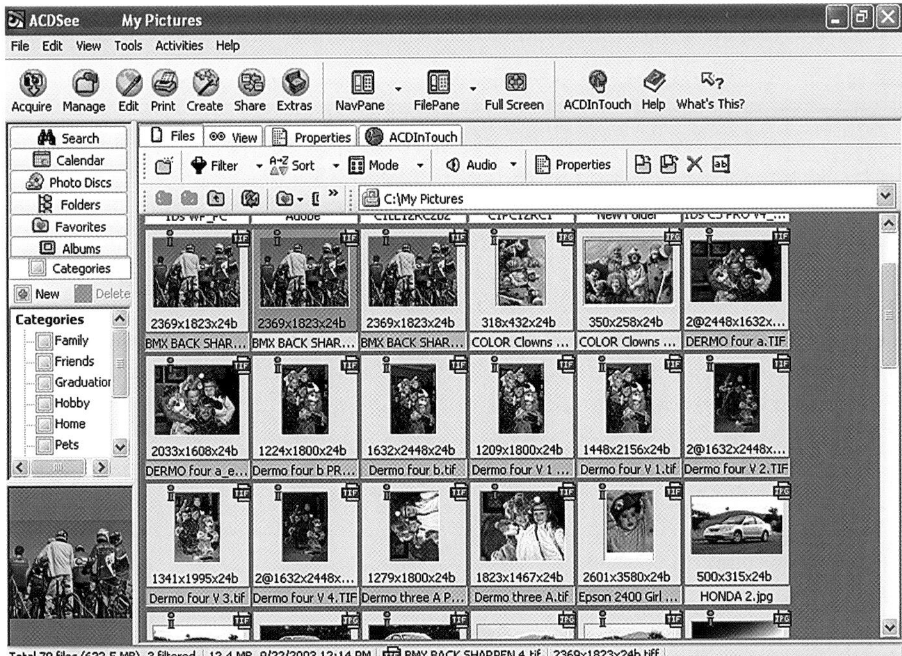

Figure 4.15: After-market browser and image-management programs often include numerous features of interest to families and serious photo enthusiasts.

My personal favorites include Ulead Photo Explorer (version 8 or later) and the ACDSee software (version 5.0.1 or later). Photo Explorer ($30) offers a convenient interface and all the features needed to organize, sort, and quickly find images. ACDSee ($50) is also user friendly, fast, and useful for managing a large volume of images, and it supports a vast range of image file formats (see Figure 4.15). Extras include tools for making slideshows with transition effects and for correcting off-kilter images, plus options for various photo printing layouts, red-eye enhancement tools, light levels, color levels, and camera shake and blemishes. All are useful for quick corrections when you're in a hurry.

RECOMMENDATION: Browser Software

Your multipurpose image-editing software or the software that was included with your digital camera may include the features you want. In that case, you have no need for the additional capabilities provided by the optional album or image-management programs. If you're not certain, it's worth taking a free trial of programs discussed here; most manufacturers provide that option on their websites.

Image-management programs such as ACDSee and CompuPic Pro are generally most useful for those who need to organize numerous images, although they offer many other features. The album software, such as Adobe Photoshop Album and JASC Paint Shop Photo, includes a browser but will be of greater interest to families. These programs include many fun features such as slideshow production and tools for creating photo album pages, calendars, and various other projects. Features of this type are rarely included in bundled software, making the additional investment worthwhile, especially for families who are likely to take advantage of these aspects of digital imaging.

Raw File Converters

As discussed in Chapter 1, images made in a digital camera's raw capture mode must be converted into a file format such as TIFF, using special software designed for this purpose. The software can also be used to correct parameters such as exposure, contrast, color balance, and saturation. Cameras that allow for raw capture are bundled with appropriate proprietary software, but such programs can be slow, difficult to use, and limited in their features; some also produce a preview image that is poor in quality.

Affordable raw conversion software (less than $100) is available from several distributors; check their websites as to compatibility with the proprietary raw files generated by your specific camera. Bibble Labs (www.bibblelabs.com) and Breeze Systems (www.breezesys.com) are two companies that offer such products, and both work quite well. Adobe's Camera Raw plug-in ($99), shown in Figure 4.16, is fast, effective, and quite versatile; it supports many cameras' raw file formats. Because the similar—but substantially more versatile—Camera Raw 2 software is built in to Photoshop CS, Adobe does not plan to upgrade their plug-in for compatibility with newer cameras. Both of the Adobe products offer a valuable function, not available with some of their competitors: interpolation for increasing the size of a raw image file while maintaining excellent quality.

If you own a Canon or Nikon digital SLR camera and want sophisticated and versatile after-market (stand-alone) raw conversion software, review the options available from Phase One (Figure 4.17) at www.c1dslr.com. The professional edition of their C1 DSLR is expensive ($499) and was designed to meet the workflow needs of prolific professional photographers and studios. The Limited Edition Phase One C1 D SLR software is more affordable and produces equally high quality. ($99; a free 15-day trial is available). It supports many Nikon and Canon SLR cameras' raw files and offers a wide range of image-enhancement features plus thumbnails of all images on a memory card.

Figure 4.16: After-market raw converter software programs generally offer greater speed and versatility than the converters bundled with most digital cameras.

Figure 4.17: While the Phase One C1 DSLR is the most expensive (and most sophisticated) of all RAW converters, the company offers several other versatile DSLR converters at very affordable prices.

RECOMMENDATION: Raw Converter Software

After working with all the software mentioned in this section, I can particularly recommend two, Adobe Camera Raw 2 and the Phase One C1 DSLR Limited Edition. Some photographers prefer the Bibble Labs or Breeze Systems software, although the versions that I tested were not as convenient as the others mentioned; check out their current versions while shopping around.

At the time of this writing, Phase One products were available only for Windows. The company was beginning to market more affordable C1 software. Available at $49, the low-priced Phase One products support only the raw images generated by a single camera, such as the Canon EOS Digital Rebel; that is all the support that most camera owners require. Links at **www.c1dslr.com** lead you to independent reviews of this company's products.

In my experience, the Phase One products are almost as versatile as the Adobe products and can produce slightly higher image quality with some cameras' raw files, but are not as easy to use. Adobe Camera Raw (plug-in or the software built in to CS) offers workflow advantages because it is part of Photoshop and can be faster to use. That feature can be important when you want to enhance and convert many raw images at one time.

By the time you read this, the Adobe Camera Raw plug-in may not be available or may not support the raw files generated by your digital camera. In that case, you can buy Photoshop CS or spend 30 minutes researching the benefits of the Bibble Labs, Breeze Systems, and Phase One C1 products. If one of these supports the raw files generated by your current camera, read online reviews and take advantage of the free downloads for a "test drive." Unless your camera was bundled with an unusually fast, convenient, and versatile raw converter, it's worth buying one of the after-market programs.

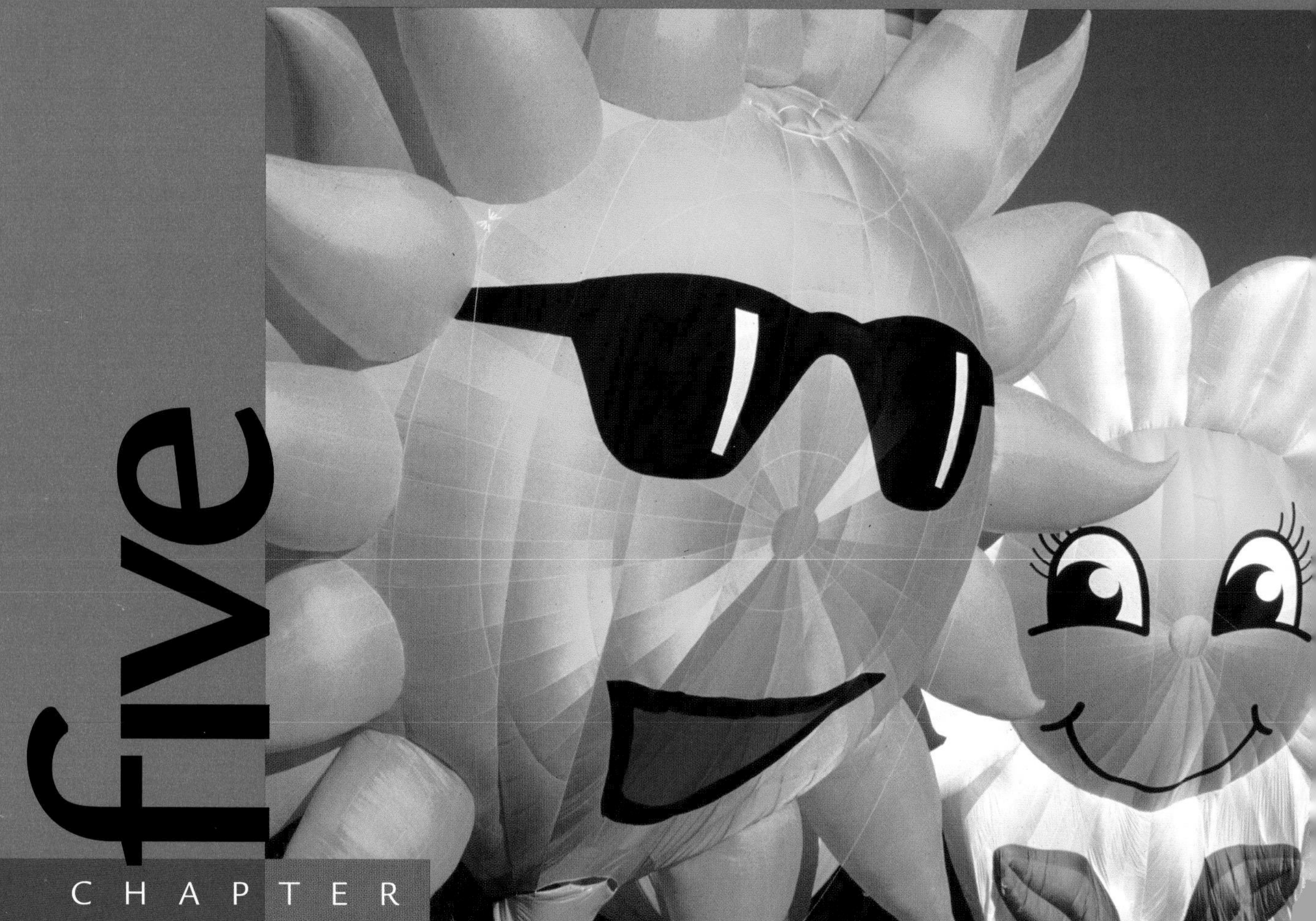

CHAPTER five

Choosing a Photo Printer

Whether you shoot with *a digital camera or scan photographs, printmaking can be one of the most rewarding facets of photography. In the past, you needed a darkroom and a great deal of time and expertise to make beautiful color or black-and-white prints from negatives. Today, anyone can make prints that are suitable for framing, without working with caustic chemicals. With a digital image, a computer, image-editing software, and a printer that's optimized for photo printing, the process need not be complicated or time-consuming.*

Two types of photo printers are most common: inkjet and dye-sublimation. Each has its own characteristics, as well as pros and cons. Because most photo-optimized printers employ the inkjet technology, I'll discuss these first and in great detail. Later I'll provide specifics on the dye-sub models, including the technology, unique features, and the specific types of printers in this category.

Inkjet Photo Printers

Most color inkjet printers employ thermal inkjet technology to deposit droplets of dye onto a sheet of paper. In this process, thousands of micro-fine droplets are heated to the boiling point so that droplets are forced through tiny nozzles in a printhead. Epson's inkjet printers use a different technology called Micro Piezo that uses vibration rather than heat to release ink droplets.

A printer's several ink colors can be combined to produce a wide range of hues and tones. This happens quickly to produce a fine pattern of closely spaced dots of ink on the

Figure 5.1: A high-quality photo printer is an essential part of the digital darkroom.

paper. Because the photo print is composed of individual dots, it is not really continuous tone like a conventional silver halide photograph. This may not be relevant. If you make a print from a high-resolution image file on photo-designated paper, at a high-quality printer setting, the ink dots should not be visible to the naked eye, and the print will resemble a continuous tone photo (see Figure 5.1).

Inkjet photo printers are versatile. They accept many types of paper, or media, from several manufacturers, as discussed in the "Inkjet Printer Paper" section later in this chapter, and you can also use them to print text and documents. In addition, inkjet photo printers are affordable. You can buy a full-featured photo printer that will produce beautiful 8.5" × 11" prints for less than $129, and you can buy a pro-caliber large-format printer that makes gallery-quality 13" × 19" prints.

Inkjet Photo Printer Features

If you are planning to buy a photo-optimized inkjet printer, you'll want to fully appreciate the primary features that are available, as well as other factors that differentiate one machine from another. This information will be valuable when you're reviewing the specifications of several models in your price range.

Number of Ink Colors

At one time, four ink colors—cyan, magenta, yellow, and black—were standard in inkjet photo printers; some models in the less than $149 range still use only four colors of ink (see Figure 5.2). Other photo printers offer six-color printing, by adding light cyan and light magenta inks. Some of these printers ship with a four-color cartridge but accept optional cartridges for six-color printing. A few models in the $300+ price range offer seven- or eight-color printing, usually by adding inks that are various shades of black and gray.

Although the best four-color photo printers can generate photos that will satisfy many viewers, it's worth paying a bit extra for a six-color printer. When you use more inks, less white space between the dots produces a smoother print without a grainy look. The additional inks offer other benefits: superior color nuances, as with skin tones that are slightly different, richer color saturation, and better color gradation (transitions) through the printer's full range of tones and colors. They can also produce superior black-white prints. Many high-end photo printers use seven or eight ink colors, producing exceptional print quality and offering an even wider range of tonal values while keeping neutral tones truly neutral, without a color cast.

Epson America Inc.

Figure 5.2: *Inkjet photo printers are more expensive than similar multipurpose printers, but Canon, Hewlett-Packard, Lexmark, and Epson (shown here is the Epson Stylus Photo 900) market some photo-optimized models that sell for less than $149.*

Ink Droplet Size

The size of the ink droplets fired by the printhead determines overall print quality, particularly the amount of fine detail the printer can produce. The droplet size is stated in picoliters (a millionth of a liter) abbreviated as pl. A 4-to-6-pl. size is common in inkjet printers, and a few machines can spray droplets as small as 2 pl. That may not sound like a major difference, but a 4 pl. droplet is 33% smaller than a 6 pl. droplet, and a 2 pl. droplet is 66% smaller than a 6 pl. droplet, based on spherical volume. Of course, the smaller the droplets, the more subtle the gradations of color, the more detail that appears in the image, and the smoother the overall appearance of the print.

Cartridge Type

Until recently, a single ink cartridge containing reservoirs of each color along with a separate cartridge for black ink was standard. Now, an increasing number of six- and seven-color photo printers, particularly Canon and Epson models, are designed with individual tanks for each of the ink colors (see Figure 5.3). Instead of replacing an entire cartridge when a single color runs out—often magenta, cyan, or the light version of these inks—you can replace only the tank that is depleted. A printer that accepts individual ink tanks can be more expensive than a comparable printer that includes all the other features and capabilities that you want. A set of six or seven tanks is also more expensive than a single multicolor ink cartridge, but can be more economical in the long run since you don't have to replace the entire cartridge when a single tank is depleted.

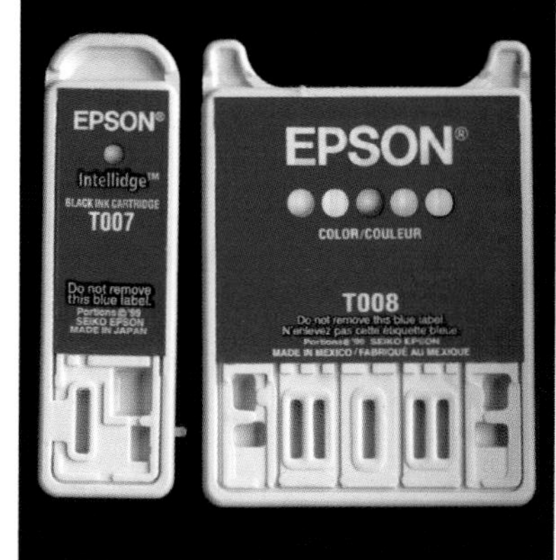

Figure 5.3: *Most of the low-priced photo printers employ one or two ink cartridges with four colors, including black. Many of the high-end models, however, use six or more inks, generally in individual ink tanks that can be replaced individually, as necessary.*

Figure 5.4: Large-format photo printers, such as this Canon i9100, can generate borderless 13" × 19" prints on sheet paper. Some Epson models can also make panoramic prints as large as 13" × 44" when using roll paper.

Paper Size and Printable Area

Inkjet printers for consumer use fall into two size categories: letter and tabloid, also called large format. Letter-size printers accept paper as large as 8.5" × 11". Some, but not all models, can make borderless 8.5" × 11" prints; others can make borderless prints only in the 4" × 6" size; larger prints will have borders. Some machines also accept roll paper, and these can also make long panoramic prints: 8" or 8.5" wide and as long as 44".

The tabloid, or large format, models—such as the Epson Stylus Photo 2200 and Canon i9100 Photo Printer (see Figure 5.4)—accept sheets as large as 13" × 19" and can make borderless prints of that size when using certain types of photo papers. The Epson 2200 also accepts roll paper for making panoramic prints: 13" wide and as long as 44".

You can also find wide-format printers, employing inkjet or other technology, that make huge prints—24", 36", 44", or 50" wide; maximum print lengths vary. These are intended for professional studios and commercial labs or service bureaus and are prohibitively expensive for all but a few consumers. (Prices start at about $3000 and go up to $100,000.)

When comparing printers, be sure to sure to check their specifications carefully for maximum printable area and the largest borderless print size that each machine can produce. Such data can be difficult to find in the specifications published by some manufacturers; you might need to contact a retailer to ask for this information. Unless you never want to make borderless prints in sizes larger than 4" × 6", I recommend buying a machine that can generate borderless 8.5" × 11" prints.

Direct Printing

Almost all photo printers can print from images in a computer, but some also offer a "direct printing" feature. These machines include a built-in card reader with slots that accept several types of common digital memory card formats (see Figure 5.5). Pop a card into the slot, and you can make prints—4" × 6" or 8" × 10" in size, depending on the printer—without turning on your computer. Some models take a different approach, offering direct printing when the printer is connected to a digital camera with a USB cable.

A few low-end printers with slots for memory cards do not allow for direct printing. The memory card reader on these printers can be used only for downloading images to a computer.

Printers that support direct printing offer some user-selectable features for basic image manipulation and editing. Check the specifications closely for the direct-printing features available with the machines you are considering.

Figure 5.5: Most inkjet printers with a direct-printing option include slots for several types of memory cards. Some models, such as this hp photosmart 7550, include a built-in image preview LCD monitor.

If your printer allows for direct printing, you might want to use this feature for snapshots or for prints that you need quickly—just don't expect the same quality you'd get if you downloaded the image to the computer and enhanced it with image-editing software. This feature can be useful when, for example, you want to hand out photos to your guests before they leave a party. Start with images that are sharp—and of adequate resolution for the intended print size—and your pictures should be fine for a scrapbook or family photo album.

In direct printing, you'll get the best results with printers that include user-selectable controls for image enhancement. Many, but not all, printers that allow for direct printing from a digital camera let you view the images on the camera's LCD monitor. Printers that can print direct from memory cards often include a built-in LCD preview monitor or connections for adding an optional ($100) monitor. This feature is very useful because it allows you to evaluate the effect of any image enhancement that you apply, using the printer's control buttons. The most affordable direct printing models are not designed for compatibility with a preview monitor. Because such machines rarely offer any image-adjustment features, a monitor is not necessary.

Resolution

Printer resolution is entirely different from image resolution. Image resolution refers to the density of pixels in a digital image. Inkjet printers produce the best quality when the image file is set to a resolution of about 300 ppi (pixels per inch). Although ppi is the correct term in this usage, it is often called dpi (dots per inch), and that can become confusing.

Printer resolution, selected in the printer driver software, is correctly expressed in dpi, because dpi refers to the number of dots of ink the printhead can apply per inch on the paper. Photo-quality inkjet printing starts at 720 dpi printer resolution and usually goes up to at least 1440 dpi, and a few, like the HP 7900 series, used eight colors of ink (see Figure 5.6).

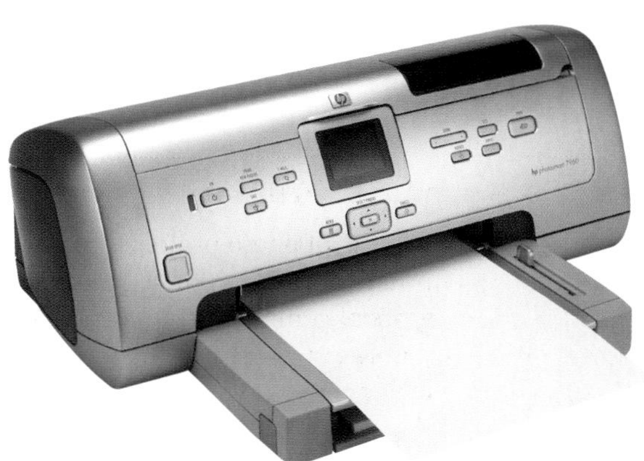

Figure 5.6: Until recently, 2800 dpi resolution and seven ink colors were the highest available in consumer grade machines.

Some recent printers offer substantially higher "enhanced" dpi such as 4800 dpi or 5760 dpi. Frankly, this is marketing hype. You will not see an improvement in your photos when printing at any setting higher than 2880 dpi for printer resolution. Even the difference between a print made at 1440 dpi and another made at 2880 dpi is noticeable only by a highly critical observer.

When using a high-quality photo printer, a setting of 720 dpi should produce good prints on matte photo paper. On glossy photo paper, 1440 dpi is adequate for making exceptional photo-quality prints, particularly when you disengage the High Speed Print option in the printer driver software. A 2880 dpi setting might produce slightly higher quality—more effectively dealing with tonal variations—that is noticeable under close scrutiny. However, the higher dpi setting consumes more ink and substantially increases the printing time. Even if you buy a 2880 dpi machine, you'll want to use the 1440 dpi setting often for faster printing and lower ink cost.

Printer Driver Software

All photo printers include software for controlling the output settings for the printer, such as quality, paper size, and other factors (see Figure 5.7). The versatility of such software varies from printer to printer. Printers in the less-than $129 category typically offer very few user-selected options. More expensive printers, particularly those in the $300+ range, include software with more options, including those for color management, image fine-tuning, page layout, and print enhancement. You can find additional details on using the most valuable of these features in Chapter 12.

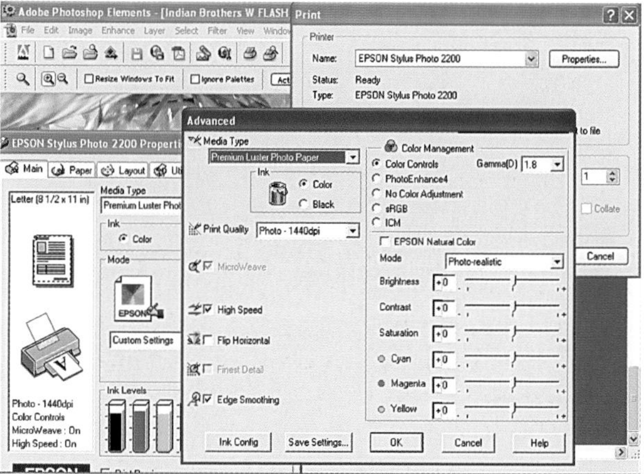

Figure 5.7: Most high-end photo printers include very sophisticated and versatile printer driver software, such as the Epson 2200 software shown here, that allows for full control over many image parameters.

Connectivity

Until recently, most printers were designed with parallel connectivity, allowing them to be connected to a computer with a parallel cable. Subsequently, some printers were designed to accept either parallel or USB cable connectivity, and others offer only USB connectivity.

The USB 1.1 connectivity has been common for some years and is substantially faster than parallel connectivity. The new USB 2, available with some new printers, allows for substantially faster data transfer than the USB 1.1 connectivity. However, in photo printing, the value of USB 2 connectivity is dubious, because printers cannot accept data at the higher speed. Nonetheless, USB 2 connectivity is useful for high-speed downloading of images from a camera or card reader and for scanning as well. In the future, printers may also take greater advantage of the higher speed of USB 2 connectivity.

Printing Speed

Printer speed determines how quickly a machine can print a photo, and it varies widely from one printer to another. Newer printers, especially the more expensive models, tend to be faster than older printers. The specifications for printers generally provide some information as to the time required to make an 8" × 10" print, but this often refers to printing documents or draft-quality photos.

The published specifications for printer speed do not relate to high-resolution *photo* printing speed, but can be useful for comparison purposes, at least among printers of the same brand. Because there is no industry standard for printer speed, each manufacturer employs a different standard for their published specs. Test reports, available on the Web and in photo magazines provide more reliable data as to actual photo printing speed: often between 3 and 5 minutes for an 8.5" × 11" print made at 1440 dpi, and longer at higher resolution settings.

Aside from the printer resolution setting, actual printing time depends on your computer's processing speed, the amount of RAM, the type of connectivity, the size of the printer's buffer, the size of the image file being processed (large files require more processing that can slow down the printing process), and so on.

Figure 5.8: All prints, regardless of the paper, ink, and technology, fade and discolor over time, as this example indicates. Although it's easy to remake a digital print, you can maximize print life by following the recommended framing and display methods.

Print Permanence

All photos eventually fade, especially when displayed in direct sunlight (see Figure 5.8). Some ink-and-paper combinations are more lightfast than others, and the resulting prints are more fade-resistant. Look for information about print longevity on the printer manufacturer's website. With some of the latest inkjet printers that use water-based dye inks, the lightfast rating varies from 20 to 50 years when the prints are framed and displayed according to the manufacturer's recommendations. Several HP machines can make prints with a lightfast rating of 73 years, when using HP Premium Plus Photo Paper. For specifics, visit www.hp.com.

The printer manufacturers' lightfast ratings are estimates based on accelerated testing by companies such as Wilhelm Imaging Research (www.wilhelm-research.com) and apply to prints made only on certain types of photo paper from the same manufacturer. The estimates are probably reliable, at least for comparison purposes, but rarely provide a lightfast rating when *other* paper types are used. The specifications assume that the prints will be framed and displayed under conditions that will minimize fading: framed, matted, covered with non-UV (non-ultraviolet) glass, and hung in an area without excessive humidity and without direct illumination from sunlight or powerful lamps. Because of the effects of UV rays, humidity, ozone, and air-borne pollutants, unframed prints fade much more quickly.

Prints made with certain pigment-based inks can be even more stable. At the time of this writing, only Epson offered consumer-grade photo printers that use pigment-based inks: the Stylus Photo 2200 and R800. The Stylus Photo 2200 can make prints with a lightfast rating of "greater than 90 years," and the R800 can make prints with a lightfast rating of 80 years, on certain Epson papers. Check www.epson.com for specifics as to current models; ; pay special attention to the type of Epson paper that must be used by each machine for the greatest resistance to fading.

In general, pigment-based inks make prints with a color gamut that is not as wide as those made with dye inks, so the prints may not appear to be as vibrant. With the latest machines, such as the Epson Stylus Photo 2200—and particularly the R800 that uses a new type of pigmented ink for greater color saturation—the difference is minimal. The prints exhibit rich, brilliant colors and deep, dark blacks for high visual impact.

If you consider print longevity important, check the manufacturers' specifications as to the lightfast ratings. Most photo enthusiasts feel that a 25-year lightfast rating is adequate, but some insist on buying only printers that can produce prints with a much longer life. Professional photographers making prints that will be sold or displayed in galleries should certainly consider a printer that uses pigment-based inks.

RECOMMENDATION: Consider Archival Issues

When inkjet photo printers were first introduced, few inks were available to produce an archival print: one that was highly fade resistant. Some early ink/paper combinations produced prints that faded quickly unless kept in dark storage; in six months or a year, color changes were obvious.

You can remake any print that has faded. But if long print life is important, buy a printer that uses lightfast inks, and use the manufacturer's most stable paper. Avoid paper that's advertised as "instant dry" because it will not make archival prints. The printer manufacturers' websites should provide longevity specifics for each printer. If the specifications do not provide lightfast rating, data, assume that noticeable fading will occur in one to three years, if the prints are on display; proper framing may extend the longevity of such prints.

Finally, if you want to make archival prints, think twice about buying an after-market paper that is said to be compatible with all brands of printers. You'll get the best results with media that are specifically matched to the dye-based or pigmented inks of a single brand of printer. Before buying any third-party paper, check the manufacturer's website for a lightfast rating; that should depend on the brand and model of the machine that you are using.

For the longest print life, use only archival photo albums or proper framing techniques. You can find additional information on maximizing print longevity on the Wilhelm Image Research website (www.wilhelm-research.com/). You might also want to take a look at a very informative article that was published in the November 2003 *Shutterbug* magazine. An interview with Mr. Wilhelm, this article includes many of his explanations of various technical issues as well as his recommendations for making archival prints. (The article should be available on the magazine's website www.shutterbug.net/features/1103sb_thearchival/.)

Other Printer Factors

You might also want to consider other factors when deciding which printer to buy. Size might be important if you have limited desk space. Noise level might be of interest if the printer will be placed close to your work area. The ability to add a roll paper holder, preferably one with an automatic paper cutter, can be useful if you plan to make numerous prints or want to make long, panoramic prints. You might want a printer that accepts thick media.

Compatibility with roll paper can be useful for anyone who will make numerous prints, but this feature is less than ideal for making 4" × 6" prints. When made on roll paper, the photos tend to curl badly and require some time under a heavy weight for flattening.

Finally, it can be useful to have some estimate as to the cost of consumables, particularly ink cartridges. The cost of paper also varies, if you plan to use the printer manufacturer's brand instead of an after-market brand. Check prices on the Web, and also check the printer manufacturers' specifications as to estimated ink consumption.

It is difficult or impossible to calculate the cost of ink per inkjet print. Some manufacturers publish estimates of the number of prints you can make with a cartridge or a set of ink tanks. These estimates are usually based on printing documents or photos at a low-resolution draft setting and not on photo printing at a high-resolution printer setting. Use such data only for comparison purposes. Because there is no industry standard for ink consumption estimates, the data is most useful for comparing printers from the same manufacturer. Regardless of the printer you buy, expect to use far more ink than the manufacturer's estimate.

RECOMMENDATION: Select the Right Inkjet Photo Printer

There's no simple method for identifying the ideal printer, because that depends on individual budgets, preferences, and printing plans. However, if you're considering a letter-size photo printer, I recommend looking for a machine with the following features: 1440 ppi or higher resolution, versatile driver software, at least six ink colors, preferably in individual tanks, ink droplets size of 4 picoliters or smaller, and a lightfast rating of at least 25 years.

The quickest way to compare the specifications for several machines of several brands is on a photo retailer's website. Also read test reports on the Internet or in photography magazines to identify the top-rated models within your price range. After you narrow the field to two or three machines, ask a local retailer to print a few 8" X 10" images so you can evaluate print quality. There's no standard as to what makes for an excellent photographic print, but look at color fidelity and tonal range: detail in both highlight and shadow areas. Then take a closer look at the print, checking for smooth gradations of color and to confirm that the ink dots are not visible. After viewing prints made by different printers, you should be able to determine which come closest to meeting your own standards.

Inkjet Printer Paper

Many inkjet photo printers accept a wide variety of media, from bond paper to photo paper to specialty paper such as watercolor or canvas. Most people tend to use only a few types because retail stores generally stock only the most popular photo papers. Those are fine as a start, but there's a wealth of other media. If you shop around on the Web, you can find specialty papers with finishes such as canvas, silk, polyester, metallic, and various textured art papers (see Figure 5.9). Each will impart an entirely different look to your images, useful

Figure 5.9: Inkjet media are available in the same brand as your printer and also in independent brands marketed by other companies.

for enhancing your artistic work or for prints that you plan to frame.

Glossy media produce prints with vibrant colors and generally with high contrast, for a very bold, snappy effect. Matte papers absorb more of the ink, causing a reduction in contrast and in color vibrancy, as well as sharpness. Matte papers work well with subdued images, of nature subjects, for example. Semigloss papers are a compromise between the two; they are similar in characteristics to the glossy papers, but without the high sheen that can produce distracting reflections or show every fingerprint. The other types of media produce an entirely different look, from artistic to dramatic (see Figure 5.10).

Inkjet Media Compatibility Issues

Every inkjet printer manufacturer offers a series of papers designed specifically for their brands of machines and their own inks. Not all their papers are recommended for use with all their printer models, so you must still check for compatibility. If you follow the manufacturer's advice on compatible paper and use the correct printer software settings for the specific medium, you're virtually guaranteed excellent results.

Many types of media are also available from independent suppliers, including some with an unusual surface and special media made from uncommon materials. Some of these are not compatible with all inkjet printers. For example, the paper might not absorb certain inks properly, which can cause ink to smudge or pool on top of the paper. If that occurs, you'll need to clean the printer's paper path, using special cleaner sheets available at most stores. Poor absorption is also common when you use one printer manufacturer's paper in another brand of printer or if you print on the wrong side of any medium.

Fabric or true canvas media can cause a jam with any printer. Very thick media can also cause a paper jam that may require repairs not covered under the printer warranty. Front- or top-loading printers are especially prone to paper jams with thick stock because they must bend the paper over a roller. A few high-end printers include a secondary straight-through paper path that will not bend the paper; this feature is intended for use with thick media (about 18 mil or thicker).

Important Inkjet Paper Concepts

It's worth knowing something about the important features and the terminology that you'll encounter when shopping for media. Although not all manufacturers provide all the following information about their products, many do so, at least on their websites.

Whiteness Denotes the brightness of the paper in percentages. The higher the percentage, the whiter the paper, leading to prints with more vibrant colors. However, you might prefer a warmer paper, perhaps closer to ivory or even to yellow. A warm paper can be appropriate for greeting cards or invitations, and it can really enhance earth-tone colors.

Weight and Thickness Terms that are often used interchangeably but that refer to different attributes. A heavier paper is usually thick and vice versa. A lightweight or thin paper is fine for photos that you plan to frame. Select thicker stock for making postcards, calendars,

Figure 5.10: Each type of paper produces a different look and feel to an image, as in this example: the first print (A) made on canvas and the second (B) on glossy paper. The difference may not be obvious in this reproduction, but it's certainly significant when examining prints.

greeting cards, and anything that will be handled often or is intended to be folded. Thickness is generally denoted in mils (thousandths of an inch), and weight is denoted in lbs/ream or grams per square meter (gsm). The higher the number, the thicker or heavier the paper. Heavy paper has a more pleasing feel than flimsy paper and is more durable.

Resin Coating Applied to glossy, semigloss, and some other papers. The coating absorbs the ink to prevent pooling, spreading, and smudging, and it also reduces subsequent fading. Some papers and fabrics are uncoated, and they allow ink to spread slightly. As a result, they produce prints that have softer detail, less sharpness, and more subtle, less-striking colors. These characteristics are appropriate for some fine art prints. Many matte, cotton rag, and watercolor papers are uncoated and seem to work well in many inkjet printers.

If you buy uncoated paper that is said to be compatible with your printer, you might need to adjust some settings in the printer software. Some manufacturers suggest setting the ink density to a low level and the printing speed to slow to minimize ink-smudging problems.

Base Refers to the actual makeup of the media: bond paper, 100% cotton rag, polyester, or other fabric, canvas, and film that resembles overhead transparency material. Some so-called canvas and fabric media are actually coated stock with a texture that resembles canvas or fabric. Although few printers are fully compatible with a true canvas or fabric base, they may produce good results with papers that merely emulate the look of such media.

Surface The finish of printing media, which can vary extensively, from the typical glossy and matte to the papers that have a flat, rough finish and different kinds of textures. Textured paper produces interesting effects because the texture becomes part of the image, adding another dimension to your prints. Certain uncoated watercolor papers produce the softest effect, resembling a watercolor painting to some extent. Artistic and nature images generally work well when printed on a textured matte, canvas-look, or watercolor paper.

RECOMMENDATION: Paper

In addition to the issues regarding the lightfast rating of any medium (discussed earlier), consider the following.

- Before trying independent brand media—whether an unusual finish or stock that is very thick—check for compatibility information in your printer's owner's manual and on the paper manufacturer's website. If using an after-market medium with an entirely different type of finish—watercolor, canvas-look, or velvet, for example—you'll need to know the most appropriate printer software setting. Check the data sheet that comes with some media, or visit the paper manufacturer's website for recommendations.
- Some paper manufacturers offer custom profiles, which should produce better results with their media with specific brands of printers, as discussed in Chapter 9. The alternative is to adjust the color controls in your printer software—in the Properties dialog box—to fine-tune the output through trial and error.
- It's worth experimenting with independent brand papers when you want to use a medium that's not available in the same brand as your printer. Although compatibility problems do exist between certain ink and paper combinations, most after-market papers work with most inkjet photo printers. You won't know how well they'll work with your printer unless you give them a try by buying a few sampler packs (a few sheets of several types of media).
- Be prepared for some artistic experimentation, adjusting color balance, saturation, sharpness, and contrast in image-editing software or the printer software. Make test prints until you find just the right combination of settings that provide the optimum results. An important part of the creative process, the paper that you select—and your printing techniques—can make a major difference. A willingness to experiment will pay dividends, helping to enhance your images.

Dye-Sublimation Photo Printers

Although inkjet photo printers are more common, several companies (Olympus, Kodak, Canon, Hi-Touch Imaging, and others) market another type of printer that employs entirely different technology. Such machines are referred to by several names: thermal dye-sublimation, thermal dye diffusion, and dye diffusion thermal transfer, depending on the exact technology that is used. Frequently abbreviated as dye-sub, this technology employs dyes that are stable and highly resistant to fading. (Specific lightfast ratings are rarely published.) The prints are made by applying heat to a ribbon; a colored gas is produced (sublimated) and impregnated into the surface of the paper. Most dye-sub printers apply a protective laminate coating to the prints, useful for greater resistance to the damaging effects of direct sunlight, humidity, fingerprints, and water droplets. Dye-sub printers are designed to print at a printer resolution of 300 dpi or 314 dpi, all that is required for exceptional prints with the dye-sub technology.

Dye-sub printers are fast and produce enduring prints, said to outlast conventional (silver halide) photographs when on display. Although print quality depend on the printer, dye-sub prints are generally sharp, with a rich, vibrant color rendition. The dyes are applied in gaseous form and produce continuous areas of color instead of actual dots on the paper; this makes for a continuous tone output. When compared with an inkjet print, a high-quality dye-sub print more closely resembles a conventional photograph; consequently, some photographers prefer dye-sub prints.

Most dye-sub printers are designed for making borderless prints that are 5.8" × 3.9", or 4" × 6", in size. Some models can only print directly from a digital camera. Others can also print from a computer when connected with a USB cable. Some of the HITI series models from Hi-Touch Imaging include slots for printing directly from some digital camera memory cards. The small-format (for making 4" × 6" or smaller prints) dye-sub printers (see Figure 5.11) range in price from $149 to $300, about the same as many larger inkjet photo printers that can generate borderless 8.5" × 11" prints.

You can also find larger dye-sub printers that can make prints with a maximum printable area of 8" × 10", such as the $1000 Kodak Professional 8500 Digital Photo Printer. This machine primarily targets professional photographers and small photo labs. At the time of this writing, a more affordable model was available, the Olympus P-400, that accepts paper as large as 8.25" × 11.7" with a maximum printable area of 7.64" × 10". Models that will make larger dye-sub prints are available too, but these are intended for use by high-volume commercial labs and are priced accordingly ($5000+).

Figure 5.11: The small-format dye-sub printers, such as this Kodak DX6000, are intended for those who do not need large prints but who want excellent quality in fade-resistant prints.

It is easy to compare the cost of consumables when comparing several dye-sub printers. That's because each machine accepts only a proprietary kit containing a supply of special paper and a new ink ribbon cartridge. With a bit of math, you can quickly calculate the exact cost per print, for paper and "ink."

As discussed earlier, dye-sub printers have certain benefits, but they have drawbacks as well. The machines are expensive when compared with inkjet printers, and consumables are also more expensive. Only a few of the large, prohibitively expensive commercial models can make prints larger than 8" × 10". A dye-sub printer requires special paper (thermal media), available only in one or two finishes and only from the manufacturer. Finally, dye-sub printers are designed exclusively for printing photos. Hence, they are less versatile than inkjet printers, which accept a broad variety of media and can also be used for printing text and documents. Dust can also be a problem in dye-sub printers, leaving blank specks on the image.

RECOMMENDATION: Dye-Sub Printers

If you already own a multipurpose printer and want a machine to use only for making 4" × 6" or postcard-size photo prints, a small-format dye-sub printer is worth considering. The dye-sub machines that can make 8" × 10" prints are less attractive because they are far more expensive than comparable inkjet printers.

The small-format dye-sub printers can produce beautiful prints that some photographers prefer over inkjet prints. If you decide to buy one, look for a model that can print directly from your digital camera and from a personal computer as well, for maximum versatility. Check the quality produced by several brands of dye-subs at a retail store, and also compare the cost of consumables.

Before making a final decision, read some test reports on the Web, and conduct some research on a retailer's website as to specifications and features of the models that produce the best prints.

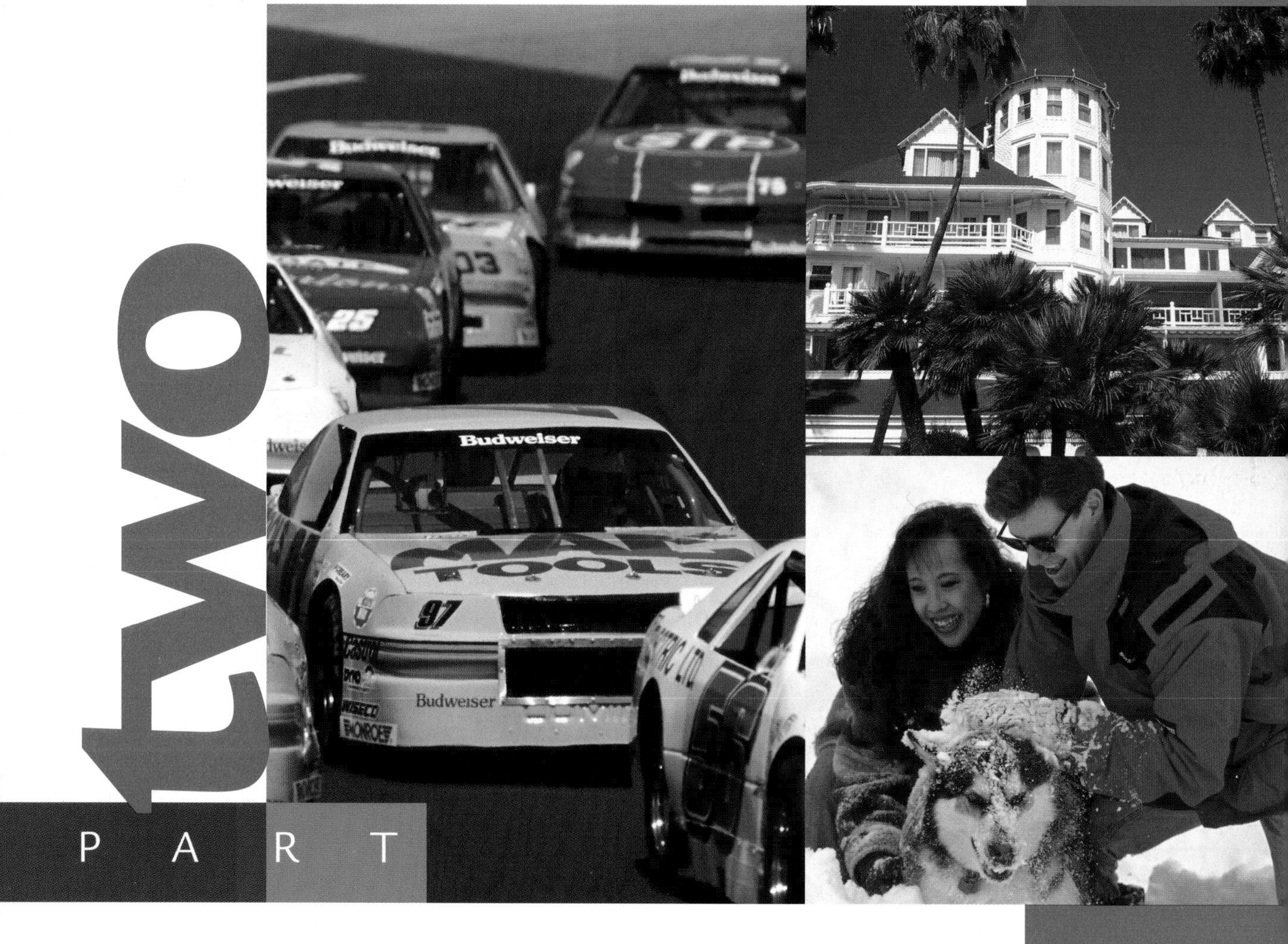
two
P A R T
Budweiser
97
Budweiser

Capture

Although digital imaging relies heavily on new technology, the traditional principles of photography apply regardless of the medium that's used. If you want to progress beyond snapshooting, apply a four-part formula: understand the essential photographic concepts; control all aspects of an image with the camera's features; take advantage of proven photographic techniques; and finally, add a dose of creativity.

As part of the capture process, the effective scanning techniques described in Chapter 8 will generate images that you can easily optimize for printing with image-editing techniques described in subsequent chapters.

six
CHAPTER

Making Digital Images

Many digital cameras are *loaded with features, ranging from fully automatic to semiautomatic to fully manual, and I mentioned most of these briefly in Chapter 1. If you own a digital camera, you should be adept at at finding and activating some of these features, as well as the built-in flash unit, while taking pictures.*

In this chapter, I'll provide a more detailed overview of all the digicam and SLR (Single Lens Reflex) camera capabilities, as well as popular accessories, and their use in making images that go well beyond the quick snapshot. But first, I'll provide an overview of the most important photographic concepts.

Essential Photographic Concepts

To appreciate the value and benefit of certain digital camera features, it is important to fully understand a few photographic concepts. Although entire books have been written on these concepts, the following brief overview should be useful as a refresher for advanced image making.

Exposure Basics

Exposure is the amount of light that will expose the camera's light-sensitive sensor in order to take a photo. Ideally, the exposure should be "correct." The image should depict the scene as our eyes perceive it, with clean whites; rich, dark blacks; midtones (such as gray) that are not excessively light or dark; and accurate detail in all important subject areas (see Figure 6.1). Two factors control the amount of light that will make the image: the length of time that the camera's shutter mechanism is open and the size of the aperture (opening) in the lens. Both factors can be controlled automatically by the camera or manually by the photographer using camera controls, as discussed later.

The shutter speed controls the length of time that light is allowed to strike the image sensor. The longer the shutter speed—1 second versus 1/1000 second, for example—the greater the amount of light that strikes the image sensor. The aperture controls the amount of light that enters during any given amount of time. Aperture size is denoted with f/numbers—also called f/stops—such as f/8. The smaller the f/number, the larger the aperture size. A wide aperture such as f/4 allows far more light to enter the camera than a small aperture such as f/11.

The "smaller the number, larger the size" concept may seem counterintuitive, but it is correct. An f/number or f/stop is actually a ratio: the focal length of a lens divided by the diameter of any given aperture that is set. Instead of concerning yourself with that technical issue, simply remember this: a wide aperture is denoted by a small f/number, and a small aperture is denoted by a large f/number.

Figure 6.1:The "best" exposure for any scene or subject is a somewhat subjective judgment. As a general rule, however, images with "correct" exposure exhibit a full range of tones—from pure white to midtones to pure black—and include detail in all important subject areas.

The amount of light required for an accurate exposure depends on the camera's ISO (International Organization for Standardization) setting. A low ISO number, such as 100, denotes low sensitivity to light. A high ISO number, such as 400, denotes high sensitivity to light. The camera's light-metering computer automatically considers this setting when calculating the aperture size and shutter speed that will produce an accurate exposure.

Many cameras provide both automatic and user-selected ISO settings. If you select the automatic feature, the camera sets a low ISO in bright light and a higher ISO in low light for much faster shutter speeds to reduce the risk of blurry images caused by camera shake or by subject movement. Manual ISO selection is preferable because image quality is higher at low ISO settings than at ISO settings higher than 200. Switch to a higher ISO setting only when you must do so to avoid blurry pictures, as discussed in the "Shutter Speed Effects" section later in this chapter.

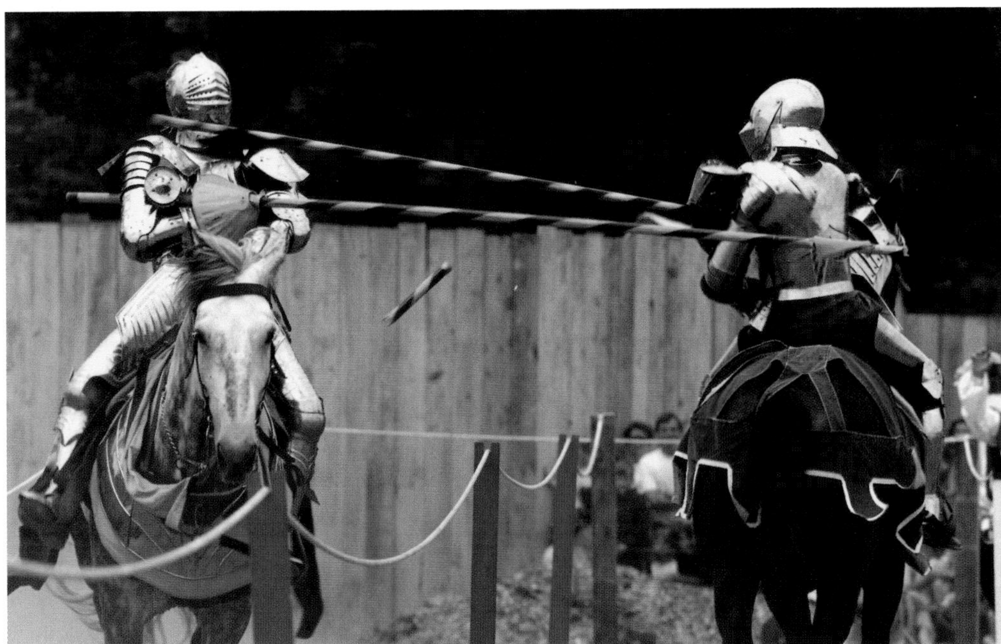

Figure 6.2: This image was made at f/4 at 1/1000 second, but many other combinations of aperture size and shutter speed would produce the identical exposure: f/2.8 at 1/2000 sec., f/5.6 at 1/250 sec., f/8 at 1/125 sec., f/11 at 1/60 sec., and so on.

Equivalent Exposure

To photograph an image with the right amount of light, you need the correct combination of shutter speed and aperture. This ensures that the image is not excessively bright or excessively dark. The camera's light-metering computer calculates the amount of light that will be appropriate for an accurate exposure, considering the brightness of the light that is reflected by the scene or the subject.

Many combinations of shutter speed and aperture size produce the same, or equivalent, exposure (see Figure 6.2). A long shutter speed and a small aperture can allow the same amount of light to strike the sensor as a fast shutter speed and a large aperture. You need not calculate which shutter speed and aperture are correct, because the camera's light-metering computer completes this task. Even in the fully manual mode, discussed later, the camera provides guidance as to the settings for a correct exposure.

"Correct" Exposure

So far, we have assumed that a camera always makes a correct exposure, producing an image that is not too bright or too dark. That's true when you photograph midtone subjects such as grass, rocks, or trees. Because all light-metering systems are designed to produce accurate exposures with such scenes, your images should be close to perfect.

However, no light-metering system is infallible. No matter how sophisticated, it will not produce an optimal exposure in certain conditions. If the subject is white (or another very light tone) or if the scene includes a vast expanse of bright snow, sand, sky, or water, the image may be too dark or underexposed. Conversely, a black lava field (or other very dark-toned subject) may be overexposed, rendered as gray: too bright.

The exposure error should not be severe (see Figure 6.3) if you're using one of the many current digicams that incorporate a highly sophisticated metering system. Such

Figure 6.3: When you photograph a white subject or a scene with an extremely bright area, most light-metering systems produce an image that is underexposed, at least to some extent.

systems, often designated as multisegment, evaluative, or matrix metering, employ a sensor with several or many individual segments and a microcomputer with artificial intelligence. These systems are designed to evaluate the various segments of a scene and to compensate for areas of high brightness.

As discussed in the "Light Metering and Exposure Controls" section later in this chapter, the sophisticated exposure systems often produce acceptable exposure even in difficult conditions. Although the system may not produce an ideal exposure, the image should not be *severely* under- (or over) exposed as it might be with a less-sophisticated metering system.

When shooting with a digital camera, a slight exposure error is not a major problem, because you can adjust the brightness in image-editing software. However, for the very best image quality, it's worth trying to make a well-exposed image in-camera. You can do so easily with the exposure controls discussed in detail later in this chapter.

Shutter Speed Effects

Although an exposure can be correct when shooting with either a fast or a long shutter speed, there is a valid reason for selecting one or the other. The shutter speed controls the effect that a moving subject produces: frozen in time or softly blurred (see Figure 6.4).

A very fast shutter speed, such as 1/2000 sec., freezes the motion of a fast-moving subject. Even a galloping racehorse covers little distance in the 1/2000th of a second that the shutter allows light to strike the

Figure 6.4: Very fast shutter speeds render motion as "frozen," as in the image on the left made at 1/1000 sec. Long shutter speeds depict motion as blurred, as in the image on the right made at 1/15 sec. while moving the camera in pace with the subject.

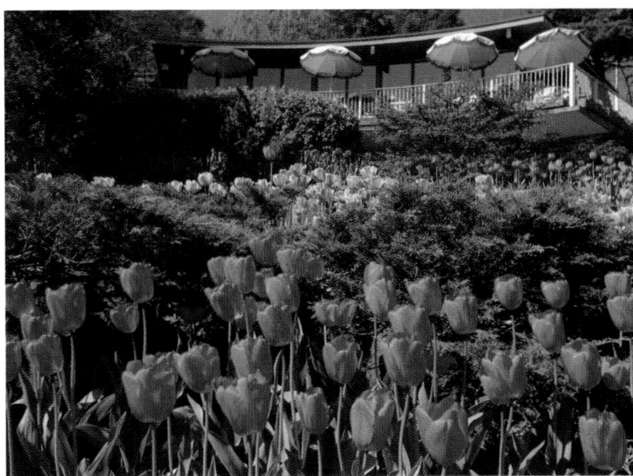

Figure 6.5 : A wide aperture produces very shallow depth of field, especially when the subject is greatly magnified, as in the image on the left (made at f/2.8 with a 500mm equivalent lens). A small aperture produces extensive depth of field, especially when subject magnification is low, as in the image on the right (made at f/16 with a 24mm lens).

image sensor. Hence, the moving horse is sharply rendered without blurring caused by its motion.

If the shutter remains open for a much longer time, say for 1/30 sec., a moving subject is not sharply rendered. The horse in a photo will be blurred, an effect that can be troublesome. Depending on your artistic goals, slight blurring might also be pleasing, because it simulates motion in a still image (see Figure 6.4b).

Aperture Effects

There is also a valid reason for selecting either a wide aperture such as f/2.8 or a small aperture such as f/16. A wide aperture produces shallow depth of field, or a narrow range of apparent sharp focus (see Figure 6.5). At f/2.8, the focused subject is sharp but the foreground and background are blurred. This effect can be pleasing, in a portrait photo, for example. If you select a very small aperture such as /16, the foreground and background are sharp, at least to some extent—useful in landscape and cityscape photography, for example.

As you set a different aperture, you cannot see the depth of field changing in a compact or SLR camera's viewfinder. If you view the scene on a digicam's LCD monitor, the change may be visible; however, the monitor is so small, the difference is difficult to detect. One way to visually evaluate depth of field is to use an SLR camera with a depth-of-field preview control, a feature that does allow you to evaluate the zone of apparent sharpness in a scene.

Control Depth of Field

In addition to the aperture size (f/stop), another factor controls depth of field, the range of apparent sharpness extending in front of the subject and behind it: magnification. When the subject is large in the frame—because it is close to the camera or because you used a telephoto lens—depth of field is shallow. When the subject is small in the frame—because it is far from the camera or recorded with a wide-angle lens—depth of field is extensive.

continues

To blur away a cluttered background, move close to the subject, or use your lens's longest telephoto setting for high magnification. Set a wide aperture: the smallest f/number available with your camera or lens, such as f/2.8 or f/4. When you want to make an image with extensive depth of field, with sharpness from foreground to background, move farther back, or use a wide angle zoom setting for low magnification. Set a small aperture: the largest f/number available, such as f/11 or f/16.

Camera Operating Modes

Once you are armed with these photographic concepts, the camera's operating modes and overrides should make sense. If you select the mode or feature to achieve the intended effect, you should be satisfied with your images. Before moving on to discuss light-metering issues, let's consider the typical operating modes available with many digicams and why you might want to use each one (see Figure 6.6).

Fully Automatic Modes

Virtually all cameras include at least one fully automatic mode, called Program (abbreviated with a *P*) or Full Auto mode. If you select this option, the camera sets both the aperture and the shutter speed based on guidance from its light-metering system. The basic Program or Full Auto mode generally selects a fast shutter speed and a moderately wide aperture. This combination helps to prevent image blur caused by camera shake and provides adequate depth of field for many situations.

The camera may also include subject-specific Program or Scene modes, for sports, portraits, landscapes, and other common subjects. When you use one of these options, the camera may set a different shutter speed/aperture combination. For example, in Sports mode, it sets a fast shutter speed to freeze motion and the relatively small aperture required to maintain correct exposure. In Portrait mode, the camera selects a moderately wide aperture to blur away a cluttered background and selects a higher shutter speed necessary to maintain correct exposure. If you select Landscape mode, the system sets a small aperture to produce great depth of field as well as the appropriate shutter speed.

COURTESY NIKON INC.

Figure 6.6: Whether you own a compact digicam or a digital SLR camera, it will include many of the modes and features discussed in this chapter. Some are accessed with analog controls, and others are available through the electronic menus.

RECOMMENDATION: Fully Automatic Modes

The standard Full Auto or Progam mode is useful for quick snapshooting if the depiction of motion and the depth of field are not important considerations. The subject-specific programs are more useful, at least in theory. Although they cause the camera to select a more appropriate shutter speed and aperture combination, the settings may not produce the motion and depth of field effects you want. Consequently, the semiautomatic modes (discussed in the next section) are more useful because they allow much greater leeway in the selection of just the right shutter speed or aperture.

Semiautomatic Modes

Two semiautomatic modes are available with many cameras: Shutter Priority, often abberevi-ated as TV (for Time Value, not television) and Aperture Piority mode, often abbrevieated as AV (Aperture Value.) If you select Shutter Priority (TV) mode, you can set a desired shutter speed; the camera responds by setting the corresponding aperture to maintain correct expo-sure. In Aperture Priority (AV) mode, you select the aperture (or f/stop), and the camera responds with a suitable shutter speed for correct exposure. These options give you much greater control over both depth of field and the depiction of motion than the subject specific Scene or Program modes.

Before selecting very fast shutter speeds, such as 1/1000 sec., review your camera's instruction manual about the operation of the Shutter Priority (TV mode). Although the exposure should be correct in most situations, not all cameras are designed to maintain correct exposure at fast shutter speeds in low light.

In Shutter Priority (TV) mode, you can control the depiction of motion: blurred with a long shutter speed or frozen in time with a fast shutter speed. This is the mode you often use for moving subjects such as sports and other action; a fast shutter speed, such as 1/250 sec., freezes most motion. Shutter Priority (TV) mode can also be useful for emphasizing motion. When you select a long shutter speed, such as 1/30 sec., most moving subjects will be blurred in your photos. You can select even longer shutter speeds to create motion blur effects. When you photograph a landscape that includes flowing water, a river or waterfalls, try a shutter speed of 1/8 or 1/15 sec. to render the water as blurred. If you prefer to freeze the droplets, set a shutter speed of 1/250 sec. or faster.

In Aperture Priority (AV) mode, you can select from the available range of apertures, and the range depends on the camera or lens you use. Often, a digicam with built-in lens provides options such as f/2.8, f/4, f/5.6, and f/8. Select the largest f/number for minimum depth of field and the smallest number for maximum depth of field. Take care when selecting small apertures (large f/numbers) in low light because the shutter speed set by the camera may be quite long, particularly at low ISO settings; that can produce blurry images, caused by camera shake.

Check for the shutter speed information on the camera's LCD data panel or in the viewfinder. (Entry-level digicams may not provide such information.) Use a tripod—or brace your elbows on something solid—if the exposure is longer than 1/60 sec. at moderate zoom settings or longer than 1/125 at long zoom settings. If using a camera with very long focal lengths, such as a 200mm or 300mm equivalent, use a firm support during exposures longer than 1/350 sec. Although you may be able to shoot handheld at longer shutter speeds, use a tripod or brace your arms on something solid to get sharper images.

RECOMMENDATION: AV and TV Modes

The semiautomatic modes are useful, providing greater control over depth of field and the effects of motion than the various Program options. As recommended earlier, do read your camera's instruction manual before selecting very fast shutter speeds in low light. If your camera will not assure a correct exposure in such situations, try another alternative: Select the widest available aperture (such as f/2.8) to cause the camera to set the fastest possible shutter speed. When you want to use an even faster shutter speed, select a higher ISO setting.

Manual Mode

Nearly all compact digital cameras include a Manual (M) mode that requires you to select both the aperture and the shutter speed. Because this option does not provide a safety net of automation to ensure correct exposure, it is intended for photographers with extensive SLR camera experience.

Select an aperture and a shutter speed, and the in-camera light-metering computer indicates whether exposure will be correct, considering the ISO and the brightness of the light. (The indication is generally in the LCD monitor with a compact digicam and in the viewfinder with an SLR camera.) As you change the aperture or the shutter speed or both, the exposure indicator will show whether the image will be over- or underexposed at your current settings.

As discussed in the "Light Metering and Exposure Controls" section, you might want to use over- or underexposure to achieve a specific effect or to produce a correct exposure if the camera's light meter does not do so. In other modes, you can use the exposure compensation control, but in M mode, you must select an aperture/shutter speed combination that will produce the necessary amount of over- or underexposure.

RECOMMENDATION: Manual Mode

Unless you are an accomplished photographer who has experience using a manual operating mode, stick with the semiautomatic modes. If you shoot an image and it appears to be too dark or too bright, set a plus or minus exposure compensation factor for the next shot. There is really no need to use Manual (M) mode to do so.

Light Metering and Exposure Controls

All digital cameras include a light-metering computer, and most include one or more features for controlling exposure. Three distinct types of light metering systems are available in digital cameras: multisegment (also called matrix or evaluative metering), center weighted, and spot metering. Less-expensive models usually offer only multisegment metering, and the more expensive models usually include two or three options. Each of the three metering types employs a different technical approach, and each is useful in different situations. Many cameras also include an AE Lock control, and most offer an exposure compensation control; these features are useful for producing even better exposures. Let's consider all these camera options individually and in greater detail.

Figure 6.7 : The most effective multisegment light-metering systems produce correct—or close to correct—exposure with "difficult" scenes that include dark shadow areas as well as bright highlight areas.

Multisegment Light Metering

The most technically advanced option, this type of exposure system works by dividing the total subject area into several or numerous segments. The light meter reads each of the areas and makes a comparative analysis of factors such as subject size and the brightness level in each part of the scene. Generally, it ignores (or deemphasizes) extremely dark or bright areas, such as the sun in a corner of the frame. Naturally, some of the multisegment (or matrix or evaluative) systems are more "intelligent" than others, employing more sophisticated artificial logic to produce an accurate exposure in most situations (see Figure 6.7).

Some multi-segment systems employ a database consisting of sample images; a microcomputer compares the brightness pattern of a scene to the database, seeking a similarity. If the similarity is found, the system applies the exposure compensation level that should produce good results with the scene that you want to photograph. Regardless of the exact technology that is used, a multisegment metering system should ensure fairly accurate exposure in difficult conditions: back lighting, for example, as with a subject against a bright sky or beach. It should also compensate (to some extent) for extremely bright subject matter, such as a snowy landscape on a sunny day, to help prevent underexposure.

RECOMMENDATION: Multisegment Light Metering

In most common shooting situations, a sophisticated multisegment light-metering system is a fine choice for good to excellent exposures. (If you are in the market for a new digicam, read test reports to identify cameras with the most effective metering systems.) You may need to use some exposure compensation in some situations, especially in strong back lighting: for example, with a person against a bright background. After making an image, check it on the LCD monitor, and reshoot if necessary, after setting some exposure compensation.

Center-Weighted Light Metering

This is the most traditional type of light-metering pattern. When it is selected, the camera's system measures the light reflecting from an entire scene, including shadows, highlights, and midtone areas. The center-weighted system then calculates an averaged exposure but gives greater weight to a large central area of the scene. For scenes of average brightness and moderate contrast, this type of meter usually produces good results. However, center-weighted meters can produce under- or overexposure with scenes that are predominantly very light or very dark in tone (see Figure 6.8).

RECOMMENDATION: Center-Weighted Light Metering

Working with a center-weighted light meter is second nature to experienced photographers who have owned 35mm SLR cameras for many years. They know when this type of meter is likely to over- or underexpose, and they have developed exposure compensation strategies that produce correct exposure. Unless you fall into this category, you will probably prefer to use multi-segment light metering instead. Although this type of system does not always guarantee correct exposure, it is often more successful than the less sophisticated center-weighted light meter.

Figure 6.8: As this example indicates, strong backlighting (a subject against bright sun, sky, water, or sand) is the most common situation that leads to incorrect exposure, especially with center-weighted metering.

Spot Metering

Similar in concept to a center-weighted light meter, a spot meter takes a reading from a much smaller area of the scene, usually the central part of the subject. Because a spot meter considers brightness only within its small area of coverage, the exposure is not affected by bright or dark surroundings as it can be with center-weighted metering.

Take a spot meter reading—by applying slight pressure to the camera's shutter release button—from an area that is not excessively bright or dark. Now, the camera makes the settings that should produce correct exposure for the subject that has been metered.

Spot metering can be useful, but remember that the exposure will be correct only if you take the meter reading from a midtone area, such as a tanned face, grass, or foliage. If the subject is not a midtone—a white swan, a bright sky, or a black cat, for example—you will not get a good exposure.

RECOMMENDATION: Spot Metering

Spot metering is recommended only for photographers who have extensive experience or training in the effective use of this technique. In most high-contrast situations—such as people against an ultrabright background—you will get better results by using an electronic flash with multi-segment light metering instead of spot metering. In images made with flash, the brightness level will be more even; the background will not be as excessively bright. If you want to experiment with spot metering, try it with distant subjects that are beyond the range of your flash: a spot-lit performer on a distant stage, against a dark (unlit) background, for example.

Autoexposure Lock

Nearly all digital cameras include a control for locking in the exposure value when you take a light-meter reading. Autoexposure lock, often called AEL or AE Lock, lets you lock in the aperture and shutter speed settings. It prevents the exposure from changing as you recompose: pointing the camera toward a brighter area of the scene, for example. This feature is most useful with spot and center-weighted light metering.

After taking a meter reading of a midtone subject area—excluding any ultrabright or very dark surroundings—press and hold the AEL button, or maintain light pressure on the camera's shutter release button. (Check your owner's manual as to how to activate its AE Lock function.) In most cases, this also locks focus. As you recompose for more pleasing framing, the exposure value (aperture/shutter speed combination) remains the same, even if the new composition includes a very bright sky or a black subject.

RECOMMENDATION: AE Lock

Use AE Lock when you decide to take a spot meter or a center-weighted meter reading from a specific part of a scene: a grassy area or a tanned face, perhaps. If your "target" is not excessively dark or light in tone or brightness, the resulting image should exhibit accurate exposure overall.

Exposure Compensation

An exposure compensation control is a standard digicam feature and can be used in the Program (fully automatic) and the semiautomatic operating modes. It may not be available in subject specific Program modes, such as Landscape or Portrait.

As discussed earlier, you may need to compensate the exposure if the camera's light meter does not produce the desired effect. Use a plus (+) compensation factor to increase exposure for making a brighter image of a light-toned or ultrabright subject (see Figure 6.9). With a black or other dark-toned subject, set a minus (–) compensation factor to avoid an excessively bright rendition.

Figure 6.9: With a light-toned subject of this type, a plus exposure compensation (+1 used in this case with center-weighted metering) is often necessary to assure correct exposure.

Although this rule of thumb might seem contradictory, it is correct: For very light subject matter, add (+) light. For very dark-toned subjects, subtract (–) light. Most light meters are calibrated to render a subject as a midtone. If you want white (instead of gray) snow, for example, increase the exposure. To render a black lava field as a rich dark black (instead of gray), decrease exposure.

Some books on photography provide numerous recommendations as to the amount of exposure compensation that you should use in various situations. These are usually based on shooting with center-weighted metering.

With digital cameras, such recommendations are less useful, for two reasons. First, multi-segment metering is the most commonly used digicam metering system. Second, minor over- or underexposure is easily corrected in image-editing software. Because multi-segment light-metering systems vary in their effectiveness in producing correct exposure with difficult scenes, it's impossible to provide a full range of guidelines for exposure compensation. However, consider the following suggestions when beginning to experiment with exposure compensation.

- For a scene or subject that is predominantly white, set a +1 compensation factor.
- For a person against an extremely bright background, as at the beach, set +1.5, or use flash and set only +1.
- If the background includes the sun, set +2, or use flash and set only +1.

For a black subject, such as a limousine, a closeup of black animals, or people dressed in black (such as groomsmen in tuxedos), set –0.5. If the entire subject is black, such as a lava field, set a –1 compensation factor.

As you gain some experience with your own camera, you'll become quite adept at judging when exposure compensation will be necessary and how much is needed to produce the desired results. The rough rules of thumb provided here should be useful for making acceptable to good exposures. Because you can make minor exposure corrections using image-editing software, the in-camera exposure need not be spot on.

RECOMMENDATION: Exposure Compensation

In digital photography, "ideal" exposure generates an image that is as bright as possible, without loss of detail in highlight areas. After taking the picture, check the LCD monitor. If necessary, reshoot the image with a different level of exposure compensation for a brighter or darker rendition. When in doubt, err on the side of slight underexposure. Avoid overexposing digital images—particularly photos with important highlight details—because you will lose detail in washed-out areas.

Autoexposure Bracketing

An increasing number of digital cameras include an option for quickly compensating your exposures. If you select the Autoexposure Bracketing (AEB) feature, you can shoot three frames in a sequence: one exposed based on the meter reading, one overexposed, and one underexposed. You can set the degree of compensation, usually from 0.5 to 2 f/stops. The higher the factor you set, the greater the exposure deviation from one frame to the next.

You can also set some exposure compensation before setting the AEB feature. For example, you might set an exposure compensation factor of +1 for a snowy landscape and then bracket in 0.5 step increments. One of the images should exhibit the optimal exposure or close to it.

RECOMMENDATION: AEB

After you develop a good instinct for the amount of exposure compensation that you need to use for various types of scenes, you will rarely need to bracket exposures. Get the in-camera exposure close to correct, avoiding over exposure, and plan to make small corrections with your image-editing software. Reserve bracketing for unusual types of lighting or for situations in which you need to shoot quickly and cannot guess the amount of suitable exposure compensation.

Other Valuable Features

In addition to exposure control, many compact digicams and digital SLR cameras offer a range of features that let you control other aspects or parameters of an image. (Flash features are discussed extensively later in this chapter.)

A camera can include controls for adjusting white balance (WB), color saturation, color tone, sharpness, and contrast as well as a manual focus feature. I mentioned these controls in Chapter 1, but it's worth looking at each in more detail as it relates to advanced digital photography. If you are shopping for a camera, you might want to know whether it's worth looking for a model that includes one or more of these features. If you already own a digicam, you might wonder which are worth using and in what types of situations. My comments and recommendations are based on conclusions formed after testing dozens of digital cameras of various types and brands.

If you shoot in a RAW capture mode, the in-camera settings for sharpness, contrast, various color factors, and white balance are applied but not locked in. Because the image is not processed until it is being converted from RAW format to an image format, you can change these parameters using tools provided in most RAW converter programs. Consequently, the features discussed in this section (except manual focus) apply to image capture in JPEG or TIFF format.

Viewing an image on a camera's small LCD monitor, it is difficult to assess the effect of any change in white balance, sharpness, color saturation and tone, contrast, or focus. This is one reason many photographers do not indiscriminately use all the image adjustment features of their cameras. Except for a specific white balance setting, it's best to leave the other options at the low or the default setting initially. After you have time to experiment with a camera's tendencies—reviewing many images on a large computer monitor—you should be able to predict when you may need to adjust contrast, sharpness, color saturation, or color tone. Keep this in mind when reviewing my comments about the various image-enhancing controls available with some digital cameras.

White Balance Control

Nearly all cameras include several white balance (WB) options. When you use the correct WB setting, the camera should reproduce whites as neutral white and grays as neutral gray. Hence, other colors should be accurate as well. Automatic WB is the default setting, but most cameras also offer five or six user-selectable options for making images with accurate white balance in specific lighting conditions: sunlight, on cloudy days, under different types of artificial lighting, with flash indoors, and so on.

Not all cameras are created equal when it comes to the effectiveness of their Auto WB systems. Some are more effective than others. In my experience, most cameras produce good to near-perfect white balance on sunny and partly cloudy days and when shooting with electronic flash indoors or out. You can easily correct any slight color cast with image-editing software. However, you might still want to use a specific WB option to make images with white balance that is closer to ideal. Afterwards, when you move to a situation with a different type of lighting, remember to re-set the WB (see Figure 6.10).

I have found that cameras rarely produce good white balance automatically on a heavily overcast day or in deep shade and under household (tungsten) lamps or fluorescent tubes. In such conditions, it is important to select the appropriate WB setting to minimize the risk of a strong blue, yellow, or green color cast. If your camera has several settings for fluorescent lighting, try each one to determine which produces the best results (without a green color cast) under a certain type of fluorescent tube system. You might still need to correct color balance in image-editing software, but this should not be difficult.

There is no WB setting for unusual types of artificial light, such as sodium vapor; under such lighting, you might need to use Auto WB and make color balance corrections after downloading the images to your computer. Use image-editing software, such as the Photoshop programs, perhaps with after-market plug-in software designed to facilitate

Figure 6.10: A serious error in WB—a strong blue cast in this case, caused by using the Sunny Day WB setting on an overcast day—can be difficult to fully correct in image-editing software.

correct color balance. As with any image that exhibits a very strong color cast, the correction process will call for some expertise.

Some cameras include a Custom or Manual WB option intended for use especially under artificial lighting. This feature is also useful in mixed lighting (several types of light sources are illuminating an area). Follow the directions in the owner's manual as to how to calibrate the system to "teach" the camera to render neutral tones accurately in the specific lighting. You might need to point the lens to a white or gray subject and press a button to calibrate the system for the specific conditions. The resulting WB may not be perfect, but it should be close to correct.

Kelvin Scale Control

Some high-end digital cameras include another option for making images with correct white balance. It allows the user to set the color "temperature" using a Kelvin scale. If you understand this color temperature scale, you can fine-tune the color balance in-camera to compensate for the color of the lighting of a scene.The Kelvin value that you set should be based on a reading taken by an accessory color temperature meter or on experience. If you set the correct Kelvin temperature value, the white balance will be accurate and your images will not exhibit any color cast.

The Kelvin Scale

A linear scale that's used to denote the color of various light sources, the Kelvin scale (named for William Thomson, Baron Kelvin of Largs, who first proposed this system) is specified in degrees Kelvin. For practical purposes in photography, think of the scale as a numerical method that defines the color of light. A low number, in degrees Kelvin, denotes the warm (orange-toned) light produced by fire, an incandescent lamp and the sun around sunset. A high number, in degrees Kelvin, denotes cool (bluish) light that we find in a shady area or on an overcast day.

Here are some typical color temperatures: candlelight, 1500 K; sunrise and sunset, 3200 K; sunshine around noon, 5000 to 5500 K; the light on a cloudy day, 6000 to 7000 K; the light in a shady area outdoors, 6500 to 7800 K. These are estimates only, and the exact color temperature can vary.

Some RAW converter software programs also include color temperature correction controls, based on the Kelvin scale; this feature is useful for correcting RAW images that exhibit a color cast caused by an incorrect WB setting in the camera.

RECOMMENDATION: White Balance

After using any digital camera for a few weeks, you'll know when it will produce good results with Auto WB and when you should select one of the other WB options. Especially when shooting under artificial lighting, one of the Custom or Manual WB options will be useful. Remember to return to another WB setting, or to recalibrate the Custom WB system when you begin to shoot in different conditions at a later time.

Color Saturation and Tone Controls

An increasing number of cameras include a feature that lets you set color saturation from low to normal (default setting) to high. I rarely find any need for this control, except with cameras that tend to produce images that are excessively saturated, with garish and artificial-looking colors (see Figure 6.11). This problem is quite common, because many manufacturers assume that we want "wet paint" colors in all our images. We can appreciate this effect for certain subjects, but not for others, such as portraits.

Low color saturation—with flat hues and tones—is much easier to correct in image-editing software than excessive color saturation because excessive saturation causes a loss of detail in highly saturated areas of an image. Consequently, you might never want to use the high-saturation setting; in fact, you'll probably most often select the low color saturation option, at least for people pictures.

A few cameras also include a control for adjusting color tone, generally to produce a blue, a red, or a yellow color cast. Boosting the blue tone slightly can be useful under household lamps (without flash) to partially counteract the yellow/orange color cast that can occur even with a tungsten WB setting. It might also be worth trying on winter days when you want to make images with a very "cool" atmosphere. Boosting the red balance can be useful for producing richer tones during a sunset; boosting the yellow can be useful in deep shade, when the camera's WB system produces a blue color cast.

Figure 6.11: Excessively high color saturation is rarely pleasing and can create loss of detail; this is most obvious on close examination, as in the closeup on the right.

RECOMMENDATION: Saturation and Tone Controls

Do not set a camera's color saturation control to high (in JPEG or TIFF capture mode) unless you know that it will produce the results that you envision based on experience. The same applies to the color tone options. Although some photographers find in-camera color tone adjustment useful—as an alternative to using specific color correction filters over the lens—you can achieve similar effects with image-editing software and with much greater fine-control and predictability. (Images made in RAW capture mode can be corrected later if your converter includes a full range of adjustment tools.)

Sharpness Control

The processor in a digital camera applies some degree of sharpening in the JPEG and TIFF capture modes. The degree depends on the camera. Some generate slightly soft images, and others produce excessively sharp images (see Figure 6.12). Some cameras include a control for adjusting the level of sharpening from low to default to high. As with color saturation, think twice about using any setting higher than the default. In fact, you might want to routinely shoot in the low sharpness setting and use Unsharp Mask in Photoshop or some other program to adjust sharpness. This method provides much greater control over the sharpening and can help to minimize problems such as sharpened artifacts and digital noise.

Figure 6.12: As this small portion of a large image indicates, very aggressive in-camera sharpening has two drawbacks: the effect appears artificial, and artifacts such as digital noise (in the sky area) are accentuated.

RECOMMENDATION: Sharpening Control

Some cameras that produce images with an artificially high degree of sharpening do not include any option for selecting a lower sharpness level. Granted, sharpness is subjective to some extent; some people like images that are aggressively sharpened, whether in-camera or with image editing software. If you fall into this category, plan to sharpen your images with software, preferably using an Unsharp Mask tool. Save the original image (without sharpening applied) in case your preferences change later; you can then return to the original image and apply a different level of Unsharp Mask. If you use a camera's high sharpness feature in JPEG or TIFF capture, you will not be able to reduce sharpness, at least not fully, and may later regret using that feature.

Contrast Control

In digital photography, contrast is generally considered as the difference in tonal value between the brightest and the darkest pixels that are recorded. Some cameras routinely produce images with high contrast: highlight areas of a scene are excessively bright, while shadow areas are excessively dark. If the camera includes a control for adjusting contrast, you might want to use that feature in some cases. In harsh, midday lighting, when scene contrast is extremely high, a low setting works well. The same applies to many people pictures, when softer contrast produces a more pleasing effect. Occasionally, a higher contrast setting can be useful, in very flat overcast day light, for example, for a more "snappy" effect.

RECOMMENDATION: Contrast Control

In images with high contrast, detail is lost in both highlight and shadow areas; you cannot later recover this detail with image editing software. When shooting in JPEG or TIFF capture mode, you might often want to use the low contrast option for producing images with gentle contrast. Because it is easy to increase contrast in image-editing software, do not use a high contrast setting in-camera. If you shoot in the RAW capture mode, the in-camera contrast setting is not relevant. Plan to set the desired contrast level in the RAW conversion software before the image is actually processed and converted to TIFF format.

Focus Control

Just like 35mm SLR cameras, digital SLR cameras allow for full control over focus, using the focus ring control on the lens. This is a simple, quick, and convenient feature, and you can see the effect of any shift in focus in the viewfinder image.

Many compact digicams also include some form of manual focus control. Typically, this feature allows you to preset focus for specific distances: 5 feet, 10 feet, 15 feet, 20 feet, and infinity, for example. A few high-end and prosumer digicams offer a more versatile manual focus control.

When viewing a scene through a compact digicam's optical viewfinder, you cannot see focus changing when using autofocus or manual focus. If you use this type of camera for manual focus, you can check the image on the external LCD monitor to try to determine if you have achieved the desired effect before taking a picture. With cameras equipped with an electronic viewfinder, you can do so in the viewfinder. In both cases, it is difficult to evaluate sharpness because the image area is too small. It is preferable to take a shot and review the image using the magnification feature in Playback mode, if available with your camera. That feature can help to determine if the intended subject area is in sharp focus.

Manual focus is most useful when you are not in a rush, when the exact point of focus is very important, or when an autofocus system has difficulty acquiring focus. You might want to use manual focus in land- and cityscapes, in extreme closeup or "macro" photography, and in portraits of people and animals (setting focus for the nearest eye), for example. Cameras that allow you to focus only at a few specific distances are not particularly useful when critical focus is essential, but are fine for vast scenes when a difference of five feet does not affect the image to a great extent.

RECOMMENDATION: Autofocus or Manual Focus

When using autofocus, you can lock focus on the most important subject element, such as the eyes in a portrait; when you subsequently recompose, focus will not shift. (Most cameras keep focus locked as long as you maintain slight pressure on the shutter release button.) Because this is a standard feature in digital cameras, you may never need to use manual focus. Even with an SLR camera, I rarely use manual focus except in the situations mentioned earlier. Anyone switching from a film camera that was often used in manual focus will probably want a digital camera that offers a versatile and convenient manual focus system. SLR cameras have this manual focus system as do some compact digicams with many manual focusing "steps"; the latter should enable you to focus at or near almost any desired point. If this is an important consideration, be sure to read test reports to determine which models are most likely to satisfy your needs.

Flash Photography with Compact Digicams

Flash has come a long way from the old days when photographers were required to make complex calculations to get a good flash exposure. Almost all compact digital cameras include a built-in flash with an automated metering system that will let you take good to excellent flash photos. These digicams generally employ a flash-metering system that bases the amount of flash output on subject distance. Flash can be used at all or most shutter speeds and in any camera operating mode.

Few SLR cameras can be used for flash photography at shutter speeds higher than 1/125 or 1/200 sec.; some cameras allow for high shutter speed flash, also called "high speed sync" but only with specific high-end flash units.

Some prosumer digicams also accept a large accessory flash unit with greater power for more distant subjects; some units also offer greater control over flash effects (they're generally $300 and up). Because an accessory flash unit is located far above the lens, the red-eye problem (discussed later) is also minimized. The operation of a compact camera's accessory flash unit is generally similar to that of the built-in flash unit, so I will not discuss this type of accessory in detail.

Select the Right Flash Mode

A compact camera's flash system—whether built in or a larger accessory unit—can be fully automatic, but some user-selected controls are available. Typical options include Flash Always On, Flash Off, "Night Scene" or "Slow Sync" and Red Eye Reduction modes. A few compact digicams also offer a Flash Exposure Compensation feature. Let's take a look at each of these options and why you might want to use them in serious image making (see Figure 6.13).

Default Mode

In its default mode, a camera fires the flash when necessary: in low light and, with some cameras, also in strong back lighting. As long as your subject is not too close to the camera or too far away, you should get a good flash exposure. Your camera owner's manual should provide specifics as to the flash range; this is essential information, and it varies from one camera to another. As a general rule, expect the maximum flash range (indoors, in low light) to be about 10 feet at the camera's ISO 100 setting, and up to 20 feet at the ISO 400 setting.

The minimum flash range may be a few feet. In extreme closeup photography, the subject can be much closer to the camera. In that case, any image made with flash might be excessively bright unless you're using a camera that's particularly effective in reducing flash output in closeup shooting.

The default flash mode is useful for general low-light photography with flash when the subject is not too close or too far from the camera. Check your owner's manual for information as to the minimum and maximum flash range at various ISO settings. Use default mode for quick snap shooting in low light, selecting the other modes when you want greater control over your images.

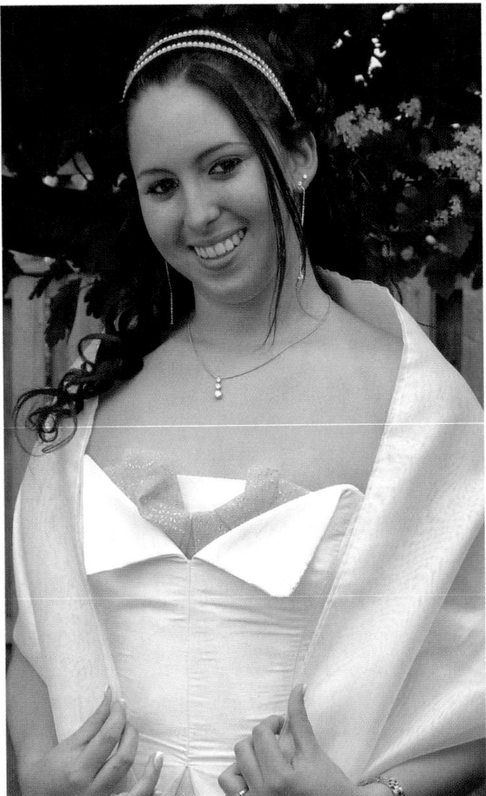

Figure 6.13: When used effectively, indoors or out, electronic flash can produce technically and aesthetically pleasing images.

Red-Eye Reduction Mode

Red-eye occurs when flash illuminates the blood vessels at the back of the eye (see Figure 6.14). If you select the Red-Eye Reduction feature, the camera emits a bright light or a series of "pre-flashes" that should cause your subject's retinas to close down before the actual exposure is made. The pre-flashes can also cause your subjects to blink, and their eyes can be closed when the actual image is made; if you often experience this problem, shoot without Red-Eye Reduction and correct red-eye in image-editing software. None of the Red-Eye Reduction flash systems are fully effective, but some are quite successful at minimizing this ghoulish syndrome. Read camera test reports if you want information as to which models are most effective.

Figure 6.14: Red-eye is common in images made with flash in low light, but you can minimize this syndrome with certain shooting techniques, and you can completely eliminate it with image-editing software. The image on the right was edited with the Red Eye Brush tool in Photoshop Elements 2.

To minimize red-eye, try one or more of these techniques.

- Brighten the room by turning on more lamps.
- Ask the subject not to look toward the camera.
- Avoid using a long zoom setting on the camera because this makes the problem more serious; shoot with a shorter zoom setting instead, and move closer to the subject.
- Use the Red-Eye Reduction mode and the other techniques for maximum effectiveness.

If red-eye is still visible in your images, use the red-eye correction tool available with many image-editing programs. If your software does not include that tool, you can use the Cloning or Rubber Stamp tool or more advanced techniques to cover the red area.

Slow-Sync Flash Mode

Also called Night Flash mode, this option is recommended for use with a nearby subject against a distant, moderately bright background at night. The most common example is a group of people sitting not far from the camera, against the background of city lights. When you select Slow-Sync mode, the camera sets a long shutter speed, such as 1/15 sec., and fires the flash as well. The flash illuminates the nearby subject, and the long exposure time ensures that a moderately bright background has enough time to register on the image sensor. To avoid blurring caused by camera shake, use a tripod to support the camera during the long exposure.

If you can find a situation in which this flash mode is appropriate and if you use a tripod, you can produce pleasing images. For some unconventional images, you can use Night Flash mode and move a handheld camera intentionally during the long exposure. Sometimes called "pan/blur," this technique produces an image with some sharp elements (frozen by the brief burst of flash light) and some blurred elements; photos of this type can be visually appealing. If you try this technique, shoot a lot of frames because many of the photos are unlikely to be successful; with some experience, you can increase your success ratio.

Flash Always On Mode

Flash is not intended only for low-light situations. In fact, an extra burst of light is often useful in bright, outdoor conditions for filling in dark shadows (see Figure 6.15). Flash can be useful for softening hard shadows that obliterate important subject detail: shadows cast by the brim of a hat over a person's face, for example. It can also fill in dark eye sockets caused by "top lighting" during the hours around noon on a sunny day. Finally, on dark overcast days, flash can help produce bright and clean colors instead of gray and muddy tones.

As mentioned earlier, flash is also valuable if the subject is against a bright background; flash can even out the overall contrast for a pleasing exposure for both the subject and the background. If you begin to use flash outdoors regularly, you might be able to make images with more pleasing lighting in order to start taking your photos beyond the snapshot in terms of technical qualities.

To be certain that flash will fire in bright situations, set the Flash Always On mode. Make sure that your subject is within the range of the flash, roughly 15 feet with a built-in flash unit used only for fill-in lighting, at an ISO 100 setting.

Figure 6.15: Outdoor people pictures made with fill flash (picture on the left) are generally more pleasing than images made with ambient light only (picture on the right).

Flash Exposure Compensation Control

Some cameras (and accessory flash units discussed later) include a feature for reducing the intensity of flash. Some manufacturers refer to this control as Flash Exposure Compensation or FEC, my own preferred term; other manufacturers call it a flash power or flash output control. It can be useful for reducing flash intensity—for a gentler burst of light that fills in shadows but does not overpower the sunlight. Experiment in outdoor photography with a –0.5 and a –1 setting; you'll soon know which works best with your own camera.

FEC can also be useful in extreme backlighting. In such situations, the subject may not be adequately bright unless you set a +0.5 or a +1 factor. And try the following advanced technique with people against a bright background of sand, surf, or sky. Set the camera's exposure compensation control (for ambient light, as discussed earlier) to –0.5 so the background will not be excessively bright. Then set the FEC to +0.5 or +1 to ensure that the subject will be brightly rendered. Experiment with various settings to achieve the effect that works best.

A control for adjusting flash output (intensity) is not essential, but it is certainly valuable in serious photography, especially for those who take a lot of people pictures outdoors. Granted, similar effects can be achieved, at least in some cases, by manipulating an image with software in your computer. However, it is a lot less complicated and less time consuming to achieve the desired effect in-camera. As well, the results are often more pleasing and more natural.

Flash Off Mode

In some situations, you might want to take pictures in low light without flash, for example, when flash is prohibited or impractical. Flash photography is not allowed in some locations, such as museums, castles, and art galleries. And flash is not practical when your subject is very far from the camera or when you want to record the interior of a vast building. In such situations, select the Flash Off mode, and shoot with ambient light only; take the necessary precautions to prevent blurry images caused by camera shake (see Figure 6.16).

There is no point in using flash, especially with a tiny, built-in flash unit, for distant subjects such as the competitors at an indoor sports event. If you do so, your images will be seriously underexposed. Select Flash Off mode in such situations. Select a high ISO setting for faster shutter speeds to reduce the risk of image blur from camera shake or subject motion.

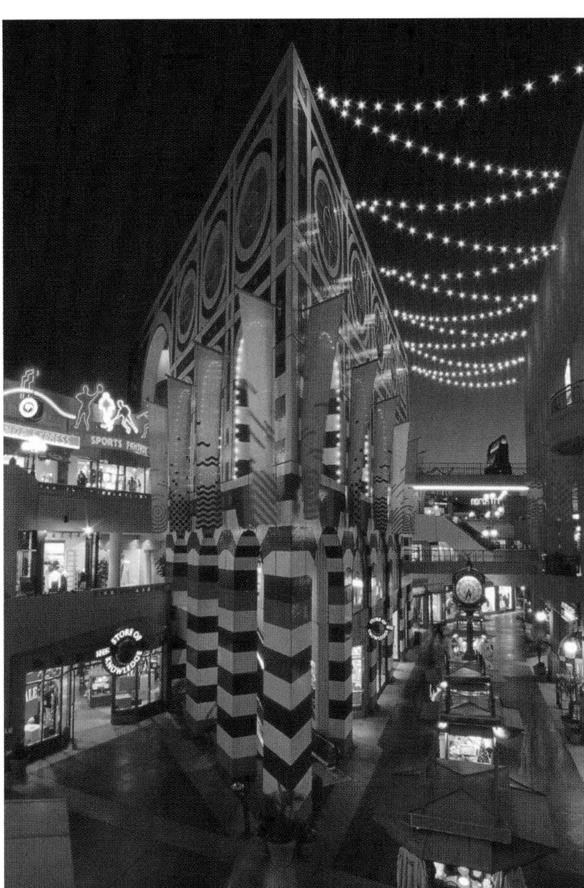

Figure 6.16: Flash cannot illuminate distant subjects or vast scenes, so turn it off in those conditions, and shoot with ambient light only, taking steps to prevent camera shake during a long exposure. This photo was captured at 1/4 sec. shutter speed with the camera on a tripod.

Flash Photography with SLR Cameras

Although they may use different technology for pleasing flash exposure, SLR cameras offer most of the same flash modes and features as the compact digicams and are used in a similar manner with the built-in unit. Not all SLR cameras include a built-in flash unit, but all accept high-powered accessory flash units, including some with very advanced features. You can mount an accessory flash on top of the camera, or use it off-camera by attaching the flash in the hot shoe with a special cable. Through electronic circuitry, the flash and camera exchange information about aperture, shutter speed, the ISO that has been set, subject distance, flash output, and other such factors.

When used with an accessory flash unit, SLR cameras employ the sophisticated flash-metering system discussed in the next section; many cameras also employ this system with the built-in flash unit. In the following sections, I'll discuss this technology and the features that can help you make pro-caliber images with an accessory flash.

The Benefits of Advanced Flash Metering

SLR cameras employ through-the-lens (TTL) flash metering. Light enters the camera through the lens that will be used to make the photos, and a light-sensitive cell reads the amount of light that will actually reach the image sensor. A computer calculates the amount of flash power needed to produce a correct exposure and selects the suitable flash output or power. In Program modes, the camera sets the appropriate aperture and shutter speed; if you're using one of the camera's semiautomatic modes, you can select a suitable aperture or shutter speed. The computer also controls flash duration for a correct exposure within the effective range of the flash unit.

When using a TTL flash unit that is fully compatible with (or dedicated to) the camera, you can shoot in most or all camera operating modes. The simplest method is to use the fully automatic Program mode for point-and-shoot operation, allowing the camera to establish all the settings. For greater control, use the camera's Aperture Priority, Shutter Priority, or Manual mode, and select your own aperture or shutter speed.

Sync Speeds

Although SLR cameras allow you to select any desired aperture and certain shutter speeds, they are not designed for flash photography at all shutter speeds. To take a picture with flash requires perfect timing between shutter and flash. The flash must first fire only when the image sensor is fully uncovered by the shutter. This perfect timing is called synchronization, and it occurs when certain shutter speeds—called sync speeds in flash photography—are used. You can shoot at very long sync speeds, but the camera will have a maximum sync speed: 1/125 sec. is common, though some models can sync with flash at up to 1/250 sec. A few cameras offer a high-speed sync feature with certain high-end flash units, employing multiple, high-speed bursts of light to allow for shooting at much faster sync speeds.

A camera's TTL flash control has several advantages over the less-sophisticated Auto Flash technology used in most compact digicams. First, the TTL exposure remains accurate even if you use a filter on the lens (that reduces light transmission), if you bounce the light from a ceiling (increasing the distance to the subject), when using a colored filter over the flash, and so on.

Current digital SLR cameras employ an advanced TTL flash system often called smart flash for greater reliability than conventional TTL systems used in some 35mm cameras. Smart flash systems control flash power so a foreground object should not be overexposed when your primary subject is farther from the camera. These systems are designed to automatically reduce flash output in bright conditions; this helps to ensure that flash gently fills in shadows without overpowering the ambient light. Finally, some of the smart flash systems also compensate automatically for backlighting or for a very bright or dark subject, for a higher success ratio of accurate exposures than conventional TTL flash metering.

Even with the most sophisticated camera/flash combination, you might not get an accurate flash exposure for an excessively close subject unless you reduce flash intensity. A flower that is a mere 6 inches from the lens will be excessively bright in your images unless you set a –1 or a –2 flash exposure compensation factor.

Also, flash range is limited, so don't use flash for very distant subjects such as a football player that is 100 yards from your seat. If your accessory flash unit features an LCD data panel, check the minimum and maximum flash range; this depends on the scene brightness and the ISO that has been set on the camera. If your flash unit does not display such information, review the owner's manual for the recommended shooting distances at various ISO settings.

RECOMMENDATION: Look for a Compatible Flash Unit

If you are thinking of purchasing a new digital SLR camera and accessory flash unit or a flash unit for a camera you already own, review the flash capabilities of several cameras on the manufacturers' websites. Avoid third-party flash units unless they are fully compatible with all important features of your camera. Also look for test reports in photographic magazines and websites; these often provide comments as to the effectiveness of a camera when used with a certain flash unit.

Photography with an Accessory Flash Unit

It is worth owning an accessory flash unit (see Figure 6.17), even a basic model, for its greater power output, which is useful for more distant subjects than a camera's smaller, built-in flash unit. The basic, compact accessory flash units are quite affordable ($100 – $150) and take advantage of advanced TTL flash metering. Although they do not include many of the advanced features discussed in this chapter or the high power output of a larger, more expensive model, they are portable and simple to use.

The larger flash units, particularly those in the $300 to $500 range, are more powerful and far more versatile. Expect to find some or all the following features with accessory flash units; some are also available with some cameras' built-in flash. The manufacturer's website provides information about features and their availability

PHOTO COURTESY NIKON INC.

Figure 6.17: Although many digital cameras include a built-in flash unit, a high-powered accessory flash, with extra features, can be useful for making images with more pleasing flash exposure.

with the various models of SLR cameras. Also check your own camera/flash owner's manuals for specifics on the equipment that you own.

Autofocus Illuminator A common feature, even on the most affordable flash units, this consists of a system that projects a beam of near-infrared light onto a nearby subject, enabling the camera to autofocus quickly even in the dark. (Some camera bodies also incorporate an illuminator of this type, but it is much smaller and, hence, less effective.) Activated automatically, the illuminator is a valuable feature that usually assures successful autofocus with subjects up to about 15 feet from the camera.

Zooming Flash Head Many accessory flash units include a feature that automatically zooms the flash head in and out, to match the focal length of the lens in use. This feature usually provides the correct flash coverage for the angle of view covered by wide-angle to short telephoto lenses. It is intended for lenses or zooms from 28mm to 85mm but works well with even longer lenses. This is a useful feature, primarily with telephoto lenses, because the zoom head concentrates all the flash light over a smaller area, providing a greater effective range for flash. Some flash units also include a built-in accessory that can be pulled in front of the flash head; use this valuable feature to spread the light when shooting with ultrawide angle lenses or to soften (diffuse) the light when desired.

Tilt/Rotate Head To allow for indirect lighting, many accessory flash units incorporate a head that can be tilted upward; some also include a swivel feature for pointing the head to the side. Use these features for bouncing light from a ceiling or a wall.

Bounce flash produces softer light than direct flash and minimizes the risk of red-eye. Do try this technique, but use a bounce surface that is white (or close to white) and not too far from the subject. This will prevent strange color casts and underexposure. The contrast in the resulting images may be low; increase it in image-editing software.

Automatic Flash Exposure Bracketing This feature is similar in concept to Autoexposure Bracketing (for ambient light) discussed earlier but is used in flash photography. When this feature is activated (on the camera or the flash unit), flash output is automatically varied by the camera, from one frame to the next, using flash exposure compensation. Preset the compensation factor that will be used for bracketing. Shoot three images of the same subject. One frame will be exposed normally; one will be exposed with greater flash output, and another will be exposed with less flash output.

Try flash exposure bracketing when you must shoot very quickly and are not sure about the amount of flash exposure that should be set, for example, in strong back lighting. If you preset the bracketing system to vary exposures in 0.5 step increments, one of your three images should exhibit fairly accurate exposure. For the best results with bright subjects or in strong backlighting, use this feature in conjunction with the flash exposure compensation control discussed earlier. Set a +0.5 or a +1 flash compensation factor—to increase flash intensity—before engaging the bracketing feature. With some experimentation and experience, you will become proficient with this advanced technique.

Flash Exposure Lock Although it is not a common feature, some digital SLR cameras, particularly Canon models, include a control for locking the flash exposure. Similar to AE Lock that's used for shooting with ambient light only, Flash Exposure Lock (FEL) can be used to set the flash exposure for an important subject area.

Pressing the FEL button (on the camera) causes the flash unit to fire a test burst that's used by the light metering system to calculate correct exposure for the primary subject. The resulting flash settings are then locked in. You can now recompose, perhaps including a bright sky in the frame, and the flash exposure remains correct for the primary subject. This is feature is useful in strong backlighting and if the subject is surrounded by very dark or very bright areas. For the best results, do not point the camera's lens toward an ultrabright or dark area when you press the FEL button.

Rear Curtain Sync This feature (activated on the camera or on a flash unit) causes the camera to fire the flash near the end of a long exposure and not at the start as in conventional flash photography. When used, this feature produces streaks of light that follow a moving subject, instead of preceding it, for an effect that appears more natural. Unless you photograph moving subjects with flash, with long exposures, you are unlikely to use this feature. If you decide to experiment with Rear Curtain Sync, set a long sync speed, such as 1/15 or 1/30 sec. Remember not to use flash for a distant subject; if you exceed the maximum range of the flash unit, your images will be underexposed.

Stroboscopic Flash This feature causes the flash to fire numerous rapid, short-flash bursts for motion studies of a moving subject, a friend's golf swing, for example. You can use this complex, advanced technique to achieve a very specific effect; it requires studying the owner's manual and a great deal of experimentation.

Remote Flash Capability When attached to the camera's hot shoe with an accessory TTL cable, a flash unit can be used off-camera; all flash features continue to operate as they do with on-camera flash. Off-camera flash can produce more pleasing flash photos than direct, on-camera flash. Whether your subject is a person, a flower or other object, you'll often get the most pleasing effect by holding the flash unit above, and slightly to the side, of the subject.

Wireless Off-Camera TTL Flash A feature that is available with some camera/flash unit combinations, this allows you to position one or more flash units off-camera, for TTL flash, without the need for connecting cables. Many, but not all, flash features continue to operate. If you intend to use only one off-camera flash unit, a TTL connecting cable is almost as convenient. Wireless off-camera flash is more useful for photographers who often use several accessory TTL flash units, a technique that is not common; for multiflash lighting, most photographers use studio-style flash units.

PC Cord In addition to accepting a TTL flash cable, for connecting a remote flash unit to the camera's hot shoe, some SLR cameras include a socket for a PC cord. This is intended for use with a studio flash system, or an old-style, fully manual flash unit for manual, non-TTL flash. Some retailers sell accessories for cameras not equipped with a PC cord socket; these slip into the camera's hot shoe and include a PC cord socket. The use of studio and manual flash units is beyond the scope of this book.

High-Speed Flash Sync Available with certain camera/flash unit combinations, this feature fires numerous rapid bursts of light, ensuring that the entire image is illuminated, even at extremely fast shutter speeds such as 1/2000 or 1/4000 sec. This allows for wide apertures (such as f/1.4) to be used even in closeups on bright days for extremely shallow depth of field or to freeze a moving subject. Do note that the High Speed Sync feature minimizes the effective range of flash so it should be used only for nearby subjects; check your instruction manual as to the effective flash range. When testing such systems, I have rarely used any shutter speed higher than 1/500 sec. If your camera has a top sync speed of 1/200 or 1/250 sec., you may never need high-speed flash sync.

In addition to the flash techniques mentioned in this section, I'll provide more specific suggestions for effective flash photography in Chapter 7.

Recommended Accessories

Compact digital cameras include a built-in lens and flash unit and generally come with batteries and the essential accessories. Hence, most owners see no need to buy any other accessories, except extra memory cards and batteries. However, a few other accessories can be valuable because they increase the versatility of a compact digicam. I've already mentioned a dedicated accessory flash unit, available for a few compact cameras. Other accessories that you might want include the following.

Wide-Angle or Telephoto Lens Converters

The built-in optical zoom lens of most digicams includes the focal-length equivalents from about 37mm (moderately wide angle) to about 110mm (short telephoto). Unless you buy a camera that offers a shorter or longer effective focal lengths, you may find a typical 3x optical zoom restrictive. You will eventually wish that you could zoom to a shorter focal length for a wider angle of view or to a longer focal length for photos of a distant subject.

Depending on your camera, you can meet either of those wishes with an accessory wide-angle or telephoto converter (see Figure 6.18). Prices for high-quality models range from $100 to $200, and higher for fish-eye or long telephoto converters. Resembling a lens for a 35mm camera, an accessory of this type attaches to the front of the camera. It incorporates the optical elements required to shorten or to lengthen the effective focal length of the camera's lens. Converters are available from the camera manufacturers and from after-market suppliers such as Tiffen, Hoya (Kenko brand), Century, and Phoenix.

Some digicams that accept accessory lenses require the use of an inexpensive adapter tube available from the camera manufacturer. Other digicams were not designed to accept lens converters. If you own a camera of that type, you may still be able to use accessory

Figure 6.18: Adapters are useful with cameras that include a built-in lens because they allow for making images with a wider angle of view or with tighter framing of a distant subject.

© The Tiffen Company

lenses with a special bracket such as a Tiffen Custom Lens Mount (less than $20). Photo retailers can provide information about the availability of a bracket for your digicam.

Attach a 0.56x wide-angle converter to a camera with a 37–110mm (equivalent) optical zoom lens, and select the shortest zoom setting of your camera. You'll get the equivalent of an ultrawide 20.7mm effect. Switch to a 2x converter, and select the longest zoom setting for a full 220mm (equivalent) telephoto focal length. You can even find fish-eye lens converters and much longer telephoto converters for wider and longer effective focal lengths. Although a camera's digital zoom feature can also be used to make a distant subject appear closer, image quality will be degraded; if high image quality is important, use a telephoto lens adapter.

RECOMMENDATION: Lenses

If you buy a high-quality lens converter and attach it to a camera with premium-grade zoom lens, the combination should produce high image quality. For the best results, use a wide-angle converter only at the shortest zoom setting and a telephoto converter only at the longest zoom setting. Some photo enthusiasts find that two converters provide adequate versatility and feel no compelling need to buy an SLR camera that accepts a full range of lenses. Others complain that two converters do not offer adequate versatility, and some mention the large size and weight of these accessories.

In my view, lens converters are useful, particularly for those who previously owned an SLR camera but now prefer a digicam with a built-in lens. If these accessories appeal to you, review the specifications closely as to their size and weight. Be prepared to pay extra for high optical quality if you often plan to make 8" × 10" or larger prints; you cannot go wrong buying a converter of the same brand as your camera. A cheap lens converter will not provide edge-to-edge sharpness in prints of that size. Avoid the very long telephoto converters that offer more than an extra 3x magnification if high image quality is important.

Accessory "Slave" Flash Unit

Most digicams incorporate a small, built-in flash unit that is useful but not very powerful. A few cameras accept a large, dedicated accessory flash unit made by the manufacturer, but most digicams are not designed for use with accessory flash. Such cameras might work with another type of accessory flash unit, called a "slave flash"; this accessory produces higher flash output than most built-in flash units ($40 to $200).

Available in brands such as Sunpak, Metz, and Phoenix, a small slave flash does not need any mechanical or electronic connection to the camera. If you simply hold a small slave flash pointing toward the subject, it is triggered by the burst of light from your in-camera flash. The extra illumination can be useful if the in-camera flash does not offer enough "reach" for a distant subject; you might also try it for brightening the background while in-camera flash illuminates your subject.

When used with a "slave flash" accessory, some digital cameras produce images that are overexposed (excessively bright). If you encounter this problem, do not use the accessory flash for closeup work. For more typical subject distances, move the accessory flash farther from the subject. In addition, some cameras do not work properly with a slave flash accessory; they generate a pre-flash burst of light that triggers the slave flash prematurely. (The same problem occurs when using a camera's Red-Eye Reduction flash mode.) Ask a retailer to check their catalog to determine whether a slave flash accessory will work with your camera.

RECOMMENDATION: Slave Flashes

Unless your camera is incompatible with any slave flash accessory, it's worth buying one of the affordable (less than $50) units if you are prepared to experiment. If you find that it produces overexposure, you might not want to use the slave flash unit for nearby subjects. Your in-camera flash should have adequate power for closeup shots in any event.

If the slave flash unit offers several settings, such as f/2, f/4, and f/8, experiment with each of these. You should find that the largest f/number causes the camera to produce minimal flash output (for nearby subjects) and that the smallest f/number causes it to produce high flash output (for more distant subjects).

Tabletop Tripod

As discussed earlier, you will find low-light situations in which flash is not allowed or is impractical. If you want to shoot with ambient light, shutter speeds can be long. In that case, you'll need to find a firm support for the camera to avoid image blur. A rigid tabletop tripod can be convenient for any lightweight digital camera. ($35 to $100.) Look for a small but solid and well-built accessory such as the Slik Mini-Pro, Manfrotto Digi-Table-Top, or the Leica Mini Tripod.

RECOMMENDATION: Tripods

When possible, set the tripod on something solid: a piece of furniture, the roof of your car, or a large, flat rock. When you cannot find a suitable object, try bracing the tripod against a door frame, the trunk of a tree, or some other vertical support. In low light, any of these techniques should produce sharp images without blur.

PC Card Adapter

If you use a laptop computer to download your images during photo trips, you can do so via the computer's PC card slot. Place the memory card in a suitable adapter, such as a CompactFlash-to-PC card adapter ($10), and insert it in the PC card slot; it is plug-and-play compatible with any computer. This eliminates the need for a memory card reader accessory or the hassle of hooking a camera up to the computer.

RECOMMENDATION: Adapters

Most adapters are intended for only one type of digital memory card. and these are fine unless you use two or more card types. In that case, look for a multiple card adapter that accepts up to four types of cards. (They run from $30 to $50.) Some PC card adapters, such as the Delkin eFilm PRO CardBus 32-bit adapter for CompactFlash cards, allow for roughly four times faster data transfer than the conventional 16-bit adapters. If you often transfer many large image files to your laptop, it's worth paying extra for the 32-bit accessory ($59, **www.delkin.com**).

Cleaning Accessories

An oversized microfiber lens-cleaning cloth is great for removing dust, fingerprints, and other smudges from a lens or LCD monitor after removing any grit or sand with a blower bulb. A small bottle of photographic lens-cleaner solution is useful too, but use only a tiny amount and only when necessary to remove stubborn smudges. Do not allow any liquid to seep behind the front element of the lens.

If you prefer not to use a liquid to remove stubborn fingerprints and other oily substances, buy a LensPen accessory, which is sold under several brand names, including LensPen, Bushnell, Kodak, Hakuba, and Carson Optical. (They're about $15.) One end includes a brush to dust away any hard particles or contaminants, and the other end features a circular pad coated with an optical cleaning compound. Apply gentle pressure on the lens, using smooth circular motions to remove any smudges. After each use, twist the cap a half turn to replenish the pad with cleaning compound. For cameras with a small lens, buy the smaller Mini-Pro model.

Memory Card Cases

Anyone who carries several digital memory cards knows that they're small and easy to misplace or lose. Fortunately, several companies now offer cases designed specifically for memory cards, such as the media storage wallets and small hard-shell cases made by Hakuba (www.hakubausa.com). Sold by photo retailers, these products are designed for holding two or more specific types of memory cards. Since I bought one of these accessories, I have not misplaced a single memory card. Highly recommended!

CHAPTER

seven

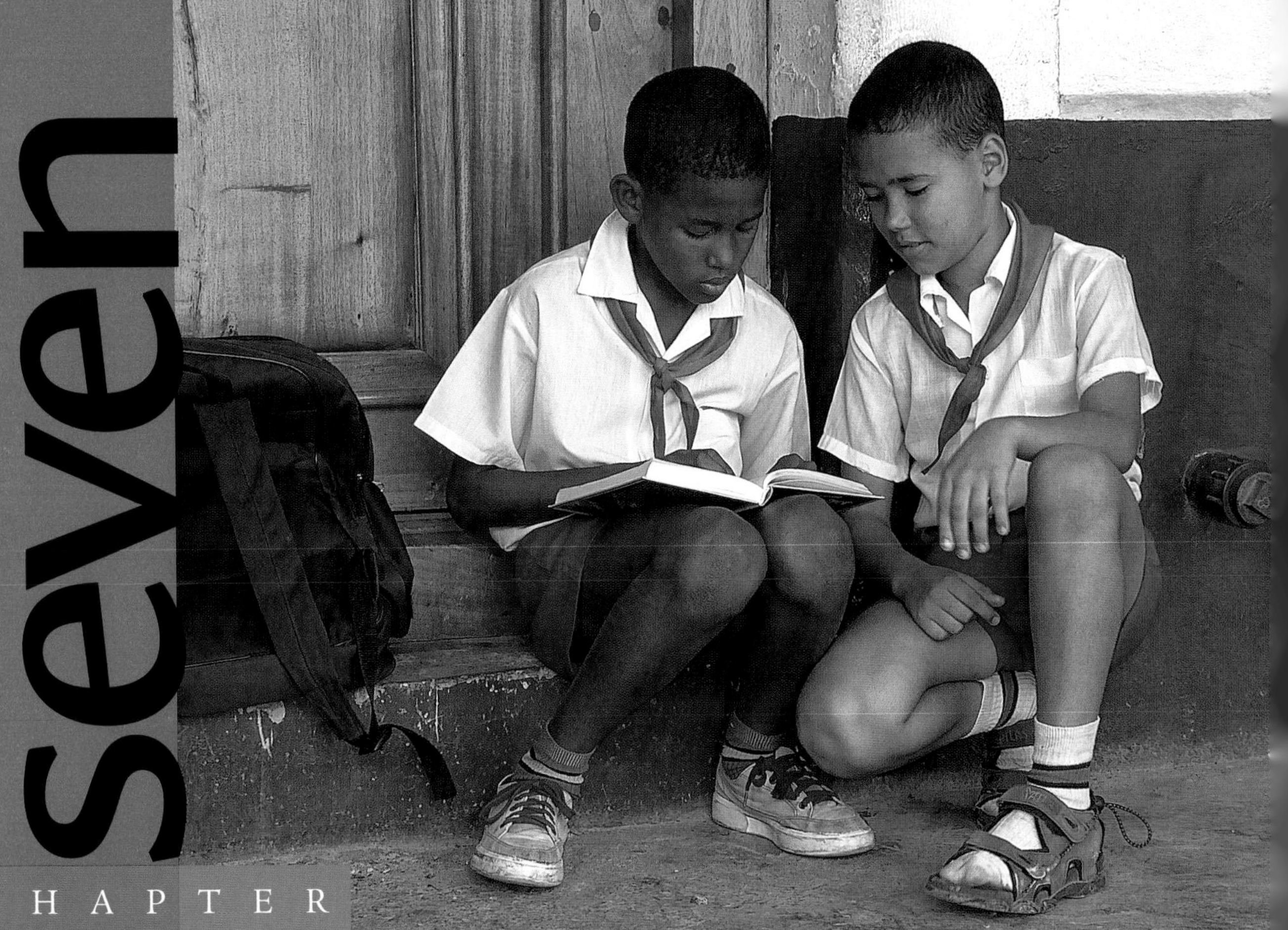

Picture-Taking Tips

With one of today's *sophisticated digital cameras, anyone can produce decent snapshots with a point-and-shoot approach, using the fully automatic camera features. On the other hand, you can take much better digital photos by using a few careful shooting techniques and some of the user-selectable controls available with most midrange and higher-level cameras. In this chapter I'll discuss methods for making technically and aesthetically superior images, with an emphasis on travel, landscape, nature, and people subjects.*

Basic Techniques for Better Images

In previous chapters, I mentioned some shooting techniques while discussing the value of certain camera features. It's worth considering these and a few others in more detail before moving on to specifics for making effective images of the most popular types of subjects.

Especially when using a compact digicam, it's easy to develop sloppy shooting techniques. With extensive automation and an LCD monitor that's convenient for framing the shots, such cameras tend to encourage a point-and-shoot approach. This can produce pictures with technical problems and little of the visual appeal that we expect from our best images. No matter what subject type you shoot, the following techniques are useful for making technically excellent digital images (see Figure 7.1).

Hold the camera steady. The primary cause of disappointing pictures is image blur produced by camera shake. When shooting with a compact digicam, this usually occurs when you use the LCD monitor for composing images, often holding the camera with one hand. The monitor provides the most accurate view of the subject, but this one-handed technique produces some unsharp images because of a lack of support.

To make sharper pictures, use the optical viewfinder instead. Hold the camera with two hands, with elbows tucked in close to your body for extra support; press the camera gently against your cheek or forehead. In low light, when flash is not practical or is prohibited, mount the camera on a rigid table top tripod or brace it against a wall for support.

When shooting extreme closeups using a digicam with built-in lens, you will need to compose using the LCD monitor to ensure accurate framing. Because the viewfinder is above the lens, it does not encompass the same subject area as the lens, a problem in extreme closeup photography. To maximize the odds of making sharp images, hold the camera with both hands and prop your elbows against your body for additional support.

Figure 7.1: It's worth the extra effort to make technically excellent images that are sharp, well exposed, finely detailed, accurately focused, and nicely lit.

Focus carefully. An increasing number of digital cameras employ a wide-area focus-detection system, using several focus points arrayed across the image area. This type of system generally focuses on the closest subject or on the largest object in a scene. Useful for quick shooting with an off-center subject, this snapshot mode may not focus on your primary subject or the most important area. In a portrait photo, for example, the camera often focuses on a person's stomach instead of the eyes, which are the essential subject area in photos of people and animals.

When the exact point of focus is important, switch to the single autofocus sensor option. Using only the small, central point, set focus for the desired subject area and recompose with slight pressure on the camera's shutter release button. This locks focus until you take the picture by pressing the shutter release the rest of the way, producing an image in which the most important subject area is in sharpest focus.

Use flash wisely indoors. Built-in flash is standard on digital cameras, and this feature is certainly useful in low light. But remember that a small flash unit has limited range, often a maximum of about 10 feet in the camera's ISO 100 setting (see Figure 7.2). A high-powered accessory flash unit may have a range of 20 feet. (Check the owner's manual for specifics as to your own equipment.) If your camera has an ISO 400 option, this can increase the effective flash range by about 50%. Even then, flash will not provide adequate "reach" for a distant bride and groom during a ceremony or the quarterback at a night football game, for example. As well, flash cannot light up the vast interior of a cathedral, castle, or cave.

In some low-light situations, you will need to shoot without flash—but, remember, the shutter speed can be quite long. You will not be able to get sharp photos at shutter speeds longer than about 1/30 sec. at the short end of a 3x zoom or at speeds longer than about

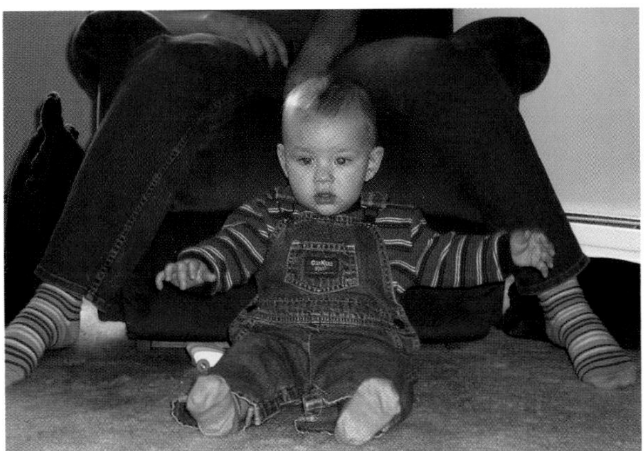

Figure 7.2: When using flash, especially in low light, move close to the subject.

Figure 7.3: People pictures taken outdoors often benefit from the use of flash to fill in shadow areas.

1/125 sec. at the long end. Use a tripod or brace your elbows on something solid. If you must handhold the camera, set the ISO to 400 for faster shutter speeds; if necessary, try ISO 800 if your camera allows. This step can be useful for producing images with less blur from camera shake, but remember this: at high ISO settings, many cameras produce considerable digital "noise," or artifacts resembling grain. That may be preferable to a grossly underexposed picture made with flash or a blurry picture made at the ISO 100 setting.

Use flash outdoors. Although flash is most often used indoors, it can be just as useful outdoors on sunny days, for filling in shadow areas, especially in people pictures. That's why most cameras have a Flash Always On mode that will cause it to fire even if the built-in computer does not consider flash necessary.

Activate flash to soften unflattering facial shadows cast by a hat, to brighten dark eye sockets, and to add a "catch light," a bright spot in the eyes that makes pictures of people and animals seem to come to life (see Figure 7.3). Also use flash in backlit conditions—against bright sky, sun, water, sand, or snow—for nicely lit photos of friends or family. The extra burst of light moderates the contrast level (between the bright background and the darker subjects), preventing one of two problems: a silhouette or grossly overexposed surroundings. On dark, overcast days, flash can help produce richer colors while adding some necessary contrast, with some shadows creating a more three-dimensional effect in otherwise "flat" lighting.

RECOMMENDATION: Outdoor Flash

To ensure that the light from flash is subtle, you might need to reduce flash intensity. If your camera or accessory flash includes a Flash Intensity or Output control, also called flash exposure compensation, consider using this feature on sunny days. Set it to a minus position, -0.5 perhaps to reduce flash output for a natural effect, with the sun providing most of the illumination. Do not set a minus factor in backlighting; in fact, you might need to use a +0.5 or a +1 factor when the background is extremely bright. If your equipment offers no method for reducing flash exposure, try this: move farther from the subject, and cover the flash head with a few layers of facial tissue to reduce the amount of flash that will illuminate the subject.

Control contrast. Images made on days with strong sunlight often exhibit extremely high contrast. In addition to a harsh overall look, shadow areas are dark and murky, and bright areas are excessively bright. You can use image-editing software to improve excessively contrasty images, but it cannot work miracles with blown-out highlight areas and dark shadow areas. It's impossible to add detail or texture that was not recorded by the image sensor.

With nearby subjects, flash can help to even out the lighting, moderating the contrast, but flash is not practical for distant subjects such as land- or cityscapes. In such situations, try one or more of the following techniques.

- If your camera has a contrast level adjustment control, select the Low setting to reduce overall contrast.
- After downloading images to a computer, use image-editing software to increase contrast if the pictures seem a bit flat. (The software is more effective in increasing contrast than in reducing contrast.)
- Whenever possible, try to take pictures when a cloud drifts over the sun, moderating contrast.

Overexposure compounds the problem of contrast by making highlight areas excessively bright. Unless a scene includes important elements in shade, it's worth underexposing slightly by setting a minus exposure compensation factor, –0.5 perhaps. After taking a picture, check the exposure in the camera's monitor, using the histogram display if it is available. If the highlight areas are still too bright, reshoot the scene with a slightly higher level of minus exposure compensation. You can correct a slightly dark image with image-editing software after downloading the pictures to a computer, using tools such as Fill Flash, Lighten, Brighten, or, preferably, the more sophisticated Levels and Curves options discussed in Chapter 10 and 11.

Shade the lens. On sunny days, stray light can strike the front of the lens and produce flare, a bright haze effect that degrades contrast and apparent sharpness. If your digicam accepts a lens hood accessory—or a tube that's intended for mounting filters—order one and use it to shade the front element. Avoid strong back lighting and side lighting by changing your shooting position. Or move around until you find a tree, a branch, or a building that casts a shadow and use that to shade the lens. You can also ask a friend to hold a cap close to your lens so it casts a shadow on the front element.

Control wide-angle distortion. Most digital cameras' zoom lenses include a wide-angle focal length, generally around 37mm. This can be useful when you need to include an entire scene or a large group of people in an image. Problems can occur if you use the wide-angle lens for portrait shots. Because you must move in very close to fill the frame with a subject, facial features will appear distorted; the nose in particular will appear to be bulbous. For more pleasing photos, move farther from the subject, and zoom to a longer lens focal length.

Wide-angle distortion can also occur when you photograph buildings, as in travel photography. To include an entire structure, it's tempting to use the wide-angle setting of the zoom lens and then tilt the camera upward. This technique creates distorted perspective called keystoning: the building appears to lean over backward. Unless you want to take advantage of this effect for creative reasons, avoid tilting the camera upward.

Use vertical framing and move farther from the subject, using a longer zoom setting if necessary; this should allow you to record an entire building without significant distortion. You can correct the remaining keystoning with some image-editing software, including some of the Photoshop programs (see Figure 7.4). Avoid any major tilting of the camera. If your images include a lot of extraneous foreground detail, crop them with your image-editing software. A high-resolution image will not be significantly degraded, and a 4" × 6" print should still be finely detailed.

Select the appropriate settings. The fully automatic camera features are great when you want to take quick snapshots, but in more serious photography, plan to make settings yourself. As discussed in Chapters 1 and 6, select the most appropriate white balance for the lighting conditions. Set a wide or small aperture to control depth of field, the range of apparent sharpness that extends behind a focused point and ahead of it. If a photo seems too bright or too dark in playback, reshoot the scene after setting exposure compensation.

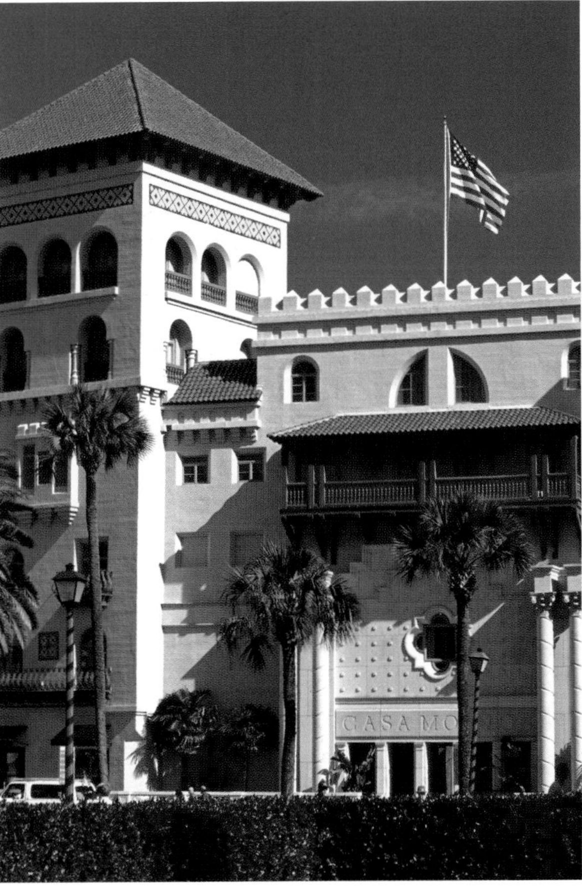

Figure 7.4: For an accurate rendition of a building or other tall subject, don't tilt the camera upward.

Digicams rarely provide an accurate display of the image exposure on their LCD monitors. If your camera offers a histogram (discussed in Chapter 1), use that feature for evaluating your exposures. If a histogram is not available, adjust the monitor brightness level. After viewing many of your images on a computer monitor, you'll know whether the camera's LCD monitor should be set to a brighter or darker level; the correct brightness level will allow you to make better assessments of exposure.

Think twice before using camera features such as the high level for color saturation, sharpness, and contrast. If you experiment with these features, you'll find that a high setting rarely produces a pleasing, natural effect. You can more effectively increase all three factors with image-editing software.

Other camera features are far more valuable. Instead of using the default setting for image quality and resolution, select the highest level for each factor. This produces the largest image file with the most pixels, with the lowest JPEG compression, for the best possible image quality. If your camera offers a RAW recording mode, use this option if you plan to make large prints. Granted, you may need to buy a high-capacity memory card to hold more of the large image files, but these are becoming quite affordable. Regardless of the card, frequently review your pictures, and delete unsuccessful images to make space for new, better images.

Advanced Shooting Techniques

Most of the basic techniques are intended to produce images that are technically satisfying—sharp, finely detailed, nicely exposed, with focus on the intended area. The more-advanced techniques address aesthetic or creative issues, primarily effective composition for making images with great visual appeal.

Granted, visual appeal, like beauty, is in the eye of the beholder. Still, most of us would agree on certain criteria. Cluttered backgrounds, partially blurred foreground objects, and tiny subjects dead-center in the frame and overpowered by irrelevant space do not make for an appealing picture. Today's high-tech digital cameras can almost take a picture for you, but they have yet to be programmed to seek out and arrange the visual elements. The following techniques are worth considering if you want to make pleasing digital photos (see Figure 7.5).

Find a clear center of interest. Instead of forcing the viewer's eye to roam around a picture, searching for something to observe, include a specific object that achieves this goal. Whether that's a Beefeater in London or a boat on the Ganges, make it the focal point of the image to achieve your intended purpose.

Exclude and simplify. Painters start with a blank canvas and add only pertinent subject matter. We photographers start with a scene with numerous elements, and we must often consciously exclude extraneous subject matter and bright areas that would pull the viewer's eye from the primary subject.

To present a clear message, a picture should generally have one strong center of interest and, perhaps, a second supporting subject. If the background is cluttered, find a better shooting angle or move your subject, if that's possible; foliage or a rich blue sky makes for a highly suitable backdrop, especially for people. No matter what types of subjects you typically shoot, greater reliance on closeups should help to improve the visual impact of your pictures.

Figure 7.5 : You will never use all the guidelines for effective composition for a single image, but keep them in mind whenever you're out shooting.

To fill the frame with your subject, walk closer to your center of interest or zoom in for tight framing for a greater sense of intimacy. When the subject is vertical—a building, trees, most people, and so on—flip the camera to a vertical orientation to avoid wasted space at the edges of a frame.

In wide-angle compositions, it's more difficult to exclude superfluous elements. Exclude competing subject matter by changing your shooting position, perhaps working from a low level to frame the subject against the sky. Defocus background clutter by using a long zoom lens setting, with a wide aperture, such as f/2.8.

Use off-center framing. In most snapshots, the subject is in the center of the image area. This placement can be effective in tight closeups of people, animals, and some colorful icons, but off-center composition is more pleasing for many other situations, especially in wide-angle photos. That's because the center of any picture is not a usual resting place for the eye and a central composition is static, not dynamic. The traditional way to create a well-balanced picture, the Rule of Thirds, is a useful guideline that suggests placing the subject one-third of the way from the edges of the frame. See Figure 7.6. (Use the focus lock technique described earlier to ensure that you subject is sharply rendered.)

Imagine that your camera's viewing screen is etched with grid lines, resembling a ticktacktoe game. (In fact, some cameras include a feature to add grid lines to the LCD monitor as an aid to effective composition.) As you view the subject—whether a blossoming cherry tree in Washington, DC, or a deserted house in a ghost town—place the subject at one of the intersecting points. This technique works equally well with a horizontal and a vertical framing and is far more effective than a dead-center, bull's-eye composition.

The Rule of Thirds can also be useful in closeup photos such as portraits. Whether your subject is a person, a pet, or a wild animal, try to compose so the most important element—the eyes—are at one of the intersecting points.

When taking pictures of moving subjects, friends walking their dog or a group of joggers, for example, leave some dynamic space in front of them. If your subjects are approaching from the right, leave lots of space on the left side of the image area for them to walk into, at least in the imagination of anyone who views your photos. Do the same with a static subject, your son looking toward the left, for example, leaving space on the left side of the frame so that he has somewhere to look within the image area.

Emphasize dramatic skies by placing the horizon low in the frame, along the lowest line in your imaginary grid. If the sky is dull, but important to the story, place it at the highest line. When the subject is quite large in the frame, as in a closeup portrait for example, place the most important subject element—the closest eye, perhaps—at an intersecting point. This is one of the two primary ways to avoid excessive empty space above the subject.

Figure 7.6: For effective composition, try to frame a scene so the primary subject element (the opening in the arch in this case) is at a point that's roughly one-third of the way in from the edges of the image area.

In many off-center compositions, especially in wide-angle images, the frame will have some empty space if the primary subject is quite small. Try to include a secondary, smaller or more distant object too. This provides a resting place for the viewer's eye as it explores the rest of the picture area.

Work the subject. Photographers using 35mm cameras are usually concerned about the cost of film and processing. Consequently, they often hesitate to really work a subject by shooting lots of frames. With a digital camera, this concern is not relevant because you can quickly delete any images that are less than ideal. Explore the subject from a variety of angles, with and without flash, at longer and shorter settings of the optical zoom lens, and so on. Generally, you'll find that you rarely capture the essence of the subject in the first shot.

Use effective visual design. If you take a college course in fine arts, you may find entire semesters devoted to the many principles of effective composition. At the risk of oversimplifying the issue, here is a brief summary of a few valuable concepts.

Compose boldly. Consider other elements of art when looking for a picture in any vast scene. Look for the rhythm of repetitive elements, a dynamic diagonal, contrasting color, texture, or shape, a unity of design, and so on.

Find leading lines. Particularly with landscapes and panoramic city scenes, it's worth trying to find some subject element that will lead the viewer's eye into the image, from left to right or from the bottom to the top. Such objects include a road receding toward a distant town, ice floes in water leading to a glacier, the graceful S curve of a river flowing from a mountain, a series of fishing boats at various distances from a village, and so on (see Figure 7.7).

Create a sense of depth. For a three-dimensional feel in a two-dimensional picture, use a wide-angle lens and include subjects in the foreground, midground, and background. A leading line plus some overlap of the elements can help produce apparent depth, whether the subject consists of a street scene or a pristine beach with colorful umbrellas.

Try diagonal compositions. Diagonals can be effective, especially when the line runs from one corner of the image to the other. Such framing can produce an image composed of two triangular sections; in that case, include important subject matter in both triangles to maintain balance. At a market for instance, place the lines of a stall on a diagonal, including colorful vegetables in one image area and a vendor in the other.

Figure 7.7: Friends who view your images may know little about the principles of visual design, but they will find your well-composed images pleasing.

With moving subjects, a diagonal composition has another advantage: it can help to convey an impression of movement or steepness. For example, for a photo of a Jeep climbing a moderate Utah hill, try tilting the camera to make the incline appear much steeper for a more dramatic image.

RECOMMENDATION: Rules Of Composition

Some of the compositional devices discussed in this chapter are often referred to as rules but are actually guidelines. Experienced photographers often break the rules for specific creative reasons—to make a point, to create tension, or to establish a mood. Before doing so, it is worth knowing and practicing guidelines that have been proven successful in both fine art and photography. After they have become second nature to you, begin to experiment. For example, you might try placing a circular subject in the center of the frame for formal symmetry, including urban clutter around an ancient monument, or placing a Civil War reenactor near the edge of a frame, so he appears to be looking out of the image area for a sense of tension. But do so knowingly and intentionally. Finally, plan to file or delete the less-than-effective images that you make while experimenting, showing only your most successful images to others.

Make Better Travel Images

Watch someone browsing through *National Geographic Traveler*, *Islands*, or *Arizona Highways* magazine, and one fact will become apparent: most people are quick to evaluate the impact of an image, flipping past any that do not capture their interest. Unless a photo offers a powerful visual statement, it won't hold their interest for long (see Figure 7.8).

After decades of saturation by television, the Web, and other media, we quickly tire of the record shots that merely present information about a location. Usually, it's the bold, graphic, stunning, or dramatic images that capture our interest. To increase the visual impact of your travel photos, consider the following techniques.

Do some research. Before leaving on a trip to any new destination, look for picture books on that area. When you arrive, check out the postcards and souvenir books that you'll find in many stores. Make a note of the most photogenic locations, and plan to visit them yourself. Without resorting to imitation, develop your own strategies for effectively communicating a sense of place. These will help to convey your intended message, satisfying a principal goal of any visual medium.

Figure 7.8: Effective travel images generally include interesting subject matter, pleasing composition, vivid colors, and, most important, people.

Add human interest to your images. Most travel pictures seem to include certain basic subjects—buildings, city scenes, and

Figure 7.9: With some self-confidence and people skills, and occasionally, a small tip, you will often be allowed to photograph people that you meet while traveling.

landscapes. Such location shots are important, but all too often they do not include people. As professional travel photographer Bob Krist (www.bobkrist.com) says, "If your friends are all landscapers and architects, they'll love your scenic and building pictures. Otherwise, people want to see pictures of people."

Frankly, we all find it difficult to take photos of strangers. Consequently, most travel pictures depict buildings and landscapes, often with a travel companion posing stiffly in front of a landmark. Sure, take such mandatory shots for your album or web page, but then go a step further. Shoot some candids of your family or friends interacting or involved in some activity. Keep your camera handy while they're canoeing in a national park, trying on a wild hat in a market, riding an uncooperative horse in Utah, and so on.

Include local people. Also plan to include some local residents in some images, to help define the essence of a place. In his book, *Spirit of Place – The Art of the Traveling Photographer*, Bob Krist recommends that you approach strangers with self-confidence, with a pleasant demeanor, and with respect and a basic understanding of the culture. Smile, make small talk, and use a bit of charm. In some areas, a tip or a small gift is considered mandatory. Street performers and artists (see Figure 7.9) earn their living from gratuities and such individuals expect a small contribution. If you want to photograph a vendor, make a small purchase from them to establish rapport.

If you don't speak the language, try a smile and a raised camera to overcome that barrier. Some people will not want to be photographed. In that case, reply with a pleasant nod and move on, until you find a more cooperative individual or group. When you do sense consent, start with a quick wide-angle shot. As your subject becomes more comfortable, move in closer, making more intimate wide-angle images. Finally, take some tight portrait shots too with a longer lens, using fill-flash to add sparkle to your subject's eyes. Conclude with a thanks and a cheerful good-bye.

A digital camera's LCD monitor can be a real icebreaker with strangers. After you take a photo of some people or their goods in a market, let them see the image. You'll probably find that they'll want you to take even more pictures, allowing you to make better compositions and tighter closeups. Others in the area will often become more cooperative too, and you'll come away with many great people pictures. Unless you are certain that you will make good on your promise, do not offer to send prints of your images to dozens of individuals.

Figure 7.10: Attend an outdoor public event if you want to take many photos of local people while traveling.

Find interesting events. People involved in unique cultural situations are ideal for evoking a sense of place. During your research, and after arriving at your destination, ask about any festivals, historical reenactments, or other celebrations taking place. An event of this type is also ideal for those who are too shy to approach strangers asking for permission to take photos. During a parade, cultural demonstration, or other outdoor group performance, photography is usually accepted or encouraged (see Figure 7.10).

If you want to take pictures of individual performers afterward, be sure to ask for permission. You may also find that some of the participants will agree to pose with your family or friends; this will allow you to make personalized photos for your vacation album or family web page.

Expand your horizons. While filling the frame is a useful technique, as discussed earlier, not every situation benefits from tight framing or the use of a long lens focal length. In a photo of a wood carver, for example, consider including the artifacts of their trade in some of the frames, using a wide-angle lens setting. Use the shortest focal length in a digicam with a built-in lens or the shortest lens available for a digital SLR camera to include both the primary subject and supporting elements. To maximize depth of field, the range of apparent sharp focus, set a small aperture (large f/number), such as f/11.

When using a wide-angle lens for buildings or trees, you may occasionally want to tilt the camera upward, using the resulting keystoning distortion for creative effects. Move in close to the subject, and tilt the camera upward at a steep angle for maximum distortion; this will make your creative intention obvious to the viewer.

Take advantage of bold colors. Most people love rich, vibrant colors, so it's worth looking for travel subjects with brilliant hues and tones. Watch for colorful artifacts, especially the symbols of tradition or culture—a decorated saddle in Mexico, a colorful mask in Venice or

Figure 7.11: Local artwork or icons with vibrant colors, enriched with a polarizing filter, often make for pleasing images in travel photography.

the Caribbean, and native handicrafts in the southwestern United States (see Figure 7.11). In a monochromatic scene, find a dash of color to act as a key element or accent. And seek out ceremonies, parades, celebrations, and festivals while traveling; you should find people costumed in a riot of color at many such events.

Use a polarizing filter. If your digital camera accepts filters, consider buying a polarizer to make outdoor images with deeper color saturation. The filter can enrich blue skies and intensify colors that would otherwise appear washed out. Rotate the filter to increase or decrease its effect, watching the changes in the camera's LCD monitor. You'll find that the polarizer is most effective when light strikes your subject from the side. If the filter does not seem to have much effect, change your shooting position relative to the sun, and try again.

Explore the subject. Some travelers are serious about making excellent images, and others find it difficult to move beyond the snapshot mode. All too often, I see people quickly snapping a shot of some great scene and getting back into their vehicles or tour buses. Although a parking area may be the single best location for a great photo, most subjects are worth exploring. Walk around until you find the ideal vantage point for a scene. If you find a beautiful background, wait until some local people walk into the scene or recruit some of your companions to do so.

Make Better Landscape and Nature Images

Since the earliest days of photography, landscapes have made a compelling subject, and we still take more pictures of outdoor scenes than of anything else, except friends and family. That's understandable, since the outdoor world does offer a lot of irresistible subjects—landscapes, gardens, trees, waterfalls, and flowers, for example. Although it's easy to take quick snapshots using a digicam's Landscape or Nature Program mode, making appealing images requires a more advanced technical and creative approach (see Figure 7.12). In addition to the techniques discussed in the previous sections, such as maximizing depth of field in wide-angle images, consider the following recommendations.

Take advantage of the best light. The color, angle, and quality of light differs throughout the day. Take advantage of the various characteristics of light to make the most effective images.

For landscapes, you'll find the most pleasing illumination in early morning and late afternoon on sunny days. At these times, your subject may be bathed in a golden glow as the reddish light produces a warmer, mellower image than the cool (bluish) light around midday.

Whether your subject is a city park, sand dunes, or red rock arches in Utah, the rich golden light will warm and enhance the scene.

Because the sun is low in the sky early and late in the day, you can also take advantage of side-lighting. Move around until the sun is to your side. Now, the shadows cast by your subjects will be obvious in the photos, helping to create a three-dimensional effect. Low-angled side-lighting also enhances texture as light skimming rock, sand, and other rough surfaces forms pockets of contrast producing a strong tactile impression.

For nature subjects—gardens, a hillside of wildflowers, or closeups of individual blossoms—the soft light of a cloudy/bright day is preferable to direct sunlight. In the diffused and even illumination, contrast is gentler, without dark shadows and extremely bright highlights; colors are richly saturated because they are not washed out by harsh light. On dark, heavily overcast days, use flash for nearby subjects to produce a brighter effect with richer colors. If your camera includes a flash exposure compensation control, try shooting with a –0.5 or –1 setting for a subtle flash effect (see Figure 7.13).

At times, you'll find that the natural light is not ideal when you first notice a photo opportunity; make a note to return at another time of day, if possible. Or wait until a cloud drifts over the sun for softer, more diffused illumination for nature subjects.

Figure 7.12: Pleasing landscape images call for effective light, framing, focus, and depth of field.

Figure 7.13: Many nature subjects benefit from soft, even illumination.

Whether you shoot a landscape or a more intimate nature subject, on a bright sunny day or in overcast conditions, use a polarizing filter as suggested earlier. This accessory can remove glare from rocks, leaves, flower petals, and water, so colors appear richly saturated instead of washed out.

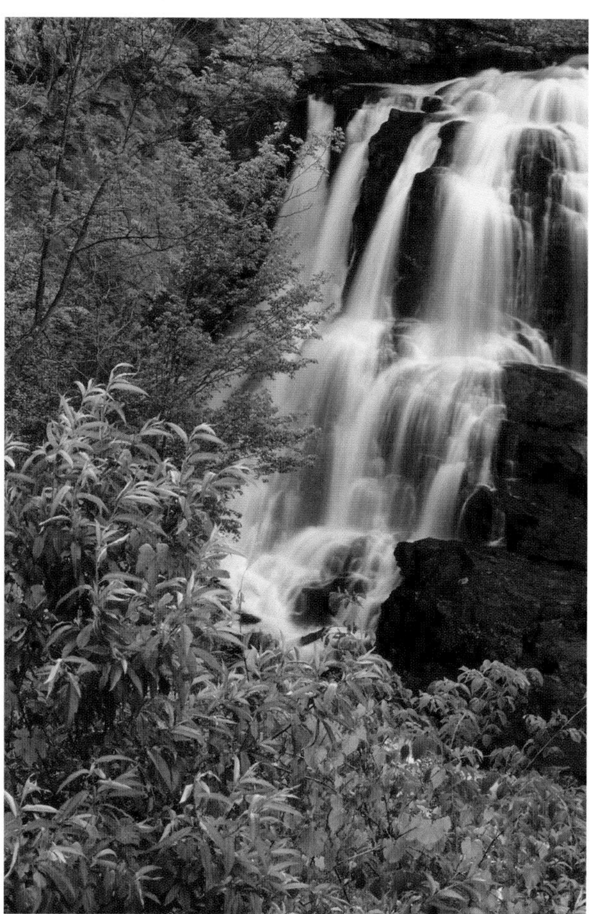

Figure 7.14: After making the usual wide-angle landscape image, zoom to a longer lens setting, and isolate individual details.

Start with an establishing shot. For the first in a series of images of a landscape or a nature subject, use the shortest end of your zoom lens to record an expansive view. Often, you'll find that the image includes many elements that will compete for viewer attention. It's difficult to tell whether the image is about a tree, the flowers, the stream, or the interesting cloud formation. Consequently, an ultrawide is not the ideal lens for snapping distant landscapes from a roadside lookout. Move in closer if at all possible to fill the wide-angle image with the most important subjects (see Figure 7.14).

Zoom to a longer lens setting. Whenever you're confronted by a vast landscape, such as a panoramic Caribbean beach at sunset, try to analyze what attracted your interest. Perhaps it was the evening light dancing across wet pebbles, the repeating pattern created by rippled sand, or pounding surf breaking over tide-worn rocks. Plan to make these appealing components the subject of a detailed photographic study using the long end of your zoom lens.

Make a series of images of individual elements that give the scene its special charm. Let each of these act as a symbol for the viewer, to represent the mood and the characteristics of this place and time. Some of your subjects will be as abstract as a contrasting color or lighting; others can be as simple as the dynamic shape of some natural form; a few may be as bold as the line created by land and water as they meet. Most of your pictures will be nothing like those of other visitors. Instead, they will reflect your own individual style, your personal interpretation of a well-traveled location.

Control depth of field. For a panoramic landscape, we usually want extensive depth of field with the foreground, midground, and background all quite sharply rendered. Use a wide-angle lens and set a small aperture such as f/11. Because depth of field (discussed in detail in Chapter 6) extends two-thirds behind the focused point and one-third in front of it, set focus for a point roughly one-third of the way up from the bottom of the image area. These techniques will maximize the range of apparent sharp focus.

In nature closeup photos, of a blossom for example, the opposite effect is preferable—very shallow depth of field. The background, or surrounding elements, should not be sharply rendered because they will compete for the viewer's attention, drawing it away from the center of interest. Use the longest zoom setting, and move in close to fill much of the frame with your subject. Select a wide aperture (a small f/number), such as f/4, to minimize the range of apparent sharpness. With a vertical subject, flip the camera to a vertical orientation so that the image includes less of the subject's surroundings.

Focus carefully. In tight closeups of nature subjects, there is little depth of field to mask any focusing error. Focus precisely on the most important subject area, a flower's pistil and stamen, for example.

Many digicams cannot focus closer than about 10" unless you select the Macro focusing mode. Unfortunately, some cameras automatically zoom the lens to a wide-angle position when Macro mode is selected; that is rarely appropriate for closeups of a small nature subject. If your camera does so, avoid using the Macro mode. Move a bit farther from the subject, and use conventional focusing with the longest zoom setting. Crop the photo with image-editing software later, in your computer, if necessary.

Use a tripod. At the long shutter speeds required when shooting landscapes at small apertures or extreme close-ups of nature subjects with high magnification, the least camera shake is amplified. If you use a tripod, your images will be sharper.

Make Better People Pictures

Digital cameras are ideal for people pictures, in part because our subjects can see an image within seconds after it is taken. This tends to make them more involved in the process and often, more likely to be cooperative when you want to make several images, using various poses. The visual feedback is also useful for the photographer, because it confirms when an image is just right, with a suitable pose and desired look. In this section, I'll provide some tips for making more satisfying people pictures, of several types (see Figure 7.15).

Despite your best efforts, many people pictures will benefit from some image enhancement. After deleting unsuccessful images—due to serious technical errors, uncomfortable poses, or poor facial expressions—plan to perfect your best photos using image-editing software. You might need to eliminate red-eye, remove blemishes, tone down a bright, distracting area, blur or crop distracting clutter, correct slight contrast, exposure, and color problems, and so on. Some of these techniques require a great deal of experience and expertise; they should not be considered alternatives to getting the image close to ideal, in-camera.

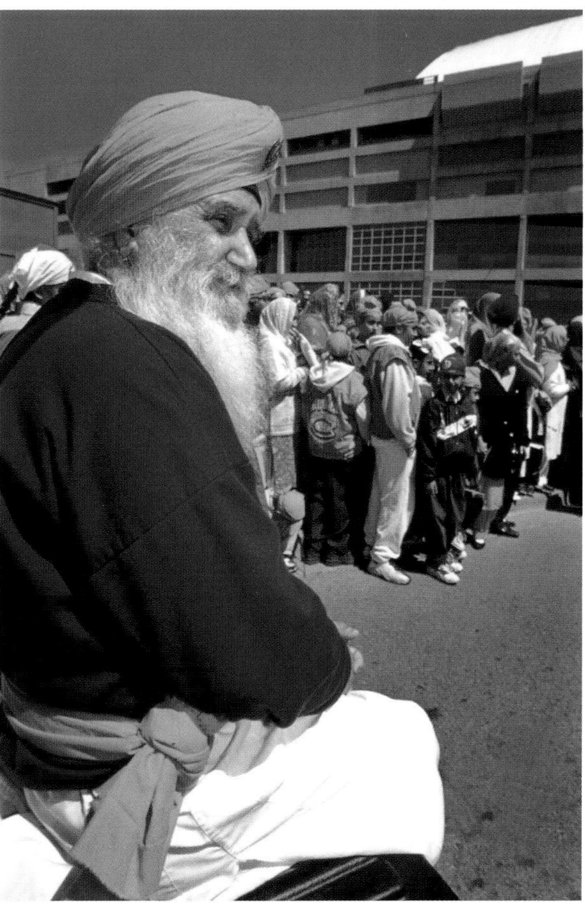

Figure 7.15: We take more pictures of people than of any other subject type, so it's worth taking the time to make pleasing images instead of snapshots.

Techniques for Making Pleasing Portraits

Most posed images are snapshots, with the subjects saying "cheese" or acting up for the camera, generally in cluttered surroundings. If you want to shoot more satisfying portrait images, you'll need to engage the subject and take greater control of the situation. The following techniques should help to produce more professional looking portrait shots.

Find a clean Background. Regardless of the location, pose the subject against an uncluttered background. Outdoors, you'll find that foliage or an area with deep

Figure 7.16: Whether you make portraits that are posed or informal, the techniques are similar.

shade or a deep blue sky work particularly well. Indoors, a plain wall is preferable to an area that includes a lot of small items as well as bright and dark areas. Although you can minimize the visibility of clutter with image-editing software, it's much easier to start with a clean background. When the surroundings are important—as in environmental portraits, depicting the subject in a location that tells us more about them—remove as much clutter as possible, and add props that help to reinforce the theme.

Shoot more verticals. Since portrait images generally feature a vertical subject, you'll often want to use a vertical camera orientation, except, perhaps, for some environmental portraits.

Use a telephoto lens setting. For a tight portrait shot, the equivalent of an 85mm to 115mm zoom setting works best for making a head and shoulders photo without getting too close to the subject and without including much of the surrounding area. (With a digicam with a 3x zoom, this will be near the long end of the zoom range.) Using a long focal length produces a flattering perspective, without the distortion that you get when using a wide-angle setting and moving in close. The greater camera-to-subject distance is also more comfortable for everyone involved (see Figure 7.16).

Perspective refers to a two-dimensional representation of a three-dimensional subject, but the full concept is difficult to define briefly. In the practical terms used in this book, accurate perspective refers to an image or lines within an image that appear normal and pleasing, as the eye expects. Pleasing perspective does not exhibit the keystoning distortion discussed earlier, exaggerated perspective (a looming foreground object), or obvious compression (objects appearing to be closer together than in reality). People pictures with normal perspective appear natural and flatter the subject.

Control the lighting. Whether shooting indoors or out, plan to use flash for even lighting in most of your images. In low-light conditions, red-eye can be a problem with on-camera flash; use the red-eye reduction flash mode and brighten all room lights to cause your subject's pupils to close down in order to reduce this ghoulish effect. Correct any remaining problem later, with image-editing software.

If you are using an accessory flash unit for indoor shooting, and if it allows you to tilt the flash head upward, try some shots with indirect illumination, bouncing the flash light from a white ceiling. This offers benefits over direct flash: it prevents red-eye and hard shadows behind the subject, and the soft illumination is quite pleasing. But bounce flash may not produce catch lights in the eyes; you may need to add some later, with-image editing software. Some flash units also rotate, allowing you to bounce flash light from a white wall; try some images with this technique too, if your equipment allows. It often produces more pleasing photos than light bounced from a ceiling.

If you prefer to use window light instead of flash, position your subject near a window; this illuminates one side of their face. Ask someone to hold a reflector (such as a large white sheet of cardboard) on the other side of the subject to bounce light that will fill in the shadow area.

Shoot from the subject's eye level. Particularly with children or with adults who are seated, avoid shooting from a position that is above the subject's eye level. For more pleasing portraits, without distortion of perspective, kneel or sit on the floor if necessary to make images in which the subject is level with the camera (see Figure 7.17).

Figure 7.17: Even when taking quick snapshots of family and friends, it's worth using some of the techniques discussed in the text.

Capture the right instant. Unless you want to make a formally posed photo, try to engage the subject in conversation or humor. Take a shot whenever the expression seems just right, shooting as many images as necessary. Generally, you'll want eye contact for a sense of intimacy. In others, ask the subject to look away from the camera, gazing into the distance, reading a book, or simply deep in (apparent) thought. When the pose seems relaxed and natural, take the picture.

Use the right camera settings. For portraits, a moderately wide aperture such as f/5.6 is often ideal; there is enough depth of field for the entire subject without excessive depth of field that would render background elements sharply.

If your camera allows you to adjust sharpness, contrast, and color saturation, set all three factors to Low. This should produce softer, more-flattering portraits with attractive skin tones. After downloading the images to your computer, adjust all three factors, as well as sharpness or blurring, as desired for the intended results.

Techniques for Taking Pleasing Candid Images

Candid images can be completely unposed, capturing subjects who are totally unaware that you are holding a camera. However, they may also be semicandid. The subject is aware that

Figure 7.18: It's difficult to take technically excellent people pictures that are totally candid; exercise a bit of control and make semicandid photos instead.

you will take some pictures, but is ignoring you and proceeding with some activity—creating a sculpture, opening gifts, playing with a pet, chatting with a friend, and so on. Because the subject is not posing per se, you might need to shoot more frames than you would in a portrait setup, in order to make a few really great images.

The semicandid photo offers greater control and is more common than a totally candid shot, particularly when it includes several people (see Figure 7.18). That's because natural interaction is almost always preferable to a posed group photo. This type of image is often ideal for family pictures, for environmental portraits (of the subject in a familiar location, involved in a familiar activity), and for images of people that you encounter when traveling.

You can provide suggestions for your subjects, but then allow them to become involved in interaction or some activity. Be ready with the camera to capture the interaction or activity as it happens. Although some of your subjects will insist on posing, they'll soon tire of that posture, and you'll start getting some candid shots. Many of the techniques discussed earlier in this chapter apply here. Other factors to consider include the following.

Plan the photo session. Before taking out your camera, discuss your plans with the subject, rearrange the surroundings and the subject's location, remove clutter and add appropriate props to reinforce any theme, turn lights on or off, and so on. Then allow your subject(s) to proceed while you take pictures from time to time.

If you're planning to make images of your children baking cookies, for example, line up all the ingredients, and get out the bowls, spoons, measuring cups, and cookie sheets in the kitchen. Remove superfluous items. Close the blinds over a window, and remove framed pictures from the wall, to prevent reflections on the glass if using flash. Coach your children as to what they should do, and shoot a series of images during the baking process. Try not to direct the action.

Some of the images might include a wide-angle shot of the spotless kitchen; the kids helping put out ingredients; closeups of individual bakers pouring or mixing; a subject licking the bowl; the kids putting the cookies into the oven; the kids wolfing down cookies later; and so on.

Be aware of equipment delays. Natural expressions are fleeting. Be prepared to shoot quickly. Remember that few digicams will make an exposure the instant that you press the shutter button; there is usually some delay, whether a half-second or two seconds. This shutter lag can mean missing a gesture or getting a shot of the back of your subject. To minimize this problem, prefocus and hold the shutter button pressed halfway. When you decide to take a picture, the shutter lag will be quite short, increasing the odds of capturing the desired moment.

When using flash, there will also be a delay after every shot, while the flash system recycles and is ready for another exposure. This delay can be quite long in low light conditions and quite short in bright light, in which flash output is minimal. Unless you want to spend a fortune on professional lighting equipment, there is really no solution to this problem. Remain aware as to when the flash is ready, usually signaled with a light in or near the viewfinder. This will help prevent the frustration of trying to take shots while the flash is still recycling.

Figure 7.19: During amateur sports events, you can generally get close to the action.

Use effective outdoor shooting techniques. When shooting in good light, do so without flash; set the camera to the burst or continuous mode so you can shoot a series of images quickly. In order to maintain a discrete distance while filling the frame, use the longest zoom setting of your camera's built-in lens. Find a shooting position that will allow you to frame your subjects so they are front-lit by the sun, while excluding clutter: parked cars, signs or picnic tables.

Try shooting sports action. If your children are involved in some team sports, you might want to shoot some semicandids of their activities (see Figure 7.19). Although you may need super telephoto lenses for professional sports, a 3x zoom or a 200mm lens on an SLR camera will work fine at children's events where you can get close to the action. If your digicam accepts a 2x or 3x telephoto lens adapter, you might want to buy one; it will allow you to fill the frame with more distant action.

When you arrive at an event, look around for a couple of suitable shooting positions that are close to the action, safe for you and for the competitors, and not in the line of sight of spectators. During a soccer game, for instance, find a position near the goal; this will allow you to get closeups of the scoring action. When you're attending any type of race, try to get close to the starting line and, later, to the finish line.

If you wait until the action gets close to your chosen position, you should get some great shots using the camera's continuous (burst) mode to shoot a series. Compact digicams do not include an autofocus mode for tracking a fast-moving subject, but you should get some good shots if you prefocus on a likely spot and use a fast shutter speed, such as 1/500 sec. Most digicams include a sports Program or an option for selecting a shutter speed; either is useful.

And a final tip: If your lens is not long enough to fill the frame with some dynamic action, take the picture anyway. Later, crop it with image-editing software until your subjects do fill the frame. The resulting (smaller) image file may not be suitable for making large, high-resolution prints, but it should be fine for 4" × 6" prints and for use on a family web page.

eight

CHAPTER

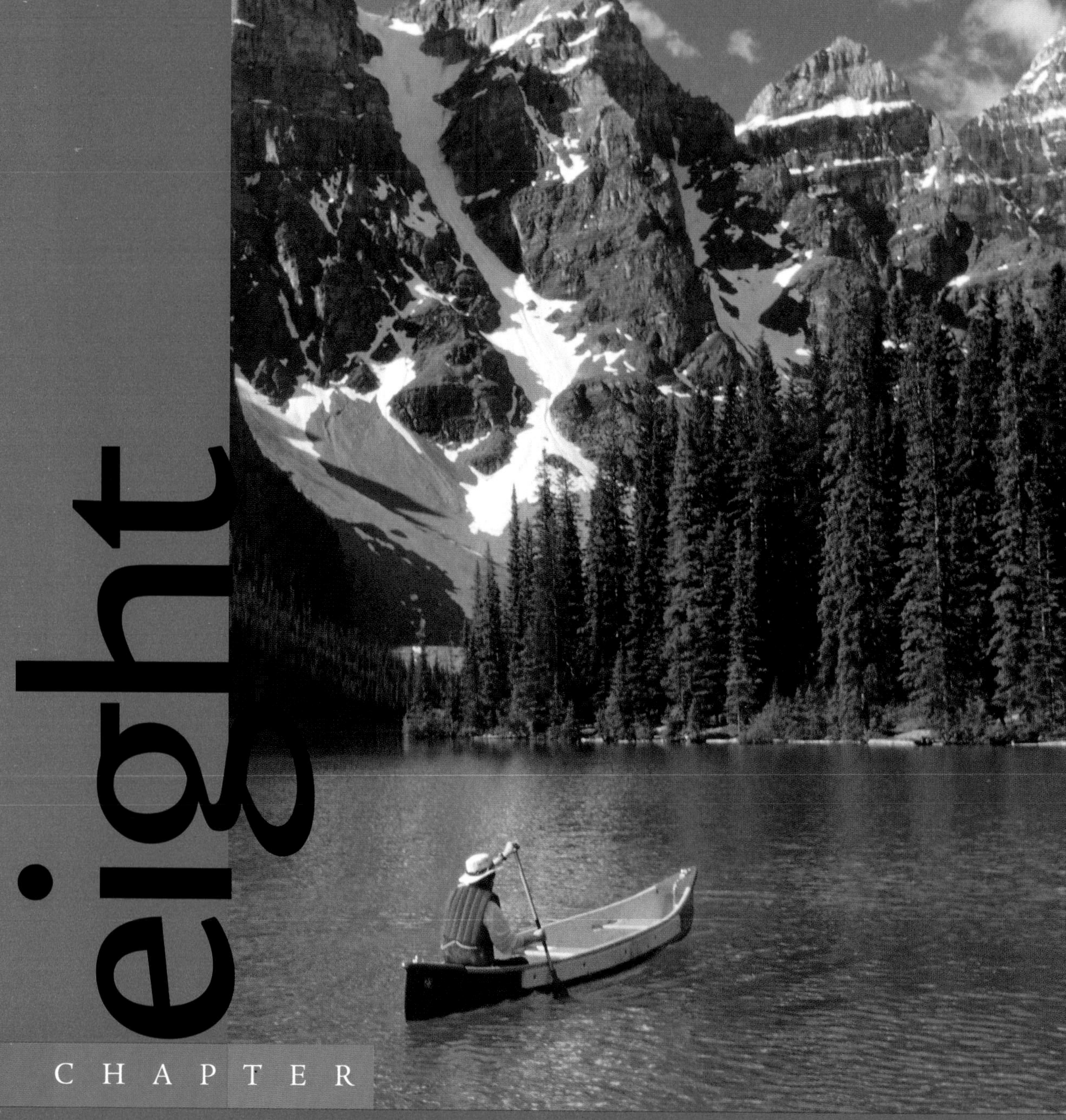

Scanning Techniques

Most of the latest *flatbed and film scanners are user friendly, incorporating features and software that allow even the novice to make good scans with the automatic features discussed in Chapter 2. Simplicity is great, but imaging enthusiasts will want to take advantage of the more-sophisticated capabilities available with the better scanners. In this chapter, I'll discuss the essential concepts and provide techniques for generating the best-possible scans, suitable for making prints of exhibition quality.*

Print-Scanning Techniques

If you decide to buy a flatbed scanner (see Figure 8.1), you will find it fairly easy to start making good scans from photographic prints. Although many flatbeds offer full automation for making a scan quickly, you will often get better results by taking some control.

After loading the scanner software and setting up your machine, follow these steps, and you'll be making good scans within 30 minutes.

1. Clean the scanner's plate glass with an antistatic cloth, a brush, or a microfiber cloth designed for cleaning camera lenses. If necessary, use a bit of a lens-cleaning solution to remove smudges. Gently clean the photograph as well. Prevention is better than the solution: spending a great deal of time later using image-editing software to remove defects.

Figure 8.1: Flatbed scanners are optimized for digitizing photographic prints and other reflective artwork.

A negative or a slide (or a larger transparency) includes substantially more image data than a print, allowing for better scans. If your flatbed scanner includes a transparency adapter, you'll want to scan a negative or a slide instead of a print as discussed in the next section.

2. Because you'll get the best scan from the largest image, select the largest available print of any subject; scan an 8" × 10" instead of a 4" × 6" print, for example (see Figure 8.2). Place it face down on the scanner's plate glass, making sure that it is not crooked.
3. To start the scanner software, press the One Touch button, open the software in your computer, or select the Import option in your photo-editing software. If the fully automatic scanning process starts, click Cancel to open the manual scanning screen.
4. Make sure that this screen indicates that the software is set for scanning a color photograph. (As discussed later, also scan black-and-white photos with the Color option.) If a preview scan is not made automatically, click Preview to produce one. Find the tool that lets you crop the image. Crop so that only the pertinent portion of the image is outlined in the Preview screen. Eliminate extraneous areas so that the image data file will not be unnecessarily large and will not slow the scanning process.
5. Check the brightness and contrast; click Auto Expose or Auto Correction if the software provides these options.
6. Access whatever additional exposure adjustment tools (such as Exposure, Adjust Highlights, and Adjust Shadows) are available, and use them to adjust the preview image until it looks just right in the Preview image. Your image should be clear and moderately bright with full detail in both light and dark areas (see Figure 8.3). An ideal exposure is as bright as possible while maintaining detail in highlight areas of the image.

Figure 8.2: If you start with a large color print of high quality, you can make an excellent scan with the techniques discussed in this section. This scan was made from an 8" × 10" print.

RECOMMENDATION: Optimizing a Print Scan

It is worth spending a few minutes with the various features of your scanner software, especially adjusting exposure, contrast, and color rendition. This reduces the amount of work you'll need to do later in image-editing software. In the "Film-Scanning Techniques" section later in this chapter, I'll discuss more advanced scanning techniques and the use of additional tools in the scanner software. Most flatbed scanners do not include all the advanced image-correction features, such as Curves, Levels, or the highly versatile Unsharp Mask tool. That's not a problem when scanning prints, because prints do not contain as much information as a piece of film, and the basic tools let you produce very good scans.

If you own a flatbed scanner with a transparency adapter and plan to scan slides and negatives, you'll want the more sophisticated capabilities available with more versatile software. In that case, you might want to upgrade to an after-market software such as SilverFast SE, available as a download for about $49 from **www.silverfast.com**. This software includes tools for intelligent auto-adjustments for exposure and sharpness, dust and scratch removal, color correction, and color cast removal, plus a feature for getting optimum results when scanning color negatives made with any of more than 100 specific films.

7. Find the color adjustment tools, and make any necessary corrections to eliminate any color cast. You might also want to increase color saturation (richness) slightly; a 10% to 15% increase can be useful unless the original photograph already exhibits a vivid color rendition. Do not increase saturation too much because that can cause loss of detail, particularly in the most saturated areas of an image.
8. Set the resolution. The software should offer several options, including one for 300 dpi, which is useful if you plan to make prints from the scan. Since most prints are produced at an output resolution of 300 dpi, a scan of 300 dpi results in an image file that can be printed at the same size as the original. Doubling the scan resolution to 600 dpi results in an image file that is four times larger, suitable for making a much larger print from the scan, useful if you own a large format printer. (The resolution is quadrupled because both horizontal and vertical resolution are doubled.)
9. The software should also include some controls for setting the size of the image file (in megabytes) or the target size (in inches) of the print that you want to make from the scan. It might also have a control for setting the magnification. These options are simply additional tools that help you determine the settings to use for a particular scan. To become familiar with these

Figure 8.3: Especially when scanning a very contrasty and excessively bright or dark print, take the extra time to make adjustments, and you can generate a digital image that is actually superior to the original print.

tools, set the target size for 5" × 7", or set the magnification to 70% to produce exactly the same result, if you are scanning an 8" × 10" print. The software will now indicate that the scan will produce an image file size of about 9MB. That is small enough to allow for fairly fast scanning and large enough to make an excellent 5" × 7" print.

10. Reset the magnification to 100%, or reset the target size to 8" × 10". Be sure the resolution is still set for 300 dpi.
11. If the software provides a feature for automatically sharpening the image, perhaps denoted as Unsharp Mask or USM, leave it off. Plan to sharpen the scan later, in your image-editing software, using that program's more effective sharpening options. (Despite its unusual name, Unsharp Mask does produce sharpening.) If your scanner software has a fully adjustable USM tool, you might want to try it. The amount of sharpening you'll want depends on the size of the scan you are making. As a starting point, try the following settings if you specified the settings in the earlier steps: Amount 25%, Radius 1.5 pixels, and Threshold 4 levels. (In Chapter 9, you'll find a full discussion of the various issues relating to Unsharp Mask.)
12. Click Scan to start the scanning process. In a minute or less, the scan should be complete, and you should be viewing the scanned image. Save this master file in a logical folder in your computer in the TIFF format.

Why save a scanned image as TIFF (Tagged Image File Format) instead of JPEG (Joint Photographic Experts Group)? Saving as a JPEG compresses the file so it's smaller, but JPEG is a "lossy" format. It discards some information during the compression process and discards more information each time that you open and resave a file. A TIFF file is much larger but preferable. Because information is never discarded for compression, optimum image quality is maintained.

Film-Scanning Techniques

As discussed in Chapter 2, you can use a film scanner or a flatbed scanner with a transparency adapter to digitize slides and negatives. A suitable high-resolution flatbed can be useful if you occasionally need to scan film and do not plan to make large prints. When using such equipment, the scanning process is similar to the steps described in the previous section, but you'll need to select a much higher resolution setting for the tiny original. When experimenting, try the highest dpi level, usually 1200 dpi or 2400 dpi, depending on the machine you're using. This will produce a high-resolution scan in a large image file.

If you want to scan many slides or negatives and want digital images of higher quality—particularly from a small 35mm film frame—consider buying a dedicated film scanner, with at least 2700 dpi resolution and a wide dynamic range, as discussed in Chapter 2. Your image files will exhibit superior color rendition, range of tones, sharpness, and definition of fine detail as confirmed by Figure 8.4.

In addition to generating scans of higher quality, dedicated film scanners typically offer another benefit: they include more versatile software that provides some of the tools that you find in image-editing programs, such as Photoshop Elements 2. You can use these tools to make precise adjustments to the image before making the scan.

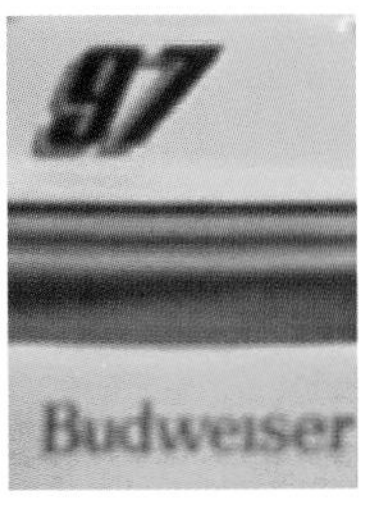

Figure 8.4: A flatbed scanner with a transparency adapter simply cannot produce the same level of quality from a 35mm film scan as a dedicated film scanner. This is confirmed by the two partial images, very small portions of the main image. The middle image was scanned by a 2400 dpi flatbed scanner, and the image on the right was scanned by a film scanner set to 2400 dpi.

It is relatively easy to make a good scan from a print; sometimes, you can do so with the automatic features in the scanner software. Making an excellent scan from film is more difficult because a slide or negative contains substantially more information and a broader dynamic range: far more tones between pure white and pure black. To record a maximum amount of information and a full range of tones, you need a scanner that has a wide dynamic range and highly versatile software that allows for making precise adjustments to certain image parameters.

Before moving on to film-scanning techniques, I want to pass on a couple of tips that are important if you want to get the maximum quality from film scans.

Buy the Best Scanner You Can Afford

If you are considering a film scanner, it might be tempting to buy the most affordable model you can find. Although 2700 dpi film scanners are available for prices as low as $229, I recommend that you budget a higher amount if you want to make scans of very high quality. That could mean spending $500 for a well-known brand, such as Nikon, Canon, or Minolta (see Figure 8.5), with the features—such as high dynamic range and color depth—recommended in Chapter 2.

Set a budget and find models within your price range on a retailer's e-store site; review their specifications as well. Then, look for reviews on the machines you are considering, through a search on the Internet, for evaluations of speed, versatility of software, image quality, and so on.

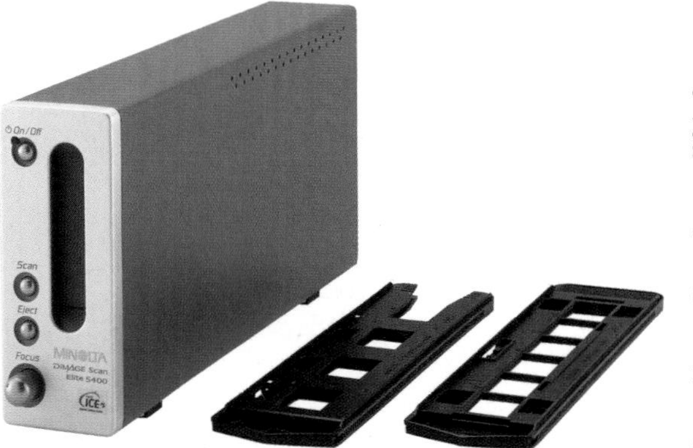

Konica Minolta Photo Imaging U.S.A., Inc.

Figure 8.5: A high-quality 35mm film scanner, with versatile software and extras such as Digital ICE for dust and scratch removal, is a wise investment if you plan to scan many slides and/or negatives.

If you will often want to make exhibition quality prints as large as 13" × 19", save up to buy a 4000 dpi film scanner. It will capture far more detail from a 35mm slide or negative than its 2700 or 2800 dpi counterpart. The price of 4000 dpi film scanners has started dropping, and you can find some new models, like the Nikon Coolscan V ED, for about $749. These affordable machines may not include all of the features of the more expensive models but they can certainly make good to excellent scans. Regardless of the price, look for a film scanner that includes software with many tools for adjusting the pre-scan image, an effective dust and scratch removal option, as well as accessories for loading numerous slides or negatives for batch scanning.

Scan at Maximum Resolution

When used at its highest resolution setting, a 2700, 2800, or 2900 dpi film scanner produces 22MB to 24MB image files that will allow you to make excellent 8.5" × 11" prints (see Figure 8.6). You should also be able to make good prints as large as 10" × 15", after increasing the file size (called resampling or interpolation) with a function in your image-editing software. For the best results, use the advanced bicubic interpolation system available in Photoshop programs and some others, as discussed in Chapter 9.

Figure 8.6: A 2800 dpi film scanner in high-resolution mode can generate images of professional caliber, suitable for making excellent prints.

High-resolution scanning does take time and produces large TIFF files that can quickly fill your computer's hard drive. It might be tempting to use a scanner's lower resolution setting to make smaller image files more quickly. Think twice before doing so. Unless you are certain that you will never want to make large prints from a scan, use the highest resolution setting to capture the most information possible. Save the large files to a CD, and make a backup copy as discussed in Chapter 3. If you occasionally need a small image file for Internet use, simply downsize a large, high-resolution TIFF file, and save it as a JPEG under another filename.

Film-Scanning Techniques

The software included with various scanners differs in its features, types of controls, options, and so on. Read your owner's manual to determine what is included and how each control is accessed. For this section, I will assume that your scanner includes many user-adjustable controls. You'll want to use these to produce scans with good color rendition, exposure, and contrast to generate a scan that will be easy to perfect in image-editing software.

RECOMMENDATION: Look for Versatile Scanner Software

Although most dedicated film scanners include versatile software, with the features discussed in this section, many flatbeds are not as well equipped. Unfortunately, it is difficult to determine what software features are included based on the specifications published by scanner manufacturers. If you are considering several flatbed scanners and want more information on their software features, review online manuals if available on the manufacturers' websites as well as reviews on the Internet or in photo magazines. You might also check with a local camera or computer store; the retailer may have scanners set up for demonstration purposes.

If you follow the steps in this next exercise, you should be able to make some excellent scans whether you use a dedicated film scanner or a high-end flatbed scanner with transparency adapter and a highly versatile software package (see Figure 8.7). The resulting images will include a great deal of information and detail from the film, allowing you to make large prints of true photographic quality. The images will also be fairly easy to optimize for printing with image-editing software, without the need for numerous advanced image adjustment techniques.

1. Select the best-possible slide or negative: a sharp, well-exposed image, with pleasing color, moderate contrast, and detail in both highlight and shadow areas. Such image evaluation is much easier to make with a slide than a negative, because a slide is a positive image exhibiting true colors, without the orange cast that you find in a negative.
2. Clean the film with an antistatic brush designed for this purpose. If fingerprints or other oil-based smudges are present, carefully clean the transparency with a solution such as PEC-12 from Photographic Solutions (www.photosol.com).

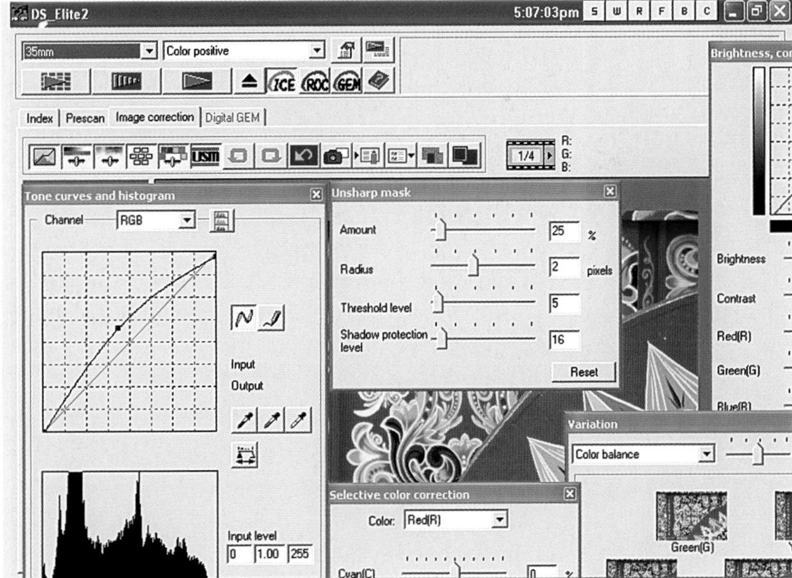

Figure 8.7: A film scanner's many image-enhancing features can seem overwhelming at first, but with some practice, you'll soon learn how and when to use each of the options.

3. Start the scanner software, and load the slide or negative into the appropriate holder, *emulsion side down*. This ensures a proper scan and allows an automatic dust and scratch removal tool to work properly.

With some films, the emulsion side is less shiny than the nonemulsion side. If you look at a slide and the image looks correct, the side *away* from you is the emulsion side.

---

4. Follow the instructions to make a pre-scan, a small, low-resolution preview image that will later allow you to view any corrections or enhancements you make. Crop the image using the tool provided so that only the pertinent portion of the image is outlined in the preview. Eliminate extraneous areas such as the slide frame. This speeds up the scanning process, minimizes the size of the image data file, and ensures an accurate histogram display (discussed later in this chapter) for evaluating scan exposure.
5. If the software provides a feature for dust and scratch removal, such as Digital ICE or FARE, activate this tool; if several settings are available, select the Normal option. Even film that looks perfectly clean will have some defects that are worth removing in the scanning process. Most defect correction tools are incompatible with Kodachrome slides or black-and-white negatives and should not be used when scanning such originals.
6. Activate the automatic features to set focus, exposure, and color balance for use as a starting point. If an Auto Contrast Correction option is available, do not activate this feature because it can cause the scan to be too contrasty (see Figure 8.8A), causing a loss of detail in highlight and/or shadow areas.
7. Fine-tune the exposure and contrast, using one or more of the correction options (see Figure 8.8B). With most images, it's important to maintain detail in highlight areas, even if that means sacrificing some detail in the shadows. Make adjustments using the Curves and Levels tools; if you do not have much experience with those advanced features, use the Brightness tool. If the image is contrasty, with dark shadows and bright highlight areas, reduce contrast slightly with Curves or with the Contrast Correction slider tool. This will minimize the loss of detail throughout the image. You can easily correct low contrast later, using image-editing software, but high contrast produces a loss of detail that cannot be completely corrected after the fact.
8. Check the color balance to make sure that it is pleasing and suitable for the subject. If you are scanning a slide, the color should be fine; little or no color correction may be required. Color negatives include an orange mask as part of the emulsion, and this can produce a color cast, an overall blue/green tone, for example. If this occurs, use the color correction tools provided in the scanner software. Each brand of software provides different color correction options, but includes some form of color balance adjustment.

As discussed in Chapter 9, it is important to work with a color-calibrated monitor when making pre-scan adjustments to ensure that your assessment of color qualities is accurate. Otherwise, your adjustments may not be accurate. With some software (such as Nikon Scan 3 or 4), monitor adjustment is not automatic, and you need to specify a display profile in the software settings. Read your scanner owner's manual for information as to steps you should take to ensure an accurate monitor image.

Figure 8.8A: If you follow the techniques in this section, you won't make technically poor scans like this one. Notice how texture has been lost in the highlight and shadow areas and how detail has been lost in the midtones.

Figure 8.8B: Although this scan might look a bit dark and low on contrast, it is ideal because it holds detail in all areas. You can easily correct low contrast in image-editing software, but excessive contrast produces a loss of detail that can never be recovered.

9. Most film scans benefit from slight sharpening to compensate for loss of sharpness caused by conversion from analog to digital form (see Figure 8.8C). You should be able to use the Unsharp Mask (USM) tool to control the extent of sharpening, with adjustments for three distinct parameters: amount, radius, and threshold. (This concept is discussed further in Chapter 9.) The amount of sharpening is based on a subjective judgment, but use conservative settings as a starting point while experimenting. It is impossible to provide recommended USM settings because these depend on the scanner software you are using. In general, a low Radius setting, a moderate Amount setting, and a low Threshold setting should work well, unless the sharpening produces digital noise or unwanted texture in the images.

Figure 8.8C: As a result of tweaking in image-editing software—lightening, adjusting color, boosting contrast a bit, and sharpening—you will have a scan that is ready to become an exceptional print.

When scanning negatives with my own 2800 dpi film scanner, I often set Amount 10, Radius 5, and Threshold 2. With slides, I prefer settings such as Amount 30, Radius 15, and Threshold 4. These may not be appropriate with your scanner, so experiment to find a satisfactory combination of settings. These values differ from those in Photoshop because most scanner software uses scales that are different from those of image editors.

If the software does not provide controls for adjusting the amount of sharpening, do not activate this feature, because it will probably oversharpen your images.

---

10. Select the resolution before making the actual scan. When scanning film, the simplest method is to set the highest optical resolution level, such as 2800 dpi, and to set the magnification to 100%. This will produce the largest possible image file. Later, in image-editing software, you can resize the dimensions to the desired print size and to a suitable printer resolution, such as 300 dpi, as discussed in Chapter 5.
11. Make the scan and save the file in your computer in the TIFF format. You can enhance and resize the image for printing or other purposes in your image-editing software.

Additional Scanning Considerations

After you have made a dozen scans from color slides or negatives using the primary steps, you might want to begin experimenting with some other tools in the scanner software. Not all scanners include some of the extra options, but if yours does, consider the following advanced techniques.

Check the histogram. When considering an image in the preview screen, you should be able to evaluate brightness as well as the shadow and highlight detail. If the software provides a histogram feature, you can use that for a more accurate check of the exposure settings. The most important consideration is to avoid clipping any highlight details. This would be indicated by a histogram that appears cut off on the highlight end of the scale. If the histogram option allows you to view individual charts for each color channel, use that option to see if you are losing detail.

Decide on color depth. Some scanner software provides the option to select color depth: 8-bit (per channel) or 12-bit. An 8-bit image is excellent with as many as 16.7 million possible colors. If you select the 12-bit option, the scan will have as many as 68 billion color values and will be saved as a 16-bit file with more tonal and color information. The scanning will take longer, and the final image file size will be twice as large as in 8-bit mode. Most image-editing software offers limited 16-bit support and will not allow you to make many adjustments to a high-bit image. Unless you are using Photoshop CS, with its extensive support for 16-bit files, you'll probably want to make scans using the scanner's 8-bit color depth setting.

Select the right color space. If the scanner software provides a Color Management option, select Adobe RGB (1998) as the working space or profile to assign to the image if you plan to make prints from your scans. Try other options too, if available, while experimenting to determine which produces the most pleasing results. For example, some Nikon film scanners offer a Scanner RGB option that is worth trying. This often produces accurate scans except with highly saturated images that should be scanned in Adobe RGB (1998) color space instead.

Eliminate excess grain. If you are scanning a very grainy slide or negative (usually from ISO 400 or higher speed film), experiment with Digital GEM or another grain-reduction feature, if available with your scanner software. At the time of this writing, Digital GEM produced the best results of all grain-control tools, particularly the latest version that's included with recent Nikon film scanners. This is probably the best solution for grain reduction, although it does soften images and introduces some digital artifacts, so it is not ideal in all respects. If you are not satisfied with the results produced by any grain-reduction tool, leave it off when scanning. You can add Digital GEM to your scanner software for $80 (www.asf.com/products/gem/), worth considering if you have many grainy slides or negatives.

Reduce image noise. Many dedicated film scanners include a multiple-pass scanning feature, intended to reduce digital noise in certain images, as discussed in Chapter 2. This feature is not often necessary because a high-quality film scanner should produce noise-free scans from most slides and negatives. Take advantage of multisampling when scanning a film frame with a large shadow area, such as a dark sky in a night photo, in which digital noise is most common. When multisampling is necessary, it's worth selecting a high level for great effectiveness, such as the 8x option. Some experts recommend 12x or 16x multisampling; that can be even more effective, but the scanning time will be frustratingly long.

Use extra care with monochrome negatives. When scanning black-and-white negatives, do so in the scanner's Color Negative mode, to capture the maximum amount of tonal information possible. You might need to reduce brightness substantially in the scanner software to avoid loss of detail in highlight areas; even then, some film scanners produce images with less than full detail. If you experience this problem, experiment with scanning in the Color Slide setting in order to capture more information. Later, in image-editing software, invert the image to a positive.

Use batch scanning wisely. Many film scanners allow for batch scanning—loading 6 or more negatives or as many as 50 slides at one time and setting the machine to scan all of them at the same software settings. (Often, batch scanning capability requires an extra-cost accessory.) This process can save a great deal of time, since the machine can complete the process while you're eating lunch or involved in some other activity. Batch scanning is appropriate only for slides or negatives that are similar in most respects, because it does not allow for individual adjustments. For the best results, do not use batch scanning for slides or negatives that require substantially different scanner software settings.

three
PART
LOBBY
FURNACE CREEK INN

Optimizing Images

Anyone with experience in a "wet" darkroom knows how challenging and time-consuming the image enhancing process can be using traditional tools and processes. By comparison, the digital darkroom contains a far greater range of control over color balance, brightness, contrast, color saturation and sharpness and the process is relatively quick. In the next three chapters, you'll find step by step guidance on color management, basic image enhancement as well as some advanced techniques to get you started in your progress along the learning curve.

CHAPTER nine

Color Management Demystified

Are your prints as impressive *as the image you see in the electronic display? Are your landscape and travel photos "clean," or do they exhibit a cyan tint? Are the colors and tones in your prints as vibrant and bright as they appear on the monitor, or do your prints seem flat and muddy by comparison? Problems such as these are common when using a monitor that does not produce an optimal display of the actual color rendition in digital image files or when a printer does not produce accurate prints.*

The solution is effective color management, a prerequisite for making prints that reflect your intentions, without a lot of frustration, trial-and-error experimentation, or a waste of ink and paper. Most photo enthusiasts dread this topic, believing that it's "too complicated." Granted, some of the concepts are not intuitive or simple, but the basic color management process need not be difficult. Professional photographers and graphic designers may need an extreme level of precision and accuracy, but hobbyists can get by nicely with the basic explanations, practical tips, and affordable accessories I'll recommend in this chapter.

The Basics of Color Management

Before proceeding to the steps in color managing your digital darkroom, it's important to understand the basic concept. At the risk of oversimplifying a complex topic, I'll offer the following explanation. Color management attempts to resolve the varying color behavior of different devices: cameras, scanners, monitors, and printers. Each device either "sees" or displays color using a different method and different primary color components and with different results.

Color management provides a method to modify or compensate for the behavior of each device. Institute an effective color management system and the colors will remain consistent through the entire process, from capturing the image to viewing it on a monitor and to making it into a beautiful photographic print.

The Key Elements in Color Management

To achieve a high level of satisfaction with any print, you must be able to trust the monitor. In other words, you must be able to work with confidence, knowing that the display accurately reflects the characteristics of the image data file (see Figure 9.1). Otherwise, the resulting print may exhibit incorrect color and tonality (brightness/contrast) that will be transferred to any print you make.

As discussed later, you can make a better print after adjusting color and tonality to compensate for the problem, but you'll be working on a trial-and-error basis. Unless you can trust your monitor to reflect the true image data, every adjustment you make will be based on a guess.

Eventually, you'll determine the steps necessary to make an image look better on a certain paper, but you may need entirely different adjustments to make a beautiful print on another type of paper. That will lead to more trial-and-error guesstimating and more wasted paper and ink. And what will happen if you send the image file to a friend or to a commercial printing service? At best, you'll get unpredictable results, because the adjustments you made to the image file are not accurate; they only appear accurate on your monitor.

If you calibrate your monitor so that it produces an accurate display of the actual image file, you can minimize disappointment, frustration, and a waste of time and money in the digital darkroom.

Figure 9.1: Although a print is not identical to an image in an electronic display, effective color management ensures that your prints come close to matching what you see on a monitor.

The Primary Color Management Steps

Entire books have been written about this topic, including Tim Grey's *Color Confidence: The Digital Photographer's Guide to Color Management* (Sybex, 2004.) These contain a great deal of valuable information and recommendations, but for the purposes of this introductory chapter, I'll discuss color management workflow in several basic steps:

1. Calibrating your monitor to produce an accurate reflection of the digital image by adjusting the black and white points as well as the midtone brightness of the display (see Figure 9.2).
2. Establishing the optimal settings in your digital camera to generate images with satisfactory exposure, color balance, and color saturation.
3. Ensuring that a scanner, if you use one, delivers satisfactory color and tonality (brightness and contrast).
4. Specifying the correct color settings in Photoshop or another image editor.
5. Taking steps to ensure that your printer produces the most accurate prints possible on each of the papers you plan to use.

COURTESY WACOM TECHNOLOGY CORPORATION

Figure 9.2: The monitor is a key component in any digital darkroom. Depending on the accuracy of its display, the monitor can either cause a great deal of frustration or complement your skills in making prints of exceptional quality.

RECOMMENDATION: Make Monitor Calibration Your Top Priority

Although logic might dictate that you consider camera and scanner issues first, I have intentionally selected monitor calibration as the starting point in this discussion. That's because the entire color management workflow hinges on monitor accuracy. Consider this worst-case scenario that can occur when working with an unreliable monitor.

You have made a technically good photo (with a digicam or scanner) and have labored to enhance the image until it appears to be perfect on your monitor. But let's say that your monitor is displaying wildly inaccurate color and tonality. In that case, the actual image is quite different from what you're seeing on the monitor.

The actual image file may include a magenta cast and excessive color saturation that's aggravated by incorrect tonality: excessive brightness and contrast. Your monitor is not displaying these characteristics because it has not been calibrated to produce an accurate reflection of the data in the image file. When you proceed to print the photo, the printer will do its job well, producing an accurate rendition of the digital image. The photo will exhibit the undesirable characteristics, because the printer software employed the actual image data and did not work from the beautiful image displayed on the monitor.

Admittedly, my example illustrates a serious problem, and many color management issues are not as troublesome. Nonetheless, I strongly recommend monitor calibration—preferably full calibration as discussed in a subsequent section—as a prerequisite to advanced image enhancement and printmaking.

Calibrating Your Monitor

What is generically referred to as calibrating a monitor actually consists of two steps:

1. Bringing the brightness, contrast, and color temperature of the display as close as possible to established standards.
2. Profiling (also referred to as "characterizing"): using measurements to determine the accuracy of the display. A monitor profile stores details about the monitor behavior and allows the display to be adjusted to compensate for inaccurate color.

You can use two distinct methods for calibration: basic "gamma adjustment" and full calibration with an after-market kit that includes a monitor sensor as well as sophisticated software. To a great extent, gamma adjustment is based on your visual assessment of monitor accuracy, and that may or may not be reliable. Full calibration, using a calibrated colorimeter sensor, is a more scientific method that produces far more reliable and precise results.

Often used in this chapter, the term *gamma* refers to a measurement of monitor brightness and contrast, denoted with numbers from 1 to 2.5 on a mathematical curve. Gamma adjustment involves altering the contrast and brightness of a display, but as you'll see, the tools that you can use, including Adobe Gamma, actually produce more effects than the mere shifting of the gamma.

If you want to try the simplest and most affordable method for testing and adjusting the appearance of images, calibrate your monitor with a software-only solution, using the technique described in the next section. If you own Adobe software, use Adobe Gamma, installed by default with most Adobe applications. Otherwise, use the ColorSync monitor calibration tool, similar to Adobe Gamma, available with Mac operating systems in the control panel. Windows doesn't provide a similar tool, so if you don't own an Adobe product, you'll need to acquire one or skip down to the "Advanced Monitor Calibration Tools" section.

Calibrating with software is definitely not an optimal solution, but it may increase the predictability of brightness and color saturation in your prints. If that doesn't provide the accuracy you want, plan to calibrate your monitor in a more scientific way, using a package with software and a "colorimeter" available for $169. The colorimeter is a sensor which can be attached to a monitor for measuring the relative intensity of a series of color samples on the display.

If you intend to buy a full monitor calibration kit, do not adjust your monitor's gamma as described in the next section. Review the information about the concepts, but skip to the "Advanced Monitor Calibration Tools" section for specifics on the equipment and techniques you'll employ.

Using Adobe Gamma for Basic Calibration

To adjust the appearance of your monitor display, use Adobe Gamma (see Figure 9.3) or the Mac ColorSync Calibrator. The software generates a color profile that describes the color behavior of your monitor. Make the *correct* monitor adjustments and settings in the utility and the new profile should allow the image editor to generate displays with greater accuracy.

You'll find discussions of profiles throughout this chapter. A profile is a file that describes the color behavior of a device, so that appropriate color values can be translated to the other devices in your digital darkroom. Think of a profile as a master translator able to translate words between any languages.

Since most of you probably have computers that include Adobe Gamma or ColorSync Calibrator, I'll provide the following steps, which you can use with either of these software programs.

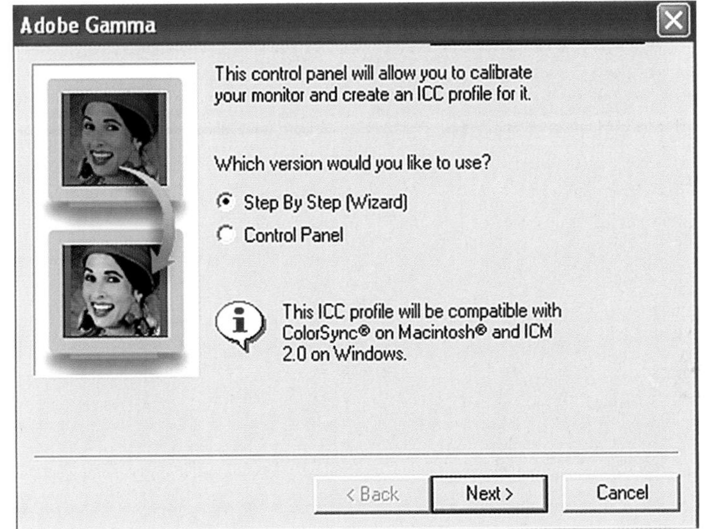

Figure 9.3: Calibrating a monitor with Adobe Gamma is a simple process and the bare minimum that's required in display adjustment.

1. Set the ambient light to a level that you generally use while working on image enhancement, preferably not too bright.
2. Open Adobe Gamma (or ColorSync Calibrator) through your computer's control panel, and follow the step-by-step instructions. Set the White Point to 6500 when prompted to do so, and set the Gamma to 2.2 (unless you share files with people who use different target values).

   The standard gamma (midtone brightness) value for Windows PCs is 2.2, a level that provides high contrast and brightness and, hence, higher color saturation in the monitor image. (Some after-market monitor calibration systems set a gamma of 2.0.) For Mac systems, the traditional value is a relatively low and flat 1.8, but it can be set to a higher level. I recommend setting 2.2 unless you often exchange image files with other Mac owners. In that case, calibrate your monitor based on their settings (often the traditional 1.8) to ensure a good match.

   When you reach steps that require you to make judgments based on a visual evaluation of the monitor display, do the best you can; consider asking for a second opinion before making your decision on the optimal settings.
3. After the process is completed, click the Finish button. The software then creates a new profile that your operating system will use to adjust all images displayed on the monitor. Photoshop (or another image-editor that can use color profiles) will employ the new profile when making its color display calculations.

The profile should now be set as the default for your system, so you should not need to take any further steps. However, you might want to confirm this. To do so on a Windows PC, follow these steps:

1. Choose Start → Control Panel to open Control Panel.
2. Click Display to open the Display Properties dialog box.
3. Click the Settings tab.
4. Click Advanced.
5. In the dialog box that opens, click the Color Management tab.
6. Confirm that the profile you created is set as the Default Monitor Profile. If not, select it from the list, or follow these steps:
   a. Click Add to open the Add Profile Association dialog box.
   b. Select the profile, and click Add.
7. Click OK twice to close the open dialog boxes, and then close Control Panel.

With Mac 9.2 and older systems, select the Apple menu and choose Control Panels → Monitors → Set Profile and choose a profile from the list of options. If you're using Mac OS X or newer, access the Apple menu and choose Preferences → Hardware → Displays → Color.

It's worth repeating the calibration process once a month because display attributes change over time, causing a shift in the display's color and brightness.

Because several monitor calibration steps are based on a visual evaluation (the user's perception), gamma adjustment settings are subjective. That's acceptable for a generalized profile that may be better than the default profile, but remember that it's still imprecise. Calibrating your monitor with Adobe Gamma is better than doing nothing at all, but I strongly recommend that you use a package described in the next section for your monitor calibration and profiling.

Advanced Monitor Calibration Tools

If you plan to make high-quality prints that reflect your creative intentions, you'll want to consider a more sophisticated alternative: a full display calibration and profiling package that's leagues ahead of Adobe Gamma in terms of accuracy. The most useful and accurate products consist of a kit that includes software and the colorimeter mentioned earlier (see Figure 9.4). This combination optimizes the gray balance of your display, produces the maximum range of colors, produces an appropriate white luminance and black point, and adjusts the display for superior color rendition with a high degree of precision. The software then builds a reliable monitor profile. Your operating system and imaging software will employ the data to adjust the colors for an accurate representation of the image file on your monitor.

In practical terms, this means that you'll be able to view a highly accurate image

PHOTO COURTESY OF COLORVISION®

Figure 9.4: A complete and highly effective monitor calibration kit includes both software and a colorimeter. The combination assures a highly reliable monitor display with accurate color rendition and tonality.

before and after you make any adjustments to enhance the tonality, color saturation, and color balance of the photo. If you use the correct printing techniques, as discussed later, your prints should closely reflect the monitor image as well as your creative intentions.

Until recently, colorimeter kits were expensive and were intended for use only with CRT monitors. Today you can buy a kit for less than $170 that's suitable for both CRT and LCD monitors. The most popular products include MonacoOPTIX with EZcolor software ($299), which you can find at www.monacosystems.com, and ColorVision Spyder, including the PhotoCAL software ($169), which you can find at www.colorvision.com.

RECOMMENDATION: Monitor Calibration Products

Both Monaco Systems and ColorVision calibration kits employ a similar concept for the sensor and software to produce great accuracy, the widest tonal range, and the largest color gamut that's possible with your monitor. Although prices may have dropped by the time you read this, the ColorVision product is likely to remain the more affordable of the two options, and it's also the one I consider the most user friendly.

In addition to the monitor calibration kits that include a colorimeter, you can buy so-called monitor-profiling software that also allows you to profile and calibrate your monitor. The best of these products—such as the DisplayMate (**www.displaymate.com**) software—is more effective than a simple gamma adjustment, but cannot match a colorimeter in terms of creating the most precise and accurate ICC (International Color Consortium) profile or adjusting your computer's display adapter video lookup table (LUT).

After testing the Spyder (with the PhotoCAL software) and the more expensive SpyderPro (with OptiCAL software), I can confirm that both offer great convenience of use as well as exceptional accuracy and consistency. Unless you are a commercial user or graphic designer, the affordable Spyder kit is all you need. The ColorVision product is highly sophisticated and will reward the user with an exceptionally accurate monitor display.

Calibrating with a Sensor and Software

Although calibration is a technically sophisticated and complex process, the actual procedure is straight-forward and takes only 10 minutes. Using a wizard, the software walks you through the procedure, step by step. It works in the following manner:

1. After the monitor has been on for at least 30 minutes, connect the Spyder sensor to your computer with a USB cable (see Figure 9.5).
2. Launch and run the software.
3. Disable Adobe Gamma in your computer so it doesn't interfere with the calibration and profile.
4. For a Windows PC and a Mac, set the target white point to 6500K. Set the target gamma to 2.2 for a Windows PC and 1.8 for Mac; 2.2 is fine for Mac too, but calibrate to 1.8 if you plan to send files to other Mac owners.

Photo Courtesy of ColorVision®

Figure 9.5: Whether you own a CRT or an LCD monitor or both, the calibration process is virtually identical when using a colorimeter that's compatible with both types of monitors.

After you complete all steps, the software makes a variety of adjustments and then generates a profile that is set as the default for your system. If you want to confirm this, follow the steps in the "Using Adobe Gamma for Basic Calibration" section earlier in this chapter. You should repeat the calibration process every month or so.

Working with a Calibrated Monitor

As you start working with your fully reliable monitor, you should find that the display produces substantially greater accuracy in terms of color values. When you make a print, it should closely match the appearance of the monitor image in color rendition and in tonal values. This seems simple enough, but consider the following before you start working with a color-calibrated monitor.

- No matter how thorough your color management system, your prints will not be identical to the image displayed on the monitor, especially prints made on certain types of paper. For example, papers with a soft finish (such as "watercolor" media) produce much softer colors and contrast than your monitor. This is a fact of life and not a problem created by any software or technique.

A print may not exactly match an image in an electronic display for other reasons. The color gamut of a monitor is different from that of a printer. In addition, a monitor emits light, making the image seem luminous, while a print is viewed only by reflected light. The color of light that illuminates a print can affect the appearance of the colors in the print.

- Images that you had adjusted previously—before the monitor calibration—may now appear to be less than ideal in terms of color rendition and brightness. That's because you made the earlier adjustments based on an inaccurate display of the images. You may now need to reopen your original (unmanipulated) image and make entirely new adjustments in your image-editing software.
- After following the printmaking advice provided in subsequent sections in this chapter (and in Chapter 13), you may not be fully satisfied with the color rendition or brightness of your prints. In that case, you'll need to determine whether your monitor or your printer is at fault. To diagnose the problem, I recommend using a standardized target image file with memory colors that you can easily evaluate.

Target image files are available from various sources, including the companion website (www.colorconfidence.com) for Tim Grey's *Color Confidence: The Digital Photographer's Guide to Color Management*. At that site, you can obtain a free download of a highly accurate PhotoDisc target.

- Download a target, open the file in your image editor without converting the colors to your working space, and print the target. Examine the image (of the target) on the monitor and on the print to determine which appears the most accurate. If this process indicates that the monitor is not reliable, recalibrate it, preferably using a colorimeter kit. If the process suggests that your printer is to blame, check your printer settings based on the information presented later in this chapter.

After calibrating your monitor, you can access the color settings in Photoshop or another image editor that supports full color management. In Photoshop on a Windows computer, choose Edit → Color Settings to open the Color Settings dialog box, as shown in Figure 9.6. In Photoshop on a Mac, choose Photoshop → Color Settings or Edit → Color Settings, depending on the operating system you are using, to open the Color Settings dialog box.

Most image-editing software does not provide as full a slate of color options as Photoshop does. If you use another image editor, check the instructions to determine whether the software provides any option other than the typical sRGB color space. Elements 2 provides a limited choice: No Color Management, Limited Color Management -Optimized for Web Graphics, and Full Color Management Optimized for Print. The last named is the most appropriate if you generally make prints from your digital images.

The Color Settings dialog box contains several options, even more if you check the Advanced Mode check box, which is unnecessary if you plan to use my recommended strategy. Although no single group of settings is ideal for everyone, you might want to start with US Prepress Defaults.

If you choose that option, the software selects settings (as shown in Figure 9.6) that work well for printing, including the Adobe RGB (1998) Color Space discussed in Chapter 10. If you

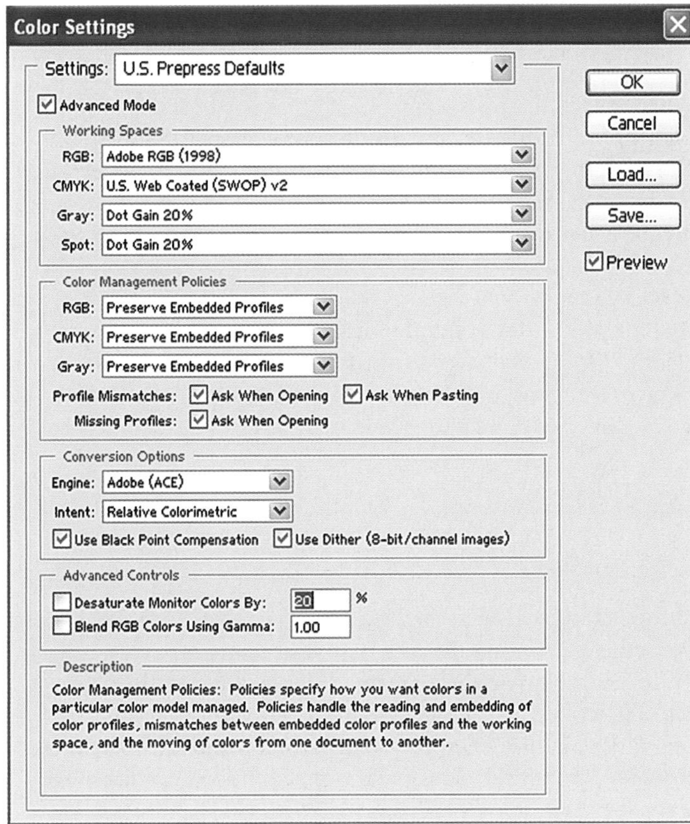

Figure 9.6: The Color Settings dialog box in Photoshop offers a vast range of options, but most users can simply select one of two combinations that are intended for their primary use: printmaking or creating web graphics.

specialize in making images for Internet use, try Web Graphics Defaults as a starting point. When you reach an advanced level in image editing, you'll want to consult one of the Photoshop books for full information on all the numerous Color Settings options as well as the purpose and the value of each.

Digital Camera Considerations

Now that your monitor is calibrated and you're using the most appropriate color settings, it's time to consider issues relating to image capture. When shooting with a digicam, you'll want to make photos that are technically satisfactory, using the techniques and camera settings recommended in Chapters 6 and 7. For the purposes of convenient color management, your images should exhibit suitable color balance, color saturation, exposure, and highlight/shadow detail. If your camera offers a choice of Color Space options, select Adobe RGB; this ensures that your camera's color space will match your image editor's working space.

The images need not be perfect, because you'll want to adjust them with an image editor in any event. Still, it's worth making the effort to optimize the images, in-camera, as part of the control process that will eventually allow you to generate prints of exhibition quality.

Color Managing Your Scanner and Printer

You may have read magazine articles that suggest that your printer and scanner should be calibrated—just as you calibrated the monitor—so they all reflect accurate information based on known standards. If you decide to do so, you can build an ICC custom profile for your scanner and build or buy custom profiles for specific printer/paper combinations. Before spending money on such products, evaluate your level of satisfaction with your scanner as well as your prints.

If you're not happy with the results that your machines produce, start by reviewing the scanning and printing techniques in Chapters 2 and 10; those were based on effective color management. If you still experience difficulties, try some of the problem-solving techniques in the following two sections of this chapter.

Before reading on, be sure that your monitor is calibrated, preferably fully calibrated with a colorimeter. Otherwise, the display will not be an accurate representation of the image data, and you will be compensating for an incorrect display instead of solving any scanner or printer problem.

Scanner Color Management Tips

A high-quality scanner is calibrated to produce good color and tonality (brightness/contrast) when the correct settings are made in the software (see Figure 9.7). As discussed in Chapter 8, a scan is only a starting point, so it need not be perfect; you'll want to enhance and perfect the image in an image editor. Nonetheless, you should find that your scans are at least highly acceptable in color and tonality. If you are experiencing difficulty in making satisfactory scans, try some of the following.

After rereading your scanner's instruction manual as a refresher about the image adjustment controls that are available, review the detailed recommendations in Chapter 8. Visit the scanner manufacturer's website regularly to find any updates to the software; these may produce better results than the earlier software.

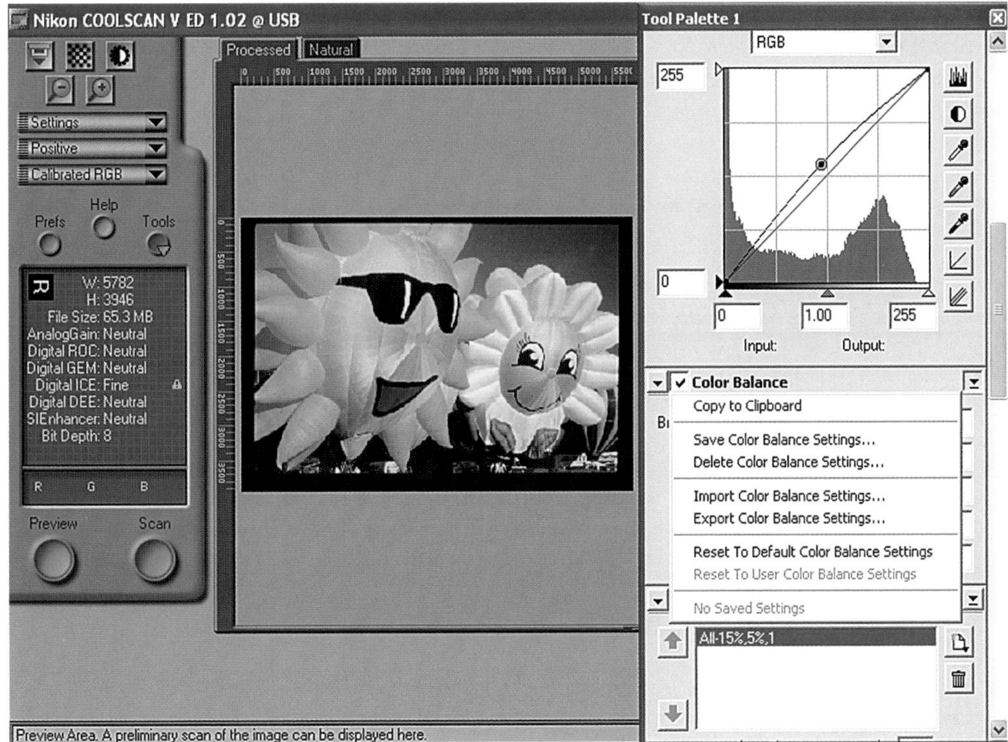

Figure 9.7: Most scanners include software that allows for extensive control over all aspects of the image. The adjustments that you make with this software are part of the color management system.

RECOMMENDATION: Experiment with Scanner Software

The software that's bundled with most scanners provides a variety of options that you can use to generate scans that meet your own needs and expectations. It's worth experimenting with all the features available in the software to determine which produce the effect that you want for any particular image.

For example, Nikon film scanners include a Scanner RGB option, in addition to the commonly recommended Adobe RGB Color Space. Scanner RGB is designed to simulate the results of "no color management" while still allowing you to use all the software tools. If you own a Nikon scanner, you'll find that this can help produce more accurate color for many images. You may also find that it does not often work well for highly saturated images. This is only one example of an option that's worth discovering through creative experimentation; others are mentioned in Chapter 8.

When you first begin using the advanced tools in the scanner software, you may find it difficult to make the optimal corrections for color and tonality. That's because many scanners do not provide a large, high-resolution preview image that would allow for effective evaluation of any adjustments and because image editing software includes more adjustment tools than most scanner software programs. This should not create a serious problem because you're not trying to generate a perfect image at the scanning stage. Instead, use the most advanced scanner software tools to adjust brightness, contrast, and color rendition as necessary, striving for excellent detail in highlights as well as in shadows, and accurate color balance. You might also consider buying third-party scanner software such as SilverFast (www.silverfast.com) that provides outstanding flexibility and control over the adjustments.

If you decide that you simply must build an ICC custom profile for your scanner, consider the MonacoEZcolor software ($299; www.monacosystems.com). The package includes a reflective and transmissive target—a reference required to determine the accuracy of scanned colors—for use with a flatbed scanner. If you want to profile 35mm film scanner, you'll need to buy another target, available on the Monaco website for $40.

Printer Color Management Tips

Just like a high-quality scanner, a printer should produce very good to excellent results using the manufacturer's standard profiles for each type of paper of their own brand. To maximize the potential of your printer, reread the instruction manual to ensure that you are following the recommendations for making the best possible prints. Also check the printer manufacturer's website for any updates on profiles for certain types of paper. An improved profile should ensure that the print will more accurately represent the color values of the image file. Then, follow the recommendations on advanced printmaking in Chapter 10.

If you are still experiencing problems, consider some of the following tips.

Make Printer Software Adjustments

When using certain papers with your printer, you may find that you cannot get a perfect print, even after following all the recommended color management and printing techniques (see Figure 9.8). For example, you may find that your printer produces a slight magenta cast when using high-gloss paper. In that case, adjust the driver software color controls, toward

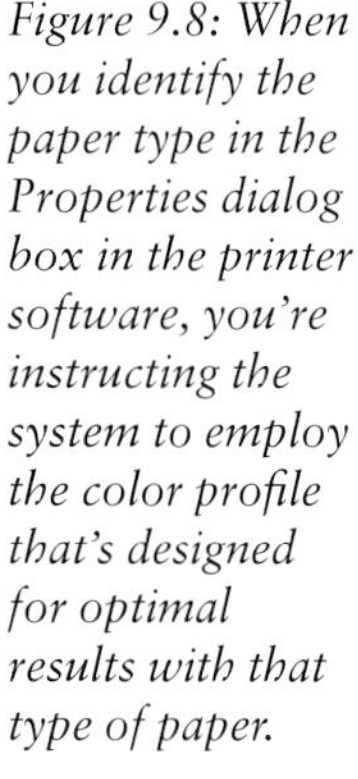

Figure 9.8: When you identify the paper type in the Properties dialog box in the printer software, you're instructing the system to employ the color profile that's designed for optimal results with that type of paper.

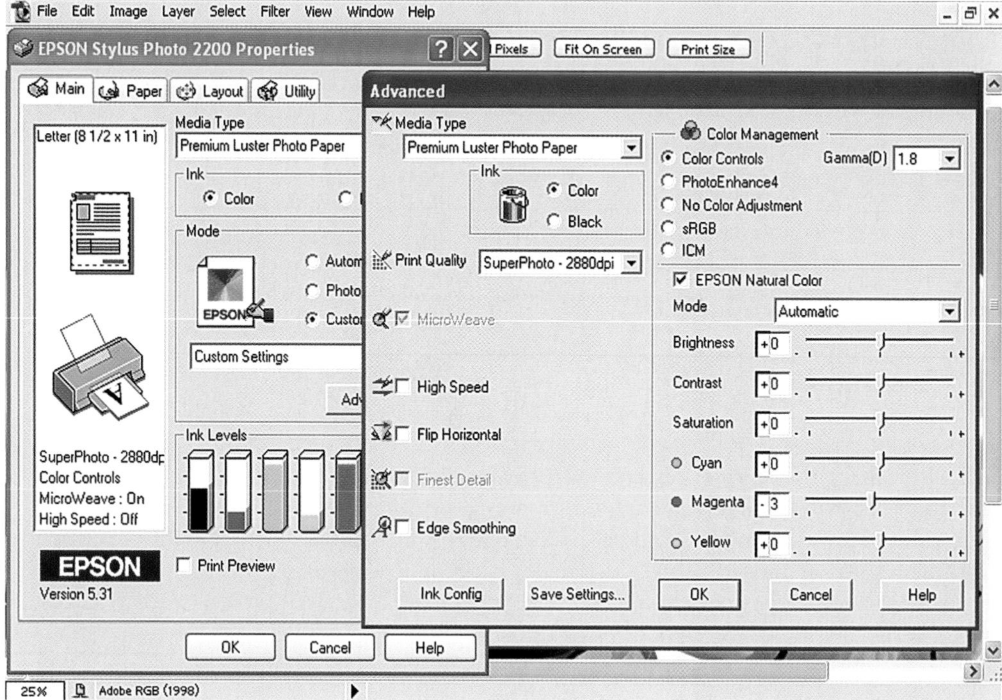

less magenta in this example. To determine the amount of correction that's necessary, make test prints, each at a slightly different adjustment level, using the same paper.

When you discover the adjustment that's required for optimum color quality, simply apply that to all subsequent prints made on the same medium. In most cases, you'll be able to save these settings in the Printer Properties dialog box so the image editor will "remember" them for quick application to subsequent prints.

Make Adjustments in Your Image Editor

The process just described requires experimentation because the printer software does not provide an accurate image preview that lets you judge the extent of any adjustment. Consequently, you might prefer to solve a consistent color-cast problem with your image editor instead, because it allows you to view the effect of any color adjustments on your monitor. Work on a copy of the original image, and retain the unmanipulated file in case you later want to use another printer or send images to others. Most photographers find this approach more intuitive because it allows for a visual evaluation and calls for making fewer test prints.

If you decide to use your image editor for printer-oriented corrections, you can minimize the time required for experimentation by using the Vivid Details Test Strip plug-in software (www.vividdetails.com). This plug-in, discussed in Chapter 12, is an aid to conventional image enhancement, but it can also be useful for determining what color adjustment settings produce the best results with a certain printer/paper combination (see Figure 9.9). You can print a series of the same image—with varying degrees of color adjustment—on a single sheet of paper, allowing you to evaluate the adjustment level that is most effective.

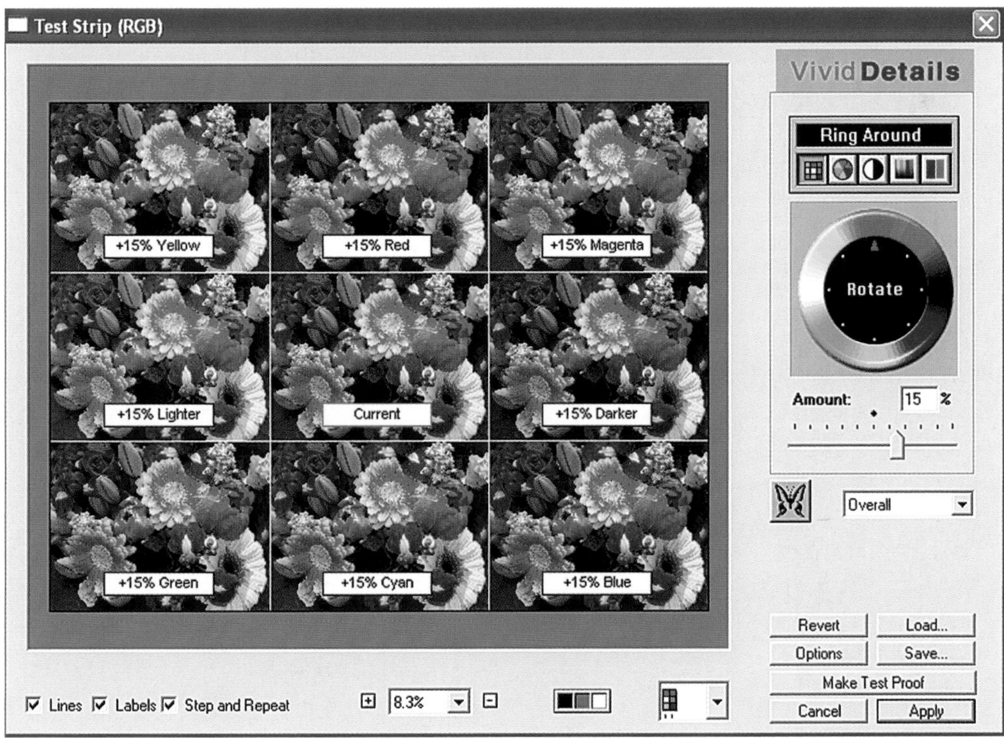

Figure 9.9: The VividDetails Test Strip plug-in is useful for determining the most appropriate color adjustments to use for making the best possible print on any type of paper.

Consider a Custom Profile

If you are simply unable to get excellent prints on certain types of media, you may need a solution for that printer/paper combination. The solution consists of a custom printer profile that describes the color behavior of the printer on a specific paper type. In doing so, it allows the instructions sent to the printer to be modified to produce the most accurate final print (see Figure 9.10).

When using a third-party paper, check the manufacturer's website for a custom profile; a few offer those for at least some of their media. If you use many third-party papers—and if you are not getting satisfactory results with your current techniques—consider buying a product that allows you to make custom profiles for any type of medium. The best products, such as the GretagMacbeth Eye One Photo system (www.gretagmacbeth.com), use a calibrated sensor device, a "spectrophotometer," but at $1500 and up, they're priced above most enthusiasts' budgets.

Before buying any product for creating your own printer profiles, it's worth reading independent reviews on several products on the web. You can usually find several—or excerpts from several reviews—on the manufacturers' websites, but plan to search for others or for the full text of any review that is quoted.

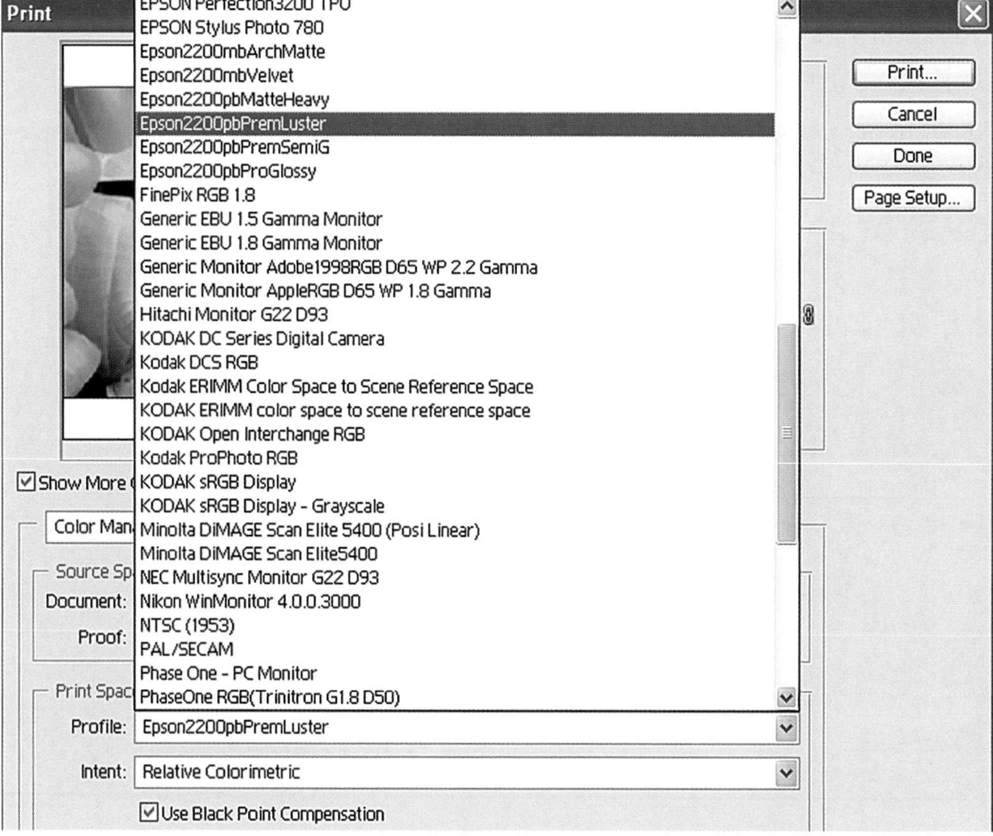

Figure 9.10: If you buy or create custom profiles for several types of paper, be sure that your printer selects the correct profile, by making the designation in the Print With Preview dialog box.

Companies that sell pro-caliber custom profiles, such as ProfileCity (www.profilecity.com), discussed in Chapter 12, use the high-end systems with a spectrophotometer and charge about $100 per profile. Such printer/paper profiles can be excellent, but you'll spend a lot of money if you use many types of media.

Figure 9.11: Designed for creating specific printer/paper printer profiles, PrintFIX differs from most of its competitors by including a special scanner that transmits data about your printer's tendencies to the ColorVision software.

More affordable options are available for making your own profiles, such as MonacoEZcolor ($299) from Monaco Systems, discussed earlier in the "Scanner Color-Management Tips" section. Products of this type may not be the most effective solution because they require that you use a flatbed scanner to read values, and that can introduce variations with data that may not be accurate.

Another similarly priced option, PrintFIX from ColorVision ($329; www.colorvision.com), employs a different approach. This kit includes a "patch reader" device that's used to "measure" (scan) printer calibration targets (see Figure 9.11), sending the resulting data to the ColorVision software. This system eliminates the need for user evaluation and, hence, the potential for user error, but the software is not available for all brands and models of printers. Several experienced reviewers have commented on the ease of use, accuracy, and effectiveness of the PrintFIX system as well as its usefulness for those who want a relatively affordable method for making profiles for many third-party papers.

CHAPTER ten

Introduction to Image Editing

Most digital images—*whether captured with a digital camera or generated by a scanner—are eventually opened in image-editing software. This is the first step to optimizing images in the digital darkroom. The next step can be simple and quick, using automated correction features, or thorough, taking advantage of many tools for fine-tuning all aspects of an image.*

In subsequent chapters, I'll provide specific step-by-step techniques for optimizing the digital image and for making exhibition-grade prints. As a prerequisite, it's essential to consider the issue of the "best" image file formats, how to get your RAW files into those formats, and the purpose and value of specific image-editing tools. These topics are covered in this chapter in detail, with recommendations as to which options are most useful or appropriate. Armed with this knowledge, you can proceed to optimize your images and make beautiful prints as detailed later in Chapters 11 and 13.

Enhancing RAW Image Files

Most prosumer digicams and SLR (Single Lens Reflex) cameras include a RAW capture mode for taking photos that will be recorded as raw data from the sensor, as discussed in Chapter 1. Before they can be opened in an image editor, these files must be converted to the JPEG or TIFF format using special software. Most converters also allow you to change many parameters, before the actual conversion, which is useful for correcting minor or major technical problems (see Figure 10.1.) Experiment with various settings, and watch the change

Figure 10.1: A RAW format file is comparable to the negative in traditional photography in the darkroom because both media allow for substantial image adjustment. Above left is before adjustment, above right is after adjustment.

that each produces to the image in the preview screen. When you are satisfied, click the OK button to apply the data to the file, which is then converted to a familiar image format.

The functions available for image adjustment vary depending on the software that you're using and range from nonexistent to basic to comprehensive (see Figure 10.2). Some cameras are sold with software that can only convert RAW format files; you must pay extra for software that allows for modifying the images before conversion. Fortunately, most camera kits include moderately versatile converter software that offers at least a few options. Using slider controls or selecting from a menu of options, you can change image parameters such as white balance, exposure, color saturation, contrast, and sharpness. You might also be able to select one or more of the following: color space (sRGB or Adobe RGB), noise reduction level, and color bit-depth (8-bit or 16-bit per channel).

The most versatile after-market converters, such as Adobe Camera Raw (www.adobe.com/digitalimag) and certain Phase One C1 products (www.c1dslr.com), include additional utilities for advanced functions such as modifying highlight and shadow detail, more aspects of color, hue, or tint, and gray balance. The Adobe product is particularly versatile, with features such as correction for optical aberrations and darkening at the corners of an image created by the camera's lens, interpolation for increasing image file size, hue and saturation adjustment in individual color channels, and color noise reduction.

But should you plan to use every single option provided by the software manufacturer? Which image parameters should you adjust in the RAW conversion software and to what extent? Which image-enhancing tools can damage the image? And which image parameters should you adjust only in your image-editing software, after converting the RAW file to TIFF? Should you take advantage of an option to increase the image file size with the interpolation system included in the RAW converter?

These and other issues would fill an entire book, especially if explored in a manner specific to each brand of converter software. Instead of trying to cover every facet of this topic, I'll address some of the issues with a step-by-step example of an effective RAW image optimization process, using tools available with most brands of converter software. I'll also provide some comments on the unique tools available in a few converters and make some recommendations as to their usefulness.

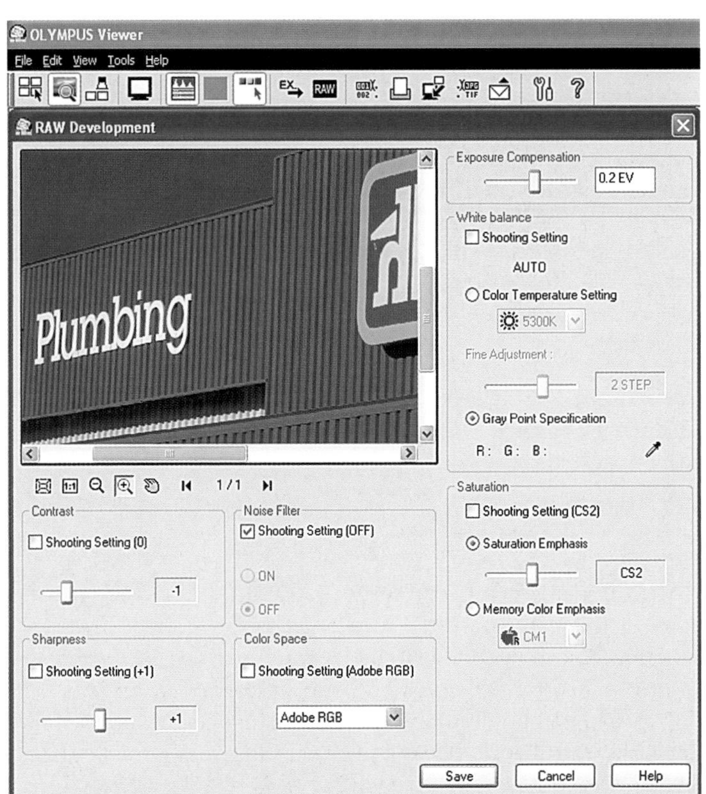

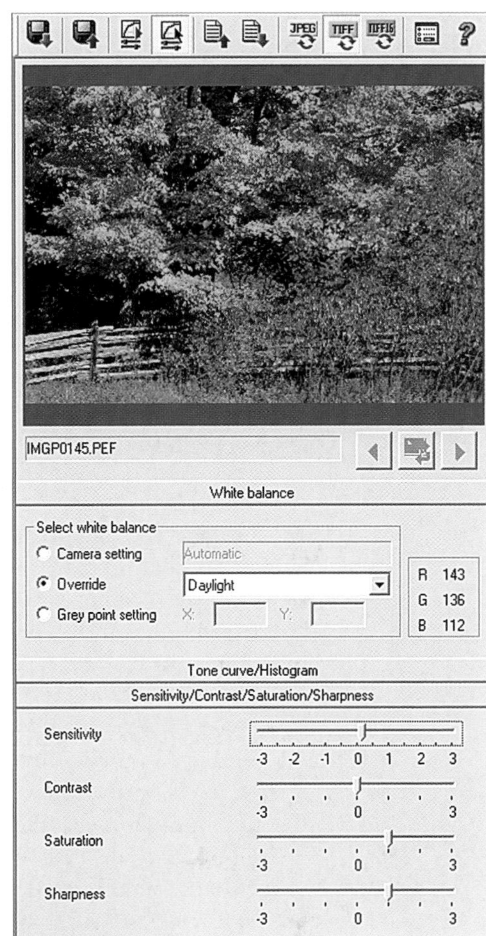

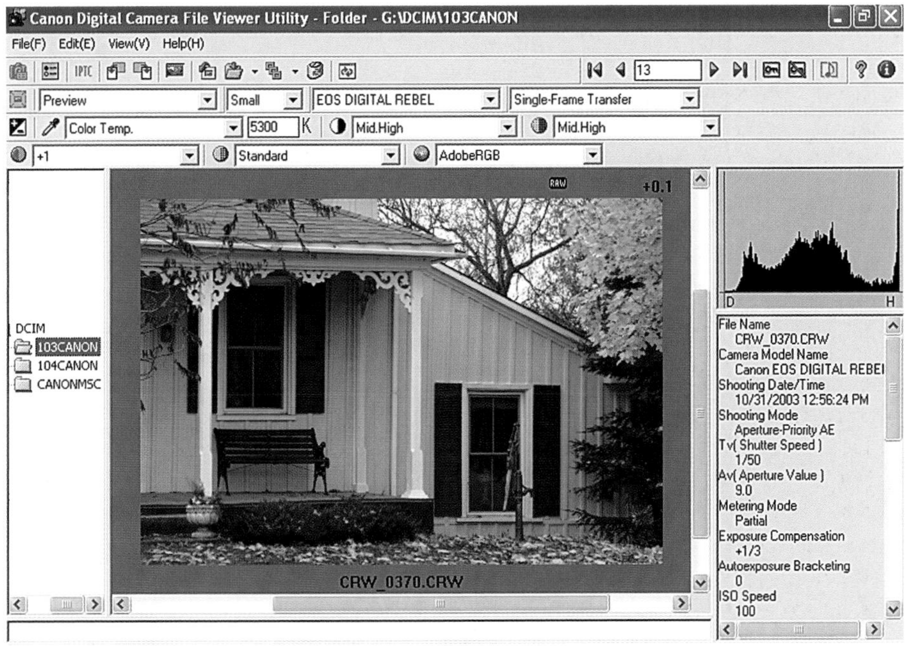

Figure 10.2: The various RAW converter programs use different types of controls but generally allow for adjusting the most important image parameters.

Convert and Adjust RAW Data Files

Just like the various brands of image editors, each brand of converter offers its own set of features and operating procedures. For the purposes of this section, I'll operate on the premise that most of you are using one of the RAW converters bundled with digital cameras.

Although I encourage the use of adjustment features in a RAW converter, the process is not intended for perfecting an image. Think of the converter as a utility that lets you improve certain image parameters so they can be easily fine-tuned in your image-editing software. After opening a RAW image in the converter (see Figure 10.3), try the following step-by-step evaluation and adjustment techniques while experimenting with the converter that you are using.

1. Evaluate the preview image critically for exposure, using the histogram graph as an aid; also check the accuracy of color balance and tone, sharpness of focus, any blurring caused by camera shake or by subject movement, color saturation, and contrast.
2. If your RAW converter includes a zoom or enlarge feature, set it for 100%, or select Large Preview Size. Check essential subject areas for sharpness. If the primary subject is not in focus, or if it is blurred by motion, you might want to move on and start with one of your sharper RAW images. (Although most imaging software includes a sharpening tool, that feature was designed to enhance a sharp image, not to correct inaccurate focus or blurring.)

The preview image in the converter might be a small, low-resolution version of the full data file, so it might exhibit jagged edges at high magnification. As long as edges seem quite sharp otherwise, proceed with this exercise.

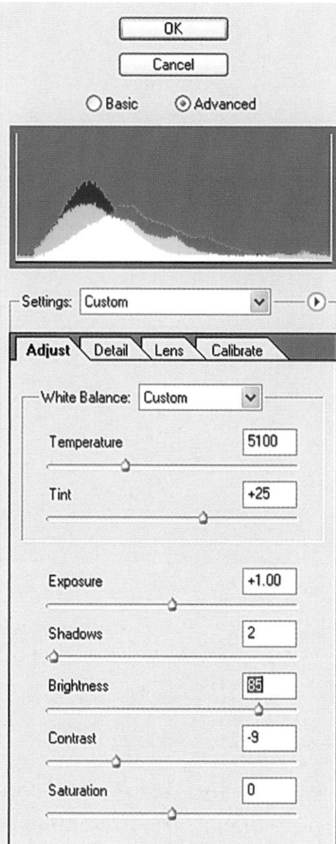

Figure 10.3: If the converter includes a histogram feature, use it to check the exposure before and after making adjustments with the software tools you're using.

RECOMMENDATION: Use "Noise Reduction" Wisely

Some RAW converters automatically apply digital noise reduction, sometimes called smoothness. Designed for reducing or eliminating the color specks that constitute noise (see Figure 10.4), this feature can make images quite soft.

Check your images closely for any digital noise; it should be most visible in shadow areas. If noise is not obvious at 100% magnification, deactivate the noise reduction feature, if your converter allows you to do so. (Some converters do not, and they automatically apply a level of noise reduction that the manufacturer deems appropriate for certain types of images.)

If the converter includes a control for adjusting the level of noise reduction, take advantage of this feature with images that exhibit noise. Experiment with various level settings until you find one that eliminates the most troublesome noise without making the image appear excessively soft. To compensate for any loss of sharpness, plan to apply a suitable level of sharpening later, as in step 9.

3. Reset the zoom to Fit Screen so the entire image is visible in the preview area. Correct any exposure error with the pertinent slider or other tools. Strive to maintain detail in important highlight and shadow areas. If the converter exhibits a histogram feature, confirm that the sliders for black point (on the left side) and for white point (on the right side) are at an appropriate position, as shown in Figure 10.3.

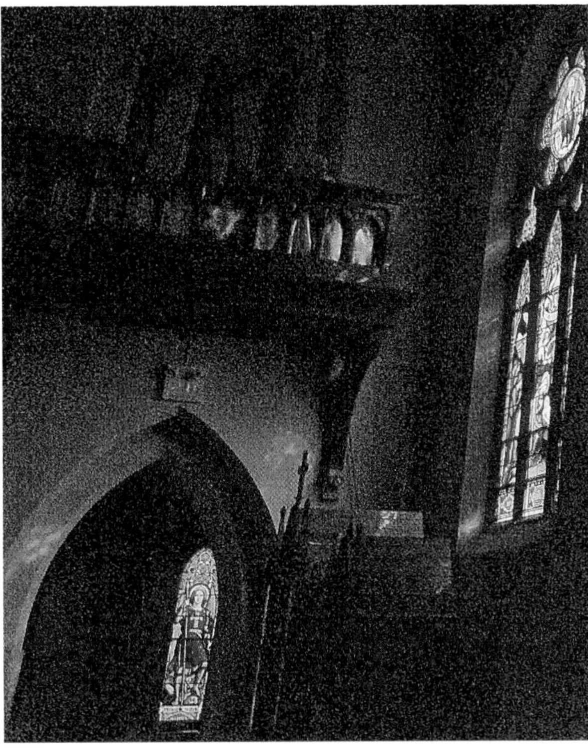

Figure 10.4: Digital noise is most prominent in images made at high ISO or during exposures longer than about a half second.

4. Evaluate the contrast of the preview image. Using the appropriate tool, adjust the contrast until the image looks just right. Because you do not want to sacrifice excessive shadow or highlight detail during conversion, moderately low contrast is preferable to high contrast. It's easy to boost contrast in image-editing software, but lost detail, caused by excessive contrast, can be difficult or impossible to recover.

   If your software includes only specific contrast-level options, select the one that best achieves your intended effect. Check the histogram display, if available. Did increased contrast produce a loss of important detail in highlight and/or shadow areas? If so, you may need to make a further adjustment.
5. While viewing the full preview image, check the color balance. If it seems suitable for the subject, and there is no obvious color cast such as green, magenta, or blue, you may not need to make any correction.

Many experts recommend adjusting color or white balance as the first step in the RAW image-enhancement process. With well-exposed images, you might want to heed that advice. However, if an image is excessively dark or bright, it is preferable to correct the exposure before attempting to make a critical evaluation of color balance.

---

6. Whether the color balance appears correct or not, experiment with some of the available white balance adjustment options. Notice the difference in the image that each produces. One of the settings should be just right for a particular image, unless it was made under unusual lighting conditions, such as sodium vapor lamps in an arena.

   If the converter includes a Color Temperature slider marked in degrees kelvin (see Figure 10.5), you can use it to fine-tune white balance by shifting it toward blue or yellow. The converter software manual should explain the kelvin scale. In a nutshell, high kelvin degrees correspond to cool (blue) light, and low kelvin degrees correspond to warm (yellow) light. Adjust the kelvin control if necessary to correct a blue or a yellow color cast, or use it to exaggerate a warm or cool color balance to meet your own interpretation of a scene.

7. Although a few images will require you to use other color balance tools such as Color Tone, Hue, or Tint, experiment with these features as well to determine the effect they produce.
8. When you are satisfied with the color balance, think about color saturation. The converter should provide a slider or a list of options that you can use to increase or decrease the depth and richness of colors. Avoid excessive color saturation because that can produce an artificial effect and a loss of detail in supersaturated areas.
9. Consider the amount of sharpening that you might apply to the image. The converter software includes a slider for adjusting sharpness or specific sharpness-level options. The default level can produce images that appear artificially sharp. Minimal sharpening is preferable to excessive sharpening, particularly for images that you plan to enhance in an image editor after the conversion. Experiment with your own converter software to determine which setting produces moderate sharpening.

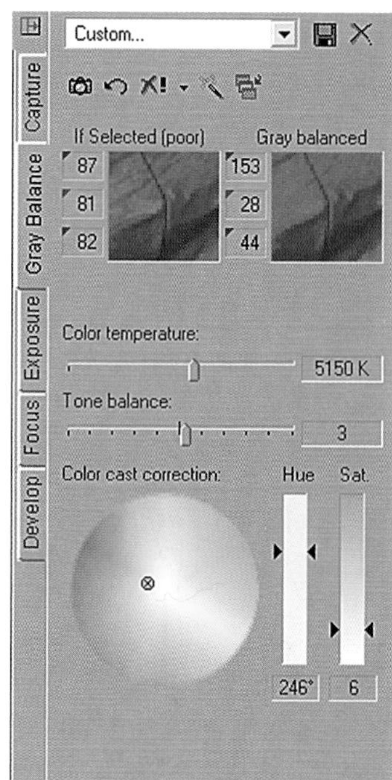

Figure 10.5: Although some converters include only a basic tool for correcting white balance, the more advanced programs offer a wide range of options, including controls for modifying hue, tone, or tint and color "temperature."

Additional Converter Considerations

After you complete these steps, you should be ready to convert the raw data file, preferably to TIFF format. Before doing so, check out any additional control options provided by your RAW converter. At least some of the following are available in several brands of software. Each will call for making a decision; consider my recommendations when deliberating as to the right choice for each option.

Consider batch processing. Some converters let you specify the adjustments that you want to make to all parameters for numerous RAW images. This can be convenient when you want to convert a series of images if their exposure, contrast, color, and all other parameters are quite similar. Adjust the first image, and then let the converter batch correct all the images while you eat lunch.

Some converters, such as the Phase One products, offer another feature that helps to optimize workflow. While the software is converting one or more images from RAW to TIFF format, it allows you to adjust other images.

Select the color space. If the converter includes this option, select Adobe RGB, instead of sRGB, for reasons discussed in Chapter 1.

Select the color depth. Most cameras produce RAW files with 12-bit (per channel) analog-to-digital conversion with extremely high tonal detail and billions of colors. The converter software provides an option to convert the images to 8-bit or 16-bit data. You might want to select 8 bit for two reasons: the image file size is 50% smaller, and most image-editing software do not support 16-bit images.

Photoshop CS provides comprehensive support for 16-bit files. Photoshop 7 offers limited support for 16-bit files, but there are complex methods for taking advantage of the extra color depth for the smoothest gradations and maximum tonal detail; these methods are detailed in some Photoshop books. You can take advantage of 16-bit conversion if you own CS or if you have acquired the expertise required for the complex process of working with 16-bit files in Photoshop 7.

Set the output resolution. Most converters offer an option to set an output resolution, such as 240 or 300 ppi. This feature is provided in RAW converters merely as a convenience, and it does not increase or decrease the actual size of the image that is output. You might want to select the setting that you often use for printing, but you can later change the output resolution in your image-editing software.

Set the output size. Some converters—including Adobe Camera Raw and the professional version of Phase One Capture One DSLR—have options that will increase the size of the image file (see Figure 10.6). If you select one of the increments—perhaps 12 megapixels for an image made with a 6-megapixel camera—the software employs sophisticated algorithms to interpolate the image to the larger size. This feature can be useful if you plan to make oversized prints and will need an image file size that is larger than the "native" output size offered for your camera.

In my tests, the Phase One Capture One DSLR (professional version) and Adobe Camera Raw software produced higher image quality than bicubic interpolation in Photoshop when doubling image file size. If your own RAW converter allows you to increase file size, compare the results that it produces with the results achieved by using bicubic interpolation in image-editing software.

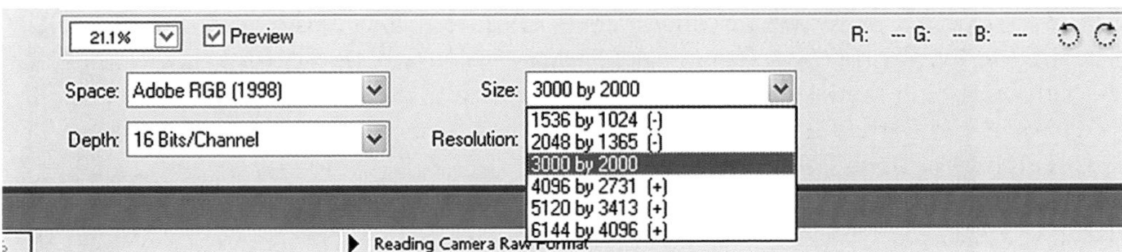

Figure 10.6: If your converter includes an option for increasing the RAW image file size, use this feature for your best images, particularly those that will be printed in large sizes.

File Formats for Image Editing

If you own an advanced image-editing program, you may have noticed that it includes numerous choices for working in various formats and for saving images in those formats (see Figure 10.7). Most are intended for images you plan to use on the Web, for use by printing or publishing companies, or for storing vector drawings, documents, artwork, and so on. Photo and imaging enthusiasts generally use JPEG, TIFF, or a proprietary or "native" format such as Adobe's PSD (Photoshop Document). Consequently, I'll discuss only these options.

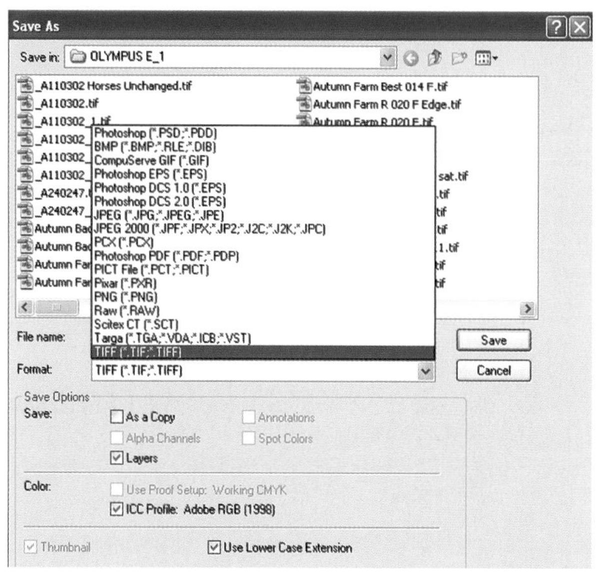

Figure 10.7: Many image-editing programs offer a wide range of options for file formats.

JPEG and TIFF Format

The issue of TIFF versus JPEG format is covered in detail in Chapter 1, so I'll just recap the pros and cons of each mode in this section. Although JPEG is useful for image capture with digital cameras, this format is not recommended for use in image editing because JPEG is lossy: some image data is always lost whenever a file is compressed (see Figure 10.8) and saved as a JPEG after any adjustment in an image editor. More important, the degradation is progressive or cumulative. Each time you modify and resave the file in JPEG format, more data is discarded and quality is further degraded. When you later open the image, the process is reversed; the values are rebuilt from the compressed data, but the subsequent image does not perfectly match the original. The degree of error depends on the degree of compression that was applied.

Although they are not in wide use, two other JPEG formats are worth noting. JPEG 2000 allows for higher compression, with a lossless option for maintaining high image quality, but is not supported by most image editors. Some Kodak digital SLR cameras and digital backs generate ERI (Extended Range Imaging Technology) JPEGs with a wide latitude that allows for substantial exposure and color correction in Photoshop, using a Kodak plug-in module. In this respect, an ERI JPEG is similar to a RAW file. Compression is lossless. Both formats have merit and deserve greater distribution and image-editor support.

Many image editors let you specify the quality that a compressed JPEG file should maintain. The highest quality level produces minimal compression, or a low "compression ratio." Select this option if you must work in JPEG, perhaps while using a laptop with limited storage space. This minimizes the loss of data and the change in the values of the image file.

Figure 10.8: When you modify and save a JPEG image (left), the quality deteriorates. Use the TIFF format (right) to maintain high image quality.

The TIFF format is preferable to JPEG for image editing because it is lossless; virtually no data is lost each time you save an image as a TIFF. This format is also universal: it is compatible with all computer platforms and image-processing applications because it supports most features available in advanced image editors. In Photoshop 7 and CS, the TIFF format supports all functions, including layers, making it an excellent choice for those who own those programs. Finally, a TIFF image can be compressed if desired, employing one or more of the lossless compression utilities discussed in Chapter 12.

Native File Formats

Some image-editing programs offer a proprietary imaging format, also called a native format because it is native to one brand of software. Typical examples include PSD, which is available with Photoshop and Elements 2. Others include CPP (Corel PHOTO-PAINT), UFO (Ulead PhotoImpact), and PSP (Paint Shop Pro). You might decide to use the native format while adjusting the images in the pertinent software.

Working with adjustment layers is an advanced image-editing technique described in Chapter 11. It involves creating special layers that contain instructions for adjusting the image. Because the layer contains no pixels, you can make adjustments without damaging the actual image. While working with a "layered" image, you want keep the layers intact when closing a file, so you can later try different interpretations with your image-editing software. That will call for saving the file in a suitable format, one that supports this feature.

The advantages of a native format depend on the image editor used; review your software owner's manual for specifics. If you own Photoshop 7, CS, or Elements 2, there is no reason to work with the Adobe PSD format because the key features of these programs support the TIFF format. If you are using an earlier version of the Adobe software, you'll need to work in PSD if you want to save a file with adjustment layers intact because you cannot save a "layered" file as a TIFF. (None of the image-editing programs provide layers support in JPEG format.)

Most image editors do not provide any options for reducing the size of a file that you save in the native format. This can create problems when you're working with layers (see Figure 10.9), as discussed in Chapter 11, because the file size can be massive: three, four, or

Figure 10.9: Most of the advanced image editors include a feature for creating adjustment layers. If you want to save layered images, do so in a format that supports layers.

more times larger than a conventional image file. Although Adobe programs automatically apply some slight compression when saving layered PSD files, the files remain large, consuming great amounts of hard-drive storage capacity.

> If you use an image editor's native format, remember this: when sending an image file to others, on a CD perhaps, save it as a TIFF unless the recipient is using an image editor that supports the format that you are using.

Primary Image-Enhancement Tools

Although it is certainly possible to produce some technically excellent digital photos—with a camera or a scanner—that don't require editing, even the best images will benefit from some fine-tuning in an image editor. And even the most accomplished photographers find that some of their images need extensive correction to qualify for the "technically excellent" rating. In the next sections, I'll discuss the tools and other functions that are most valuable for basic image correction and enhancement.

As discussed in Chapter 4, many popular image-editing software programs and at least a dozen others are on the market. Each offers a unique operating procedure and its own specific set of tools and utilities, although certain features are common. I'll discuss the most important editing functions available with most of the programs intended for imaging enthusiasts, as well as some particularly useful features available only with certain programs. The most-affordable and basic programs do not have all these features, so review the instruction manual for the program you are using for information as to its specific utilities, tools, and operating procedures.

Quick Fix Options

Many image-editing programs include several one-click options for automatically correcting certain aspects of an image, as well as simple methods for adjusting the level of correction in some tools. Adobe Photoshop Elements combines many such features into a single utility called Quick Fix (see Figure 10.10). It is intended primarily for those who want all the basic tools in a single palette and do not want to search for frequently needed tools.

When you open an image in Quick Fix (in Elements, choose Image → Enhance → Quick Fix), you'll see two preview screens side by side. This enables you to view the original image as well as the image as it appears after you make any adjustment. If you are not satisfied with an effect, simply click the Undo button to undo the last adjustment. If you change your mind after clicking Undo, you can click Redo to reapply the change. This is a great way to cycle between "before" and "after" versions of the image while deciding whether you want to keep a particular adjustment.

Quick Fix includes Auto Correction tools (discussed in detail later) that you can use to adjust contrast, levels, color rendition, and focus (sharpness). These can be useful, but for greater control, use the sliders to modify brightness, contrast, and color hue/saturation/lightness. You'll also find sliders for Fill Flash, useful for brightening shadow areas, and for Backlighting, which selectively darkens an image. Quick Fix doesn't have a cropping tool, but you can rotate and flip images.

If you are unhappy with the results when closely examining an enlarged image on your monitor, you can click Cancel to return to the original version of the image. You can also cancel all changes that you made in Quick Fix. Close Quick Fix, and then choose Edit → Undo Quick Fix from the menu at the top of the screen.

Although Elements 2 doesn't have the simplest user interface, the Quick Fix utilities make it as easy to use as any of its competitors. Take advantage of the automatic and the convenient features when you first acquire Elements 2 as the first step along the learning

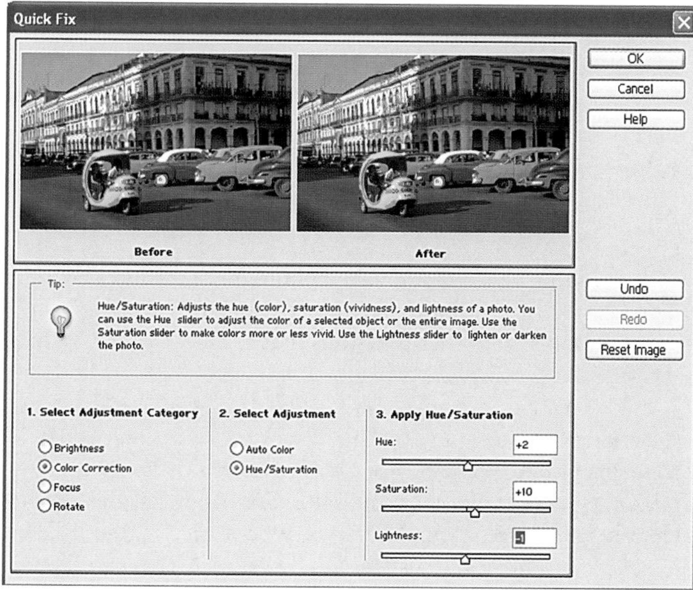

Figure 10.10: The Quick Fix feature in Photoshop Elements 2 was designed for convenient image enhancement.

Figure 10.11: In many advanced image editors, you can access numerous tools and utilities from a single location. In Adobe software, they're in the Adjustments menu.

curve with this extremely versatile image editor. (Several tools available in Quick Fix are discussed in the subsequent sections.) Because Quick Fix is unique to Adobe Photoshop Elements, I'll now discuss some of the image adjustment tools (see Figure 10.11) available with most brands of software, using the Adobe terminology for each. Some other brands use different terminology for tools that achieve the same or a similar effect. If you use Elements 2, you'll notice that several tools discussed in this section are also available in Quick Fix.

Auto Contrast and Brightness/Contrast

Auto Contrast is a simple utility that automatically adjusts contrast by turning the lightest highlights to white and the darkest shadows to black. With many images, this feature increases contrast; that does not create a problem except with images that contain important detail in the bright highlight and/or dark shadow areas.

An easy-to-use and intuitive tool, Brightness/Contrast is useful for making an image brighter or darker overall, with softer or harder contrast. You can achieve the desired effect by moving the two sliders. Brightness/Contrast is intended particularly for those who are not yet ready for the more complex features, and it does work well for overall changes to brightness and contrast.

If you're dissatisfied with the effect produced by Auto Contrast or by any other feature available with any image-editing program, you can click Cancel or Undo to cancel the adjustment. As you'll see later, you can also fine-tune the image after applying an Auto feature by using one of the advanced tools.

Those who are experienced with the more advanced tools scoff at anyone who uses the Brightness/Contrast utility in any image editor. That's unfair, because this utility can be useful for novices, a stage that we must all go through. Before progressing to the advanced adjustment tools, I used Brightness/Contrast often and made some excellent prints from the images. You will probably advance to the other utilities as well, because they provide more versatility and more precise control for greater subtlety of adjustments.

Auto Levels and Levels Adjustment

Auto Levels is another automatic tool available with many image editors. When applied, Auto Levels makes corrections to achieve black tones that are richly dark, whites that are pure white, accurate midtones, and satisfactory image contrast. Depending on the image editor, Auto Levels can also adjust color balance as it modifies the overall image to produce neutral highlights and shadows.

You should find that Auto Levels—particularly the sophisticated versions in the latest high-end programs—is effective with many images. Of all automatic tools, Auto Levels is usually the most effective overall, and it can be a good starting point before making user-selected adjustments. Often, this tool produces a pleasing combination of tonal range, contrast, and color balance. In other cases, Auto Levels can create excessive contrast, a loss of important detail in shadow or highlight areas, and inappropriate color balance. Still, it's always worth a try when you don't have much time for adjusting an image or when you aren't sure how to achieve the best results and are looking for a start in the right direction.

Available with some of the high-end programs, such as full versions of Photoshop, a Fade option allows you to tone down the effect produced by any of the auto correction tools. I find it to be most useful after applying Auto Levels or Auto Color, for gentler contrast or more pleasing color balance. (In Adobe programs, choose Edit → Fade, and change the Opacity setting to achieve the desired result.)

Available in many of the advanced image-editing programs, Levels (see Figure 10.12) is a multifaceted tool. It provides the user with extensive fine control over highlight, midtone, and shadow lightness as well as the overall image contrast. Levels consists of a histogram that offers a scientific guide to the tonal range of the image plus several adjustment controls.

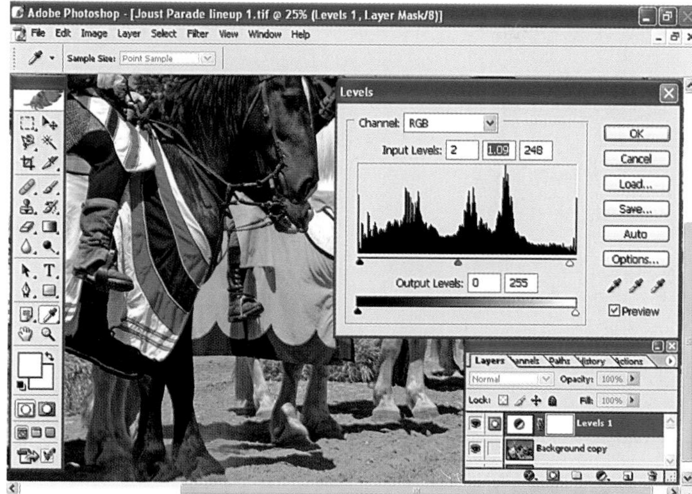

Figure 10.12: Levels is a powerful utility that is not difficult to use. This is often the first advanced feature that novices try, and they generally find its basic operation quite intuitive.

The Levels dialog box generally consists of three sliders below a graph, useful for darkening shadow areas, lightening highlight areas, and darkening or lightening midtone areas. Move a slider, and the image on your monitor changes, allowing for visual evaluation of the effect. (Drag the dialog box to the side of your monitor so it does not cover important image areas.)

To darken the darkest pixels in shadow areas, move the left (black) slider to the right. To lighten the brightest pixels, move the right (white) slider to the left. Both steps affect the midtones to some extent, and they increase image contrast. You can move the central (gray) slider in either direction to lighten or darken midtones in an image, without affecting either shadow or highlight detail. View the changes on your image as you adjust the sliders, and stop when you reach the desired effect.

In some programs, Levels includes a second set of sliders at the bottom of the dialog box, below the Output Levels indicators. You can use these to reduce image contrast, as you'll see in Chapter 11, but such changes are more effective when made with other tools.

In the advanced image editors, Levels offers other features that I have not discussed because they are not essential, can be difficult to use, and can produce unacceptable results when applied without some expertise. For example, Levels lets you adjust individual color channels—Red, Green, and Blue—for even greater fine-control but can produce strange color combinations when used without skill. Levels also offers eye-dropper tools for setting the black, white, and gray points; you might eventually want to experiment with those as you work on becoming an expert.

One of the most significant tools in your image-enhancement arsenal, Levels adjustment is covered in step-by-step detail in Chapter 13 on printmaking. This utility is not difficult to use because you can evaluate the effect of the slightest change in the image on your monitor. Try to avoid the excessive contrast that can occur when you move the black and white sliders too close to the start of the slope in the graph.

If you use Levels with a bit of care, the result should reflect your vision of what is ideal for a particular image in terms of the lightness of the various tones and the overall contrast.

Unique to Photoshop CS is the Shadow/Highlight utility. It allows you to increase detail in both dark and light areas of an image. You can also choose to add midtone contrast without affecting other areas and apply a subtle color correction tool. These functions and others are discussed in Chapters 11 and 13.

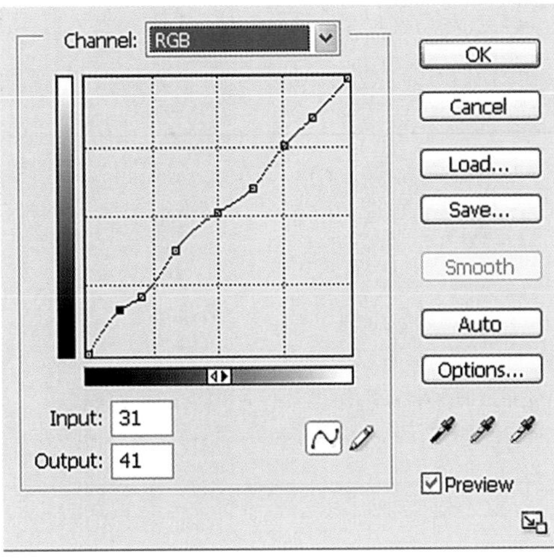

Figure 10.13: The Curves utility is useful for fine-tuning images, with small adjustments to the light and dark areas of an image, as well as to the overall contrast.

The Curves Utility

Although not provided in most of the basic programs or even in Elements 2, Curves (see Figure 10.13) is a utility that is available in Photoshop and other advanced image editors. After you become proficient with the Levels controls for adjusting highlights, shadows, and contrast, you might want to try the Curves utility for fine-tuning contrast and various aspects of brightness. This tool is not nearly as intuitive in operation as Levels and requires some study of the software instruction manual or a good book on image-adjustment techniques.

Curves works by letting you change the brightness of specific tonal values within the image, not just a black, white, and middle tone value as with Levels. Because this is a somewhat complex technique, I'll defer the explanation of using Curves to Chapter 11.

Color Correction Tools

Available in all Photoshop programs, including Elements 2 and some other brands of software, an Auto Color tool automatically corrects a color cast, at least to some extent. In Adobe programs, this tool also adjusts brightness while attempting to remove any color cast by turning grays a truly neutral shade. In some programs, Auto Color adjusts only color rendition. You might want to try this tool to determine whether it produces excellent, satisfactory, or poor results with any particular image.

Although Elements 2 and some of the basic image editors do not include a Color Balance utility, a tool of this type (see Figure 10.14) is common in other programs, sometimes labeled as a tint adjustment control. Operating procedure also differs from one brand to another, but this tool often includes sliders for shifting the balance between red and cyan, green and magenta, and blue and yellow. Use the correct slider to remove an unpleasant color cast.

The Color Balance options are valuable for correcting images with an unattractive color cast or for enhancing images by adding a pleasing color cast. You can correct a green cast, for example, produced by fluorescent lighting, by shifting the balance toward magenta. You can correct a blue cast, perhaps in images made in deep shade, by adding yellow. Add yellow and red, for example, to add a bit of "warmth" to images made in the cool light of midmorning and so on. Although it's worth developing an appreciation for color theory by reading books on image-adjustment techniques, the color correction process is quite intuitive. Experiment with the sliders, and watch the change that each makes to your image; when the effect is pleasing, click the OK or Done button to apply the modification.

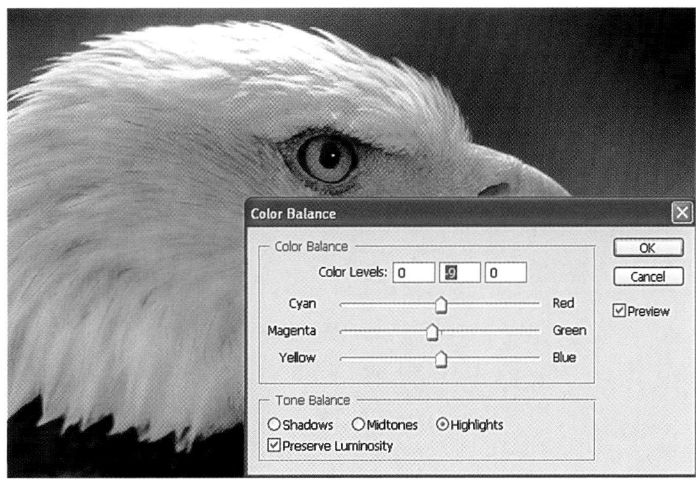

Figure 10.14: You can use a Color Balance utility to correct or emphasize a color cast by subtracting or adding the appropriate color. This image exhibits a green cast and will require a correction toward magenta, the opposite of green.

If your image editor offers a Preserve Luminosity option, be sure that this box is checked. This allows the software to fine-tune the individual color channels to maintain the same perceived brightness for all pixels in your image.

Using a Color Balance or similar utility, you can also adjust individual colors in the highlight, shadow, and midtone areas. This is useful when the amount of adjustment needed in each area varies. For example, in an image of fall colors, you might want to add yellow to the midtone leaves, but you might not want to adjust the color balance of dark tree trunks or the bright reflections from the surface of a pond. Do take advantage of this feature if it's available with the software you own.

Correcting color balance is easy when you know what color should be added or subtracted to eliminate a color cast or to add a color cast. Watch the image changing as you move the sliders, and stop when the effect is just right. On the other hand, this process can sometimes be far from simple. In images made under mixed lighting, or in images made under unusual lighting as in an arena, it's difficult to know which colors to adjust. Experiment or try one of the options discussed in the following sections.

Color Variations

If your image editor includes a Color Variations utility, take advantage of this feature for guiding your decision on the right color—and the amount of that color—to add or subtract in order to achieve a pleasing color balance. If you access the Variations utility (Photoshop's is shown in Figure 10.15), you can see thumbnails that depict your image and other samples, with increased and decreased red, green, and blue. Look for other options too, such as controls for adjusting color balance only in shadow, highlight, or midtone areas and the Color Saturation tool.

The Variations utility makes sense in theory, and some photographers use it to guide their decision on color balance corrections. In my own experience, this utility is not very useful for that purpose, but it is great for learning about color balance and the effects that you can achieve by adding or subtracting certain colors.

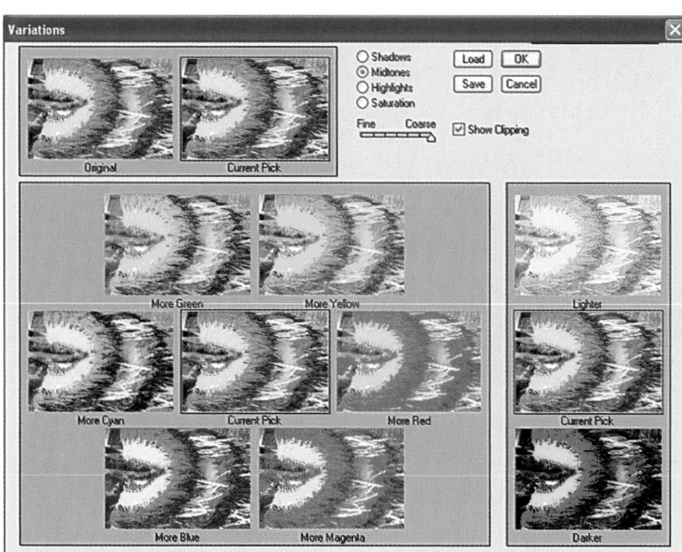

Figure 10.15: Some photographers find the Variations utility useful for correcting color balance. Others consider it most valuable for developing an understanding of color correction concepts.

The problem with Variations? The thumbnails that are displayed are too small, making it difficult to decide on the ideal thumbnail, the tiny image with just the right color adjustment. I also find that the options are limiting and that the intensity level adjustments are not very precise. I recommend VividDetails Test Strip instead (www.vividdetails.com); this Photoshop plug-in uses a similar concept as discussed in Chapters 4 and 12, but it is far more intuitive, effective, and versatile.

Hue/Saturation Utility

Available with most brands of image-editing software, a Hue/Saturation utility lets you increase or decrease the color depth or richness and shift color values (hue). Some image editors also include a Lighten control that lets you darken or lighten all colors or merely adjust one or more individual colors (see Figure 10.16). Entry-level image editors generally include only a simple saturation adjustment with a slider for intensity control.

With a sophisticated Hue/Saturation utility, you can intensify or moderate, lighten, or darken the richness of all colors or of only certain colors. Adjusting colors individually lets you achieve professional-caliber effects, without simply changing all colors to the same extent.

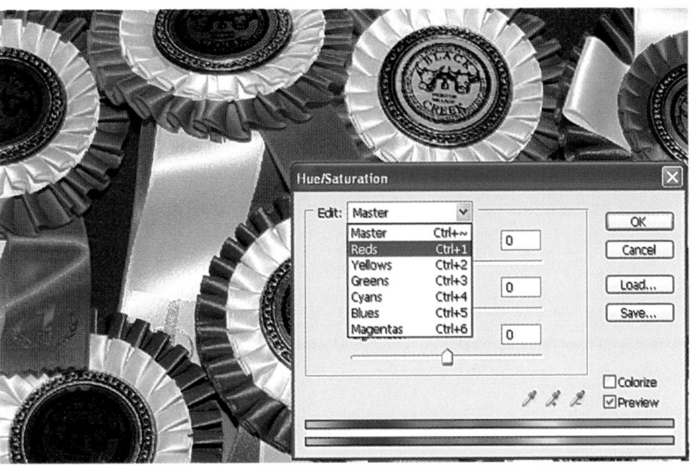

Figure 10.16: Many digital images benefit from a slight increase in color saturation. If your image editor allows, plan to adjust individual colors instead of boosting saturation for the entire image.

Some programs include eyedropper tools in Hue/Saturation for further refining the range of colors with even more precise control. It's not essential, but you might try experimenting with the "normal" eyedropper if available in your image editor. If you click a color in your image, the adjustments affect only that range of colors centered on the color you identified in the image. Try the "plus" and "minus" eyedroppers to add or subtract colors to the range that is affected by the controls.

When adjusting color saturation and lightness, strive for a natural effect, and one that is appropriate for a specific type of subject. Boosting color saturation to an excessive level can cause a loss of detail in highly saturated areas as well as colors that look artificial.

The Hue control is used to shift all color values in an image. This can be useful occasionally for adding a color cast or for fine-tuning the image when you adjust a small range of colors. You can also use the Hue control to create wild color effects that are applied to the entire image.

Unsharp Mask Filter

Discussed in great detail in Chapter 13, the Unsharp Mask (USM) filter is available in many image editors. Entry-level programs often provide only automatically applied levels of sharpening, but advanced programs offer full control over the extent of sharpening. A full USM control system (see Figure 10.17) is far more versatile than one of the automated Focus or Sharpen tools. Typically, a full USM utility lets you set three parameters for precise control over the extent of sharpening.

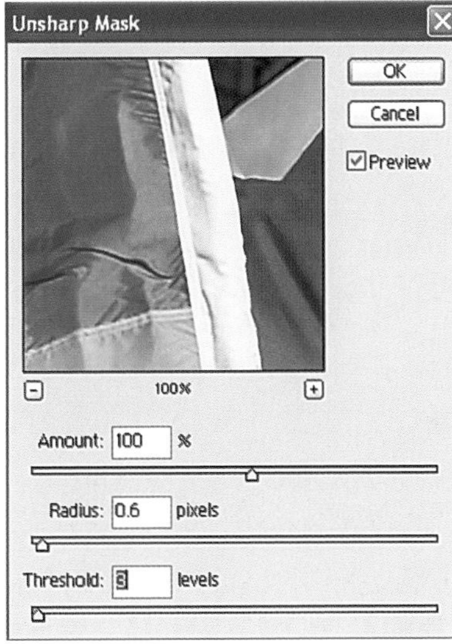

Figure 10.17: In most image editors, Unsharp Mask is the only sharpening tool that offers user-selectable settings for controlling several aspects of sharpening.

Why Is It Called "Unsharp" Mask?

Despite its unusual name, USM is indeed a sharpening tool. The term *Unsharp Mask* derives from an advanced technique used in the traditional darkroom for printing from color slides. The technique calls for making an out-of-focus copy (or "mask") of a slide and sandwiching both pieces of film in an enlarger's film holder. The process enhances the contrast of prominent edges without affecting the contrast of other subject areas and produces a print that appears to be sharper. The Unsharp Mask feature in image-editing software works in a similar manner, by digitally exaggerating the contrast between pixels and subject edges of highest contrast. The resulting image exhibits an illusion of greater overall sharpness.

Select the USM filter to open a dialog box in which you can set the Amount (in percentage), Radius (in pixels), and Threshold (in levels). The Amount setting determines the intensity of the heightened contrast. The Radius setting determines the size of the area the heightened contrast will cover. Low Radius values (0.5 to 1.0) are best for images with high detail, and higher Radius values (1.5 to 2.5) are best for images with relatively low detail. Threshold operates primarily as "noise control," allowing you to prevent the software from sharpening areas of minimal contrast, such as various tones in the sky or in people's faces.

The settings that you make for each variable control the extent of heightened contrast and apparent sharpness. You might need to experiment to find the right combination of settings for any image. For tips on USM settings that you might use as a starting point when optimizing an image for printing, review the pertinent section of Chapter 13.

Additional Sharpening Tools

Some image-editing programs, including those from Adobe, have additional sharpening options (see Figure 10.18). When these options are selected, the software applies a predefined level of adjustment; no user control is available. In Adobe programs, you'll find the following:

- Sharpen increases overall contrast but sharpens all parts of an image, including those that do not benefit from sharpening, such as flesh tones.
- Sharpen More simply applies a stronger effect.
- Sharpen Edges is more useful, because it exaggerates contrast only along distinct edges within an image.

As discussed in Chapter 4, you can also use other sharpening filters, available as Photoshop plug-ins from third-party manufacturers. Some of these products are also compatible with Elements 2 and certain other brands of image-editing software. (Check the distributors' websites for compatibility information.) The best of these filters employ a complex, multistep process that simulates the steps taken by Photoshop experts for professional-caliber sharpening.

Although it's tempting to use the "automatic" sharpening tools because of their simplicity, the Unsharp Mask filter is a far more powerful tool. In addition to producing sharpness that appears more natural, Unsharp Mask allows for fine control, in minute increments, over the sharpening effect. Occasionally, you may find that the Sharpen Edges tool achieves a desired effect; experiment with that option.

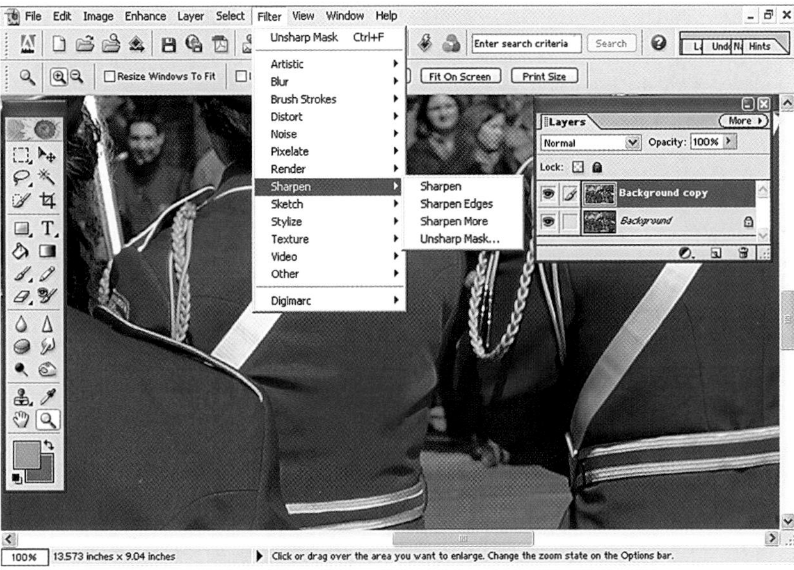

Figure 10.18: All the Adobe image editors and some other brands of software offer additional sharpening tools, but they're not as powerful as USM.

Cloning and Healing Brushes

Useful for covering up dust specks and other small defects—as well as distracting elements such as a TV antenna in a distant sky—a cloning tool or brush is available in most image-editing software. Cloning lets you take pixels from an unblemished "sample" area—a clean stretch of sky, for example—to cover defects in another area of the same color, brightness, texture, and so on.

Available only in Photoshop 7 and CS, the Healing Brush tool (see Figure 10.19) is worth noting. It is similar in concept to the cloning tool but offers a significant advantage. When you paint pixels from a sampled area onto an area with some defect, this tool copies texture from the sampled area, but maintains the lighting, tone, color, and shading of the new area. That makes the Healing Brush particularly useful for retouching portraits, for example. Use it to remove blemishes, wrinkles, and so on while creating a seamless blend: maintaining the integrity of the skin tones as well as the lighting.

A cloning brush is a multipurpose tool, and it's one of the most valuable image-editing features. It can solve problems that were difficult, time consuming, and sometimes impossible to solve with traditional photographic methods. The process is quite simple and quick, at least in its basic application. Even novices find that they can easily correct small defects effectively after a few minutes of practice.

Correcting larger areas or removing entire subject elements (such as a stop sign against foliage) calls for substantially greater expertise and a commitment of time for pro caliber results. Although the process can be frustrating, persevere; you will begin to produce retouching that appears invisible even in oversized prints. Work slowly and carefully, with maximum precision. Should you make an error, simply click Cancel, Undo, or Step Backward to undo the last step; some programs allow you to undo many previous cloning steps.

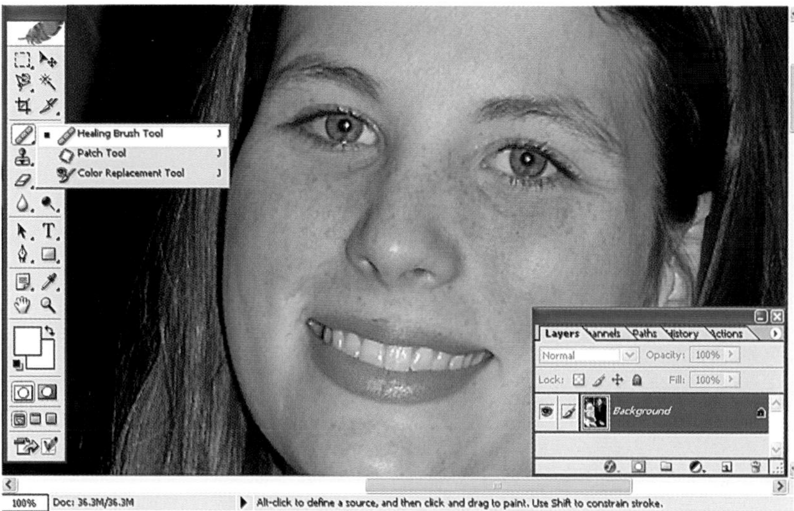

Figure 10.19: Photoshop (shown here) and most image editors include a cloning tool and red-eye removal brush, but the pro-caliber programs usually offer one or more additional options for repairing image defects.

Red-Eye Correction Tool

Many image editors include some tool for eliminating red-eye. Similar in some respects to a cloning tool, a red-eye correction tool (see Figure 10.20) affects only red areas, useful for removing red-eye in photos of people and animals. The specific operation of this tool differs from one brand of software to another but is usually quite simple and effective. For the best results, zoom in close on the eye; take care to "paint" only within the area directly affected by the red-eye; do not allow the brush to stray onto the iris of the eye.

> Photoshop CS does not include a red-eye correction tool, but it includes a new option that can be used for the same purpose. Color Replacement lets you correct red-eye by setting the mode to Color in the Options bar and the foreground color to black. From this point on, Color Replacement operates in much the same manner as the Red-Eye brush in Elements.

Other Image-Enhancement Tools

You can find many other useful utilities in advanced and pro-caliber programs. Some of these are discussed in Chapter 11, but most are beyond the scope of this book; they are well covered in books that specialize in certain brands of software such as Adobe Photoshop. Here's a quick look at a few of my favorites:

The Channel Mixer has several applications, but is most useful for converting color images to black and white. The Desaturate (in Photoshop) and Remove Color (in Elements 2) tools can also be used to convert images from color to monochrome; this is a quick and

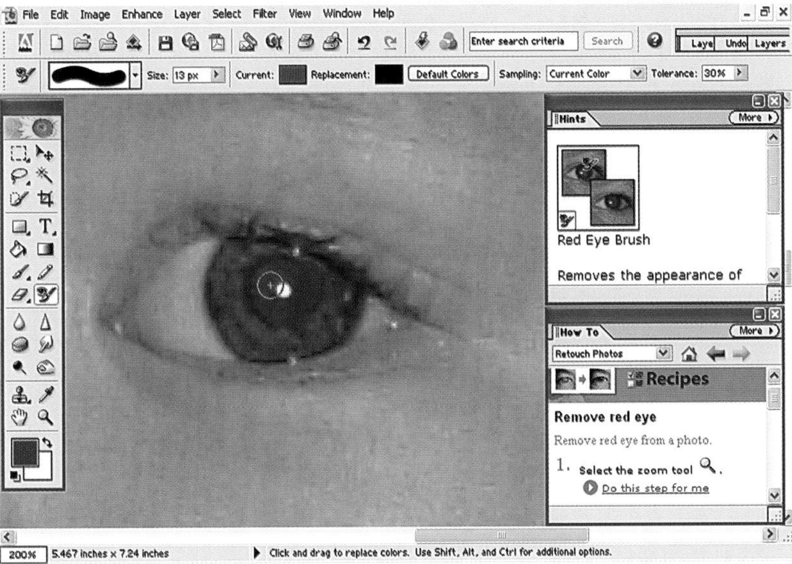

Figure 10.20: One of the most useful tools for correcting image defects, a red-eye brush is standard in many current image editors, but is not available in some of the professional caliber programs.

simple process used by novices who want black-and-white images quickly. These features are discussed in other chapters.

You'll also find some advanced tools that I will not discuss in this book. The Dodge and Burn tools let you selectively lighten or darken small areas of an image, and the Erase tool lets you erase certain types of image defects. Selection tools such as the Magic Wand and Lasso are useful for designating specific areas of an image such as the sky, a distracting road sign, and so on. After making a designation, you can apply any correction tool or filter to change only the specified image area.

Many filters are also available in some image editors and vary from brand to brand. Filters were designed for creating artistic or stylistic effects and for problem solving: digital noise removal, blurring to soften distracting areas in an image, dust and scratch removal in old photos, and more. The new Photoshop CS offers a vast range of options in Photo Filter (technically an adjustment layer) such as warming, cooling, and applying a specific color cast to your image.

CHAPTER eleven

Advanced Image Editing

If you've been reading this book *chapter by chapter, you've learned about color management and essential image-adjustment tools, plus techniques for using some of those tools and options. In this chapter, you'll find advanced image-editing techniques that will allow you to perfect your images for high-quality prints and other purposes. I'll include step-by-step instructions for use while experimenting with certain features. None of these is simple, especially when used in an advanced manner. That's why I'll also provide exercises that you can use for practicing with your own images; these will also clarify any complex concepts and help you appreciate the value of going beyond the basics in image editing.*

Enhancing Photos with Image-Editing Software

Whether you captured images with a digital camera or a scanner, and regardless of the capture mode, save your files in the TIFF format before you begin adjusting them in image-editing software. As discussed in Chapter 10, you might prefer to save files in the image-editor's proprietary "native" format instead, for some specific reason. In either case, you are now ready to begin adjusting and enhancing the photos using image-editing software.

I will assume you are using Photoshop or Elements 2 because so many people own one of those programs, and explaining the steps for each brand of image editor would make this chapter cumbersome. If you are using another advanced image editor, the specific steps might be different, but the editing concepts and techniques still apply. Review your software owner's manual as to the availability of features and specifics on how to find and apply each tool and utility.

Figure 11.1: When working with adjustment layers, you can access most image-editor features with one of the icons in the Layers palette.

Using Adjustment Layers

Before covering image adjustment and enhancement steps, it's important to consider an issue raised in the last chapter: the use of adjustment layers to modify many aspects of an image (see Figure 11.1).

Most people new to image editing make all their adjustments directly to the image file. Each adjustment affects the pixels, causing a loss of detail and degrading the integrity of the image. This can create a problem with images that require many adjustments because the damage is cumulative.

By creating adjustment layers, you can make changes to an image without cumulative damage to the actual pixels. Simply adjust the *layers*, modifying exposure, color balance, saturation, contrast, and other image parameters (see Figure 11.2). When you achieve the desired effects, the changes are effectively applied, once, to the pixels that make up the actual image. This method ensures that full data is retained in the original pixels.

All Photoshop image editors, including Elements 2, as well as Jasc Paint Shop Pro, support multiple layers within a single image file. Pro-caliber layers techniques are beyond the scope of this book, but using Adjustment layers deserves full consideration.

In addition to using Adjustment layers with masking so they affect only certain areas of an image, you can also adjust individual areas of an image by splitting each of those areas into an individual layer. For example, let's assume you have a picture of a person standing on the beach with a sunset in the background. You can select the sky and copy that selection to a new layer. Then copy the person to a new layer, and finally copy the beach and ocean to a new layer. You can then target adjustments to each of these layers individually, exercising tremendous control over the final image.

RECOMMENDATION: Adjustment Layers

Creating adjustment layers is not a prerequisite for image enhancement, and you can certainly work on the actual pixels in your image if you prefer to do so. Many image-editing programs do not even provide a facility for working with layers. But if you are an imaging enthusiast, and if your image editor supports layers, take the plunge now. Begin experimenting with this valuable option as one of the steps along the learning curve in becoming proficient in the digital darkroom.

Admittedly, the creation and use of adjustment layers can complicate the entire image-editing process, frequently adding an extra step that is not actually required for adjusting any image parameter. Working with adjustment layers will seem tedious at first, but after a few hours, you'll find that the process becomes second nature. Without even thinking about it, you'll automatically create a new layer when it is appropriate.

Think of the extra learning and experimentation time as an investment, one that will pay dividends by providing the ultimate in flexibility and control for you, the photographer. You will be able to fine-tune your images to produce exactly what you envisioned when you pressed the shutter release button. In your digital darkroom, you'll be able to try many possible interpretations of an image without damaging any pixels. If you save an image with your layers intact, you can return to it days later to make further adjustments without a loss of quality.

If you are not yet ready to begin using adjustment layers to optimize your images, flip ahead a few pages to the section "Adjusting Essential Image Parameters." Should you decide to do so, consider this final recommendation: Create a copy of your best images; rename the copies, and work only on the copies when making adjustments. Retain the original images for future access. Eventually, you will be ready to start experimenting with adjustment layers, and you will appreciate the ability to return to the original, unmanipulated image files.

Understanding Adjustment Layers

Before moving on to consider specifics about adjustment layers and the pertinent techniques, it is important to appreciate the broad concept of layers. The following analogy can be helpful in this process. Let's say you want to create a cartoon that includes a jungle setting and two characters. Start by painting the background on canvas. (Think of this as an original photograph.) While the background is drying, paint the first character on a sheet of transparent acetate, and paint the second character on another sheet. (These individual sheets of acetate are like the individual layers in a digital image, as discussed in the next section.)

No matter how many new layers you drop onto the "set" (the oil painting), the background will never be changed or damaged. In fact, if you want to change something in the underlying background—perhaps remove a branch from a tree—you can do so on another sheet of acetate; simply replace the branch with clear sky, for example.

If you want a "warmer" effect for your scene, to simulate

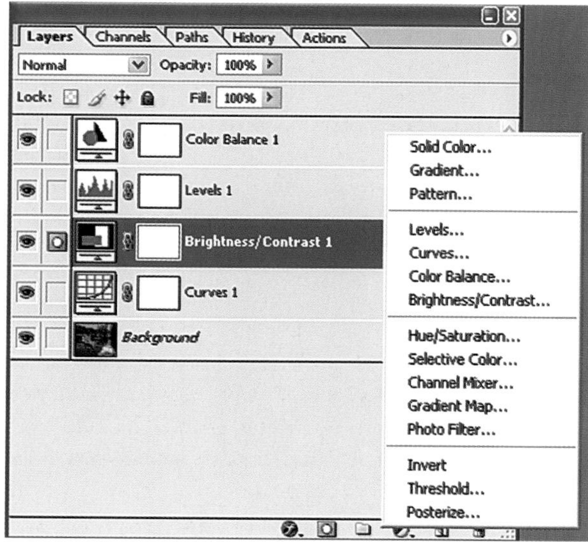

Figure 11.2: Image editors that support layers generally let you create multiple adjustment layers: at least one for each of the tools that can be used with layers.

sunset, simply add an acetate sheet with a pale orange tone. Don't worry about making a serious mistake during the adjustment process, because you will damage only a single sheet of acetate; simply discard that layer and start with a fresh layer.

The orange "warming" acetate sheet in the analogy simulates an adjustment layer in image-editing software. However, the software is far more powerful because it offers substantially more options for adjusting an image. Although an adjustment layer is not actually a "filter" like an acetate sheet, the analogy is appropriate. The software lets you make adjustments by adding additional layers to a single "document" to modify many aspects of a digital image, without changing or damaging the underlying image.

Eventually, all the elements will look just right, and you will compress all the layers into the background, creating the final cartoon. In the same manner, you can compress the adjustment layers in a digital image.

An adjustment layer (in image-editing software) is actually a set of instructions about which adjustments to apply to the underlying image layers. Instead of containing pixels, an adjustment layer contains instructions on how the software is to change the underlying image layers. For example, you can create several adjustment layers, each stacked on top of the others, above the underlying background image, as shown in Figure 11.3.

For example, you might create one adjustment layer to reduce contrast. You might then create a second adjustment layer to increase color saturation. After you complete a desired change to the adjustment layer, it affects any underlying layers. The image on your monitor changes to reflect the modification but only as a preview, because the pixels in the actual image have not yet been permanently changed.

That's a valuable aspect of working with adjustment layers. Let's say that you increased color saturation to an excessive level, producing a loss of important detail in a supersaturated area. That information is not permanently lost; you can return to the color saturation adjustment layer and change the settings to produce a more pleasing effect. You can also eliminate any adjustment layer and simply create a new layer for making your modifications.

It is even possible to "mask" an adjustment layer so that it applies only to certain areas of the image. This highly advanced technique, described in Photoshop books, provides great flexibility in optimizing your images. If the sky is too bright, darken only the sky. If the shadow areas need a color balance adjustment, target the adjustment to only those areas.

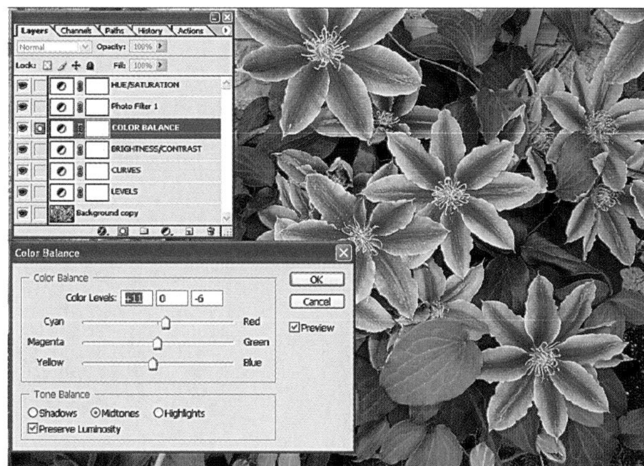

Figure 11.3: In this illustration, the background has six adjustment layers stacked above it. Separating your edits into adjustment layers makes it easy to return to any layer to make changes—to color balance in this case (the image on the right).

In Photoshop programs, you'll want to create an adjustment layer—or several adjustment layers as needed for multiple image adjustment steps—if you plan to use certain of the utilities discussed in this chapter. If you are using Elements 2, you will generally want to work with adjustment layers for modifying levels, brightness/contrast, and hue/saturation. The full versions of Photoshop add support for other valuable utilities, including the Channel Mixer (discussed in Chapter 12), Curves, Color Balance, and others.

Making Image Adjustments on a Layered File

Before actually adjusting and enhancing images, it's worth practicing with adjustment layers. If you become familiar with the process, it will become second nature to you. For the purpose of this exercise, open an image and enlarge it so that it fills your monitor screen. To work with adjustment layers, open the Layers palette in Elements 2 or Photoshop. If it does not already appear on your monitor, choose Window → Layers. You'll notice that the palette contains a thumbnail of the image (see Figure 11.4).

Now, you're ready to experiment with adjusting an image using layers. Open an image file and follow these steps. Watch the image change on your monitor as you apply each adjustment.

The full use of the image adjustment utilities is discussed in detail later in this chapter. For now, just experiment with them quickly, as part of the familiarization process for working with layers.

---

1. Click the Create New Fill Or Adjustment Layer icon (a half-black/half-white circle) at the bottom of the Layers palette to open a pop-up list.
2. From the list, select Levels, a utility for adjusting shadow, highlight, and midtone brightness, in order to open the Levels dialog box.
3. If the Levels dialog box is blocking important image details, move it to a corner of the monitor, by dragging its title bar. Make some changes and click OK to apply the modification to this first adjustment layer.
4. To create a second layer, this time for hue/saturation, click the Create New Fill Or Adjustment Layer icon to open the pop-up list as shown in Figure 11.5.
5. Click Hue/Saturation to open the Hue/Saturation dialog box.

Figure 11.4: The original image becomes the background image in the Layers palette when an Adjustment layer is created.

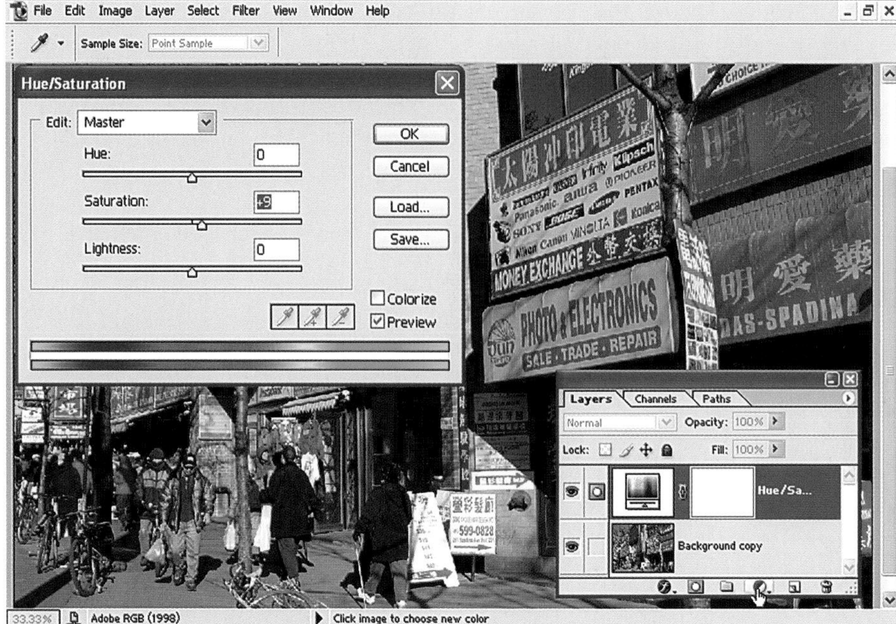

Figure 11.5: As you work with the various utilities while using Adjustment layers, you'll find that they operate in the same way as they do when you make changes directly to an image.

6. Move the slider to increase color saturation, and click OK to apply the modification to this adjustment layer.
7. Create another adjustment layer, and use it to fine-tune brightness/contrast. If you are using a full version of Photoshop, you might want to select Curves instead of Brightness/Contrast.
8. Let's say that you're not happy with the levels adjustment you made earlier, scroll through the various adjustment layer "thumbnails" in the Layers palette to find one that indicates levels. Double-click its thumbnail to open the Levels dialog box; note that the settings are exactly where you left them with the previous adjustment. Make a slight change in levels.
8. Let's say you decide that the color saturation is completely unsatisfactory, find the previous layer for this adjustment and delete the Hue/Saturation layer. (To delete a layer, drag it to the trashcan icon at the bottom of the Layers palette.) Now, you can create a new Hue/ Saturation adjustment layer and make the desired intensity settings.

Preparing the Layered File for Printing

After making all the desired modification to the adjustment layers, you might decide to apply the changes to the actual image before making a print. Follow these steps:

1. Save the layered image with all the adjustment layers intact, to serve as your master image file. If your image editor does not support layers in TIFF, save the layered file in the image editor's native format.
2. If your image-editing software (such as Photoshop) supports a Duplicate command, use it to create a working copy of the original, and close the original. (In Photoshop, choose Image → Duplicate.) If you don't have such a command, save a copy of the file by choosing File → Save As, and use this as your working file. Assign a new name to

the file, appending the word *copy* to remind you that this is your working copy of the image file. No matter what you do to this copy, you can always return to the master image, with all its layers intact. This precaution will let you change various image parameters in the future by modifying or deleting any layer.

3. You might now decide to "flatten" the working image file by merging the layers. To do so, choose Layer → Flatten Image a prudent step if you plan to sharpen the image to ensure that all pixels are sharpened to the same degree.
4. You can resize the image, set output resolution as required for a print of a desired size, and apply Unsharp Mask or another sharpening tool. These steps are described in detail in Chapter 12.

Compressing TIFF Files

As you start saving image files with intact layers, you'll find that they're very large (see Figure 11.6), consuming a lot of space on your hard drive. Since I recommend saving the original file as well, your hard drive can fill up quickly. The solution lies in compressing your images, making them smaller.

You can compress TIFF files—whether layered or not—using a variety of compression algorithms, including both lossy and lossless options. The most common compression option is LZW (Lempel-Ziv-Welch, named for its three developers). Available in most advanced image editors, LZW uses lossless compression algorithms. It can reduce a photographic image to less than half the original size, without any visible loss of image quality or detail.

Some image editors, including the Adobe products, include another option for lossless TIFF compression, ZIP. Employing the same method used by the popular WinZip software, ZIP compression produces slightly smaller files than LZW compression. However, few image browser and editing programs support ZIP compression, so it is not recommended for files you will send to others.

Some programs, such as Photoshop and Elements 2, also support JPEG compression for TIFF files. Unlike LZW and ZIP compression, JPEG compression discards data, causing a loss of detail and quality. For that reason, JPEG compression is not recommended for TIFF files.

When you save a layered TIFF file, you can select other lossless compression options in Photoshop 7 and CS to compress the actual layers in addition to compressing the underlying image. (Some other advanced image editors also offer one or both of these options.) The most common

Figure 11.6: A layered file is substantially larger than a conventional file. If your image editor allows you to save layered files in TIFF format, use your image editor's compression features to make the file smaller.

method is ZIP compression, and this is quite useful. Adobe programs offer another option, RLE (Run Length Encoding), that uses a lossless algorithm; compared to ZIP compression for layers, RLE compression provides only a modest reduction in file size.

If your image editor does not provide compression utilities, you might decide to use software such as WinZip or StuffIt. This is not recommended because few image browsers or editing programs can open the zipped files; you must first unzip them, adding an extra layer of work to the process. WinZip and StuffIt are more useful for another purpose: combining several images into a single compressed file for transmission with an e-mail message.

RECOMMENDATION: Compression

Because image editors do not offer a user-selected compression utility for files in their native formats, it's worth making TIFF your primary choice for image editing. (Confirm that the image editor you own supports all features in TIFF format.) It's worth compressing both the image and the layers, to minimize the overall size of a layered TIFF file. The only disadvantage is the extra time required for the compression and for the subsequent decompression when you later reopen the file. If your computer has lots of RAM, the delay may be no more than a second or two.

If you plan to send compressed TIFF files to others, make sure that the recipient is using software that is compatible with the compression format When in doubt, make a copy of your TIFF image, applying no compression, and send that file to others.

Adjusting Essential Image Parameters

Regardless of whether you work with adjustment layers, you'll use the same tools for adjusting images. I'll now provide step-by-step advice on correcting some of the most important technical aspects of a typical image, enhancing it for greater visual impact. If you have not yet reviewed the introductory information on adjustment tools in Chapter 10, it's worth doing so before continuing.

When working with layers, you access certain utilities from the Layers palette. If you prefer not to use layers, you can find the same utilities by choosing Image → Adjustments in Photoshop, and you can find some of the same options by choosing Image → Enhance in Elements 2.

I always recommend creating an adjustment layer when appropriate. You can ignore the suggestion if you want—it's not a prerequisite in image adjustment. Just be aware that you will be adjusting the actual pixels in your image files; work on a copy of the image, retaining the original, unmanipulated file for later use.

Optimizing Levels

After you rotate and crop an image, start the enhancement process by adjusting exposure and contrast. Unless you want to produce a print with low contrast for a specific reason (for a portrait perhaps), it's useful to have a full tonal range for high visual impact. Instead of

Figure 11.7: Some images exhibit low contrast, without pure white or completely black pixels. Adjusting blacks and whites in Levels can result in pleasing, crisp images. The challenge is in maintaining important highlight and shadow detail during the process.

exhibiting only a wide range of midtone shades, the image should include rich, dark blacks and clean, pure whites.

Levels is the primary utility that you'll use for making such adjustments, but you might want to start by trying the Auto Levels and Auto Contrast tools to determine which effect each one produces, as suggested in Chapter 9. If you plan to work with adjustment layers, create a new adjustment layer for Levels. Click the (circular) Create New Fill Or Adjustment Layer icon in the Layers palette, and choose Levels from the popup list. (If the Layers palette is not visible on your screen, choose Window → Layers to open it.) Now you can use the Levels utility to adjust highlight, shadow, and midtone areas, as well as overall contrast.

When you open the Levels utility, start by checking the histogram graph. If the histogram does not extend all the way to the black (left) or white (right) ends of the graph, your image may not contain pure black or pure white pixels. To make the image more crisp and pleasing (see Figure 11.7), adjust the sliders until the histogram extends to the black and white ends of the graph.

RECOMMENDATION: Experiment with Clipping Preview

To make an informed decision about where to position the black and white point sliders in Levels, you can use the Clipping Preview display. To access this feature in Adobe programs, hold down the Alt key (Option key on a Mac) while moving the black or white point slider. The image becomes completely (or mostly) black for the white slider and white for the black slider.

As you move the sliders, you'll start to see more pixels. The color of the pixels tells you which color channel is losing detail in those areas. If the pixels go to white (or black), they are being clipped to pure white (or black). This Clipping Preview lets you see which areas you are giving up detail in, so that you can decide how far to go in sacrificing detail to gain contrast.

Avoid moving the white point slider past the first data point, because you will lose detail in excessively bright highlights. The setting for black point is not as critical, unless there is some important detail in a shadow area; in that case, you might need to move the slider slightly back toward the left. After setting the black and white points, use the central slider to touch up midtone lightness if required.

As you experiment with the sliders, watch the lightness changing in various areas of the image. If you shift the black or white slider, notice that midtones are adjusted to some extent. The darker the shadow areas, and the brighter the highlights, the greater the overall image contrast. Unless you want to create an image with very high contrast for a specific reason, you might need to back off a bit on your black and white point settings.

The Levels utility can be frustrating. You cannot move the white point far enough to the right to darken an extremely bright highlight area. Nor can you move the black point far enough to the left to reveal detail hidden in a dark shadow area. To achieve either or both effects, use Curves or the Highlight/Shadow utility available only in Photoshop CS. If you own one of the shadow recovery plug-ins discussed in Chapter 4, you can use that tool to lighten shadows without affecting other tones in the image.

Fine-Tuning Brightness and Contrast

All image-editing programs include some basic controls for adjusting brightness/contrast, as discussed in Chapter 10. Although these can be useful, the Curves utility gives you much finer control of both parameters. Although not available in Elements 2, Curves is available in Photoshop and in some other advanced image editors. After you become proficient with Levels, try the Curves utility for fine-tuning contrast and various aspects of brightness (see Figure 11.8). This tool is not nearly as intuitive in operation as Levels and requires some study of the software instruction manual or a good Photoshop book.

You can use Curves to change the brightness of specific tonal values within the image, not just black, white, and middle tone values as with Levels. If you decide to experiment with Curves, start with the following exercises, using your own images. The more time you

Figure 11.8: Although the Levels utility is easy to use and useful for initial brightness/contrast adjustments, Curves offers greater flexibility in fine-tuning your images.

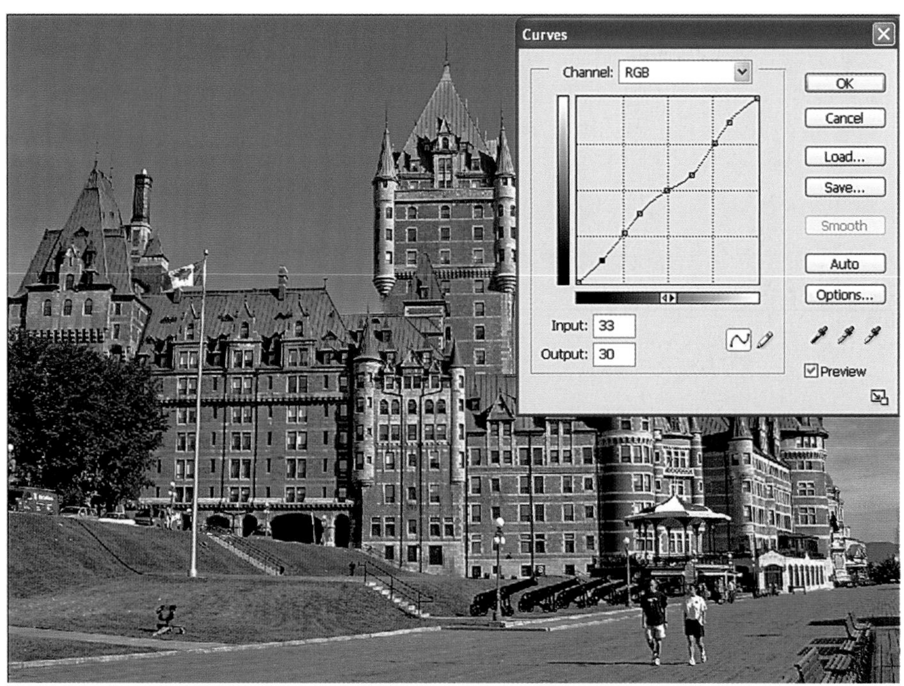

spend working with this utility, the more proficient you will become. Start each exercise by opening a new image. If you plan to work with adjustment layers, create a new adjustment layer for Curves. (Click the Create New Fill Or Adjustment Layer icon in the Layers palette.)

Since Curves is not available in Elements 2, try to achieve the intended brightness and contrast with Levels when using that program. Afterward, you might want to fine-tune the image using the Brightness/Contrast utility or using some of the tools in Quick Fix.

Using Curves: Exercise 1

Open any desired image. To slightly brighten or to slightly darken your image—without altering the black and white points—click the cursor in the center of the diagonal line in the graph; pull that point up and down in tiny increments. Watch the brightness and the contrast changing.

By adjusting this middle point, you affect the midtones, as you might with the midtone slider in Levels. However, Curves offers greater flexibility by allowing you to adjust the brightness of pixels in your image based on tonal values. You can adjust the pixels at any number of tonal values, not just the three (black, middle, white) offered by Levels. This flexibility makes Curves far more useful for midtone adjustment.

Using Curves: Exercise 2

Find an image that has a pale blue sky that is too bright and would benefit from slight darkening. If you're not sure where the pixel values fall on the curve for the sky tone, try this: Click the pertinent area of the image. As you do so, watch the curve closely. You'll notice that your clicking action places a small circle at some point along the diagonal line (see Figure 11.9).

That feedback shows you where the intended tonal value occurs on the curve. Click and hold at that point on the curve line and drag it upward or downward to adjust the sky area. You'll notice that your action also adjusts all other tones that are of similar brightness

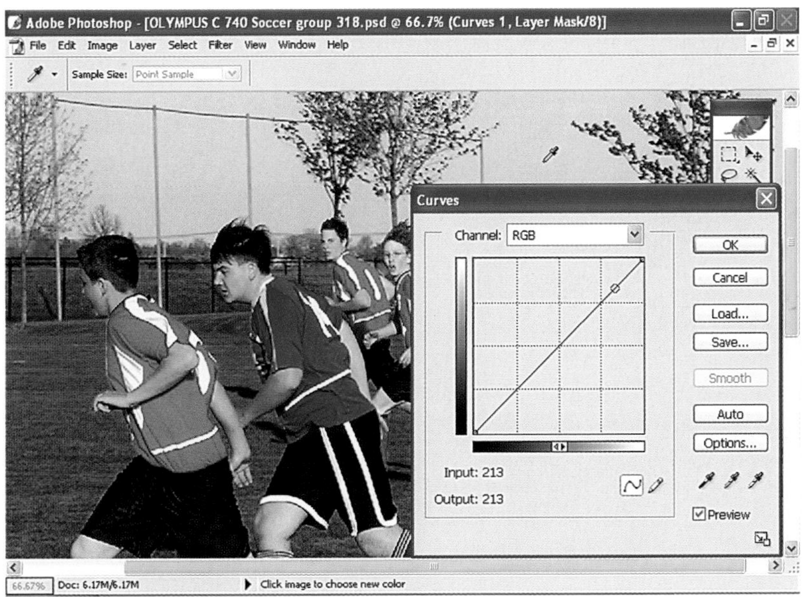

Figure 11.9: Once you know where the tonal values of an image area (the sky in this case) lie along the curve, it's not difficult to make a Curves adjustment that achieves the intended effect.

or that are darker than the sky. Make adjustments in small increments, watching the brightness and contrast changing. Stop when the overall effect is pleasing.

Using Curves: Exercise 3

Select an image that includes both highlight and shadow areas. Place your cursor at a point near the top of the line. Select the intersection that is halfway between the center point and end point of the curve line. Click that point to create an anchor point.

You can create an anchor point anywhere along the curve line, or you can create several anchor points. Simply click the desired point to do so. This allows you to fine-tune the brightness and contrast of various areas of your image based on the tonal value of the pixels. Experiment with anchor points at various locations along the curve line to adjust your image. Whenever you want to get rid of an anchor point that you created, simply click and drag it out of the Curves dialog box.

After you create the anchor, you can adjust that area of the curve. Pull it up and down to adjust the brightness of the image. The adjustments will be focused on the tonal range represented by the anchor point on the curve (the highlights in this exercise). The brightest highlight area is not affected as you adjust the sky tone; the pure white parts of the image remain pure white. This confirms the value of Curves in making make very precise adjustments to the highlights, without the risk of losing detail (clipping) in the lightest areas.

Using Curves: Exercise 4

For some images, you will want to boost contrast for a more snappy effect. You can achieve this goal by adjusting the line to create an S-curve, to increase contrast in the mid-tones, while retaining detail in highlights and shadows. The steeper you make the central portion of the curve, the higher the contrast will be.

Open an image that would benefit from increased contrast. Create an S curve by clicking the curve line at a point that's about a quarter of the way from the white end; then, click the line again, at a point that's about a quarter of the way from the black end. Click and drag the upper anchor point slightly to the left, and click and drag the lower anchor point slightly to the right. This will create a very subtle S shape. The steeper the central portion of the S, the greater the contrast of the midtones within the image. This technique offers a very sophisticated and controllable method to adjust image contrast without sacrificing highlight or shadow detail.

Using the Shadow/Highlight Utility Exercise

If you own Photoshop CS, you'll find another option that can achieve some of the same effects as Curves. A highly convenient and effective utility, Shadow/Highlight was designed to lighten shadows, darken highlights, or both. Start with an image that is underexposed and has detail that's hidden in dark shadow areas (see Figure 11.10). Later, try this utility with an image that is overexposed, with excessively bright highlights. First, create a duplicate layer for your image. (In the Layers palette, drag the image layer to the "New Layer" button at the bottom of the palette; it resembles a blank sheet of paper.) Now, in Photoshop CS, choose Image → Adjustments → Shadow/Highlight to open the Shadow/Highlight dialog box.

When the Shadow/Highlight dialog box opens, some shadow lightening is automatically applied. Move the Shadow Amount slider—and later the Highlight Amount slider—to

Figure 11.10: The original image exhibits excessively dark shadows and bright highlights that hide detail, a problem that was easily solved with the Shadow/Highlight utility in Photoshop CS.

a position that achieves the intended effects. Experiment with the Tonal Width controls to adjust the range of tonal values that should be affected. Try the Radius controls to adjust a specific area, particularly a foreground subject. If you want to boost or reduce color saturation in the adjusted area(s), use the Color Correction slider. Finally, adjust the Mid Tone Contrast slider so the midtones blend in more effectively with the adjusted highlights and/or shadows.

Optimizing Color Balance

Once you get the exposure and contrast just right, turn your mind to making the color balance ideal for any particular image. The overall color should be accurate (free of unwanted color casts) for familiar objects that represent "memory colors": an apple should be pure red, and a sky should be pure blue, for example.

That doesn't always mean that a gray object should actually appear gray. For many scenes, color balance should be appropriate to the image. Set the color balance based on your interpretation of the scene. In landscapes made near sunrise or sunset, the warm (yellow/red) color cast can be effective (see Figure 11.11). You might want to add a warm color balance to other images, taken at other times of day, for a greater sense of richness.

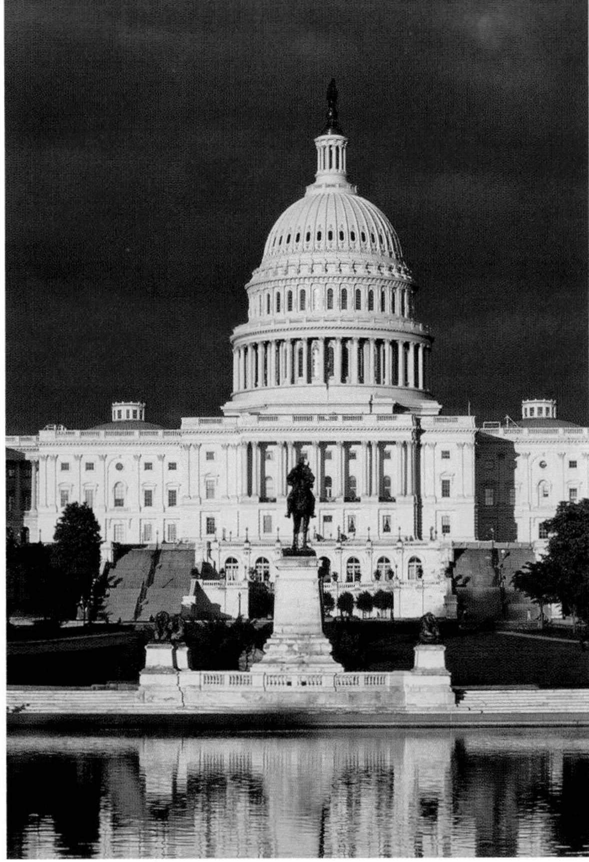

Figure 11.11: What is "correct" color balance? To a great extent, that depends on your creative intentions and what is appropriate for a particular image.

Color Balance: Exercise 1

Using an image that has been adjusted for brightness and contrast, try the Auto Color tool as a starting point. First, create a duplicate layer for your image. (In the Layers palette, drag the image layer to the New Layer icon.) Choose Image → Adjustments → Auto Color. This feature may or may not produce optimal color balance in every case. If you're not satisfied with the effect produced by Auto Color, undo it (choose Edit → Undo Auto Color), and make your own color balance adjustments.

Color Balance: Exercise 2

Experiment with the features in utilities such as Color Balance and Variations or with plug-ins such as Vivid Details Test Strip to color-adjust several images. (These tools were discussed in Chapter 10. Color Balance is not available with Elements 2 but is included in Photoshop and some other advanced image editors.) Also check out the various filters that are available in your image editor and from third-party manufacturers. The nik Sunshine Filter and Graduated Warm Yellow Filter are only two examples of plug-ins that you can use to produce a rich, warm color balance that is especially suitable for land- and cityscapes.

To evaluate the color balance of any image with greater accuracy, try this technique. Open the Hue/Saturation utility and increase saturation to 100%. Although the results will be terrible, the exaggerated effect makes it easier to identify any color cast. After you do so, cancel the Saturation setting, and use one of the options mentioned earlier to correct, modify, or exaggerate it.

Not everyone is skilled at judging the various aspects of color; some people simply differentiate colors better than others. After color adjusting several images, ask family and friends to critique them on your monitor and in prints that you make. Ask them to look for a magenta cast in particular. Many people have difficulty seeing a magenta cast, and their images often exhibit one, particularly when made with an inkjet printer that tends to emphasize magenta.

If a magenta cast is identified, the correction process will not be simple. Start by adding a bit of green in the Color Balance or Variations utility. Then, reduce color saturation in magenta only, using the Hue/Saturation utility. If your monitor image is now accurate, but your prints still exhibit a magenta cast, you'll need to make adjustments before producing a new print, as dicussed in Chapter 13.

Setting Suitable Color Saturation

After optimizing color balance for a particular image, you'll want to adjust color saturation. This too will require a judgment call, because there is no rule for the "correct" level of saturation. Some photographers love images with high saturation; when shooting film, they select Fujichrome Velvia, or Agfacolor Ultra to achieve the desired effect. Others prefer a more natural color rendition, rendering a scene the way they remember it, and often use films such as Fujichrome Sensia or the Agfacolor VISTA series.

Although some documentary photos call for great color accuracy, you might prefer more vibrant hues and tones for other types of images. Open several images and use the tools discussed in Chapters 4 and 9—Hue/Saturation and the various plug-ins—to boost the depth and richness of colors. Make your own decision as to ideal color intensity, or ask for a critique from family and friends (see Figure 11.12).

Figure 11.12: As with color balance, "correct" color saturation depends on your intentions and subject. Avoid excessive saturation that will cause a loss of detail, as in this image.

Strive to set color saturation that is appropriate for the subject: a portrait of your grandmother, wildly colorful artwork in a Mexican market, an autumn landscape, and so on. You might also want to use higher color saturation for prints made on glossy versus watercolor paper, a stylistic decision. There is no right or wrong level of saturation, but there is one caveat: excessive saturation can look artificial and cause a loss of detail in supersaturated areas.

Remember that images for viewing on a monitor should be in sRGB color space and that images for printing should be in Adobe RGB (1998) color space. (In Photoshop, you can change color space by choosing Image → Mode → Convert To Profile.) If you have used advanced color-management techniques, and your prints do not exactly match the image that you saw on the monitor, it's possible that your printer simply cannot reproduce every variance in hue and tone that your eyes can identify.

Experiment with various levels of saturation until an image looks just right on your monitor. Make a test print, evaluate it, and decide whether you should further adjust color saturation before making the final print. If you use the color management techniques recommended in Chapter 10, your print should look much the same as the image on the monitor. Naturally, there may be some difference because of the type of paper that you are using; glossy papers tend to emphasize colors, and soft-finish papers tend to make colors seem more muted.

Correcting Image Defects

No matter how careful you were while shooting with a digital camera or scanning photographs, some images will need to be cleaned up. You'll want to eliminate defects such as dust specks, scratches, blemishes in a portrait photo, and so on. You might also want to remove distracting elements—a power line, a piece of trash, or a TV antenna in the distant sky.

In Chapters 4 and 9, I suggested some techniques for using the Color Replacement tool (available only in Photoshop CS) and the Red-Eye Brush tool. Now, I'll provide a step-by-step exercise for applying the Cloning Stamp tool. You can follow the same steps when using the Healing Brush tool, available only in Photoshop 7 and CS. With the Healing Brush tool, the process is identical, but the result is different: this tool effectively duplicates texture and matches color to the destination, the area you want to repair.

Cloning Stamp: Exercise 1

Find an image that includes a small defect that you want to remove. You might want to create a new image layer, but you can also work directly on the pixels in the image. Follow these steps:

1. Zoom in on the area with a defect, enlarging the image to 300% so you can work with great precision.
2. Select the Clone Stamp tool from the Tools palette. Select a brush from the drop-down on the Options bar near the top of the screen. Start with a soft-edged brush. The size isn't important, because you can change that as you work by right-clicking your mouse. (With a Mac computer, Control-click.) For areas with relatively high detail, a soft-edged brush will blur around the edges of your brush strokes, creating a natural effect.
3. In the Brushes palette, click Brush Tip Shape, and change the Hardness setting to a value between around 50% and 85% (see Figure 11.13).

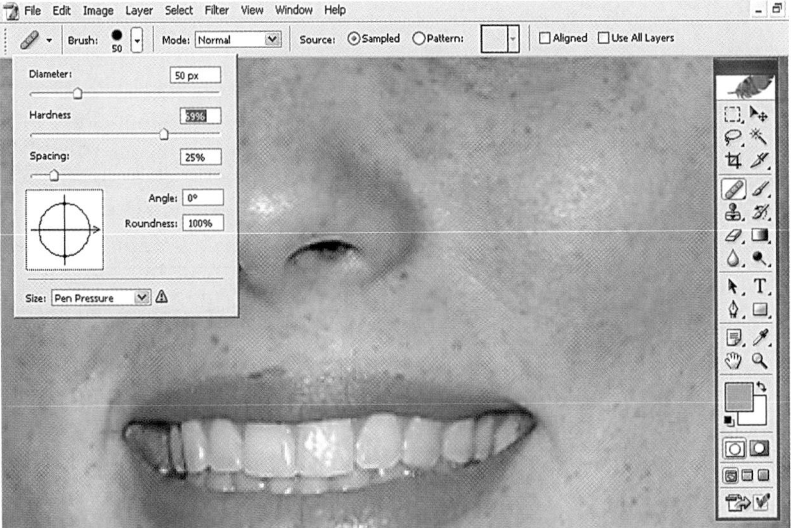

Figure 11.13: If you use some skill and the correct options available for the Cloning Stamp and Healing Brush, you can make corrections that will be invisible in the final image.

4. If you don't want to completely remove a blemish, but rather just tone it down slightly, simply reduce the Opacity setting on the Options bar. (This feature is not available with the Healing Brush tool.) When you then copy pixels, they are placed over the underlying pixels at a reduced opacity, achieving the intended effect. Experiment with different opacity levels.
5. Locate an unblemished sample area; this will be your "clone from" area, for taking pixels that you will copy onto the blemished "target" or "clone to" area.
6. Select the source or "clone from" area. To take a sample, hold down the Alt key (Option key on a Mac), click with the mouse, and then release the Alt (or Option) key.
7. Move the cursor to place the clone stamp over the "target" area that contains the defect you want to remove.
8. Left-click to cover the target with the pixels that you copied from the unblemished area. If you merely wanted to cover a tiny blemish, and if you used a suitable brush size, the process might now be finished. If not, simply repeat steps 4 through 6.

When using multiple cloning steps, select new sample points often, in order to copy pixels that are adjacent to the target area and have identical color, tone, and texture.

Cloning Stamp: Exercise 2

Find an image with a much larger "defect" that you want to remove: a sign, pole, or some other object against a background of foliage, for example (see Figure 11.14).

In order to remove this unwanted object, follow these steps:

1. Zoom in on part of the pertinent area, and select a new brush size, perhaps slightly larger than that in the previous exercise. For the most natural results, avoid using an excessively large brush. Plan to remove the defect using many individual cloning steps.
2. Select the source, or "clone from," area. To take a sample, hold down the Alt key (Option key on a Mac), click, and then release the Alt (or Option) key. Repeat the process as often as necessary.

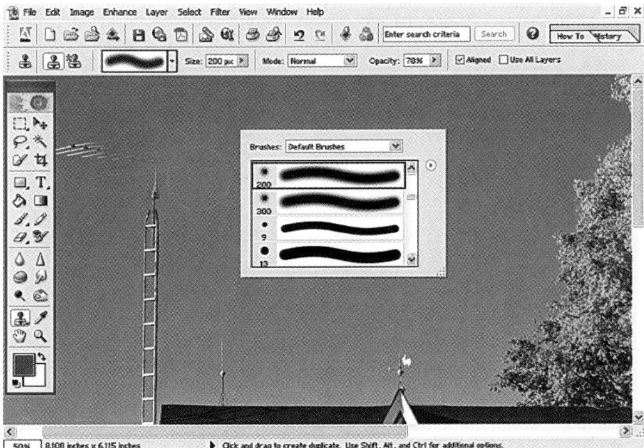

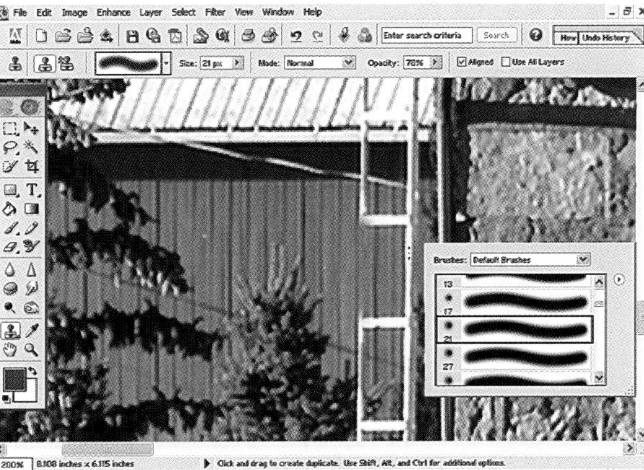

Figure 11.14: Removing a large unwanted area, such as the antenna at left, can be easy when the background is a smooth, even tone. The process is time-consuming and painstaking when the background is more complex, such as the textured wall of the barn at right.

3. As you select new sample points that are adjacent to the next small area you want to clone, avoid creating repetitive patterns; these will be obvious to anyone who views the final image.
4. If you are not satisfied with the effect produced by one or more cloning step, simply undo the effect. (Choose Edit → Step Backward.)
5. Try another cloning feature: "painting" large areas by dragging the clone stamp as you would move a paint brush, while keeping the left mouse key depressed. This feature can be useful when you want to clone large image areas. You'll find that the technique requires a great deal of patience and skill for pleasing results. In my experience, "painting" is most useful when cloning an object that protrudes into a sky area that is of consistent brightness.

Making Beautiful Monochrome Images

Although color images are certainly popular, most of us appreciate a beautiful black-and-white print. Think of the stunning Ansel Adams landscapes or the definitive Karsh portraits, with their rich blacks and luminous whites. Instead of a picture postcard view, black-and-whites can provide an impressionistic glimpse of a reality the maker intended to convey, adding emphasis to the subtleties of light and shadow. The "abstract" representation of people, places, and events often makes a more profound impression on the viewer's subconscious than a color print (see Figure 11.15).

In the past, making a beautiful monochrome image called for many hours of work with caustic chemicals in a darkroom. Today, you can make an exhibition-quality black-and-white print with a few minutes of work in Photoshop, using the techniques described in Chapter 13. Most inkjet photo printers can make good to very good monochrome prints, often better than the prints you would get from a local mini lab after shooting a roll of black-and-white film.

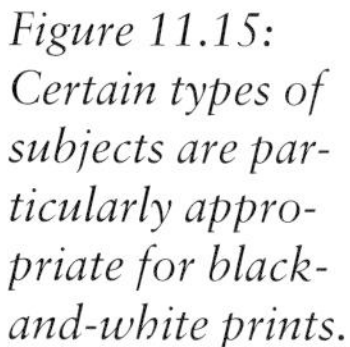

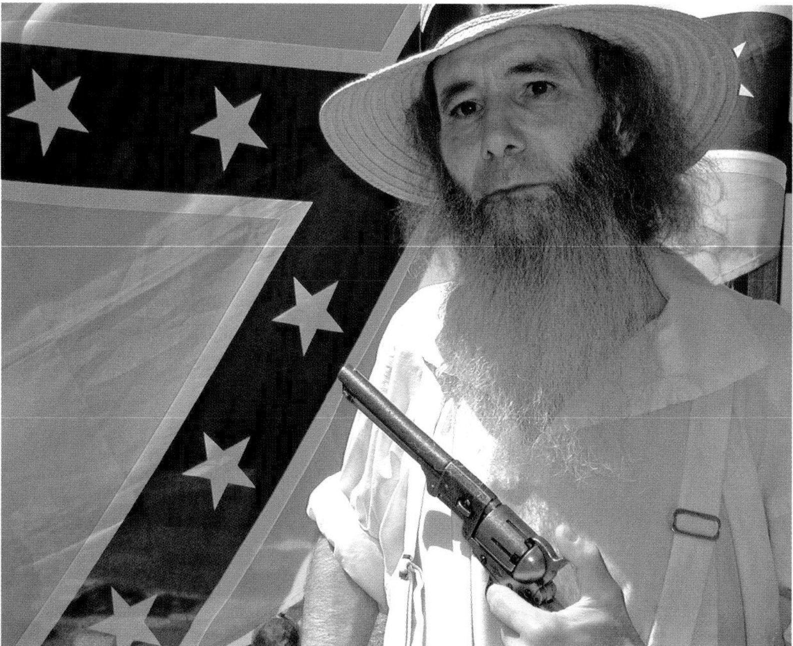

Figure 11.15: Certain types of subjects are particularly appropriate for black-and-white prints.

You can make black-and-white prints from scans of black-and-white images, from images made with a digicam's black-and-white effects mode, or from color images converted to black and white. Because most photos are made in color, I'll discuss techniques for converting those to black and white and for making the best-possible monochrome prints.

Converting Color Images to Monochrome

You can convert a color image to black and white (see Figure 11.16) using several methods. One of the simplest is grayscale conversion that discards color information, producing an image consisting of only black, white, and shades of gray. (Choose Image → Mode → Grayscale.) Although this method is often used, I cannot recommend it because it simply strips out the color values from the pixels, leaving luminosity (brightness) information behind. The effective tonal value for each color does not translate into completely accurate tonal information; that results in an image that is relatively flat and lifeless.

As in previous chapters, I am providing the commands used in Adobe Photoshop programs (including Elements 2) because these are the most popular among imaging enthusiasts. If you are using another brand of software, it will probably require entirely different commands and may or may not offer the same options as the Adobe programs. In that case, review the instruction manual or access the Help feature for specifics on features and how they are accessed.

Figure 11.16: Since my family, friends, and clients prefer color over monochrome, I generally shoot in color, knowing that I can easily convert a color image to black and white.

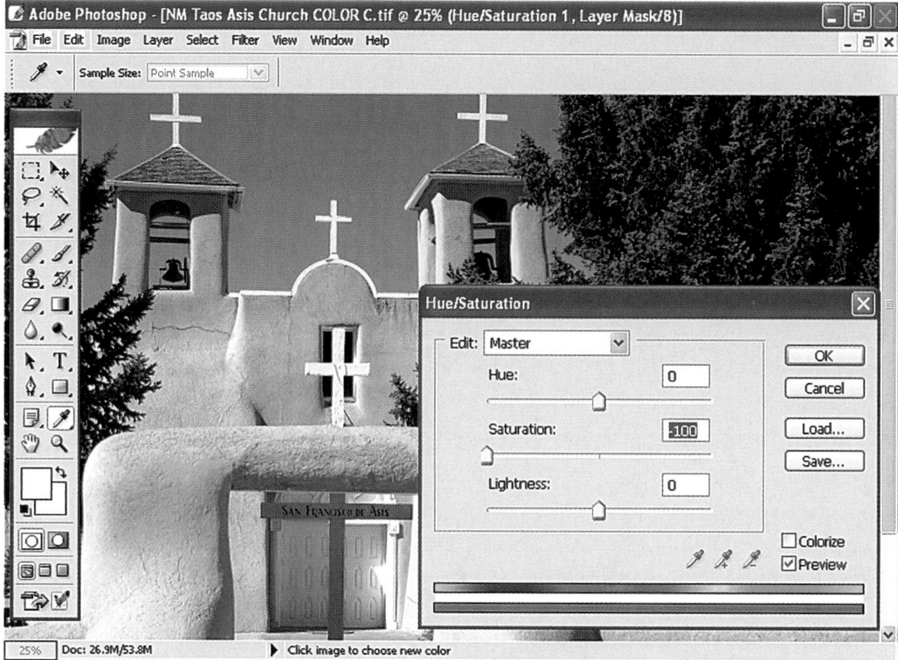

Figure 11.17: If your image-editing software does not offer a Channel Mixer (or similar) function, convert your color images to monochrome by desaturating them. This process is preferable to grayscale conversion.

Another commonly used technique is desaturation, reducing color saturation to zero with the Color Saturation control available in all image-editing programs (see Figure 11.17). This method is less than ideal too, but it has an advantage over grayscale conversion. When you totally desaturate a color image, you are still left with the extra data that is available in an RGB image. Use this option only if you are working with a program that does not offer the more sophisticated option described in the next section.

Converting with Channel Mixer

If your image editor includes a Channel Mixer option (see Figure 11.18), as most Photoshop programs do, use this feature to convert images. (Elements 2 does not include Channel Mixer.) Take the following steps and you should have a pleasing black-and-white image that should make for an excellent print.

To produce a pleasing black-and-white image that should make an excellent print, follow these steps:

1. Open a color image that you want to convert to black and white.
2. Choose Window → Channels to open the Channels palette. Click each of the color channels (Red, Green, and Blue) in turn. Each will show you a grayscale version of the image, as it appears when using only that channel.
3. Decide which channel makes the image look closest to your expectations for the final result. For the purpose of this exercise, let's say that Green is your "preferred channel." Click the RGB thumbnail in the Channels palette to return to your full-color image.
4. Create a new adjustment layer for Channel Mixer. (Choose Layer → New Adjustment Layer → Channel Mixer.) Click OK in the New Adjustment Layer dialog box.

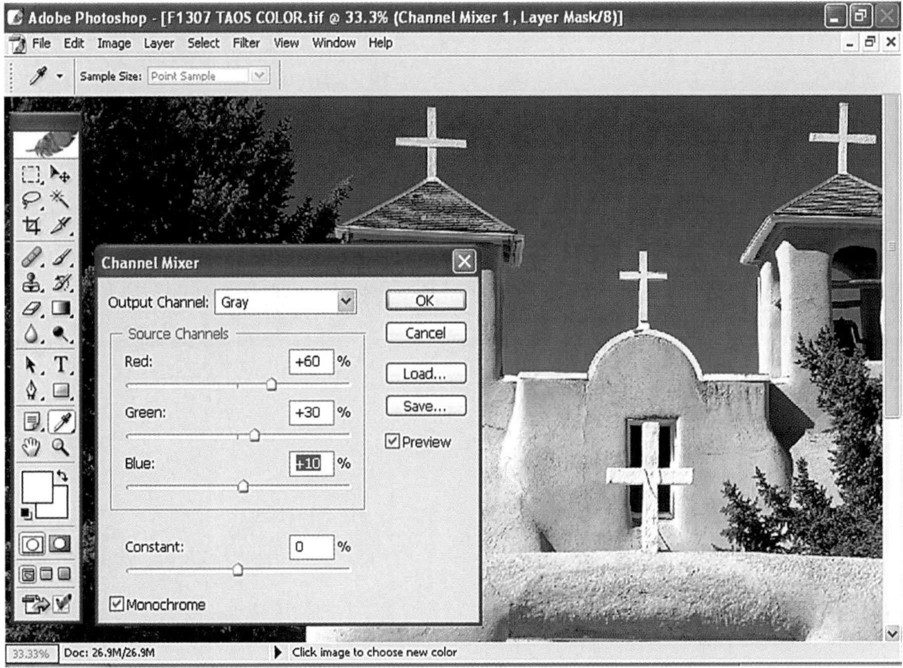

Figure 11.18: The Channel Mixer function is not difficult to use and offers a great degree of control over the final "look" of your monochrome images.

5. Check the Monochrome option in the Channel Mixer dialog box to convert your color image to black and white.
6. As a starting point, set the value for the channel that looked best in step 3 (Green in this example) to 100%. Set the other two channel values to 0%.
7. Now you can experiment with fine-tuning all three channel values to achieve the best result by setting a different percentage for each channel. Set the highest percentage for your preferred channel. Ideally, the total percentage (all three values) should equal 100% to retain accurate density in the final image, but that is just a guideline. Your final settings might be Red +20%, Green +70%, Blue +10%, but that depends entirely on the type of subject in the image and your own preferences.

You might want to try another technique instead of the method described in steps 6 and 7. Start by setting all three channels to 0%, producing a black image. Gradually increase the percentage of the preferred channel until detail in the image is quite visible, at about 80%. Gradually increase the other channels. Finally, fine-tune all three, striving for a total of about 100%, until the image exhibits the effect that you find most pleasing.

---

8. Click OK to apply the Channel Mixer. You can then fine-tune the image brightness, contrast, black point, white point, and so on, using other controls such as Levels and Curves.

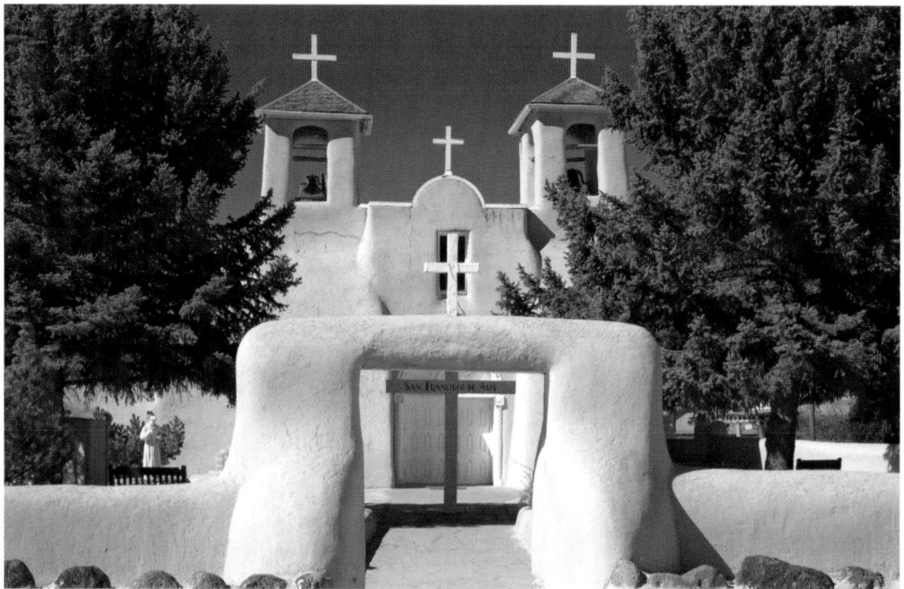

Figure 11.19: Experiment with various color balance (or hue/saturation) options to find the tone that you like best. This sepia tone was created with a Color Balance adjustment, using values of Red +28 and Yellow/Blue of –45.

Enhance the Monochrome Image

After you convert an image to black and white, you can use various tools in your image editor to enhance it for printing. Contrast adjustment is the most useful, preferably using the Levels control, to produce rich dark blacks and clean pure whites. You can also try the Curves control; make the line steeper for extra contrast, or add a slight S curve to increase overall contrast without losing detail in highlights or shadows. With more basic image-editing software, use the Contrast and Brightness adjustment tools.

Ideally, a black-and-white image to be printed should exhibit the following characteristics: deep blacks, excellent detail in highlights, strong contrast through the full range of midtones, and accurate brightness. You want to avoid a "flat" appearance with minimal contrast and blacks that aren't dark enough.

For creative reasons, you might also want to tone the photo, using various adjustments available in Color Balance; this is possible only if your monochrome image is in RGB color. For example, you might want to tone an image of an antique subject with sepia, so the print resembles an old photograph (see Figure 11.19). (Try values of Cyan/Red +30 and Yellow/Blue of –50 as a starting point.) Or add cyan and blue to produce a cool tone so the print will resemble one that has been selenium-toned in a wet darkroom. Record the settings that produce prints that are most pleasing, and use those settings as a starting point for other images.

Although I prefer to use Color Balance adjustments, the Hue/Saturation function is also useful, allowing you to experiment with various colors by simply adjusting a single slider. Start by checking the Colorize checkbox. Then move the Hue slider to change the tone to any desired color; move the Saturation slider to adjust the intensity of the tone. As a starting point for sepia toning, try settings such as 30/25 or 45/20.

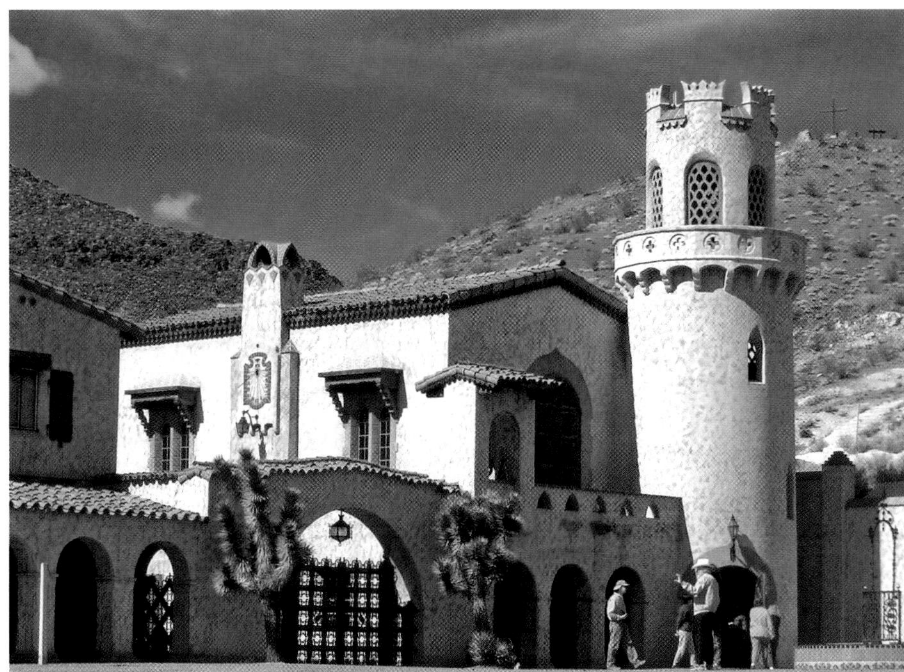

Figure 11.20: Although some of the advanced image editors include many tools that are useful for enhancing a monochrome image, you might prefer to use an after-market plug-in because of its greater simplicity and versatility. I converted this image with Digital Pro B&W plug-in, using the Orange Filter plus Manual Tweak, a 45-second process.

When you are happy with all the effects, resize the image for printing, and boost sharpness with USM or one of the after-market sharpening tools described in Chapter 13.

Black-and-White Conversion Plug-ins

The black-and-white image conversion, enhancement, and toning techniques described in these sections—as well as more advanced methods discussed in books on Photoshop—are certainly useful. However, they are somewhat complex and tedious. You can simplify the entire process and achieve many effects quickly by using plug-in software designed to automate the processes (see Figure 11.20).

The plug-ins include tools such as special filters for changing the tonal values (lightness and darkness of various colors), intensity and brightness, options for various toning effects, and so on. Read the instructions and experiment to determine which controls you find most useful; then experiment in order to view the effect that each function produces on your images. After an hour of the learning process, you should find that the plug-ins make it easy to produce professional caliber monochrome images that make excellent prints.

RECOMMENDATION: Black-and-White Plug-Ins

I can recommend two popular programs: the very sophisticated B/W Conversion, available in the Color Efex Pro! Photo Design Set ($100) from nik Multimedia (**www.nikmultimedia.com**) and the Digital B&W PRO plug-in from FM Software. (**www.fredmiranda.com/software**). Nik offers a free demo download that allows you to try all the features. FM software does not offer a free trial, but their Digital B&W PRO costs only $15 and is effective, versatile, and uncomplicated.

CHAPTER twelve

Images and the Internet

Throughout this book, *I have primarily discussed making and preparing images for printing, but many photo enthusiasts also want to share their images on the Internet. If you have devoted many hours to optimizing images for printmaking, you won't need to repeat the entire process. After a few additional steps to resize and optimize photos, you'll be able to attach them to e-mail messages and post them to one of the online photo-sharing albums on commercial websites. You might also decide to create a basic family photo web page or a gallery page that friends and relatives can visit to view your images, using one of the web-page creation programs.*

In this chapter, I'll cover the techniques required to optimize image files for Internet use and provide a few suggestions for those who want to learn more about creating web pages and full websites.

Converting Images for Internet Use

Most of your digital image files are probably quite large and have been saved in TIFF or an image editor's native format in the Adobe RGB (1998) color space. As you'll see in the next few sections, for Internet use you'll need to downscale the images, convert them to the sRGB color space, and save them as compressed JPEGs. Because Adobe's image editors offer the most options in these areas, I'll use them in this chapter's examples and exercises.

Some image-editing programs include a feature that automates the downsizing of images for Internet use (see Figure 12.1). (In Adobe image-editors, choose File → Save For Web). For the best results, don't use that utility because it doesn't let you specify a color

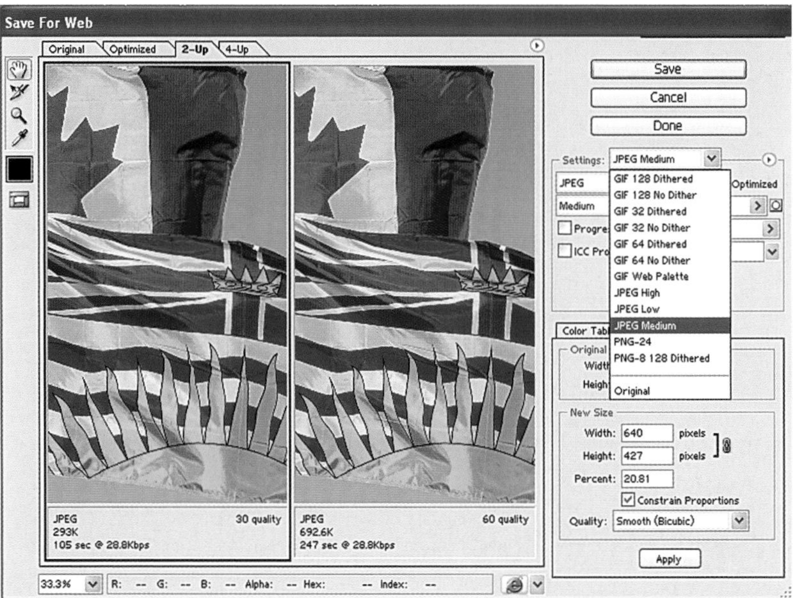

Figure 12.1: The Save For Web utility can be useful but is missing an essential feature—color space conversion.

space, and it won't work with particularly large image files. The procedure I'll recommend can produce richer color saturation when viewed on a monitor and is just as easy to use.

Setting the Color Space

As discussed in Chapters 9 and 13, Adobe RGB (1998) is a highly suitable color space for images that will be printed. For Web use, sRGB is more appropriate because it was designed to match the color space of a typical monitor for greater display accuracy (see Figure 12.2). Many image-editing programs don't let you set the color space. If you're using such a program, your images will probably be in sRGB, an ideal choice for the Internet, unless you applied a different color space in a digital camera or a scanner.

If you're working with an image that's in the Adobe RGB (1998) color space and an image editor that allows for such modifications, convert it to sRGB for Internet use. The sRGB color space helps ensure that the image is as accurate as possible on a wide range of monitors.

The advanced photo editors, including the full versions of Photoshop as well as Elements 2, let you convert images to any of numerous color spaces, as in Figure 12.2. (Choose Image → Mode → Convert To Profile to open the Convert To Profile dialog box.) I recommend the following settings:

1. In the Destination Space section, select sRGB in the Profile drop-down list.
2. In the Engine drop-down list, select Adobe (ACE).
3. In the Intent drop-down list, select Relative Colormetric; this setting maintains color accuracy.
4. Leave the Use Blackpoint Compensation check box checked to ensure that black is rendered accurately.

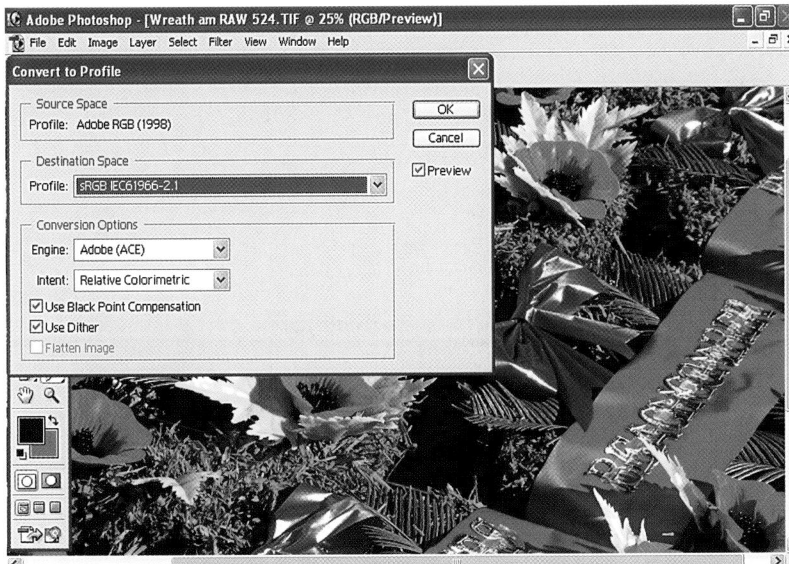

Figure 12.2: All Adobe image editors, as well as a few others, include a utility for color space conversion. Because web browsers are not color managed, they produce better results with images in sRGB, versus Adobe RGB (1998), color space.

5. The Use Dither check box should *not* be checked unless you are having a difficult time rendering accurate color for a particular image. When this option is turned on, dithering (blending pixels of two or more colors) simulates an out-of-gamut color. This can be a useful feature, but it does increase the file size in exchange for a relatively modest benefit.
6. Click OK, to apply the new color space and close the dialog box. You'll notice little or no change in the color appearance of the display because the change is rarely dramatic.

Resizing the Image

Although some Internet users have a high-speed connection and thus can transfer data rapidly, most use a dial-up connection with a 56Kbps (kilobits per second) modem. Even if you use high-speed connection, plan to downscale (downsize) your image files substantially. This step ensures that any e-mail recipient or a visitor to your online photo gallery can download or view the images without a long wait. Before we move on to consider specific steps for sizing images for Internet use, let's look at a few concepts not previously discussed in this book.

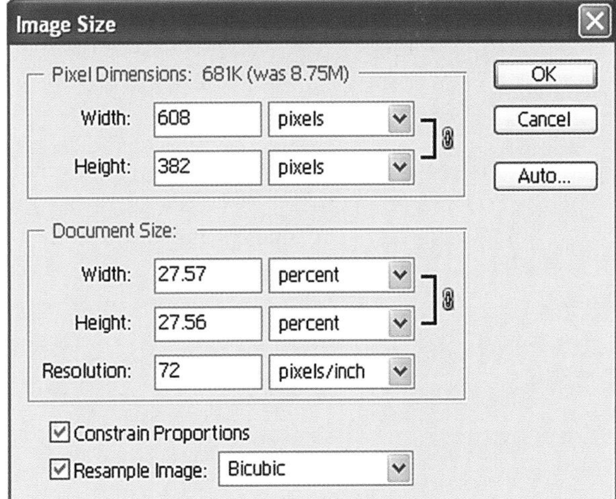

Figure 12.3: Although the process may seem complicated, it's worth taking the time to calculate appropriate dimensions for any image intended for web use.

Image Size

Whenever you consider photos for Internet use, think of the image area in terms of pixels or pixel dimensions and not in inches as you would for printmaking (see Figure 12.3). The pixel dimensions determine how many pixels across and down the image will be. The ideal file size depends on the end use of a photo.

As a rule of thumb, don't size any image larger than 1024 × 768 pixels for Internet use; these dimensions will allow an image to fill a monitor that's set to 1024 × 768, the most common monitor resolution setting. In fact, images for website use should be substantially smaller so they will load more quickly into a web browser, allowing for faster viewing. Many websites use 500 × 375 pixels for image dimensions; an image of this size will fill roughly a quarter of a monitor.

RECOMMENDATION: Calculate Appropriate Image Dimensions

Instead of using some rule of thumb or "guesstimate" as to the image dimensions, follow these steps:

1. Set your monitor display to a commonly used resolution, such as 1024 → 768. (In Windows, choose Start → Control Panel → Display to open the Display Properties dialog box. Click the Settings tab, and move the Screen Resolution slider. On a Mac, choose Control Panel → Monitor.)
2. Open an image in your image-editing software, and zoom out until it is as large as it should appear on a viewer's monitor.Remember to keep the image small.
3. Open the Image Size dialog box. (Image → Image Size or Resize.) In the dialog box [], change the unit of measure from inches to percent. Enter the percentage that is showing in the Navigator palette or in the title bar for the image. Click OK to complete the resizing.
4. The image now appears much smaller because it is not at full size. Double-click the Zoom tool on the Tools palette to return to 100% zoom. This displays the image at the size it will appear on the "average" viewer's monitor.

Using this process allows you to resize the images based on how you want them to look, rather than an arbitrary estimate of the pixel dimensions to be used.

Monitor Resolution

There is another important difference in images for the web versus those intended for printing. When you resize an image that will be printed—using inches for the dimensions—you must also set the output resolution in the Image Size dialog box. (A setting from 240 to 360 ppi is often used for printing.) When you change the resolution number (for ppi), the image file size increases or decreases.

This does not occur when sizing images in pixels. Regardless of the number you enter in the Resolution box, the file size remains constant. Nonetheless, you might want to enter 72 pixels/inch in the box. This setting is based on an old standard, the original Apple monitor display. Most of today's monitors use much higher ppi resolution, but 72 ppi is still typical for Internet use.

Many books and magazine articles refer to output resolution and monitor resolution in dpi (dots per inch) as do most individuals during a conversation. To avoid confusion with printer resolution, I always use the correct term—ppi, for pixels per inch—when discussing monitor or output resolution. Most image-editing programs also use ppi in the Image Size utility.

Image Downsizing Exercise

If you're working with one of the Adobe image editors, use the following technique to downscale your images. Other advanced software calls for a similar technique, and entry-level programs use a simplified Resize utility that asks you to enter size information. While experimenting, start with a large TIFF file that has not yet received the final sharpening process. (Final sharpening produces the best results when applied after image size is modified.) If layers are open, flatten the image. (Choose Layer → Flatten Image.) *Save this practice file under a new name so you will not overwrite an important image file.*

1. In Photoshop, choose Image → Image Size to open the Image Size dialog box; in Elements 2, choose Image → Resize → Image Size to do so.
2. Make sure that the Constrain Proportions check box is checked; this prevents distortion of the image while it is resized.
3. Check the Resample Image check box to ensure that the image is actually downsized; select Bicubic in the drop-down list box for the best results. (If you use Photoshop CS, experiment with Bicubic Sharper as well whenever you downscale an image; this interpolation option might produce greater sharpness.)

For the best results when significantly downscaling a file—from 15MB to 1MB, for example—some experts recommend doing so in small increments in order to optimize image quality. Follow the steps in this section, but start by downsizing the image to approximately 10MB, then to 5MB, and then to 1MB. It's easy to vary the resulting file size by changing the dimensions of the image; if you practice this technique, it will become second nature in a few minutes.

---

4. Set the Width and Height of the image in pixels (see Figure 12.4); for this exercise, try setting 640 pixels for the larger of the two dimensions. The other dimension is set automatically.
5. Click OK to process the changes and the image is downsized; if your image's pixel dimensions are 640 × 480, the file size is now between 800 and 900KB.

Now you can use Unsharp Mask (USM) or another sharpening tool. For the small image file, you might want to experiment with USM settings such as Amount 70% to 150%, Radius 1 pixel, and Threshold 2 levels (4 for portraits.)

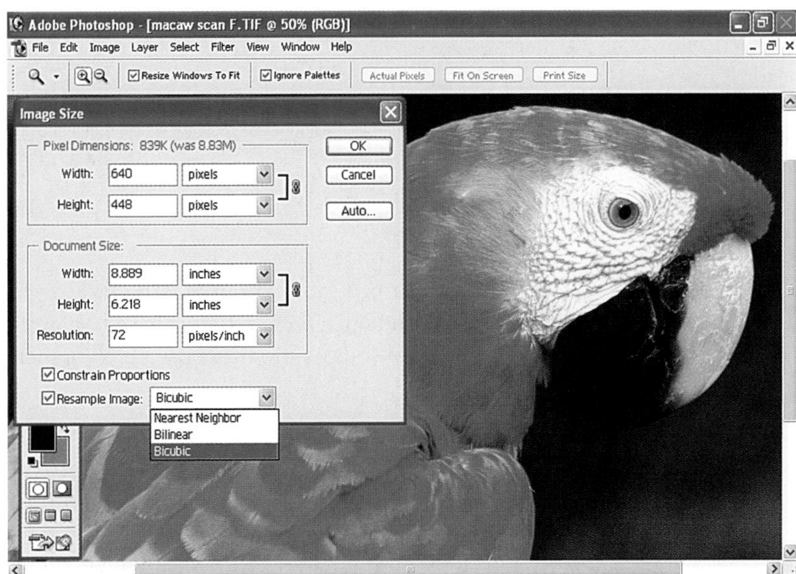

Figure 12.4 : When setting the dimensions for images intended for e-mail or a web page, do so in pixels, not in inches.

You might find entirely different settings to be more appropriate for any image; try other settings until you find a combination that is optimal. Because others will also be viewing your photos on a monitor (and not in a print), your decision about the ideal level of sharpness should be accurate.

Saving in a Browser-Supported Format

Now that you have significantly reduced the size of the image file, it's time to save it in a web-appropriate format. Few web browsers support TIFF files, and TIFF files are also very large, almost a full megabyte in the previous exercise. That's too large for most purposes, unless you're using a high-speed internet service to send an image to a friend who uses a similar broadband service. Even then, you'll probably want to send a smaller file to accelerate the uploading and downloading process. That calls for saving the image in a format that allows for significant compression, such as JPEG (see Figure 12.5).

RECOMMENDATION: Use the Most Appropriate Format

If you're attaching a file to an e-mail message, you can save the image in any format, as long as the recipient uses software that can open the resulting file. But avoid sending an excessively large file that will take the recipient a long time to download. If you plan to post images to an online photo album on a photo-sharing site, follow the recommendation provided by the operators of the website.

When saving an image file for any Internet use, JPEG is always suitable; because it's supported by all web browsers. You can compress a JPEG to a desired file-size/image-quality level and maintain high quality at modest file sizes. This format retains full RGB color because it supports 24-bit color depth (more than 16.7 million colors are available) for pleasing color rendition.

Other formats are available for web use too, with GIF (for Graphics Interchange Format) and PNG (for Portable Network Graphics) being the most common. GIF uses lossless compression but supports only 8-bit color depth for a maximum of 256 colors. GIF is most suitable for work with limited color, such as graphics, line art, and animations. PNG-24 is certainly suitable for digital images. It may eventually replace JPEG as the standard image format for Internet use, because it also supports 24-bit color and offers an advantage over JPEG: lossless compression for higher image quality. For now, JPEG remains the standard, because some older browsers do not support PNG and because few webmasters want to spend time converting to another format.

Maintaining JPEG Quality

As discussed earlier, the compression setting used when saving a JPEG file can have a significant effect on the quality of the final image. In fact, most image editors present the compression setting as "quality" setting. The higher the quality level selected, the lower the compression.

When a lower quality (higher compression) setting is used, more information is sacrificed in order to simplify the image so that it can be described in a smaller file size. This introduces a number of potential problems. The most noticeable is known as artifacts, random pixels that don't match the surroundings. For example, you might see random dark or light pixels along a high-contrast edge. These artifacts are more prevalent as you reduce the quality setting to increase JPEG compression.

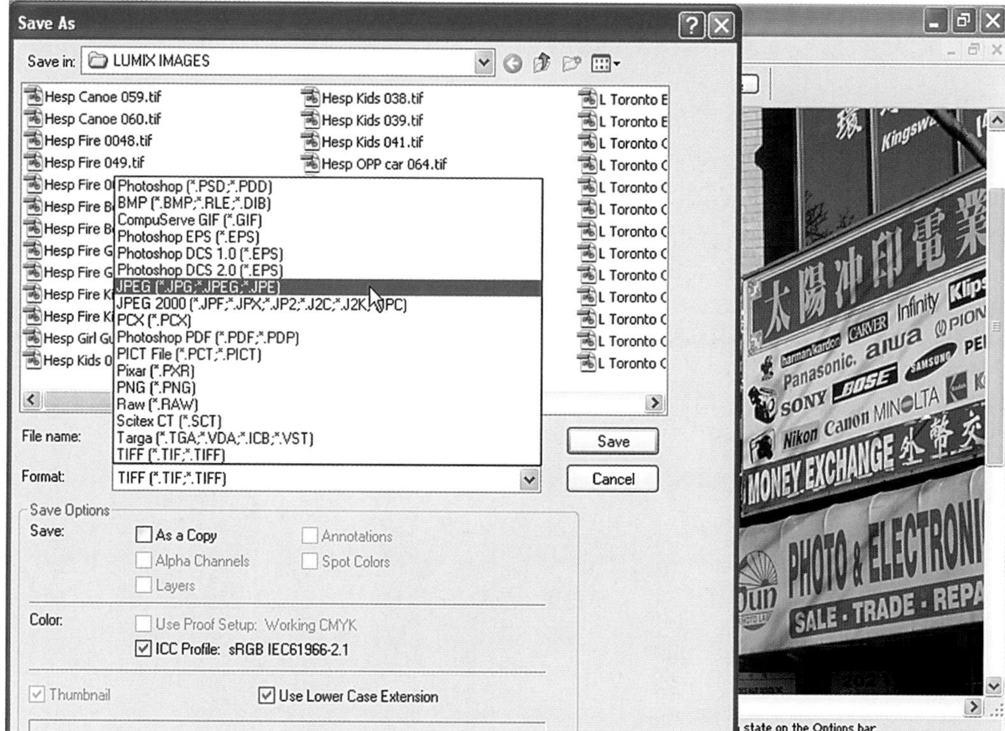

Figure 12.5: When preparing images for use on a website, you'll need to decide on the format. Select JPEG for image files and GIF for graphics and line art.

Another potential problem is loss of detail in the image. The higher compression used at low quality settings produces more changes in pixel values, which in turn results in a loss of detail within the image. Also, these changes in pixel values can make the image appear slightly soft.

Finding the correct balance between quality and image file size is particularly critical for images that will be displayed on the Web or via e-mail. Although you want to maintain the best quality possible for these images, a small file size takes precedence. Therefore, you'll want to use the smallest quality setting possible that still maintains adequate quality.

If you want to practice saving images as JPEGs, try the following for setting different quality levels, using Adobe image editors as an example. Notice especially the change in the image file size at each level. Other advanced and high-end programs offer similar options, but these options are rarely available with the $99 and under products.

1. With Adobe image editors, choose File → Save As to open the Save As dialog box. Select a location where the file should be saved, enter a new filename for the "test image," set the format to JPEG. Click OK to open the JPEG Options dialog box, as shown in Figure 12.6.
2. For the purpose of this exercise, set Quality to 12 (Maximum) in the Image Options section for the largest file/highest quality. If you are working with the 640 × 480 pixel image from the previous exercise, the resulting compressed JPEG file size will be about 325KB; that's very large for Internet use because most people still use 56Kbps modems, but useful for this exercise.

Figure 12.6: Adobe image editors and some other brands of software provide several useful features in the JPEG Options dialog box.

3. In the Format Options section, click the Baseline Optimized option. ("Standard" produces larger file sizes; Progressive is suitable for certain Internet applications too, as discussed in books on web page creation.)
4. The last drop-down list at the bottom of the JPEG Options dialog box allows you to select an option for Size. This feature will not change your image. Play around with this feature, selecting a bandwidth, from 1440Kbps to 2MBps.

The software will estimate the downloading time (in seconds) for those who will view your images on the Internet, depending on the modem they're using. This information can be useful when you are trying to decide on a Quality setting. As the dialog box confirms, low Quality settings ensure faster downloads; naturally, the image quality will be degraded.

Pay special attention to the download speed of your image especially at 56.6Kbps, the most common modem speed. When the Image Options box is set to Quality level 12, download time will be 57 seconds with a 56.6Kbps modem, and that's quite a long download time.

5. Close the file without saving it; if you want to save it, rename it so you do not overwrite your original file.
6. Reopen your original practice file. Repeat steps 1 through 3, but this time, select Quality level 8 (High). That setting provides an excellent balance between file size and image quality. If you started with a 640 × 480 pixel image, the resulting compressed file will be substantially smaller, about 114KB in size; the download time with a 56.6Kbps modem will be 19.3 seconds, quite acceptable for most people.

E-Mail Considerations

As mentioned earlier, any image file that you distribute via e-mail should be small, particularly when you plan to attach several images to a message. Otherwise, you may find that the attachments take too long to send, and the recipient encounters very long download times. Unless the recipient wants to print the image, there is no need to send a file that's larger than about 100KB after it is compressed. Many recipients of an attachment will never open the JPEG with image-editing software; they will merely view it below the text of the e-mail message, if their mail software offers this feature (see Figure 12.7).

> Some mail systems, particularly web-based services such as Hotmail, automatically bounce (reject) any message with an attachment that exceeds 1MB in size. Other mail systems may accept messages with attachments totaling up to 4MB.

When sending an image that the recipient will want to print, you might want to use higher resolution. Size the image to about 800 × 570 pixels at 72 ppi, for a 1.3MB file. This should allow the recipient to make an acceptable 4" × 6" print, at 200ppi, after upscaling the file in an image editor. If you save it as JPEG with Quality level 11, the compressed file will be about 250KB in size, small for anyone with high-speed Internet service but very large for those who use a conventional modem. If you select Quality level 8 instead, the compressed file will be substantially smaller, less than the 100KB rule of thumb. (This should allow for making an acceptable 3" × 5" print.)

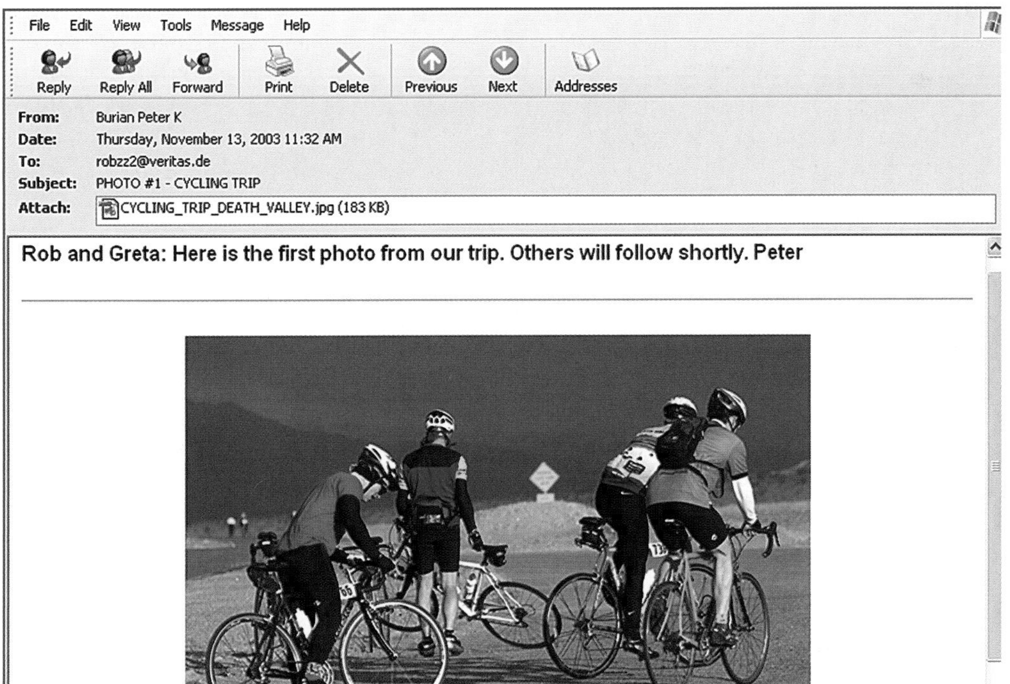

Figure 12.7: Many e-mail recipients do not open attached image files but merely view them under the text of the message. If your friends use this approach, size the images to an appropriate size such as 4x5 inches at 72 dpi.

Photo-Sharing Websites

Instead of using e-mail to send numerous photos to friends, family, and admirers, consider posting a series of images on a photo-sharing website. You can find many of these, including www.ofoto.com, www.shutterfly.com (see Figure 12.8), http://community.webshots.com/ (choose My Photos), and http://photothru.com/. To find others, use a search engine, and search on "photo sharing" or "online photo album." Check out the features and the interface of several that have been in business for at least a few years. The ideal site will be convenient to navigate, will offer adequate storage space at a reasonable fee, and will protect your images by providing you a password.

Before signing up and downloading images to an album on one of these websites, be sure to read the terms and conditions closely. For example, look for any condition that allows the site operator to sell gifts with your photos to the general public. You might be able to restrict such usage by selecting a password-protected album; in that case, share the password only with friends and family.

Some photo-sharing services are free and offer a limited amount of space, often for a limited amount of time. Others charge a monthly fee, perhaps $7 to $10. They offer substantially more storage space for an indefinite period of time—as long as you make your monthly payments.

Most free services are free because they are affiliated with a company that sells some product or service—often photo printing and photo gifts. Some of these sites include numerous ads that you—and those who visit your online album—must tolerate. On the other hand, if you are interested in ordering prints online, you'll find that some of these sites offer

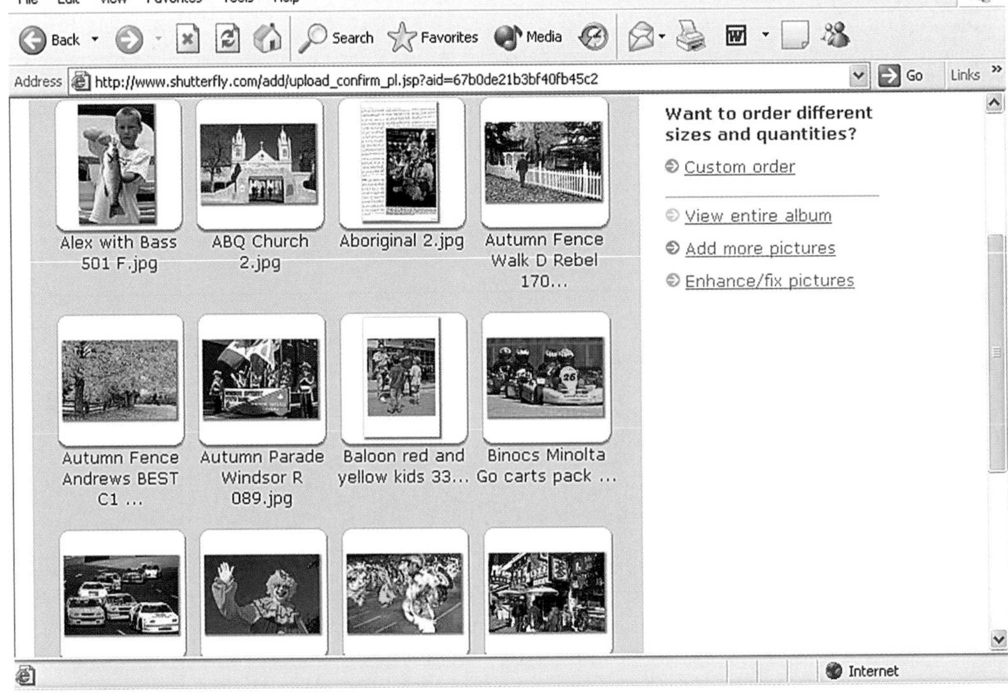

Figure 12.8: Many of the free photo-sharing websites are hosted by companies that offer printing and photo gift services.

free prints as an incentive, as well as low prices. According to articles in photo magazines, some also produce prints with image quality that rates from high to extremely high; try some free samples (if available) before ordering numerous prints.

Create Your Own Photo Web Page

If you are more adventuresome and willing to make a greater investment in time and money, consider creating your own web page or multipage website (see Figure 12.9). Check the Yellow Pages or a local newspaper to find a web-hosting service that charges a moderate monthly fee. If necessary, seek out web-hosting services with a search engine such as www.google.com. Some Internet service providers also provide free website space as part of a package or the monthly fee.

> In many cities, you can hire a college student on a part-time basis to design and build a website, generally at a modest fee. This is a lot less expensive than hiring a professional web-design firm, but you'll want to get references to confirm that the student is reliable and has the necessary expertise. Some website hosting companies offer web-design services or website-building software; ask about these options and their fees when checking out several hosting companies.

The next steps start with securing a domain name for your site, from a registration service such as www.register.com, with a URL (uniform resource locator) address such as www.zzzphotographer.com. You'll then create a web page or a multipage website, upload the data to the web server, and publicize your new web presence to attract visitors. To create a

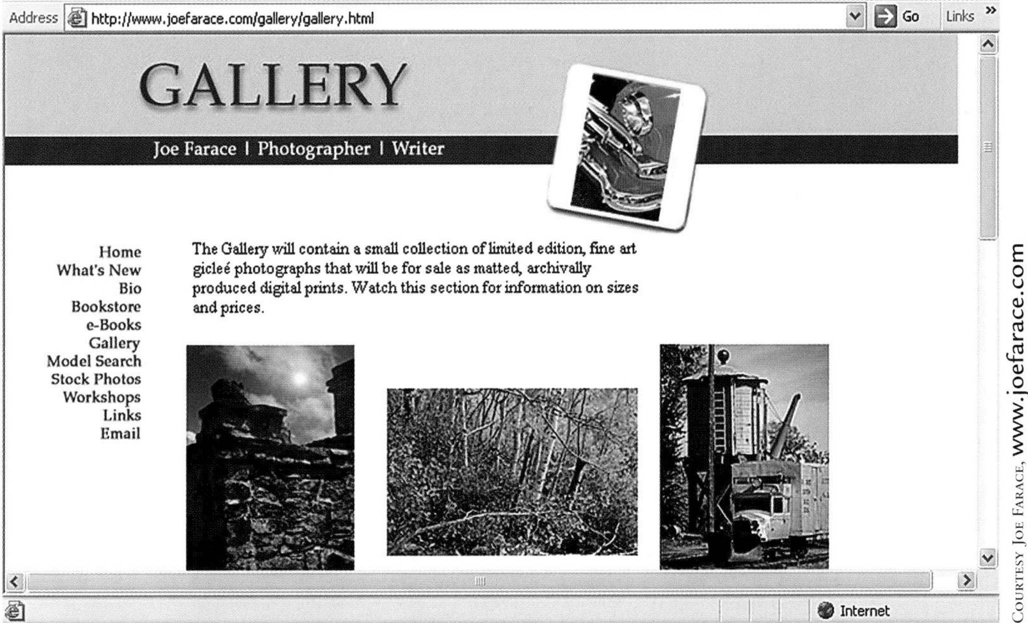

Courtesy Joe Farace, www.joefarace.com

Figure 12.9: Photographers who sell their images or other services generally need a full website. Many hire (full- or part-time) website designers, and others create the site themselves, using the software discussed in this section.

web page or multipage site, you'll want some text as well as images. That will require writing HTML (HyperText Markup Language) code or buying one of the software programs (discussed later) that will do so for you. The code consists of tag sets that identify parameters that instruct the web browser as to what to display on each page.

RECOMMENDATION: Protect Your Images from Unauthorized Use

Photographers are often concerned about the possibility of theft and unauthorized commercial use of images from their websites. This is certainly a risk but one that can be reduced by embedding a copyright notice into the images. For example, you might try this approach: Using layers in an image editor, type the copyright notice in a large, bold font in an important area where it cannot be simply cropped out, as in Figure 12.2 earlier in this chapter. Apply a layer blending option, such as Soft Light in Photoshop for a more subtle effect. You could also try embedding an invisible digital watermark of your copyright notice in each of the images. (In Photoshop, choose Filter → Digimarc → Embed Watermark.)

Or simply adopt a more pragmatic philosophy. Add a prominent warning notice on your home page about unauthorized use, but keep the images small on your website; they will be of little commercial value to anyone. Although individuals can "borrow" them to illustrate a school project or to spice up a family website, such usage is tolerated by most photographers. In fact, some allow such usage (in their Unauthorized Use warning) but specify that photo credit for the image is required.

If you are creating your first web page and do not want to devote a massive amount of time to mastering advanced software and HTML coding, look for one of the more automated programs as shown in Figure 12.10. Try the free demo versions of affordable software such as Web Easy ($40, www.v-com.com), Elibrium's Web Page Creation Kit ($30, www.elibrium.com),

Figure 12.10: If you're planning to create your first web page, consider using one of the full-featured web-publishing software packages.

Easy Web Editor ($79, http://easy-web-editor.net/), or the more sophisticated Microsoft FrontPage ($199, www.microsoft.com/frontpage). FrontPage is intended for beginners and is almost as easy to use as word-processing software; advanced web designers often criticize this software, but it works well for creating basic websites.

To accelerate the learning process, buy a book such as *Create Your First Web Page in a Weekend* (with CD) by Steve Callihan ($20) or *Easy Web Page Creation* by Mary Millhollon ($15).

If you master one of those programs and are ready to switch to more advanced software, consider ImageReady, included with full versions of Photoshop. (ImageReady can generate HTML code, but it's not an HTML editor.) This is powerful but complicated software, intended for creating web graphics and for creating basic websites from "sliced" images but not for modifying HTML files. Later, you will need to write HTML code or buy an HTML editor, as shown in Figure 12.11. Look for software such as HotDog Professional ($100), Meta Products Web Studio ($80), and Quickie Web Page ($30.) Look for reviews of these and other programs—as well as links to free trial downloads—on the Tucows website, www.tucows.com/.

You may reach a stage where you're ready for professional web design software; at that time, you will definitely want to consider top-rated software such as Dreamweaver ($399, www.macromedia.com/software) or Adobe GoLive ($400, www.adobe.com/products). The latter is included in the new Adobe Creative Suite Premium kit. ($1299; $799 as an upgrade for owners of a full version of Photoshop). Expect a steep learning curve with both of these powerful programs; with some dedication, either will allow you to produce, maintain, and update a pro-caliber website.

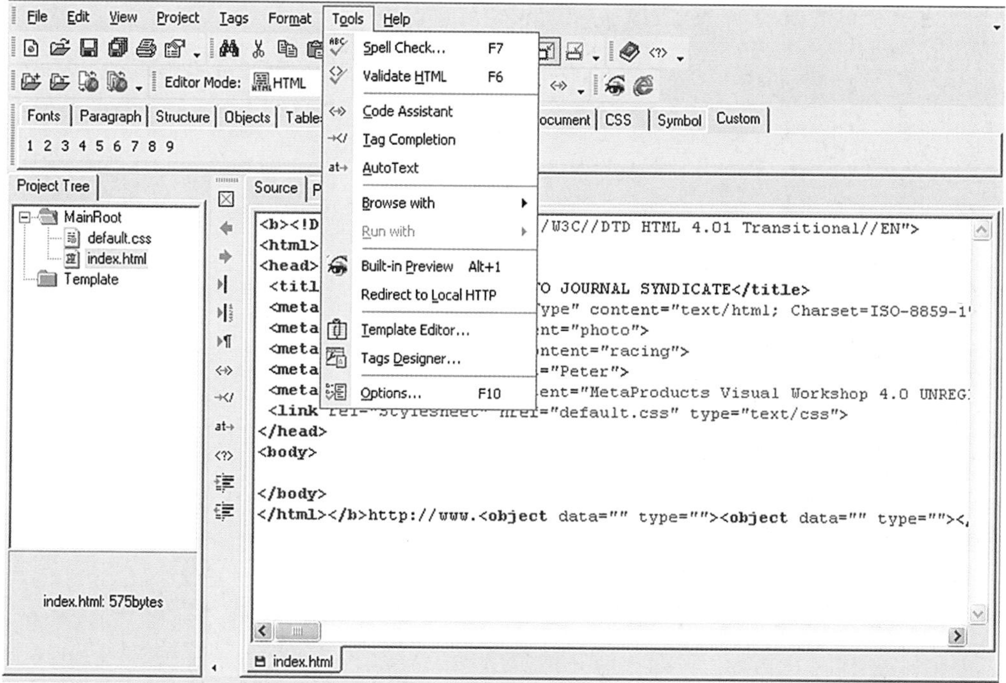

Figure 12.11: Unless you buy a full web creation program that will write HTML code, you'll need HTML editor software.

CHAPTER thirteen

Making Exhibition-Quality Prints

Although digital cameras *and scanners produce pictures in an electronic format, printed photos remain an important part of photography. We frame prints to enjoy day after day, and we appreciate the convenience of showing and sharing prints of our families, vacation trips, and important events. That makes a photo printer an important part of digital imaging. Many printers include automated features that let you produce a print without making any decisions. With machines like this, it's easy to make sharp, colorful prints that will impress most of your friends.*

And yet, competence with the automatic photo printer features is only the first step for anyone who appreciates a superb color or black-and-white print. Once you acquire a photo printer, do try its fully automatic modes and "auto enhancing features." Later, you'll want to advance to using the Custom or Manual options provided in the software, making your own settings for full control over the outputs.

As you develop advanced skills and learn effective techniques, you'll be able to make prints that match or exceed the quality produced by a professional lab. Your dedication will pay off, especially in prints that you enter in photo contests or in oversized prints that you mat, frame, and exhibit. If you use the techniques in this chapter as a starting point, you will progress to making superior prints of exhibition or gallery quality.

Basic Printing Prerequisites

A saying among computer operators applies to many aspects of digital imaging, including printmaking: "Garbage in, garbage out." If you consider that comment overly negative, think of it in positive terms: "Great quality in, great quality out." This certainly applies to printmaking, because you'll get the best results if you start with a high-resolution image file that has been optimized in image-editing software and if you use color-management techniques (Figure 13.1).

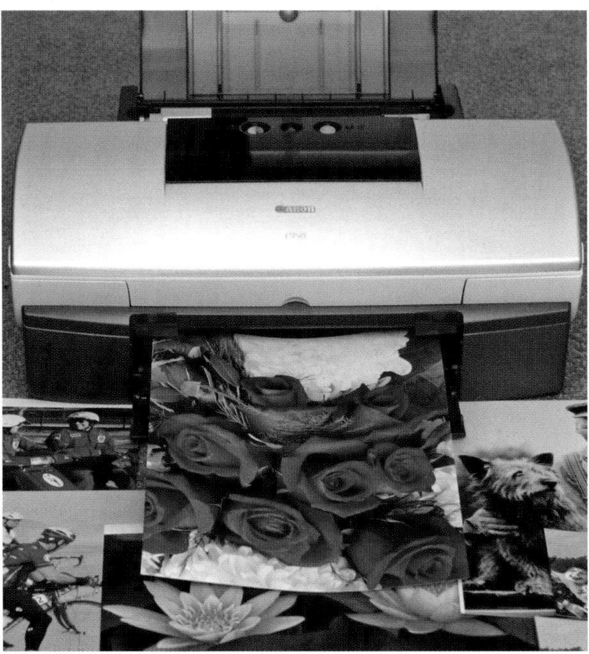

Figure 13.1: Whether you own an affordable photo printer or a pro caliber machine, you should be able to make gallery-quality prints.

All the prerequisites were described in previous chapters. Now, I'll discuss certain aspects in additional detail, as they specifically relate to printmaking, and offer some advice on extra steps that you'll want to take to make exactly the print that you envision.

Selecting a High-Resolution File

For a high-resolution print of true photographic quality, it's essential to start with an image file of adequate size. In other words, the file must contain adequate data for an intended print size.

You may have seen ads for inexpensive 3 megapixel compact digicams suggesting that you can make "great" 11" × 14" (and even larger) prints from the 8MB files that such models generate. Unless your standards for "great" quality are much lower than mine, don't believe such claims. In my experience, you need an image made by one of the very best 4 megapixel cameras to make a fine print as large as 11" × 14".

Although you can increase file size and sharpness substantially with software, the original 8 megapixel file probably does not contain enough picture data to make a very large print. The overall quality will be poor, without fine detail, adequate sharpness, accurate color, subtle tonalities, and smooth gradations. It may look "great" (acceptable) at a glance from a distance of 8', but it won't be an exhibition-quality print by any photo enthusiast's standards.

Refer to the "How Much Resolution Do You Need" sidebar in Chapter 1 as to the largest print size that you'll want to make from the images produced by various types of top-rated cameras: models that generate the highest image quality in their class. Be realistic as to the size of outputs that you can make from any digital image if you want photos that are finely detailed and crisp. Images made with most digital SLR cameras are technically superior to those made with compact digicams. In the next section, I'll explain why and will also provide some suggestions as to the largest print you might want to make from images produced with an SLR model.

Figure 13.2: Made with one of the best 4 megapixel digicams, this image file is not large (less than 12MB), but its technical quality is excellent, allowing me to make fine 11" × 14" prints.

Assessing the Image Quality

Before deciding which of your many images to print, examine them closely for their technical merits. You might be able to make larger prints than suggested in Chapter 1 if the technical quality is absolutely first rate (see Figure 13.2, for example). Let's say that you took a series of images of red rock formations in Arches National Park, using a top-rated 4 megapixel camera with a lens of superb quality, mounted on a tripod. You selected the optimal lens aperture and focal length, shot images on a day without haze or atmospheric pollution, and used the RAW or TIFF recording format at ISO 100. If you select the best of these images and optimize them for printing with image-editing software, you might be able to make 12" × 16" prints that are suitable for display. (Such large prints are rarely examined closely; from a typical viewing distance of 6 feet, most noncritical observers consider them "very good".)

Although no camera produces an image that is perfect in all respects, some images will be better than others. Examine your work at 100 percent magnification on a color-calibrated monitor; check for overall sharpness and accurate focus, particularly in essential subject areas such as the eyes in a portrait. Although it might seem logical to view images at even higher magnification for a critical analysis, stick to the 100 percent scale; at higher levels, the image is interpolated for the on-screen display, so sharpness is degraded.

If you use a digital SLR camera with the shooting techniques mentioned in the first paragraph in this section, you might be able to make larger prints than recommended in Chapter 1. That's because many SLR system lenses are superior to compact digicams' built-in lenses and because digital SLR cameras incorporate more sophisticated image processors and larger, more advanced sensors with larger pixels. If you use one of the top-rated 6 megapixel SLR cameras, such as the Pentax *ist D (see Figure 13.3), your technically best files will allow you to make (or order) very good 16" × 24" prints; some photographers have made even larger prints of impressive quality from 6 megapixel image files.

*Figure 13.3: If you want to make oversized prints of exhibition quality, it's worth buying one of the top-rated digital SLR cameras, such as this 6 megapixel Pentax *ist D.*

Setting Output Size and Resolution

Before the final sharpening for printmaking, you must set output resolution in image-editing software, and this will often call for increasing the size of the image file. (If you plan to make a very small print from a large image file, you might need to decrease the file size.) That's because digital images—whether generated by a camera or a scanner—are rarely the correct size and resolution for making a print of a desired size.

Let's say that you own a digicam that generates an 11.4MB image file with pixel dimensions of 1728 × 2304. The image was probably sized (by the camera's processor) to 32" × 24" at an output resolution of 72 ppi (pixels per inch). You cannot make a good print of that huge size from a file with pixel dimensions of 1728 × 2304, and inkjet photo printers produce the best results with output resolution around 240 to 360 ppi, when using glossy, semigloss, and other popular photo grade papers.

If you use media with a very soft surface, such as watercolor or Concord rag, you can make excellent prints, with a soft, artistic effect, with an output resolution as low as 200 ppi, and even lower according to some photographers. Try your own tests if you often print on art papers to determine the output resolution setting that produces results that you find impressive.

As mentioned in Chapter 5, printer resolution is entirely different from image resolution. Image resolution refers to the density of pixels in an image. In your image-editing software, you might set an output resolution ranging from 240 to 360 ppi. (It requires more than one droplet of ink to produce each of those pixels on paper.) When the printer actually makes prints, it uses a 1440, 2880, or higher dpi, referring to the number of dots of ink that are applied, per inch, on the paper. Do not confuse the two concepts. If you set an extremely high ppi (such as 1440) in your image-editing software, print quality will decline substantially, and the image file will be huge, possibly causing your computer to crash.

Using the image size (or resize) feature in your image editor, you change the resolution to 240 ppi, unless you generally use paper with a very soft surface. For this first step, do not check the Resample Image box (discussed later) if this feature is available in your image editor. After you click OK, the software modifies the output resolution to 240 ppi and changes the dimensions of your "document" to 7.2" × 9.6" (at 240 ppi) in this example, without changing the image file size.

Let's say that you want to make an 11.25" × 15" print using a large-format printer. That calls for a much larger image file size, with substantially more pixels, even at a moderate 240 ppi resolution. Open the Resize dialog box, set the desired dimensions, and check the Resample Image (or similar feature) box. Click OK to resize or scale up the image file, adding pixels to increase an image's physical size or resolution, using interpolation (see Figure 13.4), a sophisticated algorithm. (You must also check the Constrain Proportions or similar box to prevent distortion.) In this example, the new image file size will be 27.8MB, with pixel dimensions of 3600 × 2700, substantially larger than your original file.

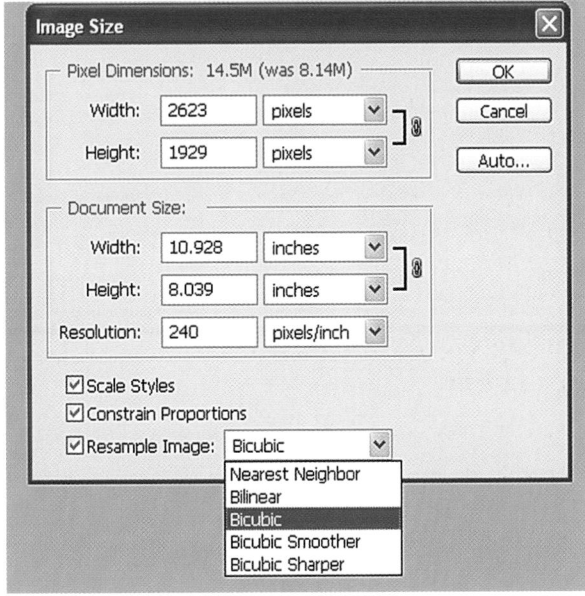

Figure 13.4: Photoshop CS has versatile resampling options, even offering two additional options for bicubic interpolation.

RECOMMENDATION: Use the "Best" Resampling Option

All Adobe image editors and some other advanced programs include three resampling options, interpolation algorightms that can scale up an image by adding pixels or scale down an image by discarding pixels. (Entry-level image editors rarely offer any user-selected options and may not even indicate the type of interpolation technology in use.) The advanced programs generally allow you to select Nearest Neighbor, Bilinear, or Bicubic interpolation. Because we generally want to scale up images for printing, I'll emphasize this process, also called upsampling. Each option uses a different algorithm to increase the physical size of an image file, using an educated guess to decide how to add pixels.

Nearest Neighbor Interpolation Selects a pixel of a surrounding color and adds that next to an existing pixel without creating any new color information. This process does not produce smooth color transitions and is most useful for line art or software screen captures.

Bilinear Interpolation Averages 4 pixels above, below, and on both sides of an existing pixel, to create new information. This produces smooth color transitions and is suitable for digital images, particularly for downsampling (reducing file size).

Bicubic Interpolation Averages an existing pixel's 8 closest neighbors (on all sides) to create new information, and adds a sharpening effect, increasing contrast to minimize pixel blurring. This is the best option for resizing digital images.

Photoshop CS is even more versatile, offering two additional Bicubic options. Bicubic Smoother is optimized for upsampling images, and Bicubic Sharper is optimized for downsampling images. Avoid using the Bicubic Sharper option unless you are upsampling a small, low-resolution image file that contains JPEG artifacts.

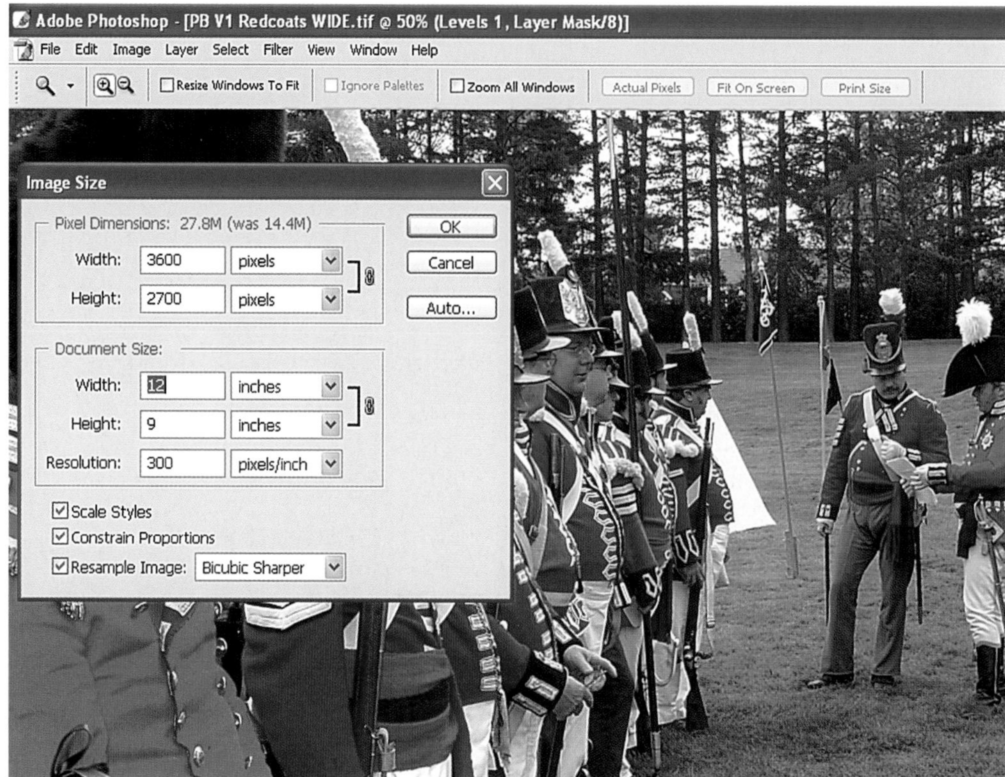

Figure 13.5: If you start with an image that is technically excellent, you should be able to double the file size without a substantial loss of quality.

The file size has been more than doubled (11.4 to 27.8MB), and that should lead you to expect some degradation of quality because the resampling technology cannot work miracles (see Figure 13.5). Many of the pixels in the current image file were created through interpolation. Inspect the image critically, at 100% magnification on your monitor, to determine the level of quality. If it looks very good—without jagged edges, "mushy" fine detail, or visible artifacts in sky or skin tones—you might want to proceed (see Figure 13.6). This image file might not allow you to produce a gallery-quality 11.25" × 15" print on photo papers but the print may still look quite good, especially when viewed from a distance of 6 or more feet.

Figure 13.6: To make a 13" × 17" print (at 260 ppi) from a 14.4MB image file of superb quality, I upsampled the file to 43.6MB. Despite the substantial amount of interpolation, print quality is surprisingly high as confirmed by this small portion (about 10%) of the image area.

RECOMMENDATION: Output Resolution and Interpolation

Most published material suggests that you use a 300 ppi setting for output resolution for making a print, increasing image file size as necessary through interpolation in your image editor. This is merely a guideline and is not cast in stone. Tests conducted by several experienced printmakers confirm that most highly rated inkjet photo printers can generate excellent prints even from files with output resolution of 240 ppi. (Naturally, the higher the size and quality of the image file, the better the prints will be.) This is possible because the interpolation technology used by the printer software is sophisticated and effective.

When you want to make a large print from an image file of moderate size, you can select one of two options.

- You can set a high-output resolution such as 300 ppi and scale up the image with resampling, using bicubic interpolation in your image editor or after-market plug-in software for high-tech scaling up. Popular plug-ins include Genuine Fractals (**www.lizardtech.com**), pxl SmartScale (**www.extensis.com**, $200), and the very affordable Stair Interpolation Pro (**www.fredmiranda.com**, $20). A plug-in is not really necessary, because bicubic interpolation, used by Photoshop and other advanced image editors, is already highly sophisticated.
- You can avoid scaling-up—or at least minimize the amount of interpolation necessary in imaging software—by setting the output resolution to a moderate level, perhaps 240 ppi. In this case, the printer software will interpolate, bringing the resolution up to the optimal level for that machine.

Which approach is preferable? In my experience, a combination of both produces the best results, if you start with an image of very high quality and if you do not try to make excessively large prints from small files. No software or technique will allow you to make a gallery-quality 16" × 24" print from an 8MB JPEG file.

Advanced image editors (particularly Photoshop CS with its additional bicubic options) do a better job of interpolation than printer software. Consequently, I recommend that you start by scaling up the image using resampling, by setting the output resolution to a moderately high amount. Check to see how much scaling up would be required for your intended print size by setting output resolution to 300 ppi, then to 280 ppi, then to 260 ppi, and then to 240ppi. (You must check the Resample Image box for this exercise.)

Unless the image quality is exceptionally high, as discussed in the "Assess the Image Quality" section earlier in this chapter, think twice about going beyond a doubling of the size of the image file because image quality will be degraded, as discussed earlier. If necessary to avoid a greater increase in file size, set output resolution to a lower level—as low as 240ppi. Then, allow the printer software to complete its own interpolation before generating the final print.

If you did not attempt to make an unreasonably large print, the second option should produce prints that are very good to superb, depending on the quality of the image file and the caliber of the image sharpening (discussed later) that you applied before making the output.

Cropping Images for Printing

Few digital images have the same aspect ratio as standard printing paper sizes. Typically, an image—from a digital camera or a scan of a 35mm film frame—will be too long. If you want to print the entire image area, you cannot use standard paper sizes. If you insist on printing at a specific size, such as 8.5" × 11", you must crop the image so that its aspect ratio matches the intended print size (see Figure 13.7).

Figure 13.7: In addition to the basic cropping tool, Photoshop (and some other programs) offer options that allow you to custom crop an image to match the aspect ratio of the intended print size.

To become familiar with this concept and the corresponding tools, open one of your images in an advanced image editor. Make sure that the Constrain Proportions box is checked if you're using software that includes this option. If you're working with an image in a portrait (vertical) orientation, set the desired width to 8.5", and the software will automatically calculate the appropriate width and display the information. You'll probably find that the length will exceed the 11" that you want for a borderless 8.5" × 11" print. You'll need to crop the length, but to what extent?

If you choose not to do this cropping to achieve the correct dimensions for the paper to be used, most printers will allow you to make a print. Naturally, a portion of the image (at one or both ends) will not be included in the output; some important subject area near the edge of the frame may be arbitrarily cropped. That's one reason it is preferable to do your own cropping, getting the dimensions down to the correct size for the print. In addition, most printers will begin laying down ink before the printhead reaches the paper, if the print dimensions are longer (or wider) than the actual paper size. This can be problematic, because the ink can accumulate inside the printer and may clog the machine or smudge the next prints that you make.

Photoshop programs (and some others) can solve this quandary, ensuring that the dimensions are correct for any intended print size (see Figure 13.7). After closing the dialog box, follow these steps:

1. Select the Crop tool.
2. In the Options bar (near the top of the screen, beside the Crop tool icon), set a specific height, width, and resolution for the print. For the purposes of this exercise, set Height to 11in, set Width to 8.5in, and set Resolution to 240 pixels/inch. (Output resolution is a separate issue discussed in the previous section.)
3. Use the Crop tool to crop the image.

The software will not allow for cropping that would produce an "incorrect" width and length because the aspect ratio is fixed, based on the dimensions that you selected. Try several cropping approaches until you are satisfied with the image area that will be included in the print.

---

4. Press Enter or double-click inside the remaining image area; in this single step, the cropping is completed, and the image is resized to fit the intended print size.

During this process, the image file size may have been increased or decreased, through interpolation; you can check that by opening the Image Size dialog box.

RECOMMENDATION: Cropping

It is preferable to make a decision on cropping any image—including not cropping—based on aesthetics instead of cropping for printing at a specific size. Still, at times you will need a certain print size, perhaps to fit a standard mat or frame. In that case, use the tools discussed in this section. They will allow you to achieve the primary goal with some versatility in cropping.

Sometimes the specific print size will not be important, but you'll want prints without borders. In that case, crop the image as desired for aesthetics using the Crop tool in image-editing software. Resize the image so it is not larger than the size of the paper that you plan to use for printing.

Remember that photo printers can only make borderless prints of specific sizes, such as 4" × 6", 8" × 10", or 8.5" × 11". If you want to make a print of some other size, use the next largest paper size; the printed area will be the desired size, with white area surrounding the image. To eliminate those borders, cut them off using a rotary print trimmer. Accessories of this type are available from photo retailers that sell darkroom supplies, such as Porter's (**www.portercamerastore.com**). Expect to pay $65 and up for a heavy-duty 18" model or $25 for a light-duty 14" model.

Optimizing Sharpness

Sharpening for printmaking is the final step after all image enhancement and resizing are completed. If you proceed with sharpening before upsampling an image, edge contrast can be excessive, and the process can exaggerate artifacts.

The correct level of sharpening is a subjective judgment, based on personal preferences. Some photographer friends make prints that seem artificially sharp to my eye, while they claim that some of my prints are "soft." When you're considering the amount of sharpening to apply to any image, think about the intended print size and the viewing distance; both factors will influence your decision. A 13" × 9" print that will usually be viewed from a distance of 6 feet may call for more sharpening than an 8" × 10" glossy that you will hand around for close observation.

In Chapter 10, I introduced the sharpening tools available in image-editing software, particularly Unsharp Mask (USM), a common filter in many programs (see Figure 13.8). USM is certainly an effective option for most images, because it allows you to exert substantial control over the level of sharpening in three distinct parameters: Amount, Radius, and Threshold in Adobe and some other image editors. (In JASC Paint Shop Pro and some other programs, you can adjust Radius, Strength, and Clipping, which are similar in concept.)

The primary issue with USM is the amount of sharpening that is most appropriate. Friends who teach Photoshop courses agree that students tend to oversharpen images that they plan to print. The instructors devote a lot of time explaining and illustrating the drawbacks of aggressive sharpening, such as excessively wide halos around the edges of objects in the images.

If you're at all like most of their students, and if you want to make exhibition-quality prints, use a lower level of sharpening than your tendencies suggest. After applying USM (or another sharpening tool discussed later), examine the image critically at 100 percent magnification on your monitor. Try making two prints of the same image, each with a noticeably different level of sharpening; show these to several friends, and ask them to select the sample they consider close to perfect.

Figure 13.8: The Unsharp Mask filter is extremely versatile, offering full control over the extent of sharpening, with three parameters.

RECOMMENDATION: The Correct Level of Unsharp Mask

What is a starting point for experimentation with the level of sharpening when using Unsharp Mask? That depends on the amount of fine detail in an image. For a print of fall foliage, with tens of thousands of individual leaves, you'll want a high level of sharpening. If the image is less complex—perhaps a colorful fishing boat against a blue sky—a lower level of sharpening is appropriate.

Keeping that in mind, consider the following settings in the USM filter for 8.5" × 11" and larger prints that you make from images produced by a 4–6 megapixel camera:

High-Detail Image Amount 200–300%, Radius 0.6, Threshold 0

Low-Detail Image Amount 75–125%, Radius 2.5, Threshold 8

"Average" Image Amount 100–150%, Radius 1.5, Threshold 4

These recommendations are merely starting points to consider in your own experimentation. For certain types of subjects, such as close-up portraits, you might want to set a lower amount and a larger threshold for a softer, more attractive rendition. My own settings for head-and-shoulder portraits are as follows: Amount 75%, Radius 2, Threshold 4; for even gentler sharpening, I'll select Threshold 8.

Other Sharpening Options

In addition to USM, some advanced image editors include a variety of other, less-sophisticated sharpening options, such as Sharpen, Sharpen More, and Sharpen Edges. As discussed in Chapter 10, Sharpen Edges is the most useful of these filters in advanced image editing, but even that option is not particularly sophisticated. For most images, USM offers the best sharpening solution for those who want to make exhibition-quality prints.

As discussed in the previous section, it's simple to apply a certain level of USM based on advice from others or on your own experience. This technique can work well, but USM sharpens everything in the image, including out-of-focus backgrounds, the pixels in a sky, any artifacts, digital noise, and so on.

Photographers with a great deal of expertise in advanced image editing often use a masking technique: deselecting areas of an image that should not be sharpened with USM. For other images, they may use special edge-only sharpening techniques discussed in instructional books on Photoshop. Unless you have developed skills with such complex techniques, consider using an after-market "intelligent" sharpening plug-in such as Intellisharpen from FM Software (www.fredmiranda.com/software; see Figure 13.9) or nik Sharpener Pro! Inkjet Edition (www.nikmultimedia.com, $100); both work well, but you might prefer one over the other. Nik offers a free demo (download) of their product; FM Software does not, but Intellisharpen is affordable ($15) and is a great choice as a first sharpening plug-in.

After all the image enhancing, resizing, and sharpening are complete, make some prints and examine them closely to decide whether they really qualify for an exhibition-quality rating. If the prints are disappointing in some respects, despite all your tweaking in your favorite image editor, check out the advanced settings in your printer's software.

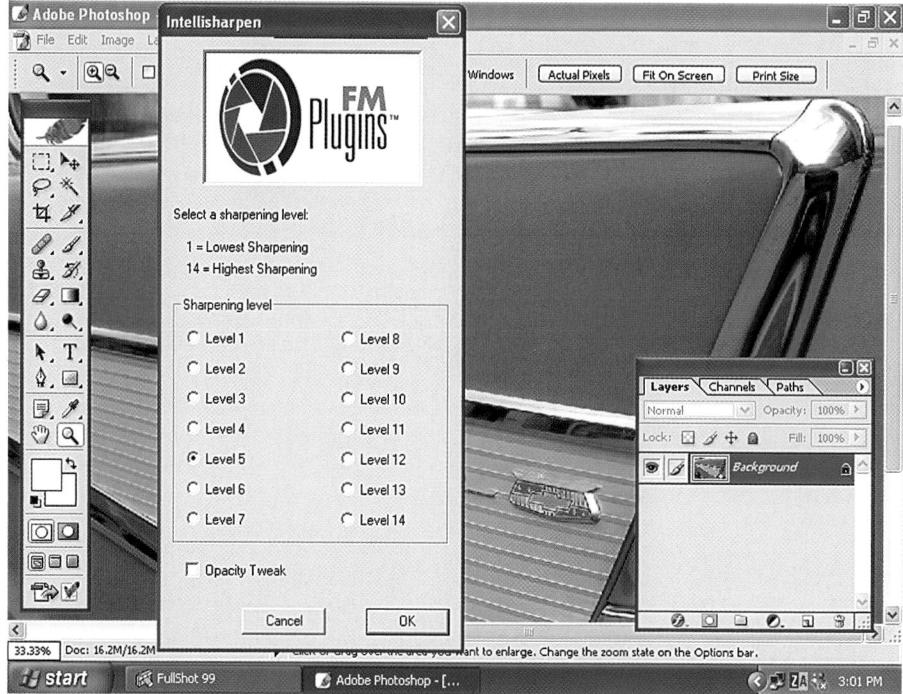

Figure 13.9: When used with some expertise, the USM filter can produce exceptional results, but an after-market sharpening plug-in, such as Intellisharpen, can be valuable for sophisticated sharpening with multiple steps, including masking.

Accessing the Printer's Custom Settings

Virtually all photo printers include software that offers a variety user-selected settings. Before experimenting with the custom settings in the Properties dialog box, make some prints using the fully automatic or default settings. If you're not fully satisfied with the results, identify the specific problem: a green color cast, excessive contrast, and so on. Then, select the Custom or Advanced section of the printer software and begin exploring the features.

The feature set depends on the manufacturer and the specific printer model, but should include options for color adjustment, print-enhancing features, print resolution or quality levels from high to low, color balance and brightness sliders, and so on (see Figure 13.10). Because there is no consistency among manufacturers on the various features, I cannot make specific recommendations as to all the settings that you might want to use, but consider the following suggestions that apply to machines with 2400 dpi (or higher) resolution capability.

Set the correct printing resolution. For high print quality, 1440 dpi is all that is generally required; with some brands of printers, this may be the second highest quality level. If you want the finest possible print, select 2400 or 2880 dpi or the highest quality level or "Best" mode, particularly when using glossy paper.

At the highest print-quality setting , more ink will be used, and printing time will be longer. The difference (between a 1440 and 2880 dpi print) will not be dramatic but should

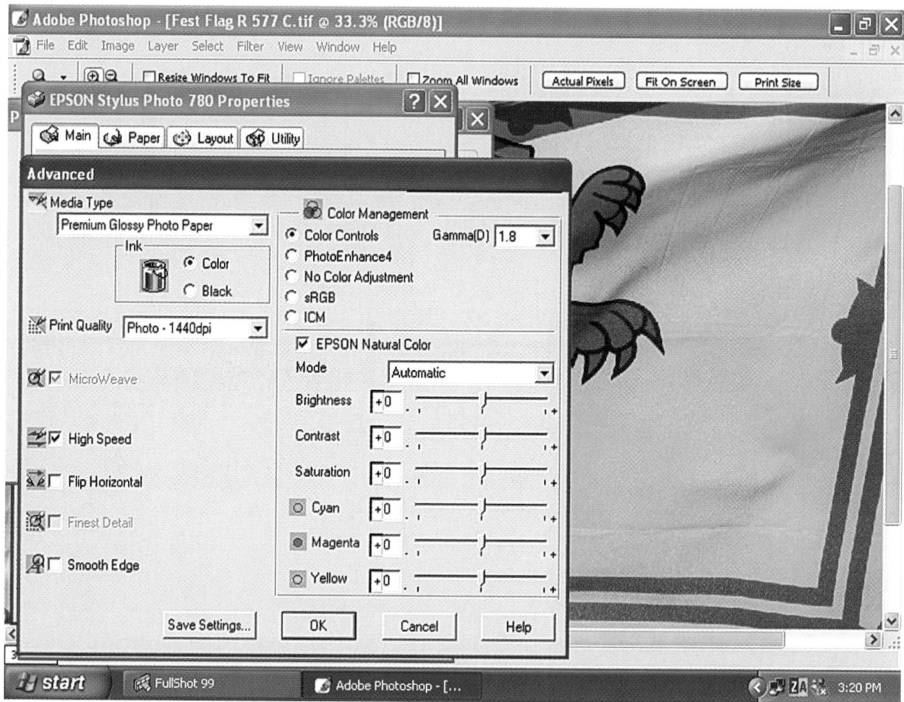

Figure 13.10: Depending on the brand and model of printer, you'll find a few or many automatic print-enhancing options.

be visible under critical examination. Some printers offer even higher dpi options, but frankly I doubt you will see any difference in prints made at such settings unless you use a magnifying glass.

With matte paper, there is no value in using any printer resolution higher than 1440 dpi because dot gain (the spreading of ink on paper) will cause those tiny droplets to blend together. With media that have an even softer finish, such as watercolor or Concorde rag papers, even a 720 dpi setting produces excellent results.

Select the correct software options. Depending on the brand of printer, its software may provide few or numerous options for adjusting color saturation, contrast, brightness, and so on. You should have adjusted all such parameters in image-editing software, so do not adjust them in the printer software. Because the printer software does not provide an accurate preview image, you cannot visually judge the effect that any change will have on the print. Reserve these controls for use after you have made many prints and know your printer's tendencies with certain types of paper. If you find that it routinely produces a slight green cast with glossy paper, for example, you might want to start setting a small increase in magenta (in the printer software) to compensate for that tendency.

Profiles and Color Adjustments

If you are using a custom profile for the specific paper type, don't plan to correct color balance in the printer software. If the software includes a Custom option such as No Color Adjustment, select that setting. Assuming that you are using the other color-management techniques described in Chapter 9, the color balance of your prints should be a close match to the image displayed on your monitor. If your printer still produces a color cast, reopen the image in your image-editing software and make the necessary change (a small increase in magenta, perhaps) before making another print with No Color Adjustment.

You might want to take advantage of a specific enhancing feature—the Photo Realistic option available with Epson printers (see Figure 13.11) and the ICM option available with Canon photo printers. In my tests of both machines, the pertinent feature helped to optimize color rendition.

Do not select features such as Digital Camera Correction, Photo Enhance, Sharpness, Smoothing, Contrast Enhancement, Digital Flash, and Noise Reduction. These were designed for improving images with low resolution, incorrect exposure, or low overall quality. When printing images of fine quality, optimized in image-editing software, such features can actually

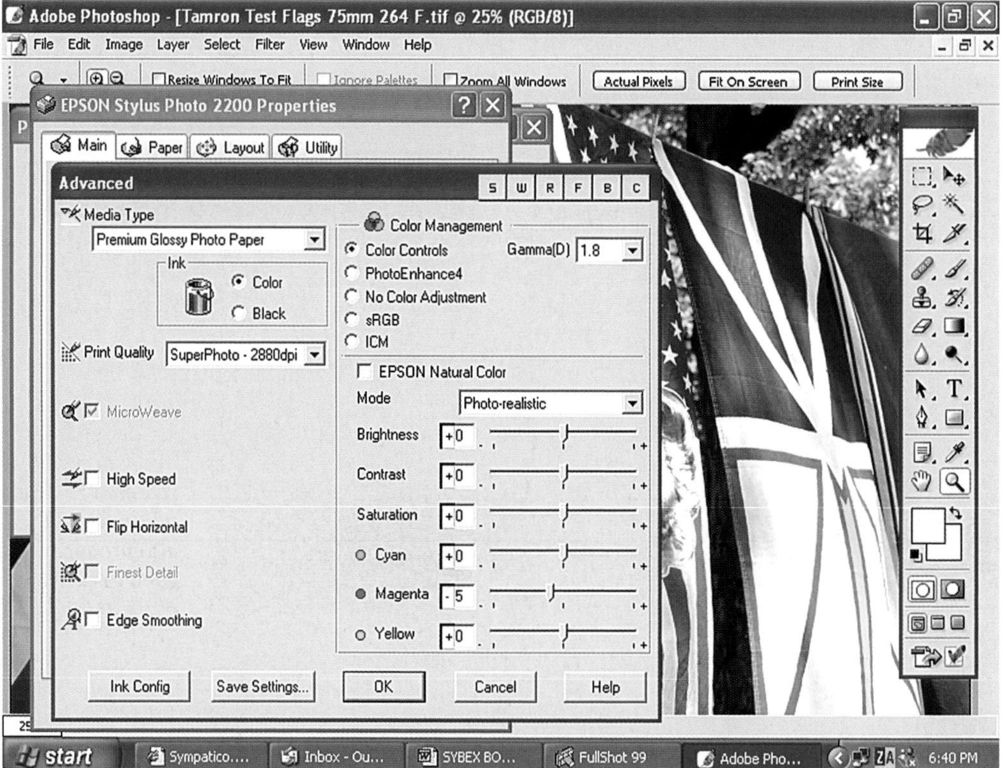

Figure 13.11: Most printers produce the best large prints at 2880 (or similar) dpi, using a single enhancing feature, such as Photo Realistic mode. If the machine consistently produces prints with less than ideal color, brightness, or contrast, try using some of the other control options.

degrade the output. They can produce an effect that is entirely different from what you intended or an effect that simply does not look natural.

Think twice about using any option that promises vivid color saturation unless you have confirmed that it produces the results you want. Often, it is better to boost saturation in image-editing software and leave this printer feature off.

Because printers produce the best quality at standard speed, set the High Speed printing feature to Off. This is particularly important when using glossy paper; high-speed printing can cause roller marks because the ink doesn't have time to dry before coming in contact with the machine's exit rollers.

Using a Color Printer for Monochrome Printing

Logic suggests that a black-and-white image—particularly one that has not been toned—should be printed with black ink only. Although a monochrome print made with only black ink might be neutral in tone, it will be pixelated and will exhibit poor tonal gradations. You'll get much better monochrome prints, with a full range of tones, by using the color inks (see Figure 13.12); do not select the Black Ink Only option in the printer's Properties dialog box.

Six- and seven-color photo printers will generally produce better monochrome prints than three- and four-color printers. Most machines generate prints with a color cast, such as magenta or blue. (Epson printers that use the new UltraChrome pigment-based inks, with a light black cartridge, produce prints that are neutral or close to that ideal.) You can remove any color cast, as discussed in the next section, but that can be a complicated process with printers that produce a strange or unpredictable color cast. If you plan to do a lot of monochrome printing, look for printer reviews on the Web and in photo magazines.

If you use standard color ink sets, try to find custom profiles for your printer/paper/ink combination. If these are not available or do not allow you to make excellent black-and-white prints, consider building your own profiles with the after-market tools discussed in Chapter 9.

Figure 13.12: Although all inkjet printers are designed for full-color printing, many machines will also produce good to excellent black-and-white prints.

RECOMMENDATION: Monochrome Inks for Printing

Several after-market ink manufacturers, including Luminos (www.lumijet.com) and Inkjet Mall (www.inkjetmall.com) offer specialized "monochrome" inks. Available for certain Epson six- and seven-color printers, these are specifically designed for black-and-white printing and can produce excellent results. (Some of these inks are not intended for use with glossy paper.) Custom ICC profiles for the after-market inks are available from the distributors, and these are worth using in order to get the best possible black-and-white prints. You might also want to try their recommended papers for monochrome printing.

Before buying after-market "monochrome" inks for your color printer, note the following. If you try these inks and then switch back to standard inks, the printhead may become clogged; in fact, these after-market inks are more prone to clogging in the first place. You will also need to purchase special flushing accessories to remove previous inks from your printer. Although flushing may work well, you can have problems with your printer caused by ink that isn't completely flushed out.

To avoid problems when switching between ink types, it is best to dedicate one printer for black-and-white printing, using it only with the after-market inks. Use your other printer with the conventional color inks. This is a great way to get some utility from a slightly older printer that you have replaced with the latest-and-greatest model.

Monochrome Printmaking Steps

Because sophisticated profiles are expensive, you'll probably start black-and-white printing using the printer's own software with built-in generic profiles for certain types of paper. Follow any advice in the instruction manual about the types of paper that are most suitable for printing black-and-white images in color RGB mode. Matte papers and semigloss papers such as luster seem to produce the best results with most printers. (For more on paper, see Chapter 5.)

Use the same steps as you would for making a color print, as discussed earlier in this chapter. After all, you are making a color print, using color inks, whether you have added a color tone or not, during the image-enhancement process discussed in Chapter 11. Depending on the printer, the paper, and the effects you created in your image file, you should be able to make an acceptable to good monochrome print on the first try.

The most typical problem is an undesirable overall color cast, often blue or magenta. After making a few prints from several image files, you'll know the printer's tendencies. If it does not produce neutral prints, you will need to access the advanced features in the printer software and use custom color controls. For a magenta cast, for example, set the magenta slider to a small minus value; for a blue cast, increase yellow slightly. Because the printer software does not provide an accurate preview of the image, this is a trial and error process.

Be sure to record the exact color correction level that produces a perfectly neutral print with a specific type of paper. If you use that setting when printing monochrome images on that type of paper, you should be able to consistently produce neutral prints. Many printers have an option for saving preferred settings for future use.

Printer Maintenance

If you expect your inkjet printer to produce the best possible outputs, and if you want to avoid frustration, be sure to follow the recommended maintenance procedures. Run the Nozzle Check, Print Head Alignment, and Print Head Cleaning options, available in the Utilities tab in the Printer Properties dialog box, as recommended by the owner's manual.

Use your printer regularly to avoid problems with clogged nozzles and poor print quality caused by inks that dry out. If you have not used the printer for more than a week or two, complete the Nozzle Check procedure and at least one head-cleaning cycle. If the printer still generates outputs with poor printing or a color cast (such as magenta), you might need to run through the cleaning process twice. Allow the machine to sit overnight, and run Print Head Cleaning again the next day. If this fails to solve the problem, you might need professional repairs; contact the manufacturer or an authorized service center.

Because each head-cleaning cycle consumes a great deal of ink, prevention is preferable to the solution. Unless you have a serious problem, clean the heads only as often as necessary.

You might occasionally need to clean the internal components of the printer to remove any excess ink caused by making borderless prints. Do not disassemble the printer; access the internal components through the top panel. Check your owner's manual for instructions on the process. If the manufacturer provided a cleaning tool, use that in the recommended manner. Otherwise, consider using dry cotton swabs to absorb and remove any ink from the accessible internal components, including the paper path. Work with caution to avoid damaging your printer; do not use any type of solvent. Unless the owner's manual recommends against it, buy a package of Paper Path Cleaning Sheets, and use one when necessary to remove ink or debris.

Appendix: Recommended Reading

To further your knowledge in various areas of photography and digital imaging, you might want to check out some of the following books, magazines, and websites.

Books

You can find dozens of great educational books on the market, including my own *National Geographic Photography Field Guide: Secrets to Making Great Pictures*, co-authored with Robert Caputo. Sybex, the publisher of *Mastering Digital Photography and Imaging*, also offers a growing library of digital photography and imaging titles on a variety of topics. Following are some recent and upcoming Sybex books.

Color Confidence: The Digital Photographer's Guide to Color Management, by Tim Grey
Mac Digital Photography, by Dennis R. Cohen and Erica Sadun
Photoshop CS Savvy, by Stephen Romaniello
Photoshop Elements 2 Solutions: The Art of Digital Photography, by Mikkel Aaland
Photoshop for Right-Brainers: The Art of Photo Manipulation, by Al Ward
Shooting Digital: Pro Tips for Taking Great Pictures with Your Digital Camera, by Mikkel Aaland
Silverfast: The Official Guide, by Taz Tally, Ph. D.
The Hidden Power of Photoshop CS: Advanced Techniques for Smarter, Faster Image Processing, by Richard Lynch
The Hidden Power of Photoshop Elements 2, by Richard Lynch

Books from other authors and publishers that I'd recommend include the following.

Creative Nature & Outdoor Photography, by Brenda Tharp
Digital Landscape Photography, by Tim Gartside
Digital Nature Photography, by Daniel Cox
Digital Photography Expert: Portrait Photography: The Definitive Guide for Serious Digital Photographers, by Michael Freeman
Digital Photography: 99 Easy Tips to Make You Look Like a Pro, by Ken Milburn
Epson Complete Guide to Digital Printing, by Rob Sheppard
How to Photograph Children: Secrets for Capturing Childhood's Magic Moments, by Lisa Jane and Rick Staudt

Learning to See Creatively: Design, Color & Composition in Photography, Revised Edition, by Brian F. Peterson
National Geographic Photography Field Guide: People and Portraits, by Robert Caputo
Spirit of Place: The Art of the Traveling Photographer, by Bob Krist
The Art of Outdoor Photography: Techniques for the Advanced Amateur and Professional, Revised Edition, by Norton Boyd

Magazines

Although a wealth of information is available on the web, many photography and imaging enthusiasts subscribe to print magazines. The following list includes publication frequency and a brief overview of the content of popular magazines; for additional specifics, visit the publishers' websites. I am a regular contributor to *e-DIGITAL PHOTO*, *Photo Life*, and *Shutterbug* but can recommend all the following titles.

The Digital Image, quarterly, from the Lepp Institute of Digital Imaging; advanced digital photography and imaging techniques provided by Tim Grey (www.leppphoto.com)
Digital Camera, bimonthly; covers digital imaging, particularly equipment (www.digicamera.com)
Digital Photographer, bimonthly; covers all aspects of digital imaging (www.digiphotomag.com)
Digital Photo Pro, bimonthly; covers all aspects of digital imaging; targets professional and advanced enthusiasts (www.digitalphotopro.com)
e-DIGITAL PHOTO, 8 issues per year; covers all aspects of digital photography and imaging (www.edigitalphoto.com)
Outdoor Photographer, 11 issues per year; extensive coverage of nature, travel, and sports photography techniques (www.outdoorphotographer.com)
PC Photo, called *Digital Photo* in some markets, 9 issues per year; covers all aspects of digital photography and imaging (www.pcphotomag.com)
Petersen's PHOTOgraphic, monthly; general photography/imaging magazine with emphasis on equipment www.photographic.com
Photo Life, bimonthly; general photography magazine with coverage of conventional and digital equipment and techniques. (www.photolife.com)
Popular Photography & Imaging, monthly; general photography/imaging magazine with emphasis on equipment (www.popphoto.com)
Shutterbug, monthly; general photography/imaging magazine with emphasis on equipment and test reports (www.shutterbug.net)

Websites

You can find information on every imaging topic on the web, but not all of it is reliable, well organized, and thorough. The following sites, however, provide valuable information and are well worth a regular visit.

Digital Darkroom Questions (www.timgrey.com); daily e-mail service. Tim Grey answers readers' questions related to digital photography, equipment, software, scanning, and printing.

Digital Photography Review (www.dpreview.com); daily news items about new equipment; thorough test reports, particularly of digital cameras, with extensive technical documentation.

FRCN Digital Imaging (www.quiknet.com/~frcn/Camera.html); lessons in photography and digital imaging, plus many reviews of imaging software.

Imaging Resource (www.imaging-resource.com); daily news items about new equipment; thorough test reports, particularly of digital cameras.

MSN Photos (http://photos.msn.com); photography and imaging magazine with practical how-to articles.

Photo.net (www.photo.net); a forum on all aspects of photography with an emphasis on effective techniques.

Photoshop User, National Association of Photoshop Professionals (NAPP) (www.photoshopuser.com); news, information, and techniques for maximizing the value of Photoshop image editors.

Rob Galbraith Digital Photography Insights (www.robgalbraith.com); news, information, and reviews about professional-level digital SLR cameras and accessories.

ShortCourses (www.shortcourses.com); numerous pages of instruction in many areas of photography and digital imaging.

Steve's Digicams (www.steves-digicams.com); daily news items about equipment; reviews of digital cameras and other types of imaging products.

Glossary

A

A/C adapter
A power adapter that allows you to plug your camera into an electrical wall outlet. Some camera kits include this accessory.

algorithm
A mathematical formula that produces results in relation to defined values. For example, algorithms are used in interpolation to determine new pixel values when an image is enlarged.

aliasing
The jagged effect produced on lines in graphics when resolution is too low or in digital images when a camera cannot resolve the fine detail.

alkaline battery
A type of nonrechargeable battery that can be used in your digital camera. Alkaline batteries drain quickly under the demands of most digital cameras.

analog
A system in which values are represented by continuously variable values, rather than a limited range of discreet values as with a digital system.

anti-aliasing
The technique that smoothes jagged effects in images caused by aliasing. Anti-aliasing combines image data from a higher-resolution image or model into adjacent pixels and produces cleaner, more natural lines.

aperture
The size of the camera's lens opening, denoted with f/numbers. A small aperture (such as f/16) provides extensive depth of field (range of sharp focus) while letting in less light. A large aperture (such as f/4) lets in more light and produces shallower depth of field.

archival
Media with long useful life, such as prints that resist fading or data storage media that are highly reliable for long periods of time, such as a CD or a DVD.

artifact

An unintentional image element or defect in image data produced by an imaging device or as a byproduct of software or algorithms, such as lossy compression. Common in JPEG images that have been heavily compressed, artifacts may appear as jagged edges or skewed lines, a "blocky" effect, color flaws and noise (resembling color specks.)

aspect ratio

The ratio between an image's width and height. Typical ratios include 3:2, 4:3, and so forth. The first number refers to the image's width, and the second refers to its height.

autofocus (AF)

An automatic system that produces sharp images by acquiring focus without user intervention.

B

backlight

A light source, such as the sun, that illuminates the subject from behind, or a bright area behind the subject. The opposite of front lighting. Backlight causes most cameras light meters to underexpose the subject because the system attempts to render the brightest area as a midtone. Use exposure compensation of flash for a more accurate exposure.

banding

The phenomenon in which gradations of tone and color in an image are not smooth; often caused by excessive editing. Working with an image in high-bit mode helps to eliminate the possibility of banding because more "steps" in tonal and color values are available.

batch processing

Altering or saving a group of images at the same time, in sequence, using the same settings in computer software, such as a RAW file converter program.

bit depth

A measure of the range of tonal and color values in a digital image file. The bit depth indicates how many bits are required to store the number of values available, which in turn determines how many total possible values there are. RGB images typically offer a bit depth of 8-bits per channel (red, green and blue), combined to produce a 24-bit image with up to 16.7 million colors. Scanners are able to scan at 8-bit per channel, with higher-end models supporting 14- or 16-bit per channel capture. Digital cameras offer 8-bit per channel capture, but in RAW capture mode they may offer 12-bit per channel. Bit depths higher than 8-bit per channel potentially offer billions of tonal and color values in the image.

blurring

A loss of image detail caused by incorrect focus, camera shake, or subject movement. Blurry pictures can be partially corrected with sharpening filters and deconvolution techniques in image-editing software.

BMP (bitmap)

Strictly speaking, a black-and-white image constructed of arrays of black and white pixels. However, in common usage, the term *bitmap* (incorrectly) refers to arrays of pixels of any colors where each pixel value is stored in sequence based on its location in the image. A graphic file format for Windows systems, it stores images as an uncompressed matrix of pixels.

brightness
The level of light reflected by a subject or emitted by a light source and detected by a digital camera's sensor.

byte
A tiny amount of data that consists of 8 bits; computers and software use bytes to transmit data and instructions.

C

calibration
In digital imaging, a term used for adjusting a device—monitor, scanner, or printer—to produce true, accurate color rendition. Calibration involves changing the behavior of a device to get it as close as possible to established standards.

capture
To acquire digital data through a camera or other scanning device.

catch light
A bright spot in a person's eyes, created by the sun, electronic flash or another light source.

CCD
charge-coupled device.

CD
Compact disc; a removable storage medium. Includes CD-ROMs (Read-Only Memory), which are intended for playback only, CD-Rs (recordable) that allow consumers to record data onto a disc one time, as well as CD-RWs (Re-Writable) that allow for recording and for erasing by overwriting previous data, using a suitable CD recorder or "burner."

CF
See *CompactFlash.*

charge-coupled device (CCD)
A light-sensitive image sensor used in many digital cameras to sample light intensity for gathering image data. A CCD array consists of a series of sensors. The values from the individual sensors are read one row at a time, with each row's data values being moved toward the output row in conveyor belt fashion as the values are read. Because CCD sensors don't have circuitry to process the signal values, additional circuitry in the camera is required for this purpose.

cloning
In image-editing software, a feature that allows you to copy a part of a photo and use that copy to replace another part of the photo. Cloning is typically used to hide flaws, distracting elements, and undesirable features.

CMOS (complementary metal oxide semiconductor)

An image-sensor chip used in some digital cameras to sample light intensity for gathering image data. CMOS sensors are less expensive, use less power, and are faster than CCD sensors. They can read all values from the sensor at one time in parallel. CMOS sensors also include circuitry at each pixel site that allows the values to be processed without additional circuitry in the camera.

CMYK

The color standard for professional offset press printing of the type used to print books and magazines. Instead of printing in red, green, and blue, this standard uses cyan (C), magenta (M), yellow (Y), and black (K) ink.

color management

A system that allows you to compensate for the variations in color behavior from device to device so that you can obtain predictable results as the image is captured, displayed, and output by the various devices in the digital workflow.

color temperature

The temperature, in degrees kelvin, of a light source. The lower the temperature, the redder the light. The higher the temperature, the more blue. Candlelight clocks in at about 2000 kelvin, and sunset, at 3000 kelvin. Daylight and flash photography both register at about 5000 to 5500 kelvin.

CompactFlash (CF)

A type of solid state memory card used in some digital cameras. Compact flash cards are built from banks of flash memory and a controller embedded in thin plastic. See also *removable media*.

compression

The use of algorithms to make data files smaller. This is accomplished by describing the data in the file more efficiently. With lossy compression, pixel values can actually be changed to better accomplish this goal.

continuous tone

In photo printing, prints whose color values continuously blend into each other and are not composed of discreet dots to simulate these smooth gradations. Dye sublimation printers, for example, produce truly continuous tone output. However, the latest photo inkjet printers produce output with ink droplets that are so small, they can be considered continuous tone devices for all practical purposes.

contrast

The ratio in brightness between the darkest and lightest elements of an image. Natural scenes should contain moderate contrast, unlike printed text, which should be highly contrasted.

CPU (Central Processing Unit)

The device that handles the mathematical processing within a computer—a main board and circuitry that transmits data to and from that chip.

CRT (cathode ray tube)

One of the two common types of computer monitors, a CRT produces a display using electron guns that fire electrons at phosphors, causing them to glow with light. CRT monitors are quickly losing favor to the smaller and lighter LCD monitors.

custom color profile

A data file of a standard format that describes the color behavior of a device. This allows software to compensate for that behavior to produce the most accurate results possible.

D

depth of field

The zone of apparent sharpness in front of the focused subject and behind it.

digital

Information made up of binary digits with discreet values limited by the storage method being used for those values and readable by a computer.

digital camera

A camera that uses a digital sensor rather than photochemical film to capture images in electronic form. The scene before the lens is translated into digital values that describe the tone and color of each pixel. In this book, we also use the term "digicam" as an abbreviation to denote cameras that are not SLR (single lens reflex) cameras and do not accept interchangeable lenses.

digital film

The medium used to store images as they are captured in digital cameras. See also *removable media*.

digital zoom

Magnifying an image by means of software within a digital camera. Digital zoom enlarges the central part of an image and discards other data to replicate the effect of using a longer lens. In effect, zoom is accomplished by cropping a portion of the total pixels within the image and then interpolating those values. I recommend against using digital zoom, except for quick snapshooting, because it degrades image quality.

digitize

To convert data into digital form, using a device such as a scanner.

download

To transfer data from a device, such as a digital camera memory card, to a computer.

dpi (dots per inch)

A measure of how many dots are used within a linear inch to represent image data. This term relates to how tightly the pixels in a digital image file are spaced together for printing. Printer manufacturers often use this term to describe the output quality of a device. Although such a use has a basis in fact, it is misleading because it refers to droplets of ink rather than to pixels in an image file.

DVD

A removable medium; originally denoted Digital Video Disc, but DVDs are now available for data storage as well. A DVD is similar in technology to a CD but offers greater storage capacity; a DVD recorder, or "burner," writes data to a DVD. (A DVD burner can also record to a CD.)

dye-sublimation printer

Also called thermal-dye transfer; this type of printer uses a head that heats a ribbon containing inks in solid form to create colored dye gas; the gas is transferred to a special type of paper to form the color image. (Sublimation refers to the conversion from a solid to a gas.) The color intensity of the dye is controlled by the heat level of the printhead. Dye sublimation produces excellent print quality with soft-edged dye spots for a smooth, continuous-tone effect. However, the printers and consumables are more expensive than those for inkjet printing.

dynamic range

The difference between the darkest and brightest values in an image. Some high-end film scanners and digital cameras can produce images with a very high dynamic range; in many such images, detail is visible in both highlight and shadow areas.

E

exposure compensation

A camera control that allows for making brighter or darker images by applying a plus or minus factor, to increase or decrease exposure.

exposure meter

A system consisting of a sensor and computing device that determines the reflectance or brightness of a scene and sets, or recommends, the camera settings that should produce a correctly exposed image, with accurate brightness. Three types of exposure meters are common. A multisegment system divides the image into several zones and evaluates the lighting pattern. A center-weighted meter primarily measures subject reflectance in a large, central area of the image. A spot meter measures reflectance in a much smaller area.

F

fill flash

Also called daylight flash and forced flash; a camera mode that causes flash to be fired at all times (often at a reduced power setting), even in bright light. It's useful for filling in (brightening) shadow areas.

filter

A camera accessory that can modify the color (and other aspects) of the light entering the lens or create special effects such as soft focus and starlike shapes around bright light points. In image-editing software, a feature that allows you to alter the pixel values in an image based on specific algorithms to cause a change in the image. With digital images, the effects can produce artistic, distorted, blurred, sharper, and many other versions of an image.

FireWire

A high-speed, serial data-transfer standard often used for transferring data from digital cameras, scanners, external hard drives, and digital memory card readers to a computer or from the computer to printers and data storage devices. Known technically as IEEE 1394, it is commonly referred to as FireWire, which is the name given to the technology by Apple. FireWire offers a maximum data transfer rate of 400Mbps. A new FireWire 800 standard will offer rates of up to 800Mbps.

first curtain flash sync

A camera mode in which the flash fires at the start of a long exposure time and not near the end of the exposure. See also *rear curtain flash sync*.

focal length

The distance between the lens and the point where light rays focus on the image sensor when light enters the lens in parallel lines. The longer the focal length, the greater the magnification that the lens provides.

forced flash

See *fill flash*.

G

gamma

A value that determines the adjustment applied to midtone values in an image or monitor display. Once the midtone value is set, it can be used as a guideline for the relative brightness of the monitor or image.

gamma adjustment

A change the midtone value of a monitor display for greater accuracy in the relative brightness.

GB (gigabyte)

A term that is often used for 1 billion bytes. It actually means 1024 million bytes or 1024 megabytes (MB).

GIF (Graphics Interchange Format)

A common file format often used for graphics and line art on the Web. The GIF format was developed by CompuServe and includes lossless compression. GIF supports no more than 256 colors, although you can define specific colors to be used for an image. GIF is usually not suitable for photographic images. Support for transparency and animation makes GIF a popular file format for web graphics.

grayscale

A colorless digital image with tone ranging from pure white to pure black, including numerous levels of gray. Color images can be converted to grayscale to produce a black-and-white image, but this is not recommended because it discards a great deal of data.

H

hue

The color (as opposed to the brightness) of a pixel. More specifically, the attribute of a color that we associate with that color, such as red, green, or blue. Hue is defined based on a measure of degrees around a color wheel, starting at zero degrees for red.

I

ICC (International Color Consortium)

A group of companies (www.color.org) that produces standards for color-management systems.

inkjet printer

A printer that sprays tiny droplets of ink onto paper to produce an image. The inks are commonly propelled either by heat or vibration. Many of today's inkjet printers use such small droplets that they can be considered continuous tone devices. See *continuous tone.*

interpolation

A method of changing the effective output size of an image file by increasing the number of pixels in the image. Special algorithms are used to calculate values for the pixels that must be added in the process. See also *algorithm.*

ISO

A measure of a film's sensitivity to light, as defined by the International Organization for Standardization. The term ISO is also used in digital imaging, although a high ISO setting does not increase the sensitivity of the sensors; it simply amplifies the signal. The ISO ranges from low at ISO 50 or 100 to high at ISO 400, and very high at ISO 800 to 1600. The higher the ISO, the faster the shutter speed that can be used to make a well-exposed image.

J

jaggies

Jagged edges within a digital image, especially noticeable in diagonal lines, usually caused by pixels that are rectangular rather than circular or by JPEG compression that produces artifacts. See also *artifacts.*

JPEG (Joint Photographic Experts Group)

An image format for digital pictures. JPEG pictures use efficient (but lossy) compression algorithms and averaging techniques to minimize image size at a cost in accuracy. When a JPEG image is modified, saved, and closed (compressed) and then reopened (uncompressed), it is not identical to the original image. The amount of degradation depends on the amount of compression and is cumulative—becoming worse the more often the image is modified and compressed. JPEG images can support 8-bit per channel color, providing greater color fidelity than GIFs. See also *GIF.*

JPEG-2000

A new standard for storing digital pictures that extends the JPEG standard to include lossless compression using wavelet technology, transparency, and other features.

K

kelvin

A temperature measurement system for light sources, using the kelvin scale. See also *color temperature.*

L

laser printer

A type of printer that uses a laser to set electrical charges along a print drum. Toner (an ink mixture) is drawn to the charged areas of the drum, and a heating element fuses the toner from the drum to paper.

layer

In image-editing software, the ability to isolate image elements so that you can work on one element at a time. These can be multiple image layers, such as would be used for a collage, or adjustment layers that allow you to apply adjustments to the image.

LCD (liquid crystal display)

A display made of a liquid crystal material sandwiched between transparent sheets. An electric charge is used to change the alignment of the crystals, which in turn affects how the light passing through is polarized. Typically, an LCD monitor on the back of a digital camera allows the photographer to view images as a preview and in playback. (With an SLR camera, preview is not available.) Computer monitors are also available with LCD technology, providing a display that is smaller and lighter than a CRT monitor. See also *CRT*.

light meter

See *exposure meter*

lithium ion battery

A type of battery that provides greater power capacity and endurance than alkaline batteries. Although most lithium ion batteries are designed for one-time-use, some lithium ion batteries can be recharged.

lossless compression

Any compression scheme that reduces the file size of an image without changing any pixel values. When the image is later decompressed, it is identical to the original. For example, TIFF compression is lossless provided that a JPEG compression option is not used.

lossy compression

Any compression scheme that reduces the file size of an image in part by changing pixel values to simplify the image. This produces a decompressed image that is not identical to the original, usually manifested in a loss of detail or color and the addition of artifacts that may appear blocky or jagged. Usually, colors have been blended, averaged, or estimated in the decompressed version. For example, JPEG compression is lossy. Each time you adjust and resave a JPEG image, you can lose valuable image information. See also *artifacts*.

luminosity

The intensity (as opposed to the color) of a pixel. See also *brightness*.

M

macro

A term denoting images made with extremely close focus. Technically, macro focusing denotes at least 1x magnification of the subject, although macro is often used to define any extremely close focus. The macro setting on a camera or lens allows you to shoot pictures from as little as an inch or two away from your subject.

MB (megabytes)

Indicates 1024 kilobytes or 1.048 million bytes of data, although MB is often used to denote 1 million bytes. In digital imaging, megabytes are most relevant in two respects: the amount of RAM in a computer (the more MB the better) and the size of an image data file (the more MB, the larger the file).

megapixel

A term for one million pixels. A one megapixel camera produces images with roughly one million pixels; a two megapixel camera produces images with roughly two million pixels, and so on.

memory card

Removable medium used in digital cameras, often called digital film. Most are solid state devices, employing flash memory, and include formats such as CompactFlash, SmartMedia, SecureDigital and the similar MultiMediaCard, MemoryStick, and the xD-Picture card. Often used to include the Microdrive (not actually a memory card but often labeled as such), a miniature hard drive in a format resembling a CompactFlash card. Most digital cameras store images on a memory card that can be removed and replaced.

memory card reader

A computer peripheral designed to accept one or more types of memory cards and used to transfer data from the card to a computer, via some form of connectivity, usually USB.

moiré

A photo artifact consisting of bands of diagonal distortions. These distortions arise from interference between two geometrically regular patterns.

N

nickel cadmium (NiCd) battery

A type of rechargeable battery that provides moderately long effective life in a camera or flash unit. Because NiCds (pronounced “nigh-cads”) contain the heavy metal cadmium, they promote concerns about proper disposal.

nickel metal hydride (NiMH) battery

A type of rechargeable battery that provides long effective life in cameras and flash units and fewer environmental concerns than alkaline or NiCd batteries. A NiMH (pronounced “nimm”) battery has less of a “memory effect” than the older NiCd batteries; you do not need to drain them fully each time before recharging.

noise

Random, unintended image values added to and distributed across a digital picture, visible as a rainbow of pixels in an image, particularly in dark areas. Noise is a common byproduct of amplification of a digital signal, such as when using a higher ISO setting in a digital camera. See also *artifact*.

O

operating system

Often abbreviated as OS, the master software that controls a computer. For consumer use, the Macintosh and Windows operating systems are most common.

optical zoom

Magnifying an image by means of a lens, with optical elements, that allows for varying the focal length. Unlike digital zoom, optical zoom maintains full image quality.

P

PC card

Memory storage medium designed for inserting in a computer's PCMCIA (Personal Computer Memory Card International Association) slot. Few digital cameras use PC cards to store photos, but adapters are available to allow the more common memory cards to be inserted into a slot on some computers, primarily laptops, called the PC card slot. Adapters are available for converting various types of removable media so that they will fit into the PC card slot.

photo paper

Paper specifically designed for use in printing photographic images; often coated to better allow the inks to bond with the paper.

Pixel

Short for "picture element," the smallest unit within an image that has a specific color value. The more pixels in a digital image, the higher the resolution, which translates into greater detail and larger potential output sizes.

plug-in

Software applications that can be installed in certain image-editing programs in order to provide additional tools for correcting images or for creating special effects.

polarizing filter

A type of lens filter that polarizes the light passing through it, allowing only light vibrating in a particular direction to pass through. Such a filter can wipe glare from nonmetallic reflective surfaces, restoring detail and increasing apparent color saturation. This filter can also enrich blue skies and help to reduce the effects of atmospheric haze for greater contrast.

ppi (pixels per inch)

The number of pixels per linear inch in an image or on a monitor. Often referred to as dpi, though that term technically refers to dots on paper, not pixels in an image.

R

RAM (random access memory)

Used for temporary storage of data in a computer or other electronic device. Most imaging applications recommend that your computer have at least 256 megabytes of RAM for fast processing; advanced users will want at least 512MB of RAM.

RAW or raw

A file format, available with some digital cameras, as an alternative to JPEG or TIFF capture. A RAW file consists of unprocessed data from the image sensor that must be processed using special RAW converter software and converted into an image file format such as JPEG or TIFF.

rear curtain flash sync

A camera mode in which the flash fires near the end of the exposure time, not at the start; intended to produce light trails that follow a moving subject. See also *first curtain flash sync*.

red-eye

An effect that appears to make a person's eyes glow red in an image. Red-eye occurs when light from electronic flash reflects from the blood-vessels (or *choroids*) directly behind the retina.

red-eye reduction mode

A solution for red-eye built in to some digital cameras. In this mode, the camera fires a series of flash bursts or projects an incandescent beam before firing the flash that will make the image. The pre-flashes are particularly effective in making people's pupils quickly contract but may also cause them to blink.

removable media

Storage mediums that can be removed from a device. Types of removable media often used with a computer or its peripherals include floppy disks, writable CDs, and cartridges with magnetic media. Removable media are portable. See also CD, DVD, *memory card*, and *digital film*.

resolution

A general term that relates to the density or quantity of information in a digital image. When referring to density, it relates to the amount of information in a given space, such as the pixels per inch in an image or dots per inch in a print. When referring to quantity, it relates to the total number of pixels, such as the number of megapixels in a digital camera. See also *ppi* and *dpi*.

RGB

Red, green, and blue, the additive primary colors and the standard set of colors used by computer systems and most digital cameras to create images. See also *CMYK*.

S

second curtain flash sync

A camera mode in which the flash fires at the end of an exposure, not at the start; with a moving subject, this can produce light trails that follow, instead of precede, the subject for a more convincing motion effect.

sensor

A general term for the light-sensitive pixel array used to record image data. See also *CCD* and *CMOS*.

serial cable transfer

A method used to transfer data from a scanner to a computer or from a computer to a printer, using a certain type of cable. Because this form of connectivity is slow, it has been replaced by faster methods. See also *USB* and *FireWire*.

shutter speed

The time during which light is allowed to enter through a camera's lens to expose the image sensor; this factor can be set automatically by the camera or by the user in manual operating mode. At very fast shutter speeds (such as 1/500 sec.), an image is unlikely to be blurry due to camera shake or subject motion. At long shutter speeds (such as 1/4 sec.), a moving subject will be blurred, and camera shake can be a problem unless a tripod (or other firm support) is used. Digital camera speed is analogous to traditional shutter speed, although some digital cameras do not come equipped with true shutters.

silver-halide paper

Traditional photochemical paper used by photo finishers for making prints; also available for consumer use in a wet darkroom.

slow sync flash

A camera mode that produces a long shutter speed and fires flash during the exposure time. This combination is intended to illuminate a foreground subject (with flash) while allowing a moderately dark background, such as a city scene, to be well-exposed, due to the long exposure time. In more typical (short) flash exposures, a moderately dark background would not be properly exposed.

T

telephoto lens

A magnifying lens with a long focal length, generally more than 50mm in terms of 35mm photography. The opposite of wide-angle lenses, telephoto lenses produce images with a narrow angle of view. Long telephoto lenses allow for making frame-filling pictures of a distant subject. Use a long telephoto lens when you cannot get close to your subject, as in wildlife photography.

thermal dye transfer

See *dye-sublimation printer*.

TIFF (Tagged Image File Format)

An image format used to store high-resolution images. Although TIFF images are often uncompressed, this format does support some compression algorithms, and most are lossless. The resulting images are identical to the original TIFF images. This makes TIFF a good choice for storing your pictures while you are working on them.

U

Unsharp Mask (USM)

A sharpening feature available in many image-editing programs, as well as the software of some scanners, USM intensifies edge contrast within an image. USM allows the user to control the exact level of sharpening, by setting a desired level in three distinct parameters.

USB (Universal Serial Bus)

A cable connection standard that provides quick and efficient data transfer. Most newer computers provide USB ports. Most digital cameras now support USB transfer in place of earlier serial cable transfers. The original USB (1.1) standard supports transfer rates of up to 12MBps, and the newer USB 2 standard supports data transfer rates of up to 480MBps.

W

watermark

A visual mark placed over an image, usually at reduced opacity, generally used to mark an image with copyright data. A non-visual digital version (called digital watermarking) adds invisible author copyright information into a picture, without noticeably altering the image.

white balance

Color balance. A camera control that allows you to manually adjust how your camera reacts to different light sources with differing color temperatures, in overcast and sunny daylight, for example. When a camera is balanced for one temperature of light and used to photograph another, the resulting image exhibits a color cast.

wide-angle lens

A lens that allows your camera to capture a wider image, with a wider angle of view. The opposite of telephoto lenses, wide-angle lenses are defined by short focal lengths, generally 35mm or shorter, in 35mm photography. Wide-angle lenses are useful for including a larger part of the scene in a single image.

Z

zoom

See *digital zoom* and *optical zoom*.

zoom lens

An optical lens with a zoom feature, allowing the user to vary the focal length and, hence, the magnification.

Index

Note to the Reader: Throughout this index **boldfaced** page numbers indicate primary discussions of a topic. *Italicized* page numbers indicate illustrations.

A

B

D

E

F

G

H

L

M

N

O

P

X

Z

Take Your Digital Images to the Next Level...

With *Photoshop Elements 2 Solutions*, noted photographer and author Mikkel Aaland has thoroughly updated his best-seller to include all the smart new features in the latest version of the program. This book is an invaluable guide for turning your ordinary images into extraordinary images. Coverage includes:

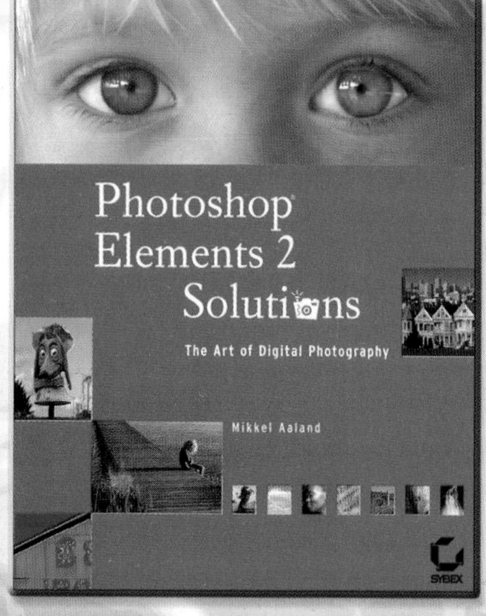

- **Getting Photoshop Elements up and running**
- **Sharpening out-of-focus pictures**
- **Touching up faces and fixing red-eye**
- **Making standout product shots**
- **Enhancing outdoor and real-estate shots**
- **Fusing photos into amazing panoramics**
- **Combining images into realistic-looking composites**
- **Optimizing photos for the web and e-mail transmission**
- **Creating PDF slide shows and professional-looking picture packages. And more...**

Photoshop® Elements 2 Solutions:
The Art of Digital Photography
By Mikkel Aaland
ISBN: 0-7821-4140-4 • US $40

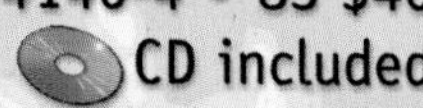

"There are several books that have been published recently about Photoshop Elements 2 and this is one of the best I have read. If you are serious about learning Adobe's Photoshop Elements 2, I would suggest you buy this superb book." —Ann Roberts, Photoshop Etc.com

CD Description

The enclosed CD comes with more than 100 practice images from the book, plus utilities to make your work easier, tryout versions of fun and useful plug-ins, and a demo of Sybex's Photoshop 6 Learning Studio software.

www.sybex.com